The Idea of a Christian University

The Idea of a Christian University
Essays in Theology and Higher Education

edited by

Jeff Astley
Leslie J. Francis
John Sullivan
Andrew Walker

PATERNOSTER

First published 2004 by Paternoster Press
Paternoster Press is an imprint of Authentic Media
9 Holdom Avenue, Bletchley, Milton Keynes, Bucks,
MK1 1QR, UK
and PO Box 1047, Waynesboro, GA 30830-2047
www.authenticmedia.co.uk

British Library Cataloguing in Publication Data

A catalogue record for this book is available from the
British Library

ISBN 1-84227-260-0

Cover design by 4-9-0 ltd
Print Management by Adare Carwin

Contents

Part Two: A Christian Curriculum?

Preface

University scholars in Great Britain who are committed to providing some form of Christian education have been hampered for decades by the failure to prevent the fragmentation of religion along a number of clearly demarcated fault lines. These include the separation of theory from Christian practice, the break between theology and education as academic disciplines, and the bifurcation of religious education itself into independent spheres. The split between theory and practice is exemplified by the migration of theology from the ecclesia to the academy. While theology has flourished as a discipline in higher education, it has more rarely been applied both educationally and in depth to the faith communities from which it sprung. If we think of theological education as the fusion of two disciplines, working either in tandem or as an innovative integrated field (as in the case of bio-ethics), then we would be hard pressed to find such a conjunction in the majority of university departments of theology. It would appear that, in higher education in the United Kingdom at least, theology is the business of theologians, education of educationalists, and theological education of nobody in particular. Its very academic homelessness is evidence of the failure of university departments of theology and of education to 'name it and claim it'.

That faculties and schools of education have not been seen as the natural home for theological education is due to the division of religious education itself into two quite different and unequal fields. The first, and by far the largest, share of the division houses what most people think of as religious education in Britain: namely the research and development of an even-handed and open-ended approach to world religions that is admirably suited for the training of specialist teachers in the state schools of a multicultural society. Its supporters can point to such potential benefits as fostering civic responsibility in young people, encouraging tolerance of diversity, and at the very least imparting knowledge of a variety of spiritual traditions. Where this approach wholly brackets out confessional truth-claims in the service of phenomenological description, it has little truck with many of the outcomes of Christian education that are intrinsic to the faith communities themselves. The net result of the division of religious education into a religious studies orientation and a confessional one, is that theological education is usually hived off to seminaries, theological colleges/courses and bible schools, where a body of knowledge rooted in both educational principles and theological tradition is often difficult to locate. The little theological education that has survived in the academy remains as a smaller and poorer relation of religious education, and is consequently under-researched and under-resourced.

It was in the light of this perceived fragmentation and marginalisation of Christian education in the mainline universities that a conversation was started in 2001 in what became known as the National Seminar on Theological Education. Meeting primarily at the Centre for Theology and Culture at King's College London, educationalists and theologians shared their insights, offered their differing perspectives, and agreed to pool their resources for a combined exercise in conciliar reflection on theological education. This initiative owes much to the St Gabriel's Programme and its Director, John Gay. They made funding available to foster partnerships between theologians and educationalists so as to work towards overcoming some of the divisions that have become endemic in Christian education.

In the event, after several consultations, the suggestion for action that met with everybody's approval came from Leslie Francis, who put forward the proposal that we should commit ourselves to a book on the idea of a Christian university. So enthusiastic were members of the Seminar for this enterprise that they decided to go beyond their original brief and extend an invitation to scholars from different countries and a variety of disciplines to participate. They were able to do this thanks to a generous grant from the All Saints Educational Trust. What has emerged is this substantial volume of original essays, bound together by a common commitment to a theologically-grounded understanding of Christian higher education. It is partly rooted in the experience of teaching in Christian higher education institutions: three of the editors and at least three other essayists have current or recent experience of working in the 'Church Colleges' sector in the UK. But it also draws on wider reflections on the experience of Christian universities in North America and Australia, and of scholars who have exercised their academic (and Christian) vocations in a range of 'secular' institutions.

The book is divided into two parts: Part One, *A Christian Calling?*, is intended not so much as an *apologia* as an airing of the debate about the desirability, purpose, and shape of a Christian university in a pluralistic culture. Part Two, *A Christian Curriculum?*, presents a more concrete view of the curriculum of a Christian university and spells out the unique contribution that Christian scholarship might bring to the university sector. Taken together, the two parts offer a comprehensive investigation from a variety of perspectives into the plausibility of a Christian university, its rationale, and its potential possibilities and problems.

The editors are most grateful to all those who have helped with this project, particularly the St Gabriel's Trust and the All Saints Educational Trust, but also the Trustees of St Hild and St Bede who fund the North of England Institute for Christian Education in which the editorial process has been located. Particular thanks are due to Evelyn Jackson for preparing the volume for publication.

Part One: A Christian Calling?

Chapter One

The Idea of a Christian University

Ian S. Markham

For many social commentators today, the idea of a 'Christian university' is nonsense. They have a cluster of related objections to the concept. First, they point to the creeping secularisation of society. With fewer and fewer people actively participating in religion, the sense that a religious ideology should dominate a university seems very unwise. After all, there are fewer and fewer people who would welcome such a vantage point. Second, they worry about the problem of pluralism. To have an institution shaped by the Christian religion poses the obvious question about all those sympathetic to other belief-systems. Third, they are not clear what the practical 'difference' will be. To require the teaching of say the 'catechism' would be unrealistic – even churches find this difficult; to argue that a 'Christian university' makes 'care a priority' is a conceit that plenty of secular or non-Christian universities would want to take issue with.

So for those of us who want to defend the concept, we have an obligation to reflect on precisely how the concept can survive in the modern period. We need to think through the issues of market (who exactly wants a Christian university), pluralism (how do we relate to religious diversity) and content (what precisely is the difference with other universities shaped by a different ideology) with some care.

The debates around the 'idea of the Christian university' echo in many respects the equivalent debate around the 'idea of a Christian society'. When T. S. Eliot published his book *The Idea of a Christian Society*, he espoused the need for society to aim for an end that transcends itself. Eliot explained that the minimum for a society to be called Christian 'would be a society in which the natural end of man –

virtue and well-being in community – is acknowledged by all, and the supernatural end – beatitude – for those who have eyes to see it'.[1] It provoked a reply by the economist theologian, Denys Munby, called *The Idea of a Secular Society*. Here Munby identifies six marks of a secular society. First, in complete contrast to the Eliot definition, 'a secular society is one which explicitly refuses to commit itself as a whole to any particular view of the nature of the universe and the place of man in it.'[2] Second, it is pluralist. Munby writes, 'A secular society is in practice a pluralistic society, in so far as it is truly secular.'[3] Third, it is tolerant. Munby believes that a secular society doesn't allow the 'disgust' that some have for homosexuality to determine the boundaries of acceptable human options in society. The fourth mark of a secular society is a minimum structure to resolve disagreements and a common framework of law. Fifth, a secular society solves problems by examination of the empirical facts; and finally, it is a society without official images.

In this chapter, I shall provide a similar contrast: I shall start with the idea of a secular university, in which we shall see that many aspects of Munby's secular society get endorsed, and argue that sociologically, historically and conceptually such an idea is flawed. I shall then move on to explain the 'idea of a Christian university' and respond to the issues outlined above of 'market', 'pluralism', and 'content'.

The significance of the secular paradigm: the idea of a secular university

The place to begin our critique of the idea of a secular university is with its roots in the secular paradigm. The debate about secularisation is complex and vast and the details of that debate are beyond the confines of this essay. It is sufficient to note that the secular paradigm has its roots in post-Enlightenment thought. It was John Locke who, famously, solved the problem of religious diversity by distinguishing between the 'public' and the 'private'.[4] The public realm does require support and maintenance of the social order (which in his day meant support for the Protestant commitment of England, which therefore entailed making Roman Catholicism a religion that could not be tolerated). The private realm is where personal preferences can be exercised. Now Locke, implicitly, (John Stuart Mill explicitly) argued that the state can and should tolerate diversity in the private realm, provided it does not undermine the conditions for order in the public realm. Given that the vast majority of religious beliefs (e.g. the doctrine of the Trinity) do not have explicit social implications,[5] then such toleration is fine.

So then 'the idea of a secular university' evolves which insists that all faiths and beliefs are permitted at the university, yet the university as a whole is ideology free. It is simply an empty space that permits the 'private' beliefs to exist under its umbrella. It is the 'hotel' model of organisation, rather than the 'family' model.[6] In a family there are expectations of shared values and cultures; prayers to a particular deity might be said over the food at mealtime. In a hotel, men and women are invited to behave in whatever ways they consider appropriate in the privacy of their own rooms, and the public spaces will be entirely neutral.

The attractiveness of the secular paradigm is compounded by a sense that an increasingly technological and scientific age finds religion increasingly implausible. Many define the secular as the 'diminishing authority of religious institutions in society'. And a powerful narrative to explain the growth of the secular is the way that religious institutions have declined in parallel with the growth of the scientific and technological narrative. One sees this very clearly in Munby's *The Idea of a Secular Society*. For Bertrand Russell, to take another example, one finds his conviction that the scientific narrative (especially in respect to the origins and structure of the world) displaces the religious one; you do not need to postulate God to explain the satisfactory harvest, when one has an understanding of the weather patterns on earth.[7]

The secular paradigm in European thought is very pervasive. It is assumed daily in the musings of many social commentators. However, there is a growing literature that questions the significance of the secular paradigm in Europe. Grace Davie provides a useful summary, when she explains that there is a growing literature that 'calls into question at least some aspects of the process known as secularization as a necessary part of modernization and that as the world modernized it would – all other things being equal – be likely to secularize'.[8] Davie then explains:

An alternative suggestion is increasingly gaining ground: the possibility that secularization is not a universal process, but belongs instead to a relatively short and particular period of European history which still assumed (among other things) that whatever characterized Europe's religious life today would characterize everyone else's tomorrows.[9]

The point is that the secular paradigm is both local and parochial. It is true that in Europe the growth of the secular has run parallel with a growth of confidence in science and technology. But this is clearly a cultural aberration: in the United States, to take the example of the most advanced scientific and technological culture in the world, religion is as robust as ever. The vast majority of Americans are deeply religious. And in the battle for the rest of the world's opinion, an enthusiasm for science and technology (which is undoubtedly there in Africa, Asia, and Latin America) is not running parallel with an enthusiasm for the secular paradigm.

Even in the United Kingdom and the rest of Europe, Grace Davie has shown that the 'secular' has not triumphed so much as has 'a decline in belonging'.[10] The church, as an institution, is outperforming the other institutions in Europe (Trade Unions, Women's Guilds, etc.). The problem, and of course it is a problem, is that institutional allegiance in Europe is in trouble. Instead of celebrating this crisis of participation, European nations should be reflecting on how to rectify this.

In addition to the sociological distortion (science and technology for most cultures do not entail secularism), there is a conceptual distortion. Science actually depends on a religious worldview. Historically, this is undoubtedly true. It was Michael Foster, in two classic articles published in *Philosophy*, who argued that it was the Christian doctrine of creation that gave birth to the possibility of science.[11] The doctrine of creation stresses the need for 'explanations' of the universe (independent of simple 'divine agency') that science can in principle investigate. In other words, in Hinduism (and other Eastern philosophies) the fact that everything is sacred makes 'scientific investigation' inappropriate. The only form of 'investigation' is a religious one because the phenomena of the universe need to be explained in 'religious terms'. However, Christians (along with Jews and Muslims) believe in a creation *ex nihilo* (out of nothing). As a result, there is a difference between God and the creation. God and the creation should not be confused. This frees up humanity to believe that the universe is 'ordered' (after all, it is created by a supremely rational deity) and therefore seek explanations, which are not 'religious' but grounded in the 'order of the universe itself'.

This flows into a related objection: it is wrong to put science into an opposition with religion. The case can be made that science needs to assume a religious framework. It is not simply an historical accident that science emerged from a religious worldview, but a theoretical necessity. Science must assume that the universe is 'ordered'. As the whole tradition of 'natural theology' has pointed out, this assumption requires some grounding. The theistic claim about the nature of the universe is precisely a claim that the order of the universe is not accidental or simply fortuitous but intended. It is precisely the belief that God created the world that enables us to have the confidence that science needs to investigate the world. If the universe is simply a massive 'accident' emerging from 'chance', then it is difficult to see how one can be confident that the universe is indeed intelligible. Yet the intelligibility of the universe is a necessary assumption of the sciences.[12]

The problems with the 'secular idea of the university' are not simply at the sociological, historical and theoretical levels, but also at the level of delivery. The 'secular' university is not only impoverished, but the secular university is also potentially socially damaging. It is impoverished because certain issues are not explored (e.g. many do not have a theology or religion department). It is damaging *in that* the *apparent* neutrality of the secular is a way of disguising a whole host of ideological convictions. Let us return to the Raymond Plant image of the 'hotel', but with one modification – let us compare the 'business hotel' with a 'retreat centre'. Hotels assume a minimal morality (providing it is legal, one can do whatever one wants); they celebrate individualism (one's obligations to fellow guests are kept to a complete minimum); and they stress a culture of 'service' in exchange for 'money'. (Thank God for the Gideons: the Gideon Bible is an important challenge to the secular assumptions of the hotel.) A hotel is in stark contrast to a 'retreat centre'. Although both provide accommodation and catering facilities, the retreat centre will not have the adult movie options and, more constructively, will have a whole host of opportunities (books, etc.) that can build up virtue and cultivate spiritual reflection.

It is an axiom of postmodernism that there is no such thing as a 'value-free' approach. The aggressive agenda underpinning the secular needs to be recognised. It is making a whole host of philosophical assumptions that are highly tendentious. In addition, these are assumptions that perhaps the majority of people worldwide would want to take issue with. However, as the analogy with the hotel should make clear, some of the attractions of the secular are theologically the attractions of 'sin'. In short, a secular society or university is temptation. The retreat centre might be exhausting and demanding (precisely because it is a place that is building up virtue) and the hotel in its lack of demands and indulgence of choice and individualism is potentially a place for the depraved satisfaction of immediate desires.

The secular paradigm is in trouble. The rest of the world thinks it is a symptom of the depravity of the West. And its associations with modernity make its ideological basis increasing problematic. Therefore this book is prescient; the time is indeed right to think through the alternative to the 'idea of a secular university'.

The idea of a Christian university

There are four features of the 'Christian university'. First, it is ideologically honest: it challenges the myth that institutions can be value-free and recognises the 'tradition–constituted' nature of us all. It was Alasdair MacIntyre who expounded the insight that all traditions are located. As MacIntyre pointed out, the secular is particularly pernicious and deceitful in masquerading as 'objective' and 'neutral', while in actual fact promoting a reductionist worldview.[13] One simple argument for a Christian university is that all institutions must have some ideology underpinning them: the secular one has an 'agnostic or atheist' ideology, while the Christian one a 'faith–based' ideology. In the contemporary debate about the nature of institutions, it is important that Christians are willing to be properly polemical about the illusion of 'objectivity' and the disguised contentious values that underpin secular institutions.

Second, the mission of a Christian university recognises that there is an attempt to inculcate certain 'faith–based' values. True education must include training in the virtues. A moral sensitivity requires cultivation. This is not simply the capacity to 'debate' moral questions and issues, one also has a strong awareness of why the Christian tradition finds certain dispositions problematic. For example, the Christian axiom that 'the taking of innocent life' is always forbidden and its implications for abortion should be discussed and understood in a Christian university. Although the university will 'respect' the student who in all conscience believes that 'abortion' might be right in certain circumstances, it is the case that the student will understand and be able to provide an account of why Christians are committed to the axiom about the 'taking of innocent life' and its implications for the abortion debate.

One assumption here is that all moral debate operates around a certain set of limited options. The sense that at secular institutions 'all options are permitted' is completely false. Most secular institutions do not permit in their classes a defence of patriarchy or anti-Semitism. This is, of course, quite right: patriarchy and anti-Semitism should be excluded as options. Both worldviews are ethically misguided and deeply damaging socially. The Christian university is willing to be more honest than the secular one and makes clear the way in which the options around certain debates are permitted. The framework of the debate shapes the options in the debate. In a Christian framework, we assume the dignity of humankind (simply because all people are created in the image of God) and therefore we exclude as options 'the legitimacy of slavery' or 'the proposal that homosexuals should be killed'. It might be objected at this point that the Christian tradition has permitted (indeed endorsed) both options at certain times in its history. This is true. However, Christian frameworks change over time and amongst the discoveries that the tradition has made is that slavery and the slaughter of homosexuals is a fundamental denial of the doctrine of the *Imago Dei*. The Christian tradition is exactly that: a tradition that 'hands on' the insights of the gospel and in so doing modifies its fundamental framework. One need look no further than the Roman Catholic Catechism to see that both slavery and homophobia are unequivocally condemned.

Once again, unlike the secular institution where the moral debate is frequently curtailed by an unthinking 'political correctness', the Christian university explicitly confines the options in the debate around certain key Christian discoveries. The difference between the two is not that secular institutions do not limit the options for moral discussion, but that the Christian university is honest about it. It is important to stress that there is still debate: the compatibility and legitimacy of homosexual relations in the context of the gospel is one such debate. And those who want to defend a norm, grounded in the creation ordinances, of heterosexual marriage as the framework for sexual relations, and those who see that the Christian tradition needs to accommodate the discovery of 'sexual orientation' and adjust its theology accordingly, are two legitimate options that can be explored at a Christian university.

The third feature of a Christian university will be the location and significance of metaphysics in the curriculum. Every student in every subject should reflect on the metaphysical underpinning of his or her discipline. This feature is simply an echo of the hope of John Henry Newman as advocated in his *Idea of a University*. Newman put it thus:

> I lay it down that all knowledge forms one whole, because its subject-matter is one; for the universe in its length and breadth is so intimately knit together, that we cannot separate off portion from portion, and operation from operation, except by mental abstraction. ... And further, the comprehension of the bearings of one science on another, and the use of each to each, and the location and limitation and adjustment and due appreciation of them all, one with another, this belongs, I conceive, to a sort of science distinct from all of them, and in some sense a science of sciences, which is my own conception of what is meant by Philosophy, in the true sense of the word, and of a philosophical habit of mind ...[14]

In practice this should involve the explicit study of the philosophy of each subject. In Britain, philosophy did deep damage to itself by spending much of the twentieth century confining the philosophical task to the 'explication of meaning' and accepting uncritically the Kantian assumption that metaphysics is impossible. Fortunately, this preoccupation with meaning has started to fade and a more constructive understanding of philosophy has emerged. Pope John Paul II sets out an appropriate vision for philosophy: it is one that forces the human mind to grapple with the ultimate questions about the nature of the universe. His challenge to theologians, in *Fides et Ratio*, is a challenge that ought to shape the curriculum within a Christian university. He writes:

> This is why I urge them to recover and express to the full the metaphysical dimension of truth in order to enter into a demanding critical dialogue with both contemporary philosophical thought and with the philosophical tradition in all its aspects, whether consonant with the word of God or not.[15]

The net result is that students in the sciences or economics or mathematics or whatever should be required to reflect on the assumptions that their discipline makes about the nature of the world. In every area, the metaphysical assumptions should be explored. Naturally the Christian university should present the spectrum: from naturalism to theism and beyond (e.g. pantheism). The distinguishing mark of a Christian university is not so much in terms of the range of options, but that the options are explored.

The fourth and final feature of a Christian university is the celebration of 'rationality' and 'conversation' in the quest for the truth. It is clear that we live in a universe in which God intended diversity. To attribute diversity to human sinfulness cannot account for what we now know about the origins of different human cultures. They emerged in different parts of the world, developing contrasting languages, and different worldviews. To insist that God was only active amongst the Jewish people is a fundamental denial of the God who is creator of the whole world and has 'numbered the hairs of each person's head'. Presumably it would have been perfectly possible for an omnipotent God to create a universe with only one religion – one that is self-evidently true – but God chose not to do this. So why is there so much diversity in this world?

The likeliest explanation is that the truth about God's world is complicated. Different cultures emerged and formulated contrasting worldviews because of the complexity of this world. After all, if economists continue to disagree about the value of interest rates as a key to controlling inflation and physicists disagree about the nature of black holes, then it is not surprising that religious people disagree about the nature of God and God's relations with the world.

Economists and physicists welcome the disagreement because it is through the process of the conversation that they can learn. So the Christian should welcome the diverse perspectives and learn from them. The Christian university is a place in which a range of vantage points are encouraged to engage in conversation and learn in humility from the process.

These four features are key to the understanding of the 'idea of the Christian university'. It is armed with these features that we revisit the criticisms of those who think that the idea of a Christian university is nonsense.

Market, diversity and content

We live in a world where both historically and today the vast majority of people are deeply religious. As with the debate over the establishment of the Church of England, some of the strongest supporters are to be found amongst the Jewish and Muslim communities. They both discern, correctly in my view, that a benign Christian influence in England is preferable to a completely irreligious heart to England. When the Salman Rushdie controversy erupted, the Church of England, unlike the secularists, could relate to Islamic hurt over the act of 'insulting the sacred'.[16] The market for a Christian university includes all people of faith: anyone who wants a faith-based framework for study. Advocates of a Christian university need to be much more aggressive in pointing out how impoverished the alternative is.

In terms of pluralism, the secular foundation for pluralism is ugly. It evades difference. The public square – to use Richard John Neuhaus' famous phrase[17] – is empty; religious expressions are confined to the realm of the personal and private. Instead of evasion, the Christian university is commitment to dialogue or conversation with difference. The hotel handles difference by letting everyone do what they like in the privacy of their room; the retreat centre handles difference by requiring everyone to share their respective narratives and engage with that difference. This is the right way to handle difference. We need a world of mutual understanding not a world where disagreements are not explored.

In terms of content, Christian universities should make curriculum amendments to their courses. There should be mission distinctiveness; there should be an overt celebration of certain values; there should be the proper study of philosophy and metaphysics in every discipline. It should make a difference. The temptation to simply embody the Christian distinctiveness in the chaplaincy or in a 'commitment to care' (which can too often become an excuse for tolerating gross inefficiency) is wrong. The Christian mission should and can make a difference. This should be reflected in the curriculum.

Conclusion

This chapter has argued that the idea of the secular university has been damaging and misguided. The time has come to replace the dull uniformity of the business hotel with attractive, well-organised, centres of study where the spiritual is celebrated and God can be truly recognised.

Chapter Two

University, Christian Faith and the Church

John Sullivan

The church once clearly formed the dominant cultural matrix from which the university emerged. It granted its mandate, sanctioned its operations, housed its students, determined the parameters of its debates, supplied the very subject matter for many of its studies and provided employment for many of its graduates (see Grant, 2001). The church and the university were intimately linked, partners in learning as a path to holiness. In this collaboration, the church was without question the senior partner. Today most universities, all over the world, function without reference to the church, whose influence is now much diminished. It remains the case, however, that the church continues to see Christian universities, like Christian schools, as potentially being central to their mission of spreading the gospel. While there is a wealth of literature that explores what might happen when Christian faith is applied to the university context, it comes from beyond the United Kingdom. (For a representative sample of recent works, from a vast and ever-expanding field, see Benne, 2001; Buckley, 1999; Dovre, 2002; Estanek, 2002; Haynes, 2002; Hughes and Adrian, 1997; Landy, 2001; Marsden, 1997; O'Brien, 2002; Sterk, 2002). This book is a modest attempt to begin to redress the balance; it offers a range of perspectives on the idea of a Christian university that emerge principally, although not entirely, from the UK context.

In this chapter I start by retrieving some useful pointers to the links between the intellectual life and the life of Christian faith. These are adapted from the work of Friedrich von Hügel (1852–1925), whose writings have usually been neglected in discussions about Christian universities. Here I show that von Hügel offers valuable guidance about five particular balancing acts of relevance to Christian educators and scholars. Then there is an exploration of what kind of salience we might expect Christian faith to have in the life of a Christian university, arguing that an explicit voice needs to be married to an invitational tone. Third, I consider which of the principal models of church fits best in the university context. It is argued that the sacramental model facilitates more healthy relationships between secular and sacred, and between intellectual and spiritual perspectives, than do the institutional, mystical, herald or servant models. Finally, some of the challenges entailed in mediating Christian faith in a university are analysed. Such mediation is shown to rely upon a host of interrelated tasks that separately and together require negotiating a range of complexly interactive factors. In the midst of pluralism some form of particularity has to be arrived at: one that promotes distinctiveness while maintaining openness.

Help from von Hügel

Baron Friedrich von Hügel was one of the great Christian scholars from a century ago. He went neither to school nor to university, having been taught privately at home by a range of tutors. Despite this, however, as an adult he systematically and rigorously became a learned auto–didact and went on to contribute significantly to debates about the mutual bearing on each other of research in biblical studies, theology, philosophy, history and science. Throughout the first twenty years of the twentieth century he found himself much in demand as a speaker in London (and other) academic circles and was invited to deliver a series of the Gifford lectures in natural theology in Scotland, although in the event he had to turn this down because of ill–health. He also was a regular visitor to many different European countries, being a fluent reader, speaker and writer in English, French, German and Italian, as well as being able to read in Hebrew, Greek and Latin. As a European scholar he was frequently at the centre of the controversies that raged over the relationship between Christian faith and the findings (and methodologies) of contemporary sciences.

A devout and faithful Roman Catholic layman, von Hügel met with much more acclaim during his lifetime from Christians outside his church than from those within it (though such recognition did eventually follow). Several features combined to make him an uncomfortable fellow-believer for many Catholics. These included his capacity to engage in critical thinking, his openness with regard to new ideas and the warmth and hospitality he showed to radical and apparently unorthodox thinkers such as Loisy and Tyrrell. He was especially challenging for those in authority at a time when the institutional church had firmly set its face against the efforts of modernisers to reconcile contemporary scholarship with religious tradition. Von Hügel was an ecumenist before this was acceptable. He offers some important pointers for the kinds of balance to be maintained by students and scholars who wish to remain faithful to Christianity, but who also intend to integrate their learning and their discipleship. Christian universities have much to learn from his spiritual wisdom and from his insights into how the intellectual dimension can and should relate to the other aspects of our lives. Here I pick out five examples of the kinds of balance he advocated and exemplified in his life and writings.

First, by stressing the beneficial effects brought about for us by a diversity of interests clamouring for our attention and engagement, he cast light on a phrase that is often used by educators, the integral, all-round (or, sometimes, holistic) development of the human person. If we are interested in many different types of subject, this will help to expand our capacities. It will also elicit from us a richness of perspective on reality, especially if we are willing to be disciplined by real engagement with these different subjects. Von Hügel indirectly provides a strong case for Christian schools and universities to offer their students a broad curriculum. For, despite the pre-eminence of the place of religion in his life, he was adamant that we need a wide range of non-religious dimensions if we are to be properly rounded, with all our faculties functioning healthily. There is mutual illumination and stimulus when subjects are studied in each other's light. Thus, there should be opportunities for interdisciplinary enquiry. This need not entail watering down each particular discipline, whose particular fields, key concepts and special methodologies should be preserved.

Second, although he was careful to draw distinctions, von Hügel saw no radical separation between the sacred and the secular, between spiritual and material realities. He saw God at work, though in different ways, in all spheres that we could enquire into. Knowledge that seemed merely secular could serve to make us re-appraise and freshly understand not only aspects of the world around us, but also our religious faith, a faith which should not be left to operate as an extracurricular activity. Thus, a recent commentator on von Hügel says, 'One of the functions of science today is to detach the church from the status quo and thus to purify it' (Hendrie, 2002, p. 68). The baron himself refers to 'the body, the stimulator and springboard, the material and training ground, of spirit' (von Hügel, 1921, p. 238). We can reach the intangible and transcendent through encounter with what is immanent and concrete. Ultimately, in this Hügelian perspective, it is our task to draw out the diversity of experience from these multiple elements and work towards some harmonisation of the complexity of life and religion. They cannot simply be left as compartmentalised or as merely juxtaposed items in our life. 'These constituents will but hinder or supplant each other, in proportion as they are not somehow each recognised in their proper place and rank, and are not each allowed and required to supplement and to stimulate the other' (von Hügel, 1908, vol. I, p. 50). Life, for von Hügel, should be considered as a journey of integration and directed towards communion with God in rhythm and relationship with the church. Integration requires many ingredients. The Christian university should guard against allowing narrowness in the range of subjects with which its students engage.

Third, von Hügel displayed a combination of the inner stability that comes from being rooted in firm foundations and a capacity for flexibility and inclusiveness that was so well summed by Tyrrell: 'A man who stands on firm ground can enjoy a freedom of movement impossible on a tight-rope' (quoted by Hendrie, 2002, p. 22). He clearly demonstrated that, provided they maintain a proper balance in their religious life, Christians should feel that their faith is quite unthreatened by new discoveries and theories, even though it must take account of, and respond adequately to them. The Christian university should try to ensure that students receive not only the benefits of formation, where they are exposed to a particular way of thinking, behaving, belonging and worshipping, but also to the challenge of 'frontier' experiences, where they encounter people, ideas and circumstances that are unfamiliar and that call into question their usual assumptions and practices (Sullivan, 2003).

Fourth, von Hügel took great care, most famously in his great work *The Mystical Element of Religion*, to advocate a balance between the claims of authority, rationality and personal experience. Although the main focus for his analysis of the interplay between the institutional, intellectual and experiential dimensions in our life was the sphere of religion, I believe that we can legitimately extend his point to the wider curriculum and community experience of Christian universities. Each of these three has something of value to offer and each of them is subject to excess and abuse, if taken on its own, without the balancing counter-work of the other two dimensions.

> To the first element, the institutional, the third will appear revolutionary and anarchic. To the intellectual side it will seem mere subjectivity and sentimentality, verging on self-delusion. The third element, in its turn, will tend to sweep aside the first element as oppressive ballast, and the second as hair-splitting or rationalism. Success in this would lead to a shifting subjectivity, dependence on a tyranny of mood and fancy and, indeed, fanaticism. (Hendrie, 2002, p. 149)

The Christian university needs to keep a watchful eye on the functioning of each of these three dimensions within its operations. As for the first dimension, a community needs to attend to the institutional requirements of organisation and structure. This will help it to be consistent in the messages it communicates, to be effective in its goals, to sustain its efforts over time, to share out its goods equitably and to engage with any degree of adequacy with external groups and agencies. It must order its life so that this is congruent with its aspirations and its mandate. Such congruence does not happen by accident or serendipity. It depends on planning, cooperation and the streamlining of effort. It also relies on the harmonisation of talents and, for economy of effort, it benefits from codes and systems of working practices, rather than responding to individual whim, inspiration, mood or initiative. Of course, an institution can slide into becoming a self-serving bureaucracy, develop a hardening of its corporate 'arteries' and 'oughteries', display an overbearing style. This stifles creativity and silences dissent. However, these are malfunctions that can and should be guarded against; they are neither automatic nor necessary.

As for the second dimension, the Christian university must also be as intellectually demanding as any other such institution. Questioning, critique, debate, an openness to alternative points of view – all these should be evident features of university life in promoting rationality. Orthodoxies, both secular and religious, must encounter interrogation.

Their assumptions must be exposed, sifted, weighed and evaluated. There must be discernment as to when doctrines slip into serving ideological purposes. When this happens, the status quo is buttressed, while particular groups are privileged, at the same time as others find that their voice and access to resources and power is denied. An emphasis on rationality has many aspects. It will include an examination of first principles, exposure of prejudice and tests for consistency. It will also lead to a comparison of the explanatory power of alternative theories and an interrogation of how well these theories match with and illuminate the data. Concepts have to be evaluated in terms of their adequacy, coherence, economy and elegance. This concern with rationality should be sensitive to the multiplicity of forms of intelligence. It should offer a sustained and in-depth intellectual engagement by students, as well as facilitating breadth and cross-disciplinary dialogue. Without the pressure to investigate, to check, to argue, to question, to analyse and to postpone, as well as to exercise judgement, the university will not be true to its role in promoting critical and independent thinking. This emphasis on rationality does not have to embrace methodological atheism. It can rise beyond technical rationality. It does not have to lead to reductionism, to excessive specialisation or to compartmentalisation of the curriculum. Authentic rationality does not entail blindness to the external environment, deafness to existential questions, or any lack of attention to the realm of emotion or the relational atmosphere in which learning takes place.

As for the third dimension, no form of education can be effective in the long-term or establish much purchase on the outlook and attitudes of students if it suppresses their voices, neglects to listen to their experiences, fails to draw upon their perspectives or ignores their feelings. A degree of plasticity is required by teachers who take into account the starting points of learners rather than simply seeking to impose some orthodoxy on them, whether this orthodoxy be religious, intellectual or political (Sullivan, 2001). It will only be via the engagement of their experience and through the perceived relevance to this experience that what is offered to them at university will be processed by them in any depth (as opposed to merely being retained in the short-term and regurgitated for assignments or examinations). Teachers have to develop pedagogical approaches that establish links between the academic disciplines and the real lives of students. On the one hand, particular concepts, categories, criteria and methodologies have to be engaged with. At the same time, university lecturers must take the actual state of their students into account – their significant experiences and relationships, their hopes and fears, their self-acknowledged strengths and weaknesses, their values and resentments. So long as this emphasis on the personal and experiential dimension is matched by attention to the institutional and intellectual dimensions described above, it should not leave students where they started from. That would merely imprison them in their past and reinforce their prejudices. It might confuse their wants with what they really need, and, through a misguided attempt to make study accessible and acceptable, slip into entertaining them or fail to offer sufficient challenge.

A fifth way that von Hügel offers a helpful model to the Christian university is the nuanced balance he maintained between the need for church affiliation and the requirements of openness and inclusiveness. On the one hand he was full of optimism that we can know something of God and God's ways, and confident that the church, as a school for sanctity, could be trusted to protect, preserve and promote salvific truth. He felt sure that a Christian flourished only within the bosom of the church, being convinced that we need to participate in its community life, to experience both the burdens and the opportunities made available through this communal life. This sense of assurance was qualified by a humble awareness that we can never know enough to be too dogmatic or over-confident in our assertions (and denials) in religious controversy. It was also modified by an awareness that the church, despite divine assistance, frequently displayed shortcomings and defects in its human agents. Our church allegiance will be checked, purified, steadied and sobered – and therefore made more wholesome – by the struggles faith has with the institution of the church (von Hügel, 1927, p. 201). This kind of friction forces us to take stock of who we are, to examine what we have committed ourselves to. It prompts us to revise our preconceptions and stimulates an expansion of our understanding.

In part von Hügel's sensitivity and balance here, between the need for ecclesial affiliation and openness, rests on his acute awareness of the limitations of his own church. Despite his fidelity, devotion, loyalty and humble obedience, he was not blind to the church's faults. In part it was also founded on his sense of the universal availability of grace. He wanted to learn from other Christian denominations and also from people of other faiths. As far as he was concerned, souls outside the church were not lost; they were safely in God's hands. Without being in any way indifferent to the question of religious truth, and without surrendering any part of his own discipleship and acknowledgement of Christ as saviour, he exercised restraint in pressing his own beliefs on others, showed respect for their own commitments and engaged robustly yet constructively in dialogue with those from whom he differed.

Salience of Christian faith in the university

Surely this combination of unashamed, indeed confident, church affiliation with openness and inclusiveness towards those who see things differently, should be an important feature in a Christian university. If a university is to deserve the attribution 'Christian' then there needs to be a willingness for its Christian claims and the embodiments of these to receive a degree of explicitness and salience in the institutional, intellectual and experiential life of its members. It is possible for reticence and restraint on the part of Christians to give the appearance of denial, to slip into abdication of responsibility and invisibility of presence. 'Too many teachers and students consider their faith a strictly private affair, or do not perceive the impact their university life has on their Christian existence. Their presence in the university seems like a parenthesis in their life of faith' (Poupard, 1994, p. 5). Where such a lament is justified, this leaves people unclear and confused about the relationship between Christian faith and university life. The Christian voice at university can be as misleadingly silent or absent as it can be inappropriately loud or intrusive.

Referring to public education in the USA, Warren Nord points out that '*most* students manage to earn their high school diplomas, their undergraduate degrees, and their professional and graduate degrees without ever encountering a *live* religious idea.' He claims that 'religious voices must be included in the curricular conversation [and] … allowed to *contend* with the secular alternatives' (Nord, 2002, pp. 10, 32; the emphasis is his). His argument is that mainstream education does not merely ignore religion but nurtures into a secular mentality (pp. 13–14). He gives as an example the teaching of neoclassical economic theory as revealed in textbooks. According to many of these, 'economics is a science, people are essentially self-interested utility-maximisers, the economic realm is one of competition for scarce resources, values are personal preferences, and value judgements are matters of cost-benefit analysis.' Yet, as Nord points out (p. 13), '*no* religious tradition accepts *this* understanding of human nature, society, and values.' Nord is not advocating a privileged place for religious voices in public universities, but he is suggesting that to deny them a place is to distort any education that claims to be liberal in nature and intention. It will simultaneously fail to facilitate an effective critique both of secular and of religious perspectives. 'Just as students should learn to think religiously about the subject matter of their typically secular courses, so they should learn something of how to think critically about religion using the methods, theories, and categories of the secular intellectual disciplines' (p. 15).

Nord also makes an interesting and pertinent distinction between learning to think religiously about the subject matter of religion and learning to think in secular ways about religion (p. 23). The latter can come about if religion is studied through the lens of history, philosophy, anthropology, psychology, sociology, and so on (on debates about the different approaches adopted in religious studies and theology, see Cady and Brown, 2002; McCutcheon, 2001; Webb, 2001). As O'Brien puts this, 'the secular view values an "arm's length" dealing with religions that results in an inability to grasp religions on their own terms' (O'Brien, 2002, p. 190). If the nature of the subject matter to be studied is to be allowed to modify the way we approach it, this should apply as much to the life of faith as it does to our study of art, drama, music or literature. That is, even though we might put questions to it that come from outside its assumptions and perspectives, perhaps questions that directly challenge its mode of operation, we also try to indwell, at least temporarily, the world as seen from within that life. We listen carefully to the voices that emerge from its living traditions – on their own terms – and we let ourselves be questioned by the various central texts, beliefs and practices that are integral to the many dimensions of religious life.

From the formative perspective granted by private prayer, public worship, collective practice and community belonging, the meaning and application of religious doctrine and moral teaching can take on particular qualities and resonances that transcend a purely logical interrogation or scholarly investigation. The theologian offers a rigorous and systematic reflection on the faith experience of a particular religious community. This reflection and analysis may well be carried out in a spirit of some detachment, but it still operates from within, and offers itself as a service to, the faith community. Integral connections between spirituality and the life of scholarship can easily be ignored (Sullivan, 2002).

Which model of church for the university?

Of course, there are many different emphases among Christians and some of these emphases fit more easily into the university than others. The question, 'what might be a suitable level of salience of Christian faith in a Christian university?' overlaps with questions about the role of the church in that setting. The nature and prime role of the church is contested among Christians. One authoritative and influential theological analysis of Christians' understanding of the church has reviewed five principal models: as institution, as mystical body, as herald or prophet, as servant and as sacrament (Dulles, 1974).

These five models have recently been set beside the idea of a university in order to consider how well they fit (O'Brien, 2002, pp. 153–158, 166, 184). Thus, the institutional model of church can be overbearing, intrusive, excessively prescriptive and threaten academic freedom. As von Hügel showed, the institutional *is* an essential dimension of Christian life, but it can be overplayed, as if it were the sole aspect. When the church is envisaged primarily as an institution, then the church in a Christian university is likely to be forthright in its articulation of truth, as it sees this, protective of orthodoxy, careful in its gatekeeping and boundary marking role, vigilant as to who is admitted and placed in leadership positions, and liable to respond to internal questioning and criticism as signs of disloyalty. Establishment might lead to an evident salience of Christian faith, but in the process a blurring occurs between the authority of the gospel and the power that comes from one's location and position within the institution.

In contrast, the mystical model pays insufficient attention to the institutional dimension and errs on the side of being excessively ethereal in its spirituality – 'vaporous' is how O'Brien puts it (p. 155). It foregrounds the divine life of the church while neglecting to take into account its human and material aspects. Thus it connects inadequately with the world that is the focus of study. As von Hügel argued, the mystical or spiritual *is* a constitutive and vital dimension of the Christian life and the life of the church. It should also flourish in a Christian university. Without proper attention to this dimension the political imperatives and the intellectual priorities would combine to dominate the individual, cumulatively leaving insufficient space for freedom of thought and for the expression of a unique response to God's invitation that each is called to give. However, too often a mystical emphasis slips into treating faith as something interior and so separate from secular realities as to render it vulnerable to accusations of irrelevance.

When the church is interpreted on the basis of the herald or prophet model, an opposition is set up prematurely between the world of faith and the disciplines of scholarly enquiry. The 'principalities' that these represent can seem at best a distraction from the gospel and at worst a denial of its supremacy. This model rightly brings out how a biblically-formed worldview differs radically from and calls seriously into question many common assumptions, both in the academy and in the wider culture (see Clouser, 1991; Dockery and Thornbury, 2002; Naugle, 2002). What it does not take sufficiently into account is that all attempts to represent the gospel are embedded culturally and therefore also linguistically and conceptually; there can be no fixed and final 'version' of Christian faith that confronts the world and the academy from outside of history and the limitations of any particular personal location or institutional setting. It can also come across as having narrow interests, neglecting von Hügel's stress on our need for the non-religious dimensions of life if we are to develop in a wholesome way. With this model, the yeast is all and the dough is missing. There is a word of challenge to proclaim; but it should not have connotations either of puritanism or of riding roughshod over the nuances yielded by intellectual engagement.

As for the servant model of the church, it can readily cooperate with any willing partners, in the academy and beyond, in the task of trying to meet the needs of the world, in promoting justice, in enhancing dignity, in advancing freedom and in working for social welfare. The Christian university should see itself and the studies it promotes as directed towards the enhancement and flourishing of life. It is right that education is envisaged as offering more than a selfish positional good, ensuring one employment, security and satisfaction. This model has the advantage that it encourages a commitment to address need regardless of where it appears and to join with many other partners in spite of differences of ideology. The church, in the light of this model, is not tempted just to care for its own members. But there are several weaknesses of this model. It can lend itself to activism at the expense of contemplation, which leads to burnout and loss of vision. It can slide into a pragmatism that borrows tools, resources, concepts, perspectives, allies and assistance indiscriminately and without discernment. Then one might find oneself and one's cause unwittingly hijacked, mis-directed or corrupted. By privileging the fruits of religious and moral life, it can fail to attend sufficiently to their personal and communal roots. By emphasising practice, it can neglect the rationale and justification that lies behind this. Yet 'without occasional attempts to devote some sustained thought to the meaning and significance of a particular Christian belief, the practices that embody that belief can become hollow, insignificant, and ultimately, unpersuasive' (David Cunningham, quoted by Amy Plantinga Pauw, in Volf and Bass, 2002, p. 41). This is hardly worthy of a Christian university.

Having identified different kinds of mismatch between these first four models of the church and the university, O'Brien summarises his verdict on them thus:

> In the other church models ... there is either a threat of encroachment (judicial [or institutional] model), abandonment (mystical), irrelevance (prophetic), or absorption (servant). In the juridical (and fundamentalist) model, one fancies that natural truth can be corrected by Revelation. The mystic abandons prosaic truth for the All. The prophet holds learning infected with sin and irrelevant to the divine command for justice and mercy. The servant accepts ordinary truth to be all that is available. (O'Brien, 2002, p. 184)

He then favours the sacramental model of the church as having most to offer the Christian university, since he believes it 'preserves the integrity of science and the sacred' (p. 184). The notion of a sacrament in Christianity is of an efficacious and visible sign of a saving encounter with God in Christ (see Macquarrie, 1997). For Christians, Jesus Christ is the primordial effective sign of God's love for the world and for humanity. The church, insofar as it lives in relationship with Christ, continues to function as a sacrament and to share his grace throughout time and across the world, being a sign and instrument of God's love for all creation. When they are responded to in faith, the encounters we call sacraments in different ways unite us to one another and bring us into greater communion with God. Sacraments are meant to serve as the great examples of what God is doing all the time in creation, rather than as the great exceptions or as out-of-the-ordinary occasions. Like presents at Christmas or on birthdays, they focus our attention on and reinforce our awareness of a love that we might lose sight of; they make explicit something implicit.

The sacramental perspective draws our attention to and makes us more conscious of the presence of God in all created reality – in nature, events, persons, rituals, words and objects. Encountered in faith and experienced in the context of worship, sacraments express and build up part of the life of the church as they signify God's presence and communicate the love of Christ that touches all aspects of life. In the specificity and limitation of a particular moment they mediate between our finiteness and the infinity of God, they incarnate or make concrete for us what otherwise might seem abstract or a distant ideal. 'The sacramental perspective maintains that one can "see" the divine in the human, the infinite in the finite, the spiritual in the material, the transcendent in the immanent, the eternal in the historical' (Cernera and Morgan, 2000, p. 213). Theologian Michael Himes says that since 'what is omnipresent is more often than not unnoticed', what the sacramental principle ensures is that 'what is always and everywhere the case must be noticed, accepted, and celebrated somewhere, sometime' (Himes, 2001, pp. 98, 91).

Christians are to be salt and light for the world. First, they should use their talents and energy to make a positive difference, to enhance life for others, to give it flavour, to encourage others to savour it as gift. Then they should witness, by word and example, that it is Christ who is the source of their strength, the focus of their attention, the goal of their future and the pathway to life and fulfilment. Witness by example precedes and has priority over witness by words. Explicit articulation of Christian faith relies very heavily for its cogency on this faith being implicitly embedded in and permeating thoroughly our everyday behaviour. However, unlike the case in the servant model, the sacramental principle does emphasise the need for making explicit, to name the source of grace and to affirm the work of God in the midst of our worldly existence. In a Christian university, in the light of a sacramental perspective, ultimately there can be no separation between the sacred and the secular, no divorce between the human and the divine, no opposition between having a vocation and being a professional. All the tasks of education, together with all the support roles that help to create the conditions such that education can proceed, seen with the eyes of faith, may be considered as elements in the path of discipleship; though not to see them this way still leaves them valid, worthy and noble human activities. As Himes puts it, 'Anything that awakens, enlivens, and expands the imagination, opens the vision, and enriches the sensitivity of any human being is a religious act' (Himes, 2001, p. 100).

University as context for mediating Christian faith

There are many types of Christian activities. These include proclaiming the gospel, worshipping God, nurturing people in faith, witnessing to this faith in various domains, offering service to those in need and thereby facilitating liberation from diverse forms of entrapment, and entering into dialogue with fellow Christians, with unbelievers or with people from other faiths. When the surrounding culture changes, these activities are understood and expressed differently in a new mixture and reassembled under a new set of priorities. The Christian university should be prominent in assisting in the process of critical and creative reappropriations of Christianity in a changing cultural context. A Christian university should play a part in discerning the signs of the times, in critiquing the surrounding culture, in calling into question its categories of interpretation, its yardsticks for evaluation and the leading metaphors that shape its thinking. This will be a task that is shared out across the various disciplines represented at the university. At the same time, the Christian university should be a place where the living tradition of the church should be interrogated and reassessed in the light of new perspectives made possible by changes in the surrounding culture. A living tradition, as MacIntyre put it, is 'an historically extended, socially embedded argument in part about the goods that constitute that tradition' (MacIntyre, 1984, p. 222). This argument faces inwards and outwards.

The Christian university requires here a high degree of subtlety, if justice is to be done to democracy and if fidelity is to be shown to

Christian tradition. Whether facing inwards or outwards, what is needed is what the philosopher Richard Bernstein describes as an 'engaged pluralism'. According to Bernstein the fundamental assumptions of democratic discussion include the following:

- The tentativeness of all knowledge;
- The infinite variety of perspectives and understandings that people bring to discussion;
- The endless nature of inquiry and the refusal to accept a definite answer;
- A genuine receptivity to other views;
- A striving for agreement that may be impossible to achieve;
- And the patience to hear out all possible opinions.
  (Bernstein, as quoted by Brookfield and Preskill, 1999, p. 14)

Neither the church nor the Christian university can ignore or fail to comply with these conditions for dialogue. However, if these are the basic 'rules' for responding to pluralism, then engagement suggests a certain (at least provisional) stability of position and principle from which to engage. There are limits to the usefulness of flexibility when engaging in dialogue; some meanings have to be fixed for argument to be possible. Some kinds of accommodation, even when intended benignly, mislead at best and betray at worst those with whom one argues. The Christian university should not seek to determine the direction or to dictate the outcome of debate, internally or externally, but it must ensure that it has something distinctive to contribute and that this contribution is offered, clearly, consistently, confidently and courageously, yet with compassion and in humility. As one recent thesis argued,

A religious tradition flourishes only to the extent that it is capable of making its central commitments available for public examination both within and beyond its boundaries. That is the condition for the public communication of those commitments, and also for their very survival. (Matthews, 2001, p. 213)

These central commitments cannot simply be repeated and applied universally. They do not operate in a manner that is sublimely disconnected from local contexts and pastoral realities. Regardless of its particular religious emphasis and its position within the spectrum of Christian tradition, the nature of a Christian university will be mediated by several factors. These include its geographical location, landmark events in its history, the gender balance, class composition and ethnic mix of students and staff, together with the level of academic ability of its intake of students. These features, coupled with the qualifications, experience and flair of its staff and the particular curriculum options available will jointly influence the type of education possible. The success with which it attracts and retains students, its financial security and the adroitness deployed in establishing partnerships and allies for various projects all have a part to play. Even in the face of a similar range of problems and opportunities that constitute a common external context for their work, and despite the central, normative features that flow from a shared Christian faith, there is still plenty of scope, given the mediating factors indicated here, for a diversity of emphasis in the mission of each Christian institution of higher education.

These diverse missions must attend to, draw from and blend together several sources simultaneously. First, Christian principles provide a degree of commonality of perspective and a set of priorities. Christian views about creation, society, the human condition, truth and moral principles will anchor and establish a framework for the educational endeavour. However, it must be acknowledged that this commonality is rendered more complex and problematical by the fact that, not only are there some important differences in interpretation about these matters between denominations, there is also increasing pluralism of interpretation within each denomination. Thus, one might find oneself in closer agreement with Christians beyond one's own denomination than with some of those inside it on certain occasions, when deciding about the bearing of Christian faith on educational issues and on institutional priorities. Second, in addition to taking into account principles drawn from Christian faith, a Christian university must also engage responsibly and prudently with the conditions and parameters laid down by legislation and government policy, both to promote their own survival and flourishing, and also to serve the common good. Third, there must be genuine consultation at the local level with all stakeholders. The mediating factors highlighted in the previous paragraph will exercise considerable weight here, but they do not predetermine decisions. These are influenced by the quality of the 'reading' of the context that goes on. They will be qualified by the sensitivity of the listening that is carried out. Each community will establish its own unique balance between caution and risk-taking. Also relevant to decisions that affect the mission is the degree to which individuals at all levels show adaptability and a willingness to sacrifice personal goals for the greater good of the whole institution. Is there evidence of imagination and creativity in harnessing energies, in building coalitions and in using synergy?

Once a mission has been agreed, there is still a great deal of mediating that remains to be done. By their very nature, institutional mission statements operate at a level above the day-to-day. They offer a general guide, a touchstone for action but they do not dictate precisely what must be done or how the ideals are to be attained. There must be room for manoeuvre and scope for initiative, at individual and team level, in the various parts of the institution; for without this there could be no real exercise of responsibility and judgement. Members of staff find they face an ongoing task in relation to the mission of mediating it, of making it concrete in particular policies and decisions. In the course of this mediation, colleagues have to internalise general principles and take ownership of them. They need to process the ideals, seeing ways to implement these. They sometimes have to translate concepts that emerged from unfamiliar contexts or which do not quite match their working environment. In responding to their university mission, they might need to remap what had seemed well-trodden territory. In applying the mission to the work of their own sector, department or team, they have to correlate and integrate different kinds of wisdom.

As an example of the kind of mediation implied above, let us focus briefly on the meeting of student needs, since pastoral care and support for students will be a feature of all universities and should certainly be prominent in Christian universities. The mission of the university provides an initial framework for the task of supporting students and meeting their needs. Then there will be specific claims made about this area of work in the university. Individual members of the academic and student services staff will internalise the institution's mission and pastoral care claims in different ways. Another factor is the amount of contact between the academic and the student services staff, the quality of relationships and communication between them, and the degree of mutual appreciation shown with regard to their respective roles, remit and requirements. Each 'unit' within an institution tends to develop its own ethos and self-understanding about its work. Thus the mission in general, policy statements about student support, and the bearing of one upon the other, may be interpreted and mediated differently by a team in sociology than by a team in theology; these may appear differently again if one belongs to a team in registry or a team whose focus is addressing special needs. Students' perceptions of their needs, their values and their expectations will influence their response to the way the institution and its staff approaches them and in turn will affect the implementation of mission. Once the wider contextual factors described in earlier paragraphs are taken into account, it can be seen that between mission and the service delivered at any particular point of need there is a long and complex journey to be made.

One central way that the Christian university can serve as a context for mediating Christian faith is in its promotion of ecumenical learning. In each of the Christian institutions of higher education at the moment, there is a generous commitment to ecumenism rather than an exclusively denominational focus. As far as one tell, this commitment to ecumenism is fully supported by the churches sponsoring these colleges. It stems from principle as well as from a pragmatic response to the reality that these colleges could not function without the presence of many students and colleagues who are either non–believers or who do not share the same version of Christian faith as the sponsoring churches. A Christian university should offer many opportunities for students and staff to pray together, to relax together, to collaborate in acts of service to those in need within and beyond the institution. It should also be a place where there are opportunities at various levels to study Christianity and its bearing on all aspects of the curriculum, community, work and of life. Some of this study should include in-depth, critical retrieval of particular denominational traditions and some of it should require ecumenical enquiry into common features of the Christian traditions. Both are essential ingredients if ecumenism is to thrive. Discernment as to what should be retained, what rejected and what modified within a tradition depends on a detailed knowledge of it, although such detailed knowledge is insufficient on its own, for it needs to be drawn into dialogue with those who start from a different perspective.

Such ecumenism will benefit especially from four types of support. First, it needs a confident and articulate team of theologians who can offer intellectual leadership in the realm of religious teaching. Second, the institution needs a strong steer from leaders who give ecumenism a high priority, for 'ecumenism is not just some sort of "appendix" which is added to the church's traditional activity. Rather, it is an organic part of her life and work, and consequently must pervade all that she is and does' (John Paul II, 1995, para. 20, p. 26). Third, a critical mass of staff and, ideally, students, should be prepared to avail themselves of the opportunities provided to engage with ecumenical sharing, dialogue and reflection and to apply the fruits of this to their studies and work. Fourth, the churches outside the university need to demonstrate their interest in it, their appreciation of its special role and their desire both to contribute to and to learn from this.

In a Christian university many people will express their Christian commitment implicitly, simply by being dedicated professionals in their daily work, whether as teachers, researchers, administrators, support staff, managers or leaders. Others will accept the responsibility of articulating publicly the Christian faith, for example as chaplains or as theologians or as members of Christian groups. Some will come to study or to work in such a place, not because of its links with a religious faith, but because of the other opportunities it affords them. Some will come to study there because they wish either to develop a relationship with a Christian community or to extend and deepen a relationship that is already important to them.

A Christian university should reflect the three theological emphases outlined by Leslie Francis: a theology of nurture, of service and of prophecy (Francis, 1993). It should be a place where those who are already Christians can experience support for this faith, the kind of support that affirms and encourages faith, but which also stretches and challenges it. Here one should have every opportunity to deepen this faith, intellectually and spiritually, and to experience a variety of ways in which it can be expressed in action. At the same time, for those who do not wish to become involved in explicitly Christian activities, the Christian university offers a high quality of education and service. For all members of the university community there should be a chance to hear Christian voices challenge gaps between rhetoric and reality in the internal running of the institution (although there will be many other voices which contribute to this critique), and offer a counter-cultural witness in the face of secular and religious establishments in the wider society. If nurture, service and prophecy each receive their rightful share of attention and energy, a Christian university will be a place where students' needs are addressed and where academic and spiritual traditions are encountered on their own terms. It will also be a place where lives and traditions are weighed in the balance for their authenticity, purpose, integrity, coherence and fruitfulness. In this way the Christian university promotes well-founded commitments and invites all its members to enter into dialogue about those commitments, and so continue their learning.

References

Benne, Robert (2001) *Quality with Soul*, Grand Rapids, MI, Eerdmans.
Blumhofer, Edith (ed.) (2002) *Religion, Education, and the American Experience*, Tuscaloosa, ALA, The University of Alabama Press.
Brookfield, Stephen and Stephen Preskill (1999) *Discussion as a Way of Teaching*, Buckingham, Open University Press.
Buckley, Michael (1999) *The Idea and Promise of a Catholic University*, Washington, DC, Georgetown University Press.
Cady, Linell and Delwin Brown (eds) (2002) *Religious Studies, Theology, and the University*, New York, State University of New York Press.
Cernera, Anthony and Oliver Morgan (2000) *Examining the Catholic Intellectual Tradition*, Fairfield, CN, Sacred Heart University Press.
Clouser, Roy (1991) *The Myth of Religious Neutrality*, Notre Dame, IN, University of Notre Dame Press.
Dockery, David and Gregory Thornbury (2002) *Shaping a Christian Worldview*, Nashville, TN, Broadman and Holman.
Dovre, Paul (ed.) (2002) *The Future of Religious Colleges*, Grand Rapids, MI, Eerdmans.
Dulles, Avery (1974) *Models of the Church*, Dublin, Gill and Macmillan.
Estanek, Sandra (ed.) (2002) *Student Affairs at Catholic Colleges and Universities*, Franklin, WI, Sheed and Ward.
Francis, Leslie J. (1993) 'Theology of Education and the Church School', in L. J. Francis and D. W. Lankshear (eds), *Christian Perspectives on Church Schools*, Leominster, Gracewing, pp. 52–66.
Grant, Edward (2001) *God and Reason in the Middle Ages*, Cambridge, Cambridge University Press.
Haynes, Stephen (ed.) (2002) *Professing in the Postmodern Academy*, Waco, TX, Baylor University Press.
Hendrie, Robert (2002) *A Church That Works: The Ecclesiology of Baron Friedrich von Hügel*, St Andrews, University of St Andrews (Theology in Scotland).
Himes, Michael (2001) '"Finding God in All Things": A Sacramental Worldview and its Effects', in Landy, pp. 91–103.
Hughes, Richard and William Adrian (eds) (1997) *Models for Christian Higher Education*, Grand Rapids, MI, Eerdmans.
John Paul II (1995) *Ut Unum Sint*, London, Catholic Truth Society.
Landy, Thomas (ed.) (2001) *As Leaven in the World*, Franklin, WI, Sheed and Ward.
MacIntyre, Alasdair (1984) *After Virtue*, London, Duckworth.

Macquarrie, John (1997) *A Guide to the Sacraments*, London, SCM.

Marsden, George (1997) *The Outrageous Idea of Christian Scholarship*, New York, Oxford University Press.

Matthews, Scott (2001) *Reason, Community and Religious Tradition*, Aldershot, Ashgate.

McCutcheon, Russell (2001) *Critics Not Caretakers*, New York, State University of New York Press.

Naugle, David (2002) *Worldview: The History of a Concept*, Grand Rapids, MI, Eerdmans.

Nord, Warren (2002) 'Liberal Education and Religious Studies', in Blumhofer, pp. 9–40.

O'Brien, George Dennis (2002) *The Idea of a Catholic University*, Chicago, IL, University of Chicago Press.

Pauw, Amy Plantinga (2002) 'Attending to the Gaps between Beliefs and Practices', in Volf and Bass, pp. 33–48.

Poupard, Paul *et al.*(1994) *The Presence of the Church in the University*, Rome, Pontifical Council for Culture.

Sterk, Andrea (ed.) (2002) *Religion, Scholarship, and Higher Education*, Notre Dame, IN, University of Notre Dame Press.

Sullivan, John (2001) 'Plasticity, Piety and Polemics', *Journal of Religious Education*, 49, 2, pp. 345–353.

Sullivan, John (2002) 'Scholarship and Spirituality', *The Downside Review*, 120, 420, pp. 189–214.

Sullivan, John (2003) 'From Formation to the Frontiers: The Dialectic of Christian Education', *Journal of Christian Belief and Education*, 7, 1, pp. 7–22.

Volf, Miroslav and Dorothy Bass (eds) (2002) *Practicing Theology*, Grand Rapids, MI, Eerdmans.

Von Hügel, Friedrich (1908) *The Mystical Element of Religion*, two volumes, London, Dent.

Von Hügel, Friedrich (1921) *Essays and Addresses on the Philosophy of Religion*, London, Dent.

Von Hügel, Friedrich (1927) *Selected Letters 1896–1924*, edited by Bernard Holland, London, Dent.

Webb, Stephen (2001) *Taking Religion to School*, Grand Rapids, MI, Eerdmans.

Wilcox, John and Irene King (2000) *Enhancing Religious Identity*, Washington, DC, Georgetown University Press.

Chapter Three

Objections to the Idea of a Christian University

Elmer John Thiessen

There are many in the academic establishment who continue to object to the very idea of a Christian university. Martha Nussbaum, for example, in her recent book *Cultivating Humanity: A Classical Defense of Reform in Liberal Education* (1997), construes tradition of any kind as inimical to the kind of free enquiry that is the heart and soul of university life.

The notion of free enquiry finds expression in the principle of academic freedom which is at the heart of the modern university. The academic establishment has by and large relegated religious colleges and universities to inferior status because of their alleged failure to uphold this principle. For example, the longstanding position of the American Association of University Professors (AAUP) is that religious schools are entitled to depart from the principle of 'full' academic freedom as long as they clearly announce their intention to do so. However, such stated intentions of accepting only 'limited academic freedom' come with a cost. Thus a 1988 subcommittee of the AAUP, studying the issue of academic freedom and tenure, stated that the 'necessary consequence' of the decision by religious institutions to invoke the Limitations Clause of the 1940 Statement of Principles on Academic Freedom and Tenure is that they forfeit 'the moral right to proclaim themselves as authentic seats of higher learning'.[1]

George Marsden, in tracing the history of the gradual secularisation of American universities, points to a parallel phenomenon in theology – the popularity during the mid-1960s of 'secular' theologies (1994, p. 417). Thus Harvey Cox, a professor at the Harvard Divinity School, devotes a chapter of his widely popular *The Secular City* (1965) to 'The

Church and the Secular University', in which he celebrates the secularisation of the university and then makes a scathing comment about churches who were responding to the rise of secular universities by establishing their own colleges and universities.

> This of course is medievalism. The whole idea of a 'Christian' college or university after the breaking apart of the medieval synthesis has little meaning. The term *Christian* is not one that can be used to refer to universities any more than to observatories or laboratories. No one of the so-called Christian colleges that now dot our Midwest is able to give very plausible theological basis for restoring the equivocal phrase *Christian college* in its catalogue. ... The idea of developing 'Christian universities' in America was bankrupt even before it began. (Cox, 1965, p. 221)

For a final criticism of the idea of a Christian university I cite another statement going back even further in time, and giving expression to an antireligious interpretation of academic freedom arising in the post-McCarthyite era when religious and political con-servativism were often conflated and assumed to be equally oppressive (Marsden, 1994, p. 433).

> Those who advocate that the university should take a definitely religious stance are in their proselytizing zeal committing themselves to a total perversion of the function of the university. They would revert to the intellectual confusion of earlier times, when a superimposed prior 'truth' retarded the advance of knowledge and thus tended to imprison the inquiring mind. To make the university a centre for the propagation of any creed, of any system of values that divides group from group, is to destroy the special quality and the unique mission of the university as a centre for the free pursuit of knowledge wherever it may lead. (MacIver, 1955, p. 138)

The aim of this essay is to answer these and other related objections to the very idea of a Christian university. I do not want to spend much time defining the notion of a Christian university – a task which has been ably addressed in other works.[2] A couple of historical obser-vations, however, might be appropriate. Universities have their origin in the Middle Ages and at that time the idea of a Christian university was not at all problematic.[3] In North America, as in Great Britain, the first universities were Christian universities. Objections to the idea of a Christian university are therefore historically conditioned. This is one of the implications that grow out of Marsden's seminal work, entitled *The Soul of the American University*.[4] Attacks against the idea of a Christian university grow out of a particular context – the secularisation of the university and the establishment of nonbelief at the vast majority of universities. This should give us some pause with regard to challenges against the very idea of a Christian university. Perhaps they are only expressions of a particular kind of narrative, an oppressive narrative at that. Despite the particularity of these attacks, however, I believe they need to be taken seriously.

One other point about Marsden's historical analysis deserves to be highlighted. The pace-setting American universities were virtually all constructed in the late nineteenth and early twentieth century and were products of a nonsectarian liberal Protestant culture (Marsden, 1997, pp. 14–15). Eventually even the vestiges of liberal Protestantism were dropped at these universities. It would seem that a consideration of the possibility of a Christian university is not as problematic given a liberal Protestant version of Christianity. Real problems are thought to arise with the linking of 'sectarian' Christianity and university education. My aim in this paper is to concentrate on a defence of Christian universities of a fairly orthodox or evangelical variety. A key to such a defence is to uncover and critically evaluate some of the assumptions that underlie the secularisation of the modern university which in turn lead to suspicions about the idea of a conservative Christian university.

Tradition and particularity

A negative assessment of tradition figures significantly in the critiques of the idea of a Christian university cited above. Running parallel to this assessment of tradition is an ideal of the university as a centre for the free pursuit of knowledge. Nussbaum, for example, construes tradition of any kind as inimical to the kind of free enquiry that is the heart and soul of university life. According to MacIver, attachment to, or the superimposition of any prior 'truth' is thought to retard the advancement of knowledge and to imprison the inquiring mind. He goes on to suggest that making a university a centre for the propagation of any creed is to destroy the special quality and the unique mission of the university as a centre for the free pursuit of knowledge wherever it may lead. Marsden has similarly shown that the original formation of the AAUP and its position concerning academic freedom assumed an ideal of free and objective scientific enquiry which would rid us of the parochial past, together with the passion, prejudice, and partisanship associated with tradition (Marsden, 1993, pp. 226–231).

There are problems, however, with both poles of this critique of the Christian university. Tradition cannot simply be described as inimical to the free pursuit of knowledge. Indeed, tradition is a necessary foundation for such a pursuit. Further, to describe the university in terms of an ideal of free and objective scientific enquiry is simply unrealistic. Both of these assumptions grow out of the Enlightenment which is also at the root of the modern ideal of the secular university.

More recent developments in the philosophy of science, the sociology of knowledge and feminist epistemology, to name but a few, have shown that the search for truth is always guided by assumptions and preconceptions which function as constraints on freedom of enquiry.[5] The Enlightenment quest for absolute objectivity is inherently futile. It is a quest for a 'view from nowhere', as Thomas Nagel has aptly described it (1986). A view from nowhere is impossible because all rational activity is 'inescapably historically and socially context-bound' (MacIntyre, 1988, p. 4). The idea of a universal and neutral rationality is now recognised to be itself an expression of a particular narrative, an Enlightenment narrative.

Or, to use the language of postmodernism, the idea of an ahistorical, non-contingent, rational self is a myth. Therefore complete objectivity is impossible. Knowledge and truth are to some degree relative to place, society, culture, historical epoch, and conceptual framework. Truth needs to be seen as located within the context of discourse communities. Scholarship, too, is necessarily situated within a present and a particular.

Postmodernism, at its core, is a reaction to the Enlightenment. At the core of the Enlightenment, which set the agenda of modernity, was a desire to search for truth apart from tradition and authority. The oral, particular, local, and timely were all viewed with suspicion (Toulmin, 1990, pp. 30–35). This same emphasis is very much in evidence in the early development of the modern secular university. Marsden highlights the fact that behind the formation of professional societies such as AAUP in 1915 was a desire 'to define and control a national culture at the expense of local cultures'. They 'were creating loyalties and self-definitions based on the scientific standards of national organisations, and thus undermining loyalty to particular institutions and their traditions' (Marsden, 1993, p. 227; 1994, p. 306). This same spirit created a suspicion of religious educational institutions.[6]

Postmodernism can be seen as an attempt to recapture pre-Enlightenment respect for tradition and that which is bound to a particular time and place. Thinking never occurs in a vacuum. It must always start from somewhere. Christian academics choose to start with a Christian worldview. Secular academics obviously start with a different worldview. Each starting point shapes and 'limits' ensuing thought and research. But it is simply mistaken to view the assumptions and preconceptions that any rational person begins with as functioning only as constraints on freedom of enquiry. While functioning as limitations in one sense, they must also be seen as preconditions of rationality.[7] In other words, they make possible the search for truth. Christian academics feel that the search for truth is better facilitated by starting with Christian presuppositions. They see their starting point 'as an academic asset, not a liability' (Hardy, 1995, p. 16). The words of Psalm 36:9 are the guiding inspiration of the Christian university: 'In your light we see light.' Considerations such as this prompt Hardy to define the Christian university as 'an elective association of scholars working in a tradition of enquiry according to constraints it accepts and believes will assist it in tracking the truth about the world' (1995, p. 16). Given the new developments in epistemology it is simply naive to ridicule the idea of a Christian university because it encourages the search for truth by starting from a particular worldview.

Liberation and free enquiry

It is also naive for critics of the idea of a Christian university to see 'free enquiry' or 'the free pursuit of knowledge' as the fundamental characteristic of the 'secular' university. There simply is not and cannot be such a thing as complete freedom or absolute freedom, as would seem to be assumed in these ideals. Freedom is necessarily defined in relation to certain constraints. The search for knowledge always takes place within a certain context. Universities too are always located within a particular environment which in fact imposes certain constraints on them.[8] The argument of the previous section also highlights the impossibility of free enquiry. The ideal of free enquiry too has its origins in the Enlightenment, where enquiry was to be freed from the constraints of tradition and authority, particularly as found in religion. But enquiry always arises from within the context of some particular tradition, as I have already argued. There simply is no such thing as free enquiry in complete isolation. Free enquiry is necessarily parasitic on tradition.

Clearly, however, we can place too much emphasis on tradition and the particularity of traditions. Surely we must also allow for the possibility of subjecting particular traditions to critical scrutiny. And here we come to a significant positive ingredient in the ideal of the university as a place of free enquiry. While I agree with the post-modernists in stressing the tradition-bound nature of all thinking, we must at the same time do justice to the fact that traditions can ossify and can even turn out to be wrong. There is, therefore, a need for critical enquiry and the freedom to engage in the same. Where the critics of the idea of a Christian university err is in assuming that a commitment to certain religious presuppositions precludes an honest and open search for the truth.

Open-mindedness is not the same as empty-mindedness (Hare, 1979, p. 53). Indeed, there are no empty minds. Locke's *tabula rasa* is a myth. Schwehn has aptly described the rhythms of intellectual life at a Christian university as including 'both a relentless questioning of what we believe and a believing of that which we question' (1999, p. 29; 1993, p. 49). MacIntyre too describes vital traditions and the institutions that bear these traditions as being constituted by 'continuous argument', and as embodying 'continuities of conflict'. 'A living tradition then is an historically extended, socially embodied argument' (MacIntyre, 1984, p. 222). There is surely no better way than this to describe the nature of Christian universities. Unfortunately, all too often their secular counterparts are unwilling or unable to engage in the same kind of critical scrutiny of their most basic presuppositions.

Relativism and the battle for truth

It should be apparent that I am distancing myself in part from the postmodernist critique of modernity and what this entails for university life. If, with the postmodernists, we stress the context-bound nature of rationality too much, there is the danger of opening the door to epistemological relativism. Indeed, the postmodernist's claim that knowledge is merely a social and political construction which privileges some and silences others requires a radical reinterpretation of the notion of freedom of enquiry. The principle of academic freedom will need to be reinterpreted in terms of protecting the rights of the silent and the marginalised, thereby enabling them to gain a voice. Such a reinterpretation along the lines of critical theory has been attempted by William Tierney (1993).

The problem with such a radical politicisation of the notion of free enquiry is that the search for truth is replaced with a battle for survival. Tierney is quite explicit in calling for a replacement of a 'consensual model' of knowledge and academic freedom with a 'conflict model in which we assume that competing interests will always exist' (1993, p. 148). Such a conflict model of the search for truth is frightening. I would suggest that we have yet to reap the full consequences of this postmodernist model being increasingly accepted in our universities. Here I can only refer to conservative critics of the academy who have, over the last decade, issued warnings about the radical orientation that currently resides in our college and university campuses.[9]

A further problem here is that without the notion of truth, or the ideal of searching for truth, we have undermined the very heart of university education and research. Indeed, what radical postmodernists like Tierney fail to realise is that without the notion of truth they have in fact undermined their own critique of the academy. Why listen to the radicals if they are merely one voice among many other relative voices? Postmodernists further invariably contradict themselves! They seem unable to avoid talking about postmodernism as better than modernism. Better in terms of what? Such evaluation seems to point in the direction of an ideal of objective and universal truth.

Here I am in agreement with a basic idea inherent in the traditional ideal of the university and its notion of free enquiry – the search for truth is important, and we need to protect the search for, and the exposition of claims to truth from arbitrary limitations. While I have stressed the limitations inherent in our search for truth and our need to be honest about these limitations, I in no way want to do away with the notion that human beings must, and invariably do, attempt to transcend these limitations in their search for universal truth (Nagel, 1986, p. 70; 1997, p. 5). Without balancing the emphasis on limitations with an equal emphasis on the need to try to transcend these limitations, we end up with epistemological relativism and the radical politicisation of the academy which we see on our campuses today. What I am proposing, therefore, is a reconciliation of the insights of modernism and postmodernism concerning epistemology and human nature, avoiding the extremes in either position.

Academic freedom

A reconciliation of the legitimate insights of both modernism and postmodernism will lead to a balanced view of academic freedom which acknowledges that while teachers and researchers are un-avoidably rooted within a tradition, they will invariably also be seeking to transcend their limitations in an ongoing search for truth. What is needed, therefore, is an ideal of 'normal academic freedom' that recognises both the need for and the limits of freedom.[10] While the notion of pure objectivity that lies behind the traditional ideal of academic freedom is an illusion, the notion of 'a view from nowhere' must be kept as a heuristic principle in order to encourage an open-minded search for truth. Of course, at a Christian university, 'the view from nowhere' will be redefined as a view from somewhere. All truth is God's truth, and thus the search for truth can and must proceed.

What does this reconciliation of the insights of modernism and postmodernism entail for the charge that the ideal of academic freedom is violated in Christian colleges and universities, or that such schools are inferior because they can only have a limited degree of academic free-dom? This charge rests on a muddled, unrealistic, and philosophically indefensible concept of academic freedom. Once this concept is updated so as to acknowledge the inescapable limitations of freedom that accompany teaching and research *in any context*, the religious commitment of these schools does not of necessity entail the absence of academic freedom.

The 'limitations clause' in the AAUP 1940 Statement of Academic Freedom unfairly singles out religious institutions as having only limited academic freedom. *All institutions have limited academic freedom.* A more honest approach to academic freedom would be to see the limitations clause as applying to *all* institutions. Here I cannot help but suggest that if the limitations clause were to be seen as also applying to secular universities, and if they were required to openly declare the boundaries to academic freedom that in fact exist, it would lead to a good deal of embarrassment about what the boundaries to research and teaching are, and how many such boundaries there are.

At the same time it should be stressed that all schools, religious as well as secular, can and should be engaged in an open and honest search for the truth. This openness, however, should be coupled with an equally open admission of the limiting context within which this search for truth is being conducted. Much more needs to be done by way of defining the proper balance between such limitations and freedom, but this cannot be undertaken in this short essay. What is important, however, is that there be honesty about the commitments within which the search for truth takes place. This is surely what objectivity is all about for the scholar and the teacher.[11]

What this revised ideal of academic freedom entails is that Christian universities should be seen as having equal status to secular educational institutions. As Marsden puts it, 'colleges and universities that represent alternate viewpoints, based on traditional Christian and other religious commitments, should be fully recognised as equally legitimate with those who have claimed universality on the basis of the alleged authority of value-free science' (Marsden 1993, p. 233).

This is not to say that there are not violations of academic freedom at Christian universities, just as there are at 'secular' universities.[12] My primary concern here is to argue that academic freedom is possible at Christian universities, and that the Christian commitment that per-vades such an institution does not in and of itself negate the possibility of academic freedom, and that the limitations to academic freedom accepted at Christian universities in no way suggest that they thereby forfeit 'the moral right to proclaim themselves as authentic seats of higher learning'.

Indoctrination

So far I have dealt more broadly with objections to the idea of a Christian university, focusing more on the intellectual climate of such institutions and the implications for faculty. The broader themes that have been considered can also be applied to the student. MacIver describes a university committed to a particular religious stance as tending to 'imprison the inquiring mind,' thus perverting the essential function of the university. The term 'indoctrination' is often invoked to describe such imprisoning of students' minds. One of the central problems of this charge is that there is much confusion surrounding the meaning of 'indoctrination'. Indeed, as I have argued at length elsewhere, I do not believe that those making the charge against education from and for commitment use the term in a coherent fashion (Thiessen, 1993). Here I will only make two additional comments in response to the indoctrination charge against Christian universities.

Underlying this charge there is again a failure to do justice to the importance of tradition in education. Charles Bailey has captured the heart of the traditional ideal of liberal education underlying the modern university when he describes it as an education which liberates a student and moves him/her 'beyond the present and the particular' (1984). Here we need to be careful because clearly there is something right about understanding liberal education in this way. Some liberation from the present and particular is surely justified. Student horizons need to be expanded. But there are some fundamental errors in seeing liberal education primarily in terms of liberating students in this way. For one, there is a tendency to view the present and the particular entirely in a negative light, as a limitation, as something from which a student must be completely liberated. It should be rather obvious that children must first of all be initiated into a particular home, a particular language, a particular culture, a particular set of beliefs, before they can begin to expand their horizons beyond the present and the particular. There is therefore a need to respect particularity and tradition. Liberal education can further be equally well described in terms of helping students to see the full potential of the particular traditions they have grown up with. Horizons are expanded at a Christian university when students come to appreciate how a Christian worldview enables them to pursue truth and to better understand the world they live in.

Another way to express the worry about 'imprisoning' or 'indoctrinating' student minds is to maintain that a Christian university will stifle student growth towards autonomy. As I have argued in my earlier writings, there is something right about understanding 'indoctrination' in terms of curtailing a student's growth towards 'rational autonomy'. But here again, we need to avoid unrealistic expectations as to the level of autonomy that any human being can achieve. I therefore prefer to talk about 'normal rational autonomy' which recognises human finiteness, the contingency of life and the degree to which human beings are interdependent.

The other central error behind this concern is to assume that starting from a committed religious stance will stifle growth towards autonomy. Exactly the reverse is the case. Some writers have introduced the notion of a 'primary culture' to describe the present and particular from which all educational growth must take place (Ackerman, 1980, chapter 5; McLaughlin, 1984). Research in the areas of developmental psychology and psychiatry by individuals like Michael Rutter, Urie Bronfenbrenner and Reuven Feuerstein, to name only three, would suggest that we can be too hasty in liberating students from the present and the particular.[13] Exposing them to plurality and a Babel of beliefs and values too soon will in fact hinder growth towards autonomy.

Here it might be objected that surely when students reach the university level of education the need for a primary culture no longer exists. Surely they should now be able to handle plurality and a Babel of beliefs. This is essentially a psychological issue. Bronfenbrenner, in his review of the research regarding the need for a stable and secure home environment, specifically raises the question of how long this need for a primary culture lasts. He replies, 'The matter is debatable, but I would suggest anyone under the age of, say, 89' (1980, p. 1). Peter Berger and Thomas Luckmann argue that all of us, whatever our age, need 'plausibility structures' in order to maintain some level of credibility for the beliefs we accept as true (1967, pp. 154–163). Brian Walsh has argued that the college stage of life (between the ages of 18 and 22) is crucial and pivotal in anyone's worldview development, and hence the importance of a Christian college or university in guiding the late adolescent process of worldview formation (1992, p. 29). Of course there needs to be a growing exposure to plurality and a Babel of beliefs. But I would suggest that this is better done within the context of a university that reflects the primary culture of the student. Hence again the need for a Christian university for Christian students.

The possibility of Christian scholarship

There is an assumption underlying my argument thus far that needs some further exploration. I have been assuming that the label 'Christian' can be applied to a university and that this will somehow make a difference. As noted earlier, it would seem that Harvey Cox questions this: 'The term Christian is not one that can be used to refer to universities any more than to observatories or laboratories.' I would suggest that Cox is here hinting that the Christian commitment of a Christian university cannot really make a difference in the teaching and research that goes on at a university. After all, science is science and whether a person is a Christian or an atheist will make no difference in an observatory or laboratory. This kind of objection to the very possibility of teaching or doing research from a Christian point of view is not at all uncommon. Indeed, the frequency of such comments prompted historian George Marsden to write a book entitled *The Outrageous Idea of Christian Scholarship* (1997). In it he recounts an address he gave at the 1993 plenary session of the American Academy of Religion. His topic, 'Religious Commitment in the Academy', created quite a stir which even spilled over into the mainstream media. John C. Green, a political scientist, made this observation:

> If a professor talks about studying something from a Marxist point of view, others might disagree but not dismiss the notion. But if a professor proposed to study something from a Catholic or Protestant point of view, it would be treated like proposing something from a Martian point of view.[14]

Of course, this kind of objection undercuts the very heart of a Christian university, and thus requires an answer. Here I can only provide an outline of a response which I have developed more carefully elsewhere (Thiessen, 2001, chapter 10).

The fundamental problem with this objection is that it rests on an epistemology of neutrality that I have already critiqued in the earlier sections of this essay. What is being assumed here is an Enlightenment epistemology and the scientific approach to knowledge which grew out of the Enlightenment. The notions of complete objectivity and a universal kind of rationality are central to this epistemology. But, as I have already argued, new developments in epistemology and the philosophy of science have seriously challenged the notions of objectivity and a universal kind of rationality. It is now generally recognised that thinking in any field is theory-laden and coloured by a host of subjective factors. But once this is acknowledged, there is nothing incoherent about the idea of a distinctively Christian approach to scholarship and the various subjects studied at a university.

What is curious is that the educational implications of the new epistemology are frequently acknowledged in academia, though, for some reason, they are not extended to include the idea of a distinctively Christian scholarship. As Marsden is at pains to point out, in mainstream academia there are now various Marxist, feminist, gay, postmodern, African–American, conservative or liberal schools of thought (1997, pp. 5–6, 52, 64, 72). The very existence of each of these schools of thought is premised on the assumption that such factors as the identities and social location of human beings have some bearing on rationality. Scholarship is in part shaped by who we are. Michael McConnell, Professor of Law at the University of Chicago, also draws attention to the existence of courses in feminist jurisprudence at most major secular law schools, though he is not aware of any course in Christian (or other religious) jurisprudence. It would seem that in mainstream academia, 'any hint of a religious approach to the subject matter would be deemed academically inappropriate,' suggests McConnell (1993, p. 315). But, surely, consistency demands that there should be room in academia for explicitly Christian points of view just as there are explicitly feminist or Marxist or liberal points of view. Such consistency would in turn call into question Cox's suggestion that the Christian commitment of a Christian university cannot really make a difference in the teaching and research that goes on at that university.

But exactly how does faith inform scholarship? I would suggest that it is precisely the difficulties involved in answering this question that have led to scepticism concerning the very possibility of Christian scholarship. Marsden, for example, talks rather vaguely about 'faith-informed scholarship', or about a Christian perspective 'influencing' a curriculum (1997, pp. 10, 62, 65, 67, 70). I want to try and define this a little more precisely.[15]

The notion of a worldview is useful in explaining how faith might inform scholarship. A worldview (derived from the German word *Weltanschaaung*) is a way of seeing the world. It is like a set of sunglasses which often colour everything that we see. Walsh and Middleton describe the Christian worldview as a 'transforming vision' which makes us look at the world in a different way from, say, a naturalistic framework (1984).[16] Other worldviews make us see the world differently once again. For example, Schumacher has given us a classic statement on the difference between a Buddhist approach to economics over against the standard Western capitalist approach (1973, chapter 4).

Here it might be objected that while a Christian worldview might make a difference in certain areas of scholarship, for example, the humanities and the social sciences, it is difficult to see what difference it might make in the hard sciences.[17] In order to explain why this might be so I would like to draw on some useful descriptions and analogies of the structure of knowledge provided by the Harvard philosopher, Willard Van Quine. Quine suggests that we need to look at what we believe in terms of a system of interlocking beliefs which we use in trying to explain experience. 'The beliefs face the tribunal of observation not singly but in a body,' he maintains (Quine and Ullian, 1978, p. 22). Elsewhere, Quine goes on to suggest that there are varying degrees of importance in the beliefs of a belief-system (1961, p. 42). Beliefs in the interior of the field are more central and basic than empirical statements that arise at the periphery of our belief-system. I like to think of our belief-system as a series of concentric circles, at the core of which is a particular worldview. This worldview, or the basic presuppositions of our worldview, lead to the next circle of beliefs, namely philosophical theories, which in turn lead to scientific theories, which in turn finally lead to the making of specific claims. All beliefs, however far removed from the centre of one's belief-system, are influenced by one's basic presuppositions to some degree. Such influence can be compared to the diminishing ripples caused by a stone cast into a pond. The influence of one's basic presuppositions are very evident in the philosophical theories one adopts, but less so with regard to specific claims about the colour of one's shoe, $2 + 2 = 4$, or the chemical composition of common salt. But even in mathematics and chemistry, different interpretations of these disciplines become evident as any book on the philosophy of mathematics or the history of science will show.[18] A Christian worldview will therefore make a more obvious difference in the humanities and social sciences, which I believe are closer to the centre of a belief-system, and hence are the more important courses at any university.

Here one qualification must be introduced. While distinctive, Christian scholarship will of necessity also share many things in common with the scholarship at a secular university. Here we must avoid the fallacy of either-or. It is possible to affirm at one and the same time that one's belief-system is unique, and that it shares truths with other belief-systems. This can be illustrated by thinking in terms of a series of ellipses, each representing a different worldview, but all overlapping to some degree. Each ellipse is unique, and yet there is some common ground. This illustration is meant to do justice to the fact that we invariably find that there is a partial convergence of differing worldviews or differing belief-systems.[19]

Why is there such an overlap? We live in the same world. Regardless of our worldviews, we have a common source of data, which imposes constraints on the extent to which we can interpret reality. Human nature is roughly the same. We are trying to understand the same reality. We are striving for the same truth. Hence, it should not surprise us that the work done at a Christian university will to some extent resemble the work done at a 'secular' university. The underlying justifications and interpretations of this work will be very different however. Thus there is nothing outrageous about a Christian university doing distinctively Christian scholarship or teaching from a distinctively Christian perspective.

Tolerance and social cohesion

There is a hint of another objection to Christian universities in the quotation from Robert MacIver cited at the beginning of this essay. MacIver suggests that 'to make the university a centre for the propagation of any creed, of any system of values that divides group from group, is to destroy the special quality and the unique mission of the university.' I have already dealt with the primary concern of this quotation, namely the relation between the religious commitment of, for example, a Christian university and its ability to fulfil the mission of any university to be a centre for the free pursuit of knowledge. But MacIver is hinting at another problem with a religious university. It is based on a system of values that divides group from group. The university, for MacIver, also has a social mission, and that is to foster social cohesion. It must therefore focus not on particularity which divides us, but on that which unites – universal values. Other writers are even bolder in maintaining that a focus on particularity will foster intolerance and divisiveness in a society.[20]

These concerns create problems for the very idea of a Christian university, because it is based on a division which clearly divides those who are Christian from those who are not. Further, it is obvious that if one accepts the idea of a Christian university, one must also, in the interests of fairness, defend the idea of a Muslim or a Hindu university. I am here assuming a certain context, that of multicultural and multi-religious society.[21] The objection often raised against such a pluralistic system of university education is that it would not contribute to social cohesion, that the isolating of students into separate religiously-oriented universities would lead to a kind of 'voluntary apartheid' (Halstead, 1995).

Here it is important to keep in mind that, as various writers have shown, the political purpose of social cohesion was of more concern than a purely educational agenda in the founding of public education in America, for example.[22] This extended also to various levels of higher education, at the top of which the founding fathers envisioned a national university, which in all its functions was to be carefully attuned to the need for national cohesion (McClellan, 1985, pp. 35–36). While the early universities in America were clearly Christian in orientation, increasing concerns about sectarianism led to the gradual secularisation of the universities, as Marsden has carefully documented (1994). Indeed, these concerns about sectarianism eventually have led to a widespread opinion that having a plurality of church-related universities in a country is divisive. Hence also the opposition to the very idea of Christian universities on the part of many academics.

What I find curious about those who raise this kind of objection is that these same people are generally strong defenders of religious pluralism and multiculturalism. They just have a different under-standing of the nature of pluralism. They would, for example, identify the plurality of the secular university as an advantage over that of a monolithic Christian university. The secular university accommodates diverse points of view and provides the opportunity for dialogue between students from diverse backgrounds, including diverse religious orientations. There is certainly something to be said for this characterisation of the secular university and its implicit criticism of the Christian university. However, there is an important question that needs to be raised here. What kind of plurality are we talking about? I would suggest that the plurality being espoused by defenders of the secular university is a plurality of individuals. Indeed, the liberalism that is at the heart of the modern university typically does not see cultural membership as a primary good.[23]

Marsden further argues that despite the emphasis on multiculturalism and pluralism at American universities since the 1950s, 'American university culture is still shaped by a powerful impulse towards homogeneity and uniformity' (1997, p. 19). The subtitle of his 1994 work sums up the history of the American university – 'from Protestant establishment to established nonbelief' (1994). Marsden concludes: 'Pluralism as it is often conceived of today seems to be almost a code word for its opposite, a new expression of the melting-pot ideal. Persons from a wide variety of races and cultures are welcomed into the university, but only on the condition that they think more-or-less alike' (1994, p. 432). Alasdair MacIntyre has shown that these same dynamics are also present in the universities of Great Britain.[24] Interestingly, Marsden argues in a 'concluding unscientific postscript' not only for a greater acceptance of a pluralism of viewpoints within the secular university, but also for an acceptance of a plurality of institutions of higher learning (1994, pp. 436–440).

Indeed, there is empirical evidence to support the claim that a plurality of institutions of higher learning would be a better way to fostering social cohesion within a pluralistic society.[25] Why is this so? Because forced assimilation is always counter-productive. Because the key to foster social cohesion in a society is to recognise particularity. Here we need to face the question of whether it is best to start with unity or plurality. I would suggest that nature really dictates the proper order. As already pointed out, we all begin the human journey with particularity. Universality can only grow out of the particular, and this is best accomplished if it is done gradually and slowly within the context of universities that reflect particular identities. These are the kinds of insights that are behind the growing acceptance of the need for a 'politics of recognition' (Gutmann, 1994).

Conclusion

Let me conclude by drawing on a recent paper given by Brian Wash and Steven Bouma-Prediger, 'With and Without Boundaries: Christian Homemaking Amidst Postmodern Homelessness'.[26] Walsh and Bouma-Prediger introduce the metaphor of home which parallels an overriding theme of this essay – an emphasis on particularity and the need for a primary culture and plausibility structures. This need is rather acute in a world where there is so much disorientation. And this disorientation is in part rooted in the postmodern Zeitgeist of our time despite its seeming emphasis on particularity. Walter Truett Anderson speaks of postmodernism as 'the age of overexposure to otherness' (1995, p. 6). Postmodernism is rather allergic to the establishing of boundaries. It stresses the constructed character of all boundaries and hence the need to have them questioned or deconstructed. The result of all this questioning and deconstruction, unfortunately, is a widespread feeling of homelessness. But we need boundaries. We need places that we call home. As Caroline Westerhoff puts it, 'Boundaries are lines that afford definition, identity and protection – for persons, families, institutions, nations. … A boundary gives us something to which we can point and ascribe a name. Without a boundary, we have nothing to which we can invite or welcome anyone else' (1999, p. 7). We have here also the hint of the expansive possibilities of a boundary and a home. Although boundaries can exclude, although they can serve as 'fortresses of self-protection', they need not be exclusionary. They can also serve as places from which we can play the host to other persons and to other ideas. A Christian university will therefore function in two different but essentially related ways for its students. It will at one and the same time be a home which provides security and peace for its inhabitants, and also a place of orientation from which students will be able to explore and take possession of the wider world around them.[27]

References

Ackermann, Bruce (1980) *Social Justice in the Liberal State*, New Haven, CT, Yale University Press.
Anderson, Walter Truett (1990) *Reality Isn't What it Used to Be: Theatrical Politics, Ready-to-Wear Religion, Global Myths, Primitive Chic, and Other Wonders of the Postmodern World*, San Francisco, CA, Harper and Row.
Astley, J. and L. J. Francis (eds) (1994) *Critical Perspectives on Christian Education: A Reader on the Aims, Principles and Philosophy of Christian Education*, Grand Rapids, MI, Eerdmans and Leominster, Gracewing.
Bailey, C. (1984) *Beyond the Present and the Particular: A Theory of Liberal Education*, London, Routledge and Kegan Paul.
Berger, Peter L. and T. Luckmann (1967) *The Social Construction of Reality: A Treatise on the Sociology of Knowledge*, New York, Doubleday.
Bloom, Allan (1987) *The Closing of the American Mind*, New York, Simon and Schuster.
Bronfenbrenner, Urie (1979) *The Ecology of Human Development: Experiments by Nature and Design*, Cambridge, MA, Harvard University Press.
Bronfenbrenner, Urie (1980) 'On Making Human Beings Human', *Character: A Periodical about the Public and Private Policies Shaping American Youth*, 2, 2, pp. 1–7.
Burtchaell, James Tunstead (1998) *The Dying of the Light: The Disengagement of Colleges and Universities from their Christian Churches*, Grand Rapids, MI, Eerdmans.
Ciocchi, David M. (1994) 'Orthodoxy and Pluralism in the Christian University', *Faculty Dialogue*, 21, pp. 31–62.
Cox, Harvey (1965) *The Secular City*, New York, Macmillan.
Clouser, Roy A. (1991) *The Myth of Religious Neutrality: An Essay on the Hidden Role of Religious Belief in Theories*, Notre Dame, IN, University of Notre Dame Press.
D'Souza, (1991) *Illiberal Education: The Politics of Race and Sex on Campus*, New York, Free Press.
Ernest, Paul (1991) *The Philosophy of Mathematics Education*, London, Falmer.
Garry, Anne and Marilyn Pearsall (1989) *Women, Knowledge and Reality*, Boston, Unwin Hyman.
Geiger, Roger L. (1986) *Private Sectors in Higher Education: Structure, Function and Change in Eight Countries*, Ann Arbor, MI, University of Michigan Press.
Gleason, Philip (1995) *Contending with Modernity: Catholic Higher Education in Twentieth-Century America*, New York, Oxford University Press.
Glenn, Charles Leslie (1988) *The Myth of the Common School*, Amherst, MA, University of Massachusetts Press.
Gutmann, Amy (ed.) (1994) *Multiculturalism: Examining the Politics of Recognition*, Princeton, NJ, Princeton University Press.
Halstead, J. M. (1995) 'Voluntary Apartheid? Problems of Schooling for Religious and Other Minorities in Democratic Societies', *Journal of Philosophy of Education*, 29, 2, pp. 257–272.
Hardy, Lee (1995) 'Between Inculcation and Enquiry: The Virtue of Tolerance in the Liberal Arts Tradition', paper presented at the RUNA (Reformed University in North America) Conference, Grand Rapids, MI, March 24–25, pp. 5–26.
Hare, William (1979) *Open-Mindedness and Education*, Kingston and Montreal, McGill-Queen's University Press.
Hamilton, Neil W. (1995) *Zealotry and Academic Freedom: A Legal and Historical Perspective*, New Brunswick, CT and London, Transaction.

Heie, Harold and David L. Wolfe (eds) (1987) *The Reality of Christian Learning: Strategies for Faith-Discipline Integration,* Grand Rapids, MI, Christian University Press.

Hirst, Paul H. (1974) *Moral Education in a Secular Society,* London, University of London Press.

Holmes, Arthur (1987) *The Idea of a Christian College,* revised edition, Grand Rapids, MI, Eerdmans.

Horn, Michiel (1999) *Academic Freedom in Canada: A History,* Toronto, University of Toronto Press.

Kimball, R. (1990) *Tenured Radicals,* New York, Harper and Row.

Kuhn, Thomas S. (1970) *The Structure of Scientific Revolutions,* second edition, Chicago, University of Chicago Press.

Kymlicka, Will (1989) *Liberalism, Community and Culture,* Oxford, Clarendon.

McClellan, B. Edward (1985) 'Public Education and Social Harmony: The Roots of an American Dream', *Educational Theory,* 35, 1, pp. 33–42.

McConnell, Michael W. (1993) 'Academic Freedom in Religious Colleges and Universities', in William W. Van Alstyne (ed.), *Freedom and Tenure in the Academy,* Durham and London, Duke University Press, pp. 303–324.

MacIntyre, Alasdair (1984) *After Virtue,* second edition, Notre Dame, IN, University of Notre Dame Press.

MacIntyre, Alasdair (1988) *Whose Justice? Which Rationality?,* Notre Dame, IN, University of Notre Dame Press.

MacIntyre, Alasdair (1990) *Three Rival Versions of Moral Enquiry: Encyclopaedia, Genealogy, and Tradition,* Notre Dame, IN, University of Notre Dame Press.

MacIver, Robert M. (1955) *Academic Freedom in Our Time,* New York, Columbia University Press.

McLaughlin, T. H. (1984) 'Parental Rights and the Religious Upbringing of Children', *Journal of Philosophy of Education,* 18, 1, pp. 75–83. Reprinted in Astley and Francis, 1994, pp. 171–83.

Marsden, George M. (1993) 'The Ambiguities of Academic Freedom', *Church History,* 62, pp. 221–236.

Marsden, George M. (1994) *The Soul of the American University: From Protestant Establishment to Established Nonbelief,* New York, Oxford University Press.

Marsden, George M. (1997) *The Outrageous Idea of Christian Scholarship,* New York, Oxford University Press.

Matthews, Michael R. (ed.) (1989) *The Scientific Background of Modern Philosophy: Selected Readings,* Indianapolis, IN, Hackett.

Middleton, J. Richard and Brian J. Walsh (1995) *Truth is Stranger Than It Used To Be: Biblical Faith in a Postmodern Age,* Downers Grove, IL, InterVarsity.

Mouw, Richard J. and Sander Griffioen (1993) *Pluralisms and Horizons: An Essay in Christian Public Philosophy,* Grand Rapids, MI, Eerdmans.

Nagel, Thomas (1986) *The View From Nowhere,* New York, Oxford University Press.

Nagel, Thomas (1997) *The Last Word,* New York and Oxford, Oxford University Press.

Newman, John Henry (1912) *The Idea of a University,* London, Longmans, Green and Co.

Nussbaum, Martha (1997) *Cultivating Humanity: A Classical Defense of Reform in Liberal Education,* Cambridge, MA, Harvard University Press.

Quine, W. V. (1961) *From a Logical Point of View,* second edition, Cambridge, MA, Harvard University Press.

Quine, W. V. and J. S. Ullian (1978) *The Web of Belief*, second edition, New York, Random House.

Rauch, Jonathan (1993) *Kindly Inquisitors: The New Attacks on Free Thought*, Chicago, University of Chicago Press.

Rawls, John (1987) 'The Idea of an Overlapping Consensus', *Oxford Journal of Legal Studies*, 7, 1, pp. 1–25.

Relph, Edward (1976) *Place and Placelessness*, London, Pion.

Russell, Conrad (1993) *Academic Freedom*, London, Routledge.

Rutter, Michael (1972) *Maternal Deprivation Reassessed*, Harmondsworth, Penguin.

Rutter, Michael (ed.) (1980) *Developmental Psychiatry*, Washington, DC, American Psychiatric Press.

Schrecker, Ellen W. (1986) *No Ivory Tower: McCarthyism and the Universities*, New York, Oxford University Press.

Schumacher, E. F. (1973) *Small is Beautiful: Economics as if People Mattered*, New York, Harper and Row.

Schwehn, Mark R. (1993) *Exiles From Eden: Religion and the Academic Vocation in America*, New York and Oxford, Oxford University Press.

Schwehn, Mark R. (1999) 'A Christian University: Defining the Difference', *First Things*, 93, pp. 25–31.

Sharron, H. (1987) *Changing Children's Minds: Feuerstein's Revolution in the Teaching of Intelligence*, London, Souvenir Press.

Sloan, Douglas (1994) *Faith and Knowledge: Mainline Protestantism and American Higher Education*, Louisville, KY, Westminster Knox Press.

Thiessen, Elmer John (1993) *Teaching for Commitment: Liberal Education, Indoctrination and Christian Nurture*, Montreal and Kingston, McGill-Queen's University Press and Leominster, Gracewing.

Thiessen, Elmer John (2001) *In Defence of Religious Schools and Colleges*, Montreal and Kingston, McGill-Queen's University Press.

Tierney, W. G. (1993) 'Academic Freedom and the Parameters of Knowledge', *Harvard Educational Review*, 63, 2, pp. 143–160.

Toulmin, Stephen (1990) *Cosmopolis: The Hidden Agenda of Modernity*, New York, Free Press.

Van Brummelen, Harro (2001) 'Core Values in Christian University Education', *Journal of Education and Christian Belief*, 5, 1, pp. 75–88.

Walsh, Brian (1992) 'Worldviews, Modernity and the Task of Christian College Education', *Faculty Dialogue*, 18, pp. 13–35.

Walsh, Brian J. and S. Bouma-Prediger (2003) 'Education for Homelessness or Homemaking? The Christian College in a Postmodern Culture', *Christian Scholar's Review*, 32, 3, pp. 281–296.

Walsh, Brian J. and J. Richard Middleton (1984) *The Transforming Vision: Shaping a Christian World-View*, Downers Grove, IL, InterVarsity.

Westerhoff, Caroline (1999) *Good Fences: The Boundaries of Hospitality*, Boston, Cowley.

Wolterstorff, Nicholas (1980) *Educating for Responsible Action*, Grand Rapids, MI, Eerdmans.

Young, Michael F. D. (ed.) (1971) *Knowledge and Control: New Directions for the Sociology of Education*, London, Collier-Macmillan.

Chapter Four

A Christian University Imagined: Recovering Paideia in a Broken World

Andrew Walker and Andrew Wright

Introduction

It might seem an unnecessary exercise to try and imagine a Christian university when empirically North America is replete with Christian institutions of higher education, and Continental Europe is no stranger to them either. But in Great Britain, by contrast, there is virtually nothing on the home front from which we can draw inspiration. Admittedly there are religious colleges of higher education that have recently obtained university status as constituent colleges of larger academies (St. Mary's, Strawberry Hill, for example),[1] or have been granted university status in their own right (such as the University of Gloucestershire).[2] But these institutions can more accurately be said to be religious in origin rather than orientation. This being so they do not display a critical Christian engagement with the secular world which we would see as an essential hallmark of a Christian university.

One might argue that at least we could draw on North American experience as a spur to our imagination. This begs the very real question as to whether the two educational contexts are comparable. Constitutionally the United States is secular and forbids religious education in schools, but faith communities are free at the tertiary level to provide religious alternatives to State educational provision. Conversely, in the United Kingdom the State is not formally secular and this is reflected in the fact that religious education is not only encouraged but is also compulsory in State schools. Furthermore, since the 1944 Education Act, England and Wales have encompassed both secular and church schools as part of the State educational provision for children. In higher education, however, there is neither compulsory provision for religious education nor is there a significant role, outside of departments of theology and religious studies, for Christian participation.

But it is not only the incomparability of British and American educational systems that leads to hesitation in drawing on American experience to help envision a Christian university: many private colleges in the United States with the imprimatur of denominational approval are in fact, like the few British examples we cited above, often Christian universities only in name.[3] In Houston, Texas, for example, while we know that Baylor is Baptist, it is not the case that it is in any substantive sense a confessional institution any more than Pepperdine University in California is overtly a reflection of the principles and precepts of the Churches of Christ.

We certainly acknowledge that there are many Christian universities in America, from Notre Dame to Duke, which make a positive Christian contribution both to scholarship and to the larger community, but we also observe that some of the many Christian colleges that sport curricula dominated by their religious commitments are also deeply rooted in Protestant sectarianism (Bob Jones University in North Carolina, Liberty University in Virginia, and Oral Roberts University in Oklahoma, readily come to mind). Arguably the opposition to, and sometimes separation of, such universities from the mainstream of American society contribute by their very isolationism to the fragmentation of late modernity. It is precisely this fragmentation – the slippage and splintering of pluralism into oppositional segments – which we wish to resist through our imagined Christian university.

Our vision of such an academy might be thought of as merely academic or at best utopian, but in the language of phenomenologist Alfred Schutz (1967, p. 148) we will lay claim to the term 'phantasy'.[4] For Schutz a phantasy is akin to Coleridge and Rilke's notion of imagination linked to the practical application of human projects in the *Lebenswelt*. Phantasy, for Schutz, is the mind's blueprint for the actualisation of an idea. Our blueprint for a Christian university is that it should become the training ground[5] for the reclamation of Christian tradition – partially buried as it is under the rubble of dislodged and disordered discourses caused by the implosion of the so-called Enlightenment Project.

According to Alasdair MacIntyre, this disorder is marked by 'different, incommensurable and fragmented rationalities' (Smith, 2003, p. 312; cf. MacIntyre, 1985). By their refusal to offer tradition parity with reason in the modern era, or even a subservient role, the founding fathers of the Enlightenment were stoking the fires for a meltdown of rational paradigms when, as they were bound to, instrumental and pragmatic programmes finally burned themselves out. Lyotard's famous definition of postmodernism as 'incredulity towards metanarratives' (1984) was a recognition that the grand theories of modernity – of positivism, evolutionism, pragmatism, and modernism – had themselves disintegrated into snatches, tropes and remnants of crumbling traditions. A Christian university, as we imagine it, must refuse to be victims of this process of disintegration. What is needed, in the face of it, is not something new but something better.

In order to achieve this it seems to us not enough for a Christian university to become merely another player in the academic game. Throwing our hat into the ring is hardly a mission statement or a *raison d'être*. To become a training ground, as we put it, for the recapitulation of the Christian tradition is to set our faces against the shattered Ozymandias of the Enlightenment and build a university on altogether sounder foundations. This does not, as we envision it, entail a Christian academy that will eschew other perspectives, or demonise plurality, for we do not wish to stifle debate or anathematize alternative perspectives. But it does signal that such a university will be the ground on which we can take a stand – for a distinctive *Weltanschauung*, for a particular God. Yet this enterprise is really about more than that: it will also be a commitment to a particular way of conceiving and doing education. This education, this training ground, calls for nothing less than a Christian *paideia*.

The origins and unity of Christian *paideia*

The classical Greek notion of *paideia*, while sharing the same root as the word pedagogy (*paidagogos*), did not so much refer to the principles and practices of teaching as to the formative task of transmitting a cultural heritage in order to school virtue and cultivate character (Jaeger, 1965). The concept of *paideia* can also be found in the New Testament (which should not surprise us as it was written by Hellenistic Jews). 2 Timothy 3:16f, for example, describes the Hebrew Scripture as profitable 'for instruction in righteousness': such a training, for those who belong to God, ensures that they will be proficient and 'throughly furnished unto all good works'.[6]

In the light of the biblical record and the predominance of Hellenistic thought in antiquity, we can safely say that something approaching the classical notion of education as *paideia* was adopted by the early church (Jaeger, 1961). Though Christian teachers were quick to adopt the humanist notion of *paideia* as character formation (*kalos k'agathos anthropos* – 'the good and virtuous person'), the Christian doctrine of the Fall made it impossible for them to adopt, without qualification, the accompanying Greek doctrines of self-discovery (*gnoth s'auton* – 'know thyself') and recollection (*anamnesis*).[7]

The appropriation of classical *paideia* into a Christian theological framework was pioneered by Clement of Alexandria. Speaking of his ground breaking work in the *Paedogogus* and *Stromata*, Pannenberg (1994, p. 36) declared that his thinking 'has systematic importance for the interpretation of salvation history as divine education of the race'. Proclaiming Christianity as 'true gnosis', Clement gave short shrift to the speculative systems of his Gnostic opponents. But like Justin Martyr and Irenaeus before him, he welcomed certain aspects of Greek philosophy as a kind of 'propaedeutic by which men's minds are trained to receive the full truth' (Lampe, 1978, p. 64). 'Hellenistic philosophy,' Clement said, 'comprehends not the whole extent of the truth, and besides is destitute of strength to perform the commandments of the Lord, yet it prepares the way for the truly royal teaching; training in some way or other, and moulding the character, and fitting him who believes in Providence for the reception of the truth' (Clement of Alexandria, 1994, p. 318).

As Barth observes, the 'royal teaching' Clement refers to is derived not from natural knowledge rooted in human effort and will, but from 'God's revelation, by which we are authorised and commanded to view and conceive Him according to the measure of our incapable capacity' (Barth, 1957, p. 200). For Barth it is clear that Clement understands the true source and foundation of *paideia* to be in God Himself as He is revealed in Christ. The Christian virtues of love, faith and knowledge, then, 'are not matters of formal instruction and are not gained like wisdom that is implanted by teaching – they derive through communion with God and arise in the soul as it is kindled in that union with him' (Torrance, 1995, p. 167). In effect Clement stripped Hellenistic *paideia* of its pre-Christian ontology, and gathered what remained into 'a bouquet of the best and finest that he has found in the religions of all peoples to lay at the feet of the Word made flesh' (von Balthasar, 1984, p. 25).

The synthesis between the classical and Christian *paideia* was firmly embedded into the Christian tradition by the fourth century. As Pelikan has shown (1993, p. 176), although the Cappadocian Fathers could boast of Christian *paideusis* as the first of the many advantages the church held over Hellenism, and considered classicism to be deficient and corruptive in the light of revelation, they were by no means fideists in the mould of a Tertullian, nor did they totally turn their back on the learning of antiquity. They criticised rhetoric in rhetorical tones, argued against neo-Platonic *apophasis* in *apophatic* language, attacked the sterility of logic with Aristotelian syllogisms, and did not spurn the benefits of Hellenistic education if used wisely. Gregory of Nazianzus made use of a much admired analogy (echoed centuries later by Gregory Palamas in his debates with the Western monk Barlaam) to help make the case for not totally abandoning the methodology of the Greek schools. He argued that medicinal properties could be extracted from the venom of snakes but one took great care not to be bitten by the hideous reptile.

In short, the Fathers were not averse to classical learning, or neglectful of the benefits of Platonic idealism, Aristotelian logic, or Stoic psychology. They were quite prepared to sup with the devil, but insisted on the necessity of using a very long spoon. Or to put it another way, the classical tradition was not eschewed but rather incorporated into the Christian worldview, rather like druidic symbols in Britain were exorcised of their pagan implications and redeployed as liturgical signifiers in Celtic Christian practice and worship.

It is not possible to outline the substantive features of early Christian *paideia* for none have survived. But in the didache and mystagogies of the Greek fathers we get a glimpse of their holistic approach to education which was a combination of theological teaching grounded in the Trinity, spiritual formation, and detailed pastoral guidance. The letters of Basil of Caesarea in the fourth century (1994) and the orations of Gregory Nazianzus and John Chrysostom are rich sources (Manley, 1990).[8] Despite the apparent absence of detailed educational programmes in the early centuries, however, there is no doubt that the essential features of Christian *paideia* – knowledge of God leading to self-knowledge, schooling in the virtues, spiritual formation, and worship and contemplation of God – were acknowledged and practised (though unevenly) by most of Christendom until at least the start of the Enlightenment.

Such a view is affirmed by Kelsey, who has identified what he believes to be an historical and ecumenical continuity in Christian approaches to education, rooted in the notion that to 'understand God is to have a kind of wisdom or *sapientia*' (Kelsey, 1992, p. 34). Speaking of theological education in particular, but with relevance to the purpose of all Christian education, he draws attention to four distinctive dimensions of *paideia*-as-wisdom at work within the Christian tradition: (i) discursive reasoning, driving an academic study of theology grounded in *theoria* and directed towards *scientia divina* and *scientia dei*; (ii) practical action, focusing on questions of how Christians ought to act appropriately and responsibly in the world, since to 'understand God is to understand God's will for me in this particular situation'; (iii) spiritual formation, moulding the Christian character of students; and finally, (iv) doxological contemplation, attending to God, the true object of theological knowledge, through prayer, worship and meditation (p. 47).

Kelsey acknowledges that the precise relationship between each of these tasks varies greatly within different Christian traditions and at different periods of Christian history, and suggests that the balance achieved between them inevitably leads to different Christian 'forms of life'. Nevertheless, he insists that despite such diversity the integrity of theological education is dependent on maintaining the unity of all four dimensions of Christian *paideia*. They cannot be separated from one another without diminishing the enterprise of Christian education. In the light of Kelsey's summary of Christian *paideia* and our desire to imagine a Christian university that reconstitutes it, two questions clearly present themselves: (i) What happened to this baptised *paideusis?*; (ii) What would an imagined Christian university look like that was predicated on *paideia?*

The fragmentation of *paideia* in the modern secular university

Farley has argued that 'the education whose centre is *theologia* is an ecclesial counterpart to *paideia*, focusing as it does ... on a sapiental knowledge engendered by grace and self-disclosure' (Farley, 1994, p. 153). Such a view, we believe, only holds if *theologia* is centred in the ecclesia, or at the very least in a confessional seminary where *paideia* also can thrive. It is our contention that theology underwent significant changes in its transfer to the modern secular academy which resulted not only in it ceasing to be ecclesial but also, in conjunction with other factors, led to the loss of Christian *paideia*.

The drive for academic specialisation spearheaded by the natural sciences, led theology itself to be broken down into sub-texts to comply with the canons of modern university disciplines. These sub-texts were themselves divided into two camps. The first we might call pure or academic theology, which included Old and New Testament hermeneutics (with appropriate levels of Hebrew and New Testament Greek) and dogmatics/systematic and historical theology (supplemented by classical Greek, Latin, and since the nineteenth century, German). The second camp, which we might call applied theology, included homiletics, pastoral theology, missiology and, in more recent times, practical theology. But in this break-down and sub-division of theology in the modern university there has been no room for spiritual formation, one of the foundational practices of Christian *paideia*. If vestiges of it survive at all they do so by being translated into second order studies of liturgics, types of Christian spirituality or varieties of mysticism in world religion (where competing truth-claims are bracketed out in phenomenological reduction). The most glaring omission in theology departments, however, and one of Kelsey's hallmarks of *paideia*, is the absence of Christian worship. Without a liturgical structure to underscore theological discourse there can be no doxological punctuation of the Christian narrative, no theological grammar to frame the semantic core of salvation history, no chance of restoring the primal vision and educational unity of a Christian *paideia*.

If Christian *paideia* has struggled to maintain a hold inside theology departments, within other non-theological university departments operating in the full glare of secular modernity it has stood no chance of even making an entrance. By its very nature *paideia* affirms a necessary unity between the contemplation and worship of God, true knowledge, the cultivation of character and intellectual engagement with the world. Furthermore, according to the precepts of *paideia,* the process of education itself is assumed to possess intrinsic value, the meaningfulness and truthfulness inherent in the object of study impacting directly on the life–world of the learning community. This goes against the grain of 'value free' and objectivising studies; given such a secularised rhetoric, *paideia* must sound like gobbledegook.

Paideia was able to thrive in the ancient world because for both Plato and the biblical writers the cosmos was essentially teleological, possessing an ultimate meaning, purpose and destiny of direct existential relevance to humanity. Indeed, it was impossible to build character in any authentic manner in the early centuries of the Christian era without reference either to something like the vestiges of the Platonic forms innate in the soul, or to the trinitarian God and the *Imago Dei.* The advent of modernity, however, brought with it a naturalistic metaphysic that affirmed a morally neutral universe devoid of any inherent teleological goal or eschatological end. As modern science learnt to describe the universe through the neutral language of mathematics and geometry, so the motion of the planets came to be understood in terms of their spatio-temporal relationships, rather than through any reference to the ultimate meaning and purpose of the order-of-things.

As a result, as Arthur Koestler has famously argued in *The Sleepwalkers* (1989), religion was prised from natural philosophy (science), the spiritual separated from the temporal, metaphysics from physics, eternal verities from empirical certainties. Newton was able 'to bring mathematical order into phenomena, and so expound the immutable laws of nature in terms of the causal and mechanical connections that constitute the system of the world' (Torrance, 1980, p. 24). This led directly to 'the discarding by scientific thought of all considerations based upon value concepts, such as perfection, harmony, meaning and aim, and finally the devalualization of being, the divorce of the world of value from the world of facts' (Koyre, 1957, p. 276). The teleology of a morally, aesthetically and spiritually meaningful universe gave way to the purposeless infinity of space and time. As Gunton notes, the 'divorce of the natural and moral universes is perhaps the worst legacy of the Enlightenment, and the most urgent challenge facing modern humankind' (Gunton, 1985, p. 25). The stripping from reality of any ontological meaning, purpose, and value in the modern era undermined the legitimacy of *paideia*. With the pursuit of knowledge no longer possessing any intrinsic significance for personal and social development, let alone for ultimate human destiny, the traditional unity of a Christianised and holistic conception of education as *paideia* was fragmented.

This fragmentation enabled the emergence of a range of distinctively modern pedagogies clearly identifiable by virtue of their uncoupling of personal and social development from the pursuit of truth. John Locke's 'traditionalist' pedagogy, for example, was concerned, like Dewey after him, simply to induct students into the prevailing norms of society. He viewed education as essentially a pragmatic activity, concerned to provide the young bourgeoisie gentleman with 'the knowledge of a man of business, a carriage suitable to his rank, and [the ability] to be eminent and useful in his country according to his station' (Axtell, 1968, p. 197). The cultivation of virtue, wisdom, breeding and learning was driven not by *paideia* as in the past but ultimately by eudemonistic concerns: 'a sound mind in a sound body, is a short, but full description of a happy state in this world' (p. 114). Locke's confidence in the efficacy of education enabled him to bypass the Christian doctrine of original sin: 'of all men we meet with, nine parts of ten are what they are, good or evil, useful or not, by education' (p. 114).

Rousseau like Locke also rejected original sin, but in contradistinction to the English philosopher he attempted to lay the radical foundations of a 'progressive' pedagogy designed to enable students to develop naturally in accordance with their intrinsic good-nesss (Rousseau, 1986). He did not advocate a process of socialisation into the traditions of society because he saw them as the corrosive influences of a corrupt and flawed civilisation. On this reading of education, the task of the teacher is a far cry from the spirit of classical and Christian *paideia*. Instead of inducting students into a normative cultural heritage, the role of the teacher was to provide an environment in which young persons were free to explore their inner selves, encounter their natural God-given innocence and thereby establish their true identities. This child-centred but anti-cultural pedagogy adopted the classical model of education as *anamnesis*, but adapted it to a Romantic framework.

However, the Enlightenment tendency to dislocate the natural and moral universes left Rousseau's belief in the natural goodness of humankind as a formal proposition 'hanging in the air' with no substantial content, empirical weight or moral prescription to ground it. Indeed Rousseau's 'back to nature' pedagogy which, among other things, lionised the 'noble savage', was not philosophically connected to human agency or the gnomic will. His rejection of both ethics (what Kant was to call 'practical reason') and rationality as the measure of humankind is summed up in his Romantic reposte to Descartes' *cogito ergo sum* − *je sense, donc je suis*. In effect, then, 'goodness' for Rousseau was little more than 'a rallying point for the disengagement from the traditional culture thought necessary by the Enlightenment' (Bantock, 1980, p. 282).[9]

Modern pedagogies such as Locke's and Rousseau's, which in their different ways divorced fact from value and separated the pursuit of truth from the cultivation of character, militated against the four aspects of *paideia* identified by Kelsey, and contributed to their loss in the translation from Christian education to the curriculum of the modern secular university.

(i) Discursive reasoning, once it was separated from any concern for the formation of character, provided the basis for the notion of the university as a site of research and scholarship primarily concerned with the production of neutral, objective and value free knowledge.

(ii) Teaching became an adjunct to research rather than intrinsic to it (though space was made for practical action in the arena of professional studies, where the university took responsibility for the professional training of medics, lawyers, teachers and ministers of religion, and more recently for the development of transferable skills).[10]

(iii) Education as spiritual formation found itself ousted from the classroom altogether and relegated to the extra curriculum of the modern university. The cultivation of character is now rarely an intentional goal of a university education. Rather, it constitutes a secondary outcome of spending three years as an undergraduate living away from home in the company of fellow students in a campus environment and engaging in the practices of student voluntary societies.

(iv) Finally, Kelsey's fourth dimension of paideia − contemplation of the object of study − appears to have little place, either formally or informally, in the university; perhaps the best the modern academy hopes for is that the more committed and enthusiastic student will be driven by a love for his or her subject. With such an abortive view of contemplation it would be possible to love theology without any regard for God. And it is impossible to imagine students being able to worship God in 'spirit and in truth' without ridicule or condemnation in contemporary secular university lecture rooms.

The tensions and contradictions of the modern university are not, of course, only due to the gradual abandonment of the original unity of Christian *paideia*. The fragmentation of knowledge, and the bifurcation of teaching and research, has also been exacerbated by the postmodern turn. However, while theologians have been adroit in exploiting the contradictions of postmodernism (Milbank, 1993; Walker, 1996), there has been remarkably little theological reflection on the broken unity of *paideia* and scant attention has been paid to exploring the pathology of the health of modern education. Despite the paucity of theological thinking on tertiary education, at various points since World War Two, commentators have spoken of a series of crises in higher education which, if not exactly couched in theological language – though this does not hold for Carmody (1996), Fisher (1989) and Pelikan (1992) – has certainly reflected moral concerns apposite to theological discourse.

These crises in the academy have been variously attributed to: insecurity in the face of potential nuclear threat (Moberly, 1949), moral relativism (Sorokin, 1941; Wilshire, 1990), and a loss of integrity rooted in indifference to any deeper purpose of education beyond the trivial and superficial (Bloom, 1987; Blamires, 1963). In Britain, Scott (1984) has described as a crisis the fact that universities are under-resourced, and asks whether there might not also be a crisis of purpose. Reeves (1988) criticises a market-led approach in which the second of two vital aspects of education, 'education for delight', has been squeezed out by over-emphasis on the first, 'education for capability'. She sees lack of delight and celebration as also symptomatic of a 'crisis in spirituality' (p. 86) among academic staff, and calls universities to return to a concern with the whole person, by uniting and piecing together what in the contemporary world has become alienated and fragmented. Carmody (1996) argues that preoccupation with research and publication leads to the neglect both of teaching and of dealing with ultimate human questions, while Fisher (1989) is concerned with a general loss of unity and purpose. Most famously, in Pelikan's (1992) diagnosis, a storm is breaking upon the university system because of a lack of consideration of the university as an *idea*. It seems to us that these crises are all related to the absence of an imaginative vision of what universities should be. And, as the writer of Proverbs reminds us: 'Where there is no vision, the people perish' (Prov. 29:18).

The phantasy of a Christian university

And this brings us to the second of our two questions: 'What would an imagined Christian university look like that was constituted by *paideia*?' Once again, we will allow ourselves the luxury of drawing on our collective imagination, putting to one side more down-to-earth pragmatic and practical issues and concerns. Though we do not wish to suggest the latter are unimportant, we draw sustenance from Martin Luther King's preference for dreaming over strategic planning. Hence, it is dreaming and envisioning that will govern our response to the second question.

Our vision for a Christian university, our phantasy, should it come to pass, will not be without risk. If a Christian university is to be a training ground (*paideia*) for the reclamation of Christian tradition, it must refuse to succumb to the dominant secular discourse of the modern academy. This requires an opening out of existing philosophies of higher education to theological interrogation and consequently, given the paucity of such interrogation in recent years, a willingness to move into uncharted territory and heed the prophetic call to 'Enlarge the site of thy tent, and let them stretch forth the curtains of thine habitations' (Isa. 54: 2). However, this does not mean that we need to create something new. Modernity, we suggest, has singularly failed to refute the patristic vision of *paideia*, or replace it with something better; rather it has simply obscured and distorted it in a fragmentary and incoherent manner. Hence the educational task in hand is not so much the creation of a new vision as the recovery of an old one, tried and tested by centuries of Christian experience.

A phantasy of a Christian university that seeks to recover *paideia* is necessarily derived from the larger vision of the personhood and nature of God. Admittedly, this vision is mediated by theology (Carmody,

1996, p. 200), but theology as it takes its bearings from God is open to divine disclosure (Ramsey, 1976, p. 147). Disclosure facilitates an act of theological imagination, one that is concerned not only with *theoria* but also with the *implications* of knowing God (Todd, 2000, p. 37). God's disclosure of Self as Father, Son and Holy Spirit is not just a question of revelation: it carries with it both educational and missiological ramifications for the people of God. As the community of faith they seek to understand and respond to what it means to be accepted, sent and called by God into the brokenness of the world (Seymour and Miller, 1990, p. 24).

This sense of a calling – to seek for justice and reconciliation – should, it seems to us, be normative for a Christian university. In order for this to be realised, however, there needs to be a threefold approach to recovering *paideia* as the training ground on which Christians who have heeded the call of God can be equipped intellectually and spiritually for the task of healing and restoration.

The first approach is to ensure that research and teaching is rooted in the knowledge of God. Such knowledge requires a unified (though not uniform) curriculum rather than a loosely connected grouping of autonomous faculties: as Elshtain reminds us (2001, p. 135). The noun university derives from *universitas*, meaning something encompassing, and there is a certain irony in the fact that modern secular universities, despite their presuppositions about the narrowness of Christian colleges, have eschewed this breadth and unity in favour of specialisation that is all fission and fragment. In the light of this fragmentation an integrated vision of education must address itself to bringing dislocated and oppositional academic disciplines into harmony (Kazanjian and Laurence, 2000; MacIntyre and Dunne, 2002). The disjunction between religion and science, for example, may be a contingent fact of history, but as McGrath has shown, the deep structures of science and theology are not in opposition to each other (McGrath, 2001–2003). In the same vein, a Christian university will eschew the absolute distinction between fact and value in which knowledge is divided into scientific and mathematical precision, on the one hand, while the liberal arts and the humanities are shunted off to the realm of opinion and subjectivity, on the other hand. Such a recapitulated Christian *paideia*, like that of the Cappadocians in the fourth century, will be responsive to the best of the surrounding non-Christian culture.

The second approach necessary for the recovery of *paideia* for a Christian university will be to treat teaching and research not as ends in themselves but as instrumental to the health of the student community, and through them for the church and society as a whole. Students in our imagined university, far from being epiphenomenal to the central task of the pursuit of knowledge, will be both recipients of and contributors to the scholarly life. This mutual giving and receiving will foster the spirit of *paideia*, through establishing a habit of ascesis: Christian education will be concerned, therefore, not only with acquiring a body of knowledge (academic disciplines) but in establishing schooling (personal discipline) in Christian spirituality, virtue and character. Without the connection between knowledge and moral character, *paideia* will remain a pipe dream incapable of becoming the training ground for reclaiming the Christian tradition and hence ministering to the world.

This brings us to the third and most fundamental approach of ensuring that *paideia* will provide the training ground for a recapitulation of the Christian tradition: the pursuit of knowledge and formation of character, to be truly Christian, must begin and end in the worship and glorification of God. St. John Chrysostom's oft quoted aphorism captures the synergy of intellectual and spiritual development we are trying to convey: 'When you pray,' he said, 'always keep your mind in your heart.'

This three-fold approach for recovering *paideia* for a Christian university, since it will take place within a predominantly secular context, will be by definition missionary in character. Christian engagement with the larger culture has long been faced with the secular strategy of sidestepping the challenge of the gospel by insisting on the privatisation of Christian faith. The response to this challenge has tended to be polarised: on the one hand in the direction of a docetic–like sectarian disengagement from the world, and on the other in the direction of an ebionite–like liberal compromise with it. Our exercise in theological imagination, our phantasy, leads us to believe that a Christian university must establish a genuine incarnational engagement with our culture that neither compromises the integrity of the faith nor retreats into isolation.

It was the late Lesslie Newbigin who argued that if the gospel were true then it must be public truth that is not hidden away beneath our privatised bushels (Newbigin, 1991). The gospel should be proclaimed in the market place, for we are not only declaring our Christian faith but also demonstrating to the academic mainstream a form of scholarship that relates one's personal belief in God to what everything else one thinks about (Marsden, 1997, p. 4).

To relate one's faith to every aspect of life is not to court triumphalism: Christians are to serve a secular world which, despite its estrangement from religion, is held in existence by God. Acknowledging the 'analogy between divine and human political justice in which the poor are lifted up and the prisoner released', Colin Gunton (1988, p. 192) insists that Christians must strive to establish the universal justice realised in Christ. However, there is a fundamental difference between the way in which the justice of God is achieved in Christ – a refusal to exercise coercion – and by the way in which fallen human societies tend to realise it. The transforming power of God's justice became a reality in the world through the crucifixion of Jesus: God conquered the world not through raw power, but in self-giving weakness, humility and service. Hence the missiological task of a Christian university is not to be opposed to the world, but to be present within it 'as a particular way of being human, a living reminder of the true basis and end of human life' (p. 193). God's granting to non-Christians the freedom to live their lives outside of the kingdom of God must not be undermined by Christian attempts to enforce God's rule. This suggests that there can be no return to Christendom, to the Constantinian settlement of the early fourth century in which Christianity was established as the official state ideology without the prior approval of pagans.

A Christian university will have house rules (*paideia* is not an option) but it will be open house, a place of refuge and hospitality, a focus of integration and reconciliation, a 'city that is set on a hill' (Mtt. 5:14). In the context of contemporary society we would be missioners simply by existing: it is acolytes we are looking for, not proselytes.

Conclusions

A Christian *paideia*, as in the early centuries of the church, will see as part of its remit the responsibility to fulfil the Christian duty to uphold the common good. Such a duty is clearly expressed in the Service of Holy Communion in the *Book of Common Prayer:* 'give wisdom to all in authority; and direct this and every nation in the ways of justice and of peace; that we may honour one another, and seek the common good.' This is in accord with the *Augsburg Confession*: 'since lawful civil ordinances are good works of God, Christians must work to uphold these works' (Grane, 1987, p. 166). Luther's reading of the Augustinian doctrine of the two kingdoms has frequently been interpreted as giving priority to the *civitas Dei*, with Christian commitment to the *civitas terrena* limited only to the need to protect society from a descent into anarchy. However, as Bernhard Lohse points out (1999, p. 320): 'for Luther the Christian is a citizen of both kingdoms ... Indeed, one must state that the Christian is first a citizen of the kingdom of the world and only then a citizen of the kingdom of God ... Since God is also at work in the temporal government, there is ultimately no conflict, since the divine will is authoritative in both kingdoms and governments.'

This positive reading of the Christian responsibility to preserve the common good is the necessary antidote to the dangers of a strident partisanship that seeks to deny the diversity in the modern world. But it is also a contribution to the practices of tolerance and hospitality so necessary in a pluralistic society. In this respect a Christian university will join in partnership with other institutions committed to the common good, which we can define as the sum total of social conditions that allow people to reach fulfilment more fully and more easily.

Society prospers wherever human rights are upheld, human dignity preserved, security established and peace maintained. Since this is the will of God for all humankind, a primary task of a Christian university engaging with its secular surroundings is to work towards the commonwealth of all. However, a Christian university that has recovered *paideia* will also contribute to the common good by living its 'form of life' and bearing witness to the one true God and Father of all. This witness will be embodied in the faculties of scholars and the student community but it will also have a distinctive voice in the public square: for the prevailing assumptions about the secular university's role in society deserve to be challenged. Without such a broader spiritual and philosophical engagement with our culture, as we said in our introduction, a Christian university is not worthy of the name.

References

Axtell, J. L. (ed.) (1968) *The Educational Writings of John Locke*, Cambridge, Cambridge University Press.

Bantock, G. H. (1980) *Studies in the History of Educational Theory. Volume One: Artifice and Nature 1350–1765*, London, Allen & Unwin.

Barth, K. (1957) *Church Dogmatics, Volume 2/1: The Doctrine of God*, Edinburgh, T & T Clark.

Basil of Caesarea (1994) 'On the Holy Spirit' and 'Pastoral Letters', in P. Schaff and H. Wace (eds), *The Nicene and Post-Nicene Fathers*, Second Series, Volume 8, Edinburgh, T & T Clark, pp. 109–327.

Blamires, H. (1963) *The Christian Mind*, London, SPCK.

Bloom, A. (1987) *The Closing of the American Mind*, New York, Simon & Schuster.

Carmody, D. L. (1996) *Organizing a Christian Mind: A Theology of Higher Education*, Valley Forge, PA, Trinity Press International.

Cherryholmes, C. H. (1988) *Power and Criticism: Poststructural Investigations in Education*, New York, Teachers College Press.

Clement of Alexandria (1994) 'The Stromata, or Miscellanies', in A. Roberts and J. Donaldson (eds), *The Ante-Nicene Fathers*, Volume 2, Edinburgh, T & T Clark, pp. 299–568.

Elshtain, J. B. (2001) 'What Have We Learned?', in R. E. Sullivan (ed.), *Higher Learning and Catholic Traditions*, Notre Dame, IN, University of Notre Dame Press, pp. 131–147.

Farley, E. (1994) *Theologia: The Fragmentation and Unity of Theological Education*, Eugene, OR, Wipf & Stock.

Fisher, B. C. (1989) *The Idea of a Christian University in Today's World*, Macon, GA, Mercer University Press.

Grane, L. (1987) *The Augsburg Confession: A Commentary*, Minneapolis, MN, Augsburg Publishing House, 1987.

Gunton, C. E. (1985) *Enlightenment and Alienation: An Essay Towards a Trinitarian Theology*, Basingstoke, Marshall, Morgan & Scott.

Gunton, C. E. (1988) *The Actuality of Atonement: A Study of Metaphor, Rationality and the Christian Tradition*, Edinburgh, T & T Clark.

Jaeger, W. (1961) *Early Christianity and Greek Paideia*, Cambridge, MA, Belknap/Harvard University Press.

Jaeger, W. (1965) *Paideia: The Ideals of Greek Culture*, Oxford, Oxford University Press (3 volumes).

Kazanjian, V. H. and P. L. Laurence (eds) (2000) *Education as Transformation: Religious Pluralism, Spirituality, and a New Vision for Higher Education in America*, New York, Peter Lang.

Kelsey, D. H. (1992) *To Understand God Truly: What's Theological About A Theological School?*, Louisville, KY, Westminster/John Knox Press.

Kierkegaard, S. (1967) *Philosophical Fragments*, Princeton, NJ: Princeton University Press.

Koestler, A. (1989) *The Sleep Walkers: A History of Man's Changing Vision of the Universe*, Harmondsworth, Penguin.

Koyre, A. (1957) *From the Closed World to the Infinite Universe*, Baltimore, MD, John Hopkins.

Lampe, G. W. H. (1978) 'Christian Theology in the Patristic Period', in H. Cunliffe-Jones (ed.), *A History of Christian Doctrine*, Edinburgh, T & T Clark, pp. 23–180.

Lohse, B. (1999) *Martin Luther's Theology: Its Historical and Systematic Development*, Edinburgh, T & T Clark.

Lyotard, J.-F. (1984) *The Postmodern Condition: A Report on Knowledge*, Manchester, Manchester University Press.

MacIntyre, A. (1985) *After Virtue: A Study in Moral Theory*, London, Duckworth.

MacIntyre, A. and J. Dunne (2002) 'Alasdair MacIntyre on Education: In Dialogue with Joseph Dunne', *Journal of Philosophy of Education*, 36, 1, pp. 1–19.

Manley, J. (ed.) (1990) *The Bible and The Holy Fathers*, Menlo Park, CA, Monastery Books.

Marsden, G. M. (1997) *The Outrageous Idea of Christian Scholarship*, New York and Oxford, Oxford University Press.

McGrath, A. (2001–2003) *A Scientific Theology*, Edinburgh, T & T Clark (3 volumes).

Milbank, J. (1993) *Theology and Social Theory: Beyond Secular Reason*, Oxford, Blackwell.

Moberly, W. (1949) *The Crisis in the University*, London, SCM.

Newbigin, L. (1991) *Truth to Tell: The Gospel as Public Truth*, Grand Rapids, MI, Eerdmans.

Pannenberg, W. (1994) *Systematic Theology*, Volume Two, Edinburgh, T & T Clark.

Parker, S. (1997) *Reflective Teaching in the Postmodern World: A Manifesto for Education in Postmodernity*, Buckingham, Open University Press.

Pelikan, J. (1992) *The Idea of the University: A Reexamination*, New Haven, CT, Yale University Press.

Pelikan, J. (1993) *Christianity and Classical Culture: The Metamorphosis of Natural Theology in the Christian Encounter with Hellenism*, New Haven, CT, Yale University Press.

Ramsey, I. T. (1976) 'Towards a Theology of Education', *Learning for Living*, 15, 4, pp. 137–147.

Reeves, M. (1988) *The Crisis in Higher Education: Competence, Delight and the Common Good*, Milton Keynes, Open University Press.

Rousseau, J.-J. (1986) *Emile*, London, Dent.

Schutz, A. (1967) *The Phenomenology of the Social World*, Evanston, IL, Northwestern University Press.

Scott, P. (1984) *The Crisis of the University*, London, Croom Helm.

Seymour, J. L. and D. E. Miller (1990) 'Openings to God: Education and Theology in Dialogue', in J. L. Seymour and D. E. Miller (eds), *Theological Approaches to Christian Education*, Nashville, TN, Abingdon Press, pp. 7–26

Smith, R. (2003) 'Thinking With Each Other: The Peculiar Practice of the University', *Journal of Philosophy of Education*, 37, 2, pp. 309–324.

Sorokin, P. A. (1941) *The Crisis of Our Age*, New York, Dutton.

Todd, A. (2000) 'What is Theological about Theological Reflection?', *British Journal of Theological Education*, 11, 1, pp. 35–45.

Torrance, T. F. (1980) *The Ground and Grammar of Theology*, Belfast, Christian Journals.

Torrance, T. F. (1995) *Divine Meaning: Studies in Patristic Hermeneutics*, Edinburgh, T & T Clark.

Usher, R. and R. Edwards. (1994) *Postmodernism and Education*, London, Routledge.

von Balthasar, H. U. (1984) *The Glory of the Lord: A Theological Aesthetics, Volume II, Studies in Theological Styles: Clerical Styles*, Edinburgh, T & T Clark.

Walker, A. (1996) *Telling the Story: Gospel, Mission and Culture*, London: SPCK.

Willows, D. (2001) *Divine Knowledge: A Kierkegaardian Perspective on Christian Education*, London, Ashgate.

Wilshire, B. (1990) *The Moral Collapse of the University: Professionalism, Purity and Alienation*, Albany, NY, State University of New York Press.

Wright, A. (2004) *Religion, Education and Post-modernity*, London, RoutledgeFalmer.

Chapter Five

Sedes Sapientiae: Newman, Truth and the Christian University

Denis Robinson

Introduction and background

The public career of John Henry Newman, in many ways, can be summarised as the pursuit of the rather biblical question, What is truth?[1] Newman worked and taught in a time when the very foundations of knowledge and truth were being called into question by developments in philosophy, the natural sciences, culture and politics.[2] Newman saw his intellectual endeavours on behalf of truth as a call to reinvigorate the church and, indeed, society as a whole. In this essay, I propose to consider Newman's arguments on behalf of truth, particularly as they relate to his unique contribution to epistemology. In the second part, I will apply his thought *on thinking* to his philosophy of education, particularly as expressed in *The Idea of a University,* but also in other places. Finally, I will consider the way in which Newman's idea of a university, growing out of his epistemology, is necessarily that of a *Christian* university, not only as an institution among others, but as the very seat of wisdom.[3]

Newman's public career began at a moment of decided crisis in English society and Anglican theology.[4] For many, religion, with its internecine wrangling and confessional violence, had become out-dated, a mode of thought easily (and perhaps with some relief) discarded in light of newer, more predicable and serviceable intellectual developments. However, the abandonment of religious forms and culture had left a lacuna in the English spirit. Like Thomas Carlyle, his near contemporary, Newman profoundly regretted this seeming desertion of religious belief, this National Apostasy. Like the Sage of Cheyne Row and others, such as the novelist George Eliot and the poet Matthew Arnold, Newman felt bereft that the seemingly discarded God of Anglicanism had left no successor in his wake, no deity to stir the inner reaches of the spirit and inspire women and men to heroism. While it was easy enough to observe the transformations in English culture, the passing away of agrarian ways of life and the growth of industry, it was less obvious what the decease of many religious institutions and sentiments entailed in terms of their successors. It was an age, to quote the loquacious Carlyle in which 'all human dues and reciprocities have been fully changed into one great due of *cash payment* ... and man's duty to God has become cant, a doubt, a dim inanity, "a pleasure of virtue" '.[5] It was, in a word, the Age of Bentham and Utility.

Newman, like Carlyle, lamented the impoverishment of the world wrought by faithlessness and the abandonment of the church. Many if not most of the prominent intellectuals of early and mid-Victorian England had already cast off conventional confessionalism in favour of intellectual agnosticism. Rather than lament the death of God and wail at his funeral however, Newman considered another approach, because in his estimation, God had not become smaller; rather, the human instruments of perceiving God, that is to say epistemologies, had become smaller. This smallness of perception was the fault not only of near-sighted philosophers but also of myopic religion.

The critic in Newman may well have sympathised with Carlyle, writing in 1843 on the state of the nation: 'England is full of wealth, or multifarious produce, supply for human want in every kind; yet England is dying of inanition.'[6] The social and cultural fibre of the people had become emaciated from a want of spiritual nourishment despite the rise in affluence that characterised mercantile and industrial Victorianism, a surplus of imperial proportions. Thinkers like Eliot, Arnold, Charles Dickens and John Ruskin also understood this bankruptcy. In their own ways, they lamented the loss of *largeness* that the complexity of the old order represented. They saw that the new effortless and simplistic answers to life's perennial problems led to the stagnation of culture and society.

What precipitated this seeming need for epistemic simplicity? One aspect that must be considered was the very complexity of the old social order and worldview. The Middle Ages, as thinkers like Carlyle and Ruskin were to rediscover in the nineteenth century, was a time imbued with a highly multifarious symbolic order. This order was sustained only by its multiple meaning(s) and symbolic systems being perpetuated in a communitarian medium. There were so many signs and symbolic essentials of this worldview that the entire community was necessary to give it life. The tide of individualism, which may well have begun at the time of the fourteenth-century plagues, isolated minds to think for themselves, to create world orders for themselves, and finally to *doubt* for themselves. The decay, even suspicion of social structures brought about by the reformations and enlightenments necessitated a turn to more simplistic hermeneutics and epistemologies. Once the community was discarded as an epistemic gravitational centre, direct and immediate knowledge is the only real recourse for *individuals* knowing.

Another factor that certainly played into the development of a narrow scientific epistemology and a narrower natural religion in England was the question of the controversies surrounding religion in the sixteenth and seventeenth centuries. The Deists, a chief target for Newman, were inspired to simplify the nature of religion and religious knowing in order to find the point of commonalty among warring religious factions.[7] The dramatic advances in science brought about as a result of the empirical revolution, particularly advances in the practical science of medicine, helped to instil optimism in the scientific point of view. As a result, a large chasm developed between faith and what now passed for reason. The gap in significance created by the advance of the religion of reason was filled by the swell of Evangelicalism – that is, emotional religion, fideism.

Religion, therefore, for those who chose to continue its practice in the nineteenth century, was an either/or proposition. It was either completely rational and scientific, a proposition that Hume had seriously injured so that no right-thinking person could hold it, or it was an emotional leap into the unknown wilds of Evangelical excess and enthusiasm. This Kierkegaardian proposition was unacceptable to Newman. For Newman:

> Truth is too sacred and religious a thing to be sacrificed to the mere gratification of the fancy, or amusement of the mind, or party spirit, or the prejudices of education, or attachment (however amiable) to the opinions of human teachers, or any of those other feelings which the ancient

philosophers suffered to influence them in their professedly grave and serious discussions.[8]

Modern religion, either rational or enthusiastic – all individually centred – had made a muddle of the legacy of the church by forcing the mystery of the truth of God into the confines of intellectual structures unsuited to contain or even approximate its magnanimity. Some like Eliot moved away from the church, becoming an agnostic seeker to find God in the sympathetic epistemology of the community. Here she had to forge her own path because what was needed was a third way, a *via media*, literally a *Middlemarch*, but this entailed a complete rethinking of thinking. Newman remained firmly within the church, even if he changed confessional allegiance, to solve the problems of the narrowing of epistemology and created an entire new vision of education and ecclesiology, indeed, of religion itself.

Newman and truth

Newman made many important contributions to the development of religious thought in the nineteenth century. In some ways, as Avery Dulles and others have observed, he was unappreciated in his own time, but has become the (often unnamed) source of many of the advancements that characterise twentieth-century theology, including the Second Vatican Council.[9] Newman's understanding of conscience, his appreciation of the role of the laity in church life, and his extensive writings on spirituality have all played an essential role in contemporary discourse. Arguably, Newman's most original and significant contribution to thought is his contribution to epistemology. Thought about truth pervades all the works of Newman. His great Catholic work, *An Essay in Aid of a Grammar of Assent* is his most systematic, but certainly not his first contribution to this area of discourse.[10]

Newman's creative contribution to epistemology has four distinct components. The first is the somewhat simplistic insight that truth is complex. The second is that the pursuit of truth is always imbued with a moral aspect, a place in a life of action. In other words, knowledge is not passive; it has consequences. The third is that truth is a product not of individual and isolated reflection but of the life and vigour of the community. And the fourth is that truth, in its ultimate sense, is a particular Christian truth.

First, truth is complex. Truth, for Newman, begins with the insight (for him a phenomenological insight) that nothing comes to us immediately and directly; we have to work for what we know. This is his first direct challenge to the simplistic epistemologies of reason and emotion. For Newman, there are no instantaneous enlightenments. There are no Newtonian 'Eurekas!' or Wesleyan 'Alleluias!' Coming to know something is a process that involves a great complexity of insights, some rational and scientific, some historical, some emotional, and some whose origin may remain mysterious. In other words: 'The idea which represents an object or supposed object is commensurate with the sum total of its possible aspects, however they may vary in the separate consciousness of individuals.'[11] For Newman, this development involves a kind of peripatetic process, that is, a *purposeful* consideration and re-consideration of various points of view and opinions from various disciplines.

> Ordinarily an idea is not brought home to the intellect as objective except through *this variety*; like bodily substances, which are not apprehended except under the clothing of their properties and results, and which admit of being walked round, and surveyed on opposite sides, and in different perspectives, and in contrary lights, in evidence of their reality.[12]

Some of the factors that contribute to this walking around an object include abstract definitions and notions. In the Christian context these certainly include specific doctrines and teachings of the faith. But knowledge of Christianity, as knowledge of anything, is not merely the grasping of abstract concepts. In the *Essay in Aid of a Grammar of Assent,* Newman makes the distinction between what he terms notional and real apprehension, to which a person might give notional or real assent. Notional apprehension is deductive and scientific. We know a thing is true because it is logically conclusive. It is syllogistically correct. Mathematical propositions are an example of notional apprehension. Notions, however, do not arrest the imagination, which is central to Newman. Real apprehension, on the other hand, is that by which we know a thing to be the case, not from the force of syllogism and deductive conclusion alone, but from a variety of factors that offer proof. Newman defines this type of coming to knowledge as the exercise of what he terms the illative sense. A collection of weak evidences (notions, images, historical occurrences, emotions) make a strong evidence. Newman equates such knowledge to the construction of a cable, whose fibres, taken separately, could never be strong enough to support anything, but which combined together are very strong indeed.

> We conceive by means of definition or description; whole objects do not create in the intellect whole ideas, but are, to use a mathematical phrase, thrown into series, into a number of statements, strengthening, interpreting, correcting each other, and with more or less exactness approximating, as they accumulate, to a perfect image.[13]

Truth, then, for Newman is always the product of an elaborate process of construction.

> There is no one aspect deep enough to exhaust the contents of a real idea, no one term or proposition which will serve to define it; though of course one representation of it is more just and exact than another, and though when an idea is very complex, it is allowable, for the sake of convenience, to consider its distinct aspects as if separate ideas.[14]

The illative sense constructs knowledge through practice, an active and pursued process of intellection, and indeed, of the whole person. For Newman this was a natural instinct in the human person. It is a kind of truth, of education, that extends beyond cognition and presses on to a reality that cannot be reduced to the simplistic categories of argumentation. As Newman says in *The Idea of a University*:

> We know, not by a direct and simple vision, not at a glance, but, as it were, by piecemeal and accumulation, by a mental process, by going round an object, by the comparison, the combination, the mutual correction, the continual adaptation, of many partial notions, by the employment, concentration and joint action of many faculties and exercises of the mind.[15]

If this is the way knowledge is attained, the process of education must somehow emulate and facilitate this process. Truth as a complex assemblage is in proportion to what Newman refers to as the actual state of things, which is understood in contrast to the *simplicity* of theory. There is a subtlety in the construction of truth that is elusive to those who strive for facile answers. 'Divine Truth should be attained by so subtle and indirect a method, a method less tangible than others, less open to analysis, reducible but partially to the forms of Reason, and the ready sport of objection and cavil.'[16] Truth is complex because the world is complex, and the God who created the world is complex, and therefore it is not only foolish but futile to seek simple answers in the face of overwhelming complexity. Indeed, all simple and straight-forward answers will be intuited by the person as shallow. Newman writes:

> it seems incredible that any men, who were really in earnest in their search after truth, should have begun with theorizing, or have imagined that a system which they were conscious they had invented almost without data, should happen, when applied to the actual state of things, to harmonize with the numberless and diversified phenomena of the world.[17]

Patience, then, is an essential element in the pursuit of truth. 'Rashness of assertion, hastiness in drawing conclusions, unhesitating reliance on our own acuteness and powers of reasoning, are inconsistent with the homage which nature exacts of those who would know her hidden wonders.'[18] Newman asserts: 'Accordingly the Poet makes Truth the daughter of Time. Thus at length approximations are made to a right appreciation of transactions and characters. History cannot be written except in an after-age.'[19]

In several places, Newman contrasts this complex pursuit of truth with the spirit of heresy, a spirit all simple and straightforward. For Newman, heresy and indeed all sin is a failure of the imagination, a failure, in a sense, to shake things up and to *realise* complexity. It is a kind of pre-Sartrian 'bad faith' that chooses ready-made answers to complex questions over the inconvenience of living. 'The world overcomes us, not merely by appealing to our reason, or by exciting our passions, but by imposing on our imagination.'[20] There is need here for pursuit. Once the inquirer 'settles' for anything less than the greatness of this truth, then a kind of idolatry sets in because the inquirer believes that the object of inquiry has been 'attained'.

Second, the acquisition of truth for Newman is never passive, as the writing on a *tabula rasa*. Rather its primary conduit is always a sense of *earnestness* in the seeker. 'It is obvious that to be in earnest in seeking the truth is an indispensable requisite for finding it.'[21] The pursuit of truth produces restlessness in the seeker that cannot be satisfied and yet the perception of the object as something great, indeed ultimate, generates the energy for further pursuit. For Newman authentic ideas and truths must be what he termed 'living': 'When an idea, whether real or not, is of a nature to arrest and possess the mind, it may be said to have life, that is, to live in the mind which is its recipient.'[22]

Truth for Newman is a kind of convergence of factors witnessing to the truth that Newman terms 'antecedent probabilities'. These are generated not through the processes of syllogistic reason, or in the armchair reflections of amateur philosophers, but in the lived experience, that is, the daily activity of the person. Truth is not an isolated pursuit but one that unfolds in every aspect of the human person. For Newman, any distinction between the seat of education and 'real life' is false. The witness of experience, the vicissitudes of youth, the example of other people, the chance encounter with nature, a powerful experience of art, the poetic imagination, all of these have the same power to inform as the pages of a book. All of these things are assimilated over time, often in ways we control, manipulate and understand, but often as a result of simply *being in the world*. 'As fresh and fresh duties arise, or fresh and fresh faculties are brought into action, they are at once absorbed into the existing inward system, and take their appropriate place in it.'[23] In Newman's estimation, the directness of reason – cold rationality – can never serve as a proof, the evidence of which is built up over time and the subject of innumerably antecedent factors.

> Faith, then, as I have said, does not demand evidence so strong as is necessary for what is commonly considered a rational conviction, or belief on the ground of Reason; and why? For this reason, because it is mainly swayed by antecedent considerations. In this way it is, that the two principles are opposed to one another: Faith is influenced by previous notices, prepossessions, and (in a good sense of the word) prejudices; but Reason, by direct and definite proof.[24]

The strength of proof generated by this convergence does not admit to any (at least successful or determinative) attempt at analysis: 'First, every part of the Truth is novel to its opponent; and seen detached from the whole, becomes an objection.'[25] In other words, what is grasped by this pursuit is only understood in its assemblage, and attempts at analysis yield only failure and doubt. Faith, for Newman, like truth, is a principle of action:

> Faith is a principle of action, and action does not allow time for minute and finished investigations. We may (if we will) think that such investigations are of high value; though, in truth, they have a tendency to blunt the practical energy of the mind, while they improve its scientific exactness; but, whatever be their character and consequences, they do not answer the needs of daily life.[26]

In other words, there is the necessity of the maintenance of a kind of parabolic tension that becomes the very hallmark of the pursuit. What is gained by education, by the pursuit of truth, rather than satisfying, impels the seeker to greater heights. To employ a Gadamerian expression, the horizons change and develop over time so that there is a constant tension to pursue further. Tension, indeed, is the essence of truth. The resolution of tension is a sign of error. Denial of tension is the essence of ideology and heresy. Christianity is defined by tension. It *necessarily* maintains the tension by denying resolution to questions and maintaining an endless hermeneutic stance that mirrors the depth of the object of its intellection: for Newman, the Divine Reality.

> It is indeed sometimes said that the stream is clearest near the spring. Whatever use may fairly be made of this image, it does not apply to the history of a philosophy or belief, which on the contrary is more equable, and purer, and stronger, when its bed has become deep, and broad, and full.[27]

Truth, for Newman, is contained not in argument but in the power of the truth to generate moral action precisely by means of tension:

> On the other hand, that its real influence consists directly in some inherent moral power, in virtue in some shape or other, not in any evidence or criterion level to the undisciplined reason of the multitude, high or low, learned or ignorant, is implied in texts, such as those referred to just now: 'I send you forth as sheep in the midst of wolves; *be ye, therefore*, wise as serpents, and harmless as doves.'[28]

Indeed, the shortcoming of pure reason is the inability to work, to propel, to generate, and to inspire. No one was ever inspired to devote their lives to a mere notion. For Newman, then, nothing can be perceived as true that does not have a consequence. If I say, for example, that I believe in God, that I have perceived, at some level, the truth of the Deity, then I must act upon that is some way. I cannot have a passive faith just as I cannot have a passive education. There are no truths that are good *simply* to know. The perception of Truth changes lives, it necessitates conversion and movement, which, in turn, propels the learner, the believer toward increasing knowledge and truth. Perceptions that arouse complacency or a mere satisfaction in knowing are not really the truth for Newman. Finally, all of these activities and pursuits instil in the person a commitment to their further pursuit, a habit of the mind and of the personality:

> Whereas in him who is faithful to his own divinely implanted nature, the faint light of Truth dawns continually brighter; the shadows which at first troubled it, the unreal shapes created by its own twilight-state, vanish; what was as uncertain as mere feeling, and could not be distinguished from a fancy except by the commanding urgency of its voice, becomes fixed and definite, and strengthening into principle, it at the same time develops into habit.[29]

Third, for Newman, the pursuit of truth always takes place within the context of the community. Truth, for Newman is never privatised. It needs the presence of others to inspire and augment its development. It only thrives in a critical and mutually corrective atmosphere. Just as the perception of truth necessitates action, so this action necessarily has ramifications in the life of the community. Here his stance is in direct opposition to that of the enthusiastic religion of his Evangelical colleagues. There is no privatised revelation or truth. 'Truth is not the heritage of any individual, it is absolute and universal; mankind ought to seek and profess it in common.'[30] Indeed, for Newman, truth can only be acquired in a context. 'And others, not being able to acquiesce in the unimportance of doctrinal truth, yet perplexed at the difficulties in the course of human affairs, which follow on the opposite view, accustom themselves gratuitously to distinguish between their public and private duties, and to judge of them by separate rules.'[31]

Therefore, in Newman's estimation, there is always the need to, in a sense, 'grow where one is planted'. That is to say, the community provides the proper arena for growth and there is no need to look beyond it for confirmation of the truth, yet un-revealed.

Finally, the fullness of truth is manifested in the active living of a life of faith. Secular learning and institutions of education can benefit from Newman's insights on epistemology only to a certain point because Newman was convinced that the fullness of truth is not open to all. Indeed, 'She refuses to reveal her mysteries to those who come otherwise than in the humble and reverential spirit of learners and disciples.'[32] Truth, however, is instinctual in the hearts of those who believe and practice faith. 'Nay, such confessors have a witness even in the breasts of those who oppose them, an instinct originally from God, which may indeed be perverted into a hatred, but scarcely into an utter disregard of the Truth, when exhibited before them.'[33] Faith, Christian belief *and* practice, however, are not to be understood as another aspect of knowledge, or even of the highest knowledge. For Newman, the insight of Christianity is the epistemological ground of knowledge. For Newman the object of pursuit in the context of Christian faith is the truth of the divine reality, the central aspect of which is the matter and form of revelation. God as divine reality is, in Newman's estimation, not only the source of truth but the only goal of truth finally worth pursuit. This in no way denigrates any other branch or discipline of learning, in fact it enhances the disciples by making them essential components in the construction of the Great Truth, the divine reality. But herein lies the paradox for Newman. The nature of this divine reality is its very inexhaustibility, that is, what we know when we know God is the infinite itself and pursuit of God is the ultimate pursuit in that it can never be exhausted. What it yields is the same paradox one encounters in education. For the educated person, the more one knows, the more one knows what one does not know. The horizons shift and the pursuit is endless. The paradox of God is the same. The more the believer 'knows' God, the greater, deeper, and broader the divine reality becomes. God is not something to be grasped, rather God is the energy, as it were, of grasping, one with which to be in relationship. '[This pursuit of God] becomes an active principle within [believers], leading them to an ever-new contemplation of itself, to an application of it in various directions, and a propagation of it on every side.'[34] The truth here sometimes yields paradoxical and parabolic contradictions that can, nevertheless, be held in perfect tension because of the nature of the truth pursued. In this way, the incarnation, with its inherent and irresolvable tension, becomes the central teaching of Christianity, the core of its parabolic life.

> [I]n this sense I should myself call the Incarnation the central aspect of Christianity, out of which the three main aspects of its teaching take their rise, the sacramental, the hierarchical, and the ascetic. But one aspect of Revelation must not be allowed to exclude or to obscure another; and Christianity is dogmatical, devotional, practical all at once; it is esoteric and exoteric; it is indulgent and strict; it is light and dark; it is love, and it is fear.[35]

In the above we see the full force of Newman's complicated epistemology: I know that I know, an artistic or poetic knowing that is not reducible to easy categorisations. All truth is poetical for Newman. Even the sciences are poetical in that they are super-saturated with meaning, a meaning that cannot be reduced to simple analysis or formulae.

The truth that faith yields is not the product of academic or even intellectual reflection alone. Rather, it is open and part of the faith *experience* of every Christian person. 'No irreligious man can know any thing concerning the hidden saints. Next, no one, religious or not, can detect them without attentive study of them. But, after all, say they are few, such high Christians; and what follows? They are enough to carry on God's noiseless work.'[36] Newman also requests that we:

> Next, consider the extreme rarity, in any great perfection and purity, of simple-minded, honest devotion to God; and another instrument of influence is discovered for the cause of Truth. Men naturally prize what is novel and scarce; and, considering the low views of the multitude on points of social and religious duty, their ignorance of those precepts of generosity, self-denial, and high-minded patience, which religion enforces, nay, their scepticism (whether known to themselves or not) of the existence in the world of severe holiness and truth, no wonder they are amazed when accident gives them a sight of these excellences in another, as though they beheld a miracle; and they watch it with a mixture of curiosity and awe.[37]

Newman compares this instinctive perception of truth to that of a leader. 'Firmness and greatness of soul are shown, when a ruler stands his ground on his instinctive perception of a truth which the many scoff at, and which seems failing.'[38] Truth, however, for Newman always requires a preparation not of the mind alone but also of the heart. 'For is not this the error, the common and fatal error, of the world, to think itself a judge of Religious Truth without preparation of heart?'[39]

Truth and education

Newman wrote *The Idea of a University* one hundred and fifty years ago. What can his insights offer students, teachers and administrators of the twenty-first century? First, I think Newman proposes a challenge to our way of conceiving education. We have largely discarded the 'liberal arts' model of education in favour of the utilitarian model proposed by thinkers of the nineteenth century, a trend Newman abhorred. Are people better educated as a result? More crucially, are the universities of today making a significant contribution through their educational endeavours to the advancement of communities? Have we become aware of our mutual dependence or are we isolated by our method-ologies and singular hypotheses? As teachers and tutors, are we inspiring students to a lifelong quest for wisdom or do we teach and promote our subjects in such a way that students are interested only in 'what is on the examination'? More concisely, are the universities of today terminal, utilitarian training academies or are they, in every possible sense, including the divine, seats of wisdom?

When Newman set out to redefine what was meant by truth, reason, knowledge and other epistemological categories, his re-appropriations had necessary consequences for the task of education. By way of example we might consider an analogous scenario in the history of philosophy. Those who think as Socrates thought about the reality of innate ideas and the faculty of anamnesis, will necessarily approach the question of education in a different way from those who have a Lockian epistemology. Professor Socrates will apply a maieutic method, whereas Dr. Locke will employ a distributive pedagogy. In other words, if Newman reinvented epistemology he necessarily reinvented education and he was, of course, aware of this. Newman overcomes the simplistic epistemologies of reason and emotion with an appeal to

complexity. For Newman, this appeal was rooted in an acute
observation of the real action of the human agent. Newman begins his
understanding of knowledge and education with a phenomenological
observation:

> It is the characteristic of our minds to be ever engaged in passing judgment
> on the things which come before us. No sooner do we apprehend than we
> judge: we allow nothing to stand by itself: we compare, contrast, abstract,
> generalize, connect, adjust, classify: and we view all our knowledge in the
> associations with which these processes have invested it.[40]

What we might term Newman's holistic approach to education cannot be construed as a product of his later thought. From the beginning
of his teaching career, Newman saw education as the formation of the
whole person. He insisted in his journal that, 'education ... has always
been my line.'[41] In his early days as an Oxford don, Newman was
obsessed with the idea of reforming the tutorial system as it then
existed. When he became a tutor at Oriel in 1826, Newman viewed his
responsibilities not only in an academic way, but also in a spiritual
way.[42] Newman wrote:

> The most important and far reaching improvement has been commenced
> this term: – a radical alternation ... of the system. The bad men are thrown
> into large classes – and this time saved for the better sort who are put into
> very small lectures, and principally with their own Tutors quite familiarly
> and chattingly.[43]

Many of Newman's ideas about the very personal and 'chatty' nature of
education stem from his appreciation of the monastic culture of
education represented by the school of St Benedict. Newman saw these
Benedictine models as educational institutions that considered the
formation of the whole person. The formation of the religious or
spiritual aspect was necessary in Newman's estimation because only
insofar as one grasped God as epistemic category could authentic and
complete learning take place.[44]

In light of Newman's epistemology, what can be known and how it is
known is actualised in the places of learning, the university.

There is no other way of learning or of teaching. We cannot teach except by aspects or views, which are not identical with the thing itself which we are teaching. Two persons may each convey the same truth to a third, yet by methods and through representations altogether different. The same person will treat the same argument differently in an essay or speech, according to the accident of the day of writing, or of the audience, yet it will be substantially the same.[45]

Epistemologically speaking, then, the university betrays several characteristics, which are related to the epistemological considerations above mentioned. First, the university provides an educational pro-gramme that is *necessarily* and *purposefully* broad and comprehensive. Second, education is an engagement of the whole person and is an active integration of the various and varying factors presented in the educational programme. Third, education is not a solitary pursuit, but takes place within the context of a community of learners and teachers. Finally, for Newman the only authentic university is a Christian university.

First, the educational process replicates the process of intellection itself. It is fuelled by the illative sense active in the individual learner, but also in the institutions themselves as community of learners. The problem of education as Newman saw it in his time was the problem of isolation and fragmentation. A strictly utilitarian approach to the question had led to a vision of education as focused on specialised training in a particular science or skill. With the rise of the education of utility, promoted for example by Bentham, Henry Brougham and the *Edinburgh Review,* there was a concomitant denigration of the importance of classical education and religion. In this vision, if disciplines were not practical, they were useless. In this way, education was the product of a monocular epistemology. The integrative value of classics and religion was set aside as too complex. They were not measurable and observable enough. They had no immediate utility. The pursuit of learning was isolated into disciplines and *specialised.* For Newman, however, the authentic task of the university was *purposefully* to complicate the process of education by the introduction of a density, even convolution, of learning that belies the simple conveyance of information and techné. Newman states:

This process of training, by which the intellect, instead of being formed or sacrificed to some particular or accidental purpose, some specific trade or profession, or study or science, is disciplined for its own sake, for the perception of its own proper object, and for its own highest culture, is called Liberal Education; and though there is no one in whom it is carried as far as is conceivable, or whose intellect would be a pattern of what intellects should be made, yet there is scarcely any one but may gain an idea of what real training is, and at least look towards it, and make its true scope and result, not something else, his standard of excellence.[46]

The university promotes a vision of education that is integral and complex. Here the key is in the promotion. 'A UNIVERSITY may be considered with reference either to its Students or to its Studies; and the principle, that all Knowledge is a whole and the separate Sciences parts of one, which I have hitherto been using in behalf of its studies, is equally important when we direct our attention to its students.'[47]

In Newman's estimation, however, the university does not simply provide the means by which an individual or the group can access knowledge from different disciplines; it rather designs its curriculum in such a way that 'going around' is necessary and cooperation is essential. As Newman rather poetically expressed it:

Thought and word are, in their conception, two things, and thus there is a division of labour. The man of thought comes to the man of words; and the man of words, duly instructed in the thought, dips the pen of desire into the ink of devotedness, and proceeds to spread it over the page of desolation. Then the nightingale of affection is heard to warble to the rose of loveliness, while the breeze of anxiety plays around the brow of expectation.[48]

The scholar must *necessarily* approach her topic from varying perspectives and angles in order to appropriate its content. This is a value almost completely neglected in modern seats of higher learning. It is a question of methodology. The practice of theology, history, religious studies, and indeed any discipline has, in the past two hundred years, increasingly become immured in methodologies. The techné of history and theology, to use the two most applicable examples, began as a vehicle for discovering 'truth' (von Ranke and Troeltsch). The question asked by the formulators of techné was (and is) 'how can we discover the truth?' Of course, the positivist question itself was predicated on a belief in the final outcome that truths, truth or even truth could be discovered and in fairly straightforward ways. It was (and is) a decidedly modern, predetermined, foundational approach. Methodologies provide rules, systems of analysis, skeletons upon which to hang the sinews of a discipline. For Newman, however, it is necessary to be aware of 'the harm which has been done to the interests of science by excessive attachment to system.'[49] Methodologies are embarrassed by phenomena that are inconvenient and do not splice easily into the established techné of the methodology. Such phenomena invariably get exiled to the hinterlands of a discipline. For example, theological method cannot *measure* mystical experience, so it comes within the provenance of 'spirituality'. The messy work of parishes is now 'pastoral theology'. In such instances, methodologies are forced into the corner of delimitation. Ironically, it can be the case that methodologies come to limit the very expansiveness they sought initially to explore. History or theology, or any other discipline, becomes that which the methodology can determine. If it is not observable through the lens of a particular techné, it is not history or theology, or whatever. Here we see the need to remove the classics, with their determined parabolic and 'mythic' approach, from utilitarian curricula. Narrowing the areas of study by way of method solidifies (some might say calcifies) the answers that are possible.

Efforts at demilitarising the sometimes-burdened methodologies of the disciplines have been termed (pejoratively?) postmodern, because they seem to throw out the epistemological baby with the cultural bathwater. Is this necessarily the case, however? Does a new, a different approach to a discipline, or even a purposefully interdisciplinary approach to learning imply the lack of foundations?

Of course, the advent of the postmodern merely points to the fact that while the modern vision held sway in the past three hundred years, it was not the only vision. Completely outside the confines of the prevailing methodologies, history has gone on and theology has continued, among and between the parameters of the established methodologies. The Catholic Church labelled efforts such as these 'modernist' in the late nineteenth century. Later 'modernism' itself became the established methodology. Theologians and historians who have not worked within the accepted rules of the game may have been classified 'bad' or even 'heretical' historians and theologians, yet their work remains.

Being immured in a methodology may well have the effect of isolating and segregating the disciplines, even disciplines once seen as meaningfully compatible. Theology cannot speak to history, because we have no common method or language. Yet thinkers both affable and inimical to Christianity have continued to work within a multi-dimensional disciplinary substratum. There have been historical theologians and theological historians, although their work today, viewed from the vantage point of later methodologies, might be labelled primitive, naïve or basically wrong.

A serious consideration of the complexity of Newman's epistemology not only necessitates the development of a common language, but also the absolute need for disciplines to be in dialogue. I can say nothing about literature until I have consulted botany. In this way:

> in the number of these special ideas, which from their very depth and richness cannot be fully understood at once, but are more and more clearly expressed and taught the longer they last – having aspects many and bearings many, mutually connected and growing one out of another, and all parts of a whole, with a sympathy and correspondence keeping pace with the ever-changing necessities of the world, multiform, prolific, and ever resourceful.[50]

Interdisciplinary study, in light of Newman's epistemology, is not *merely* a good idea or an educational philosophy that promotes a well-rounded student. It is essential in the basic sense of that word. The university *creates* the environment for enacting the very process of intellection that Newman asserts is natural. 'I have said that all branches of knowledge are connected together, because the subject-matter of knowledge is intimately united in itself, as being the acts and the work of the Creator.'[51] The student is inevitably polymathic, parabolic and, finally, poetical.

Second, in Newman's estimation education is not a passive activity of the mind. It is, rather, a *way* of life. If ideas, as Newman opines, are not merely the desiccated specimens of mental process decaying in the japanned specimen boxes of Victorian methodologies, but living and breathing impulses; then they must be shown vigorous in the activity of the academic community. All that a person is and was, she brings to the particular kind of learning that is disclosed in the university. What one learns in the institution is informed and magnified, indeed given credence, by antecedent experiences, both named and un-named. The student is inspired to learn because all that he has done before has prepared him and compelled him to continue the journey of education. There is a tension inherent in the university education that instils life and vigour. The tension brings the learner to the institution and sustains her presence there. We do not go to university for answers, but to be inspired. I learn not so much to know facts or things, but to know what there is to know and thus arouse me to greater learning and living. The central message of the university, then, in Newman's epistemology is that learning is something acquired, it is a relationship that one commits to, not for a time of training or preparation but for life. In other words, the university inspires the student to a parabolic way of living, an imperative to continue to grow and develop. In its curricula, therefore, universities must *excite* this growth. Students do not need to *acquire* facts from varied disciplines, they need to learn to think and live by walking around truth in all its incarnations and in all its angles. Universities inspire learners not to knowledge as a goal but to the wisdom that a life of learning instils. In this light Newman can claim, 'that Knowledge, in proportion as it tends more and more to be particular, ceases to be Knowledge'.[52]

Third, for Newman the university must always be conceived as a community of learners and not as individuals pursuing knowledge and truth, however parabolically, for their own ends. In terms of his epistemology, as we have seen, there is a limit to what the individual can know in and of himself. True learning only comes within the context of a community, living and working together and observing and respecting the growth in one another. Each person has something to contribute to the creation of the whole. Here we see the early Benedictine model at work again. Like a monastery, the university depends on cooperation, not only between individuals but also between disciplines and branches of learning. For Newman, the *sui generic* nature of the individual and his collection of intellectual insight is duly enhanced by dialogue with others:

> The throng and succession of ideas, thoughts, feelings, imaginations, aspirations, which pass within him, the abstractions, the juxtapositions, the comparisons, the discriminations, the conceptions, which are so original in him, his views of external things, his judgments upon life, manners, and history, the exercises of his wit, of his humour, of his depth, of his sagacity, all these innumerable and incessant creations, the very pulsation and throbbing of his intellect, does he image forth, to all does he give utterance, in a corresponding language, which is as multiform as this inward mental action itself and analogous to it, the faithful expression of his intense personality, attending on his own inward world of thought as its very shadow: so that we might as well say that one man's shadow is another's as that the style of a really gifted mind can belong to any but himself. It follows him about *as* a shadow. His thought and feeling are personal, and so his language is personal.[53]

Self-will, self-motivation or auto–didacticism is counter-productive because the fullness of truth can never reside in an individual. In theological terms, Newman understood this as truth dwelling in a complete way only in the sense of the faithful, a kind of Aristotelian *phronema* beating in the heart of the church. Wisdom for Newman is not the province of the isolated sage speaking from the mountaintop; it is the collected wisdom of women and men, young and old, of all classes and 'levels' of education. Newman likens this collected wisdom to the generation of language.

> Language itself in its very origination would seem to be traceable to individuals. Their peculiarities have given it its character. We are often able in fact to trace particular phrases or idioms to individuals; we know the history of their rise. Slang surely, as it is called, comes of, and breathes of the personal. The connection between the force of words in particular languages and the habits and sentiments of the nations speaking them has often been pointed out. And, while the many use language as they find it, the man of genius uses it indeed, but subjects it withal to his own purposes, and moulds it according to his own peculiarities.[54]

All have a piece to contribute like a jigsaw puzzle and the picture can never be complete until all have contributed. So the university becomes the community of learners whereby this collaborative wisdom is shared. 'It will give birth to a living teaching, which in course of time will take the shape of a self-perpetuating tradition, or a *genius loci*, as it is sometimes called; which haunts the home where it has been born, and which imbues and forms, more or less, and one by one, every individual who is successively brought under its shadow.'[55] Comparisons and contrasts are made between and among disciplinary concerns. Seeming differences that are collected and stored arouse critical awareness. The only heresy in this context is deafness, a refusal to listen to others because of the conviction that one has attained the answers for oneself, or one's discipline is complete without the wisdom of the others. But here, as we have seen above, some work is required. A common language is needed. A method is vital. This seems to be one of the foremost challenges to university education today. Newman certainly saw it as his greatest challenge. However, there is no other way of learning or of teaching.

Of course, Newman, ever faithful to his epistemology, viewed any truly successful university as necessarily a Catholic university. 'If the Catholic faith is true, the University cannot exist external to the Catholic pale.'[56] Newman's insistence on the point, however, should not be interpreted simply in doctrinaire language. The assertion is more epistemological than creedal. For Newman, the paradox of education and the paradox of God were analogous, the more one knows, the more one knows one does not know. 'And so in the intellectual, moral, social, and political world. Man, with his motives and works, his languages, his propagation, his diffusion, is from Him. Agriculture, medicine, and the arts of life, are his gifts.'[57] God as the endless *fons sapientiae* is the last and greatest object of study, a subject that leads the person not to knowledge but to relationship, which is the source of wisdom itself.

> The word 'God' is a Theology in itself, indivisibly one, inexhaustibly various, from the vastness and the simplicity of its meaning. Admit a God, and you introduce among the subjects of your knowledge, a fact encompassing, closing in upon, absorbing, every other fact conceivable. How can we investigate any part of any order of Knowledge, and stop short of that which enters into every order.[58]

Newman describes it thus in *The Idea of a University*: 'To Him must be ascribed the rich endowments of the intellect, the irradiation of genius, the imagination of the poet, the sagacity of the politician, the wisdom (as Scripture calls it), which now rears and decorates the Temple, now manifests itself in proverb or in parable.'[59] In other words, only the inclusion of God in the equation of education provides for the necessary interpretive key to understanding truth. The engine of the illative sense generates truth in all disciplines. From a phenomenological point of view, this is as true in the 'secular' university as it is in the Christian or Catholic university. There is a grace in the Catholic university, however, in that Christians who learn, who enact the illative sense in a purposeful way, who live their faith not only intellectually but *really*, know more profoundly what they are knowing, that is, they know the divine reality and the sense in which the divine reality is the paradoxical propulsion of all knowledge. 'You see, Gentlemen, if you trust the judgment of a sagacious mind, deeply read in history, Catholic Theology has nothing to fear from the progress of Physical Science, even independently of the divinity of its doctrines. It speaks of things supernatural; and these, by the very force of the words, research into nature cannot touch.'[60] When Pilate asks Jesus 'What is truth' in the passion narrative of John's Gospel, the paradox is of course that the teacher is the very thing taught.

References

Beford, R. D. (1979) *The Defense of Truth: Herbert of Cherbury and the Seventeenth Century,* Manchester, Manchester University Press.

Carlyle, T. (1843) *Past and Present,* London, Humphrey Milford.

Dulles, A. (2002) *John Henry Newman,* London, Continuum.

Herbert of Cherbury, E. (1937) *De Veritate,* Manchester, Manchester University Press.

Hylson–Smith, K. (1997) *The Churches of England from Elizabeth I to Elizabeth II,* London, SCM Press.

Ker, I. (1988) *John Henry Newman: A Biography,* Oxford, Oxford University Press.

Merrigan, T. (1991) *Clear Heads and Holy Hearts: The Religious and Theological Ideal of John Henry Newman,* Louvain, Peeters Press.

Newman, J. H. (1845) *An Essay on the Development of Christian Doctrine,* London, Longmans, Green and Co.

Newman, J. H. (1852) *The Idea of a University,* London, Longmans, Green and Co.

Newman, J. H. (1868) *Fifteen Sermons Preached before the University of Oxford,* London, Longmans, Green and Co.

Newman, J. H. (1872) *Historical Sketches I,* London, Longmans, Green and Co.

Newman, J. H. (1978–1984) *The Letters and Diaries of John Henry Newman,* Oxford, Clarendon Press.

Robinson, D. (2003) *The Mother of Wisdom: The Parabolic Imperative in the Early Work of John Henry Newman,* Louvain, Louvain Studies.

Robinson, D. and T. Merrigan (eds) (2003) *Theology and Religious Pluralism,* Louvain, Louvain Studies.

Qualls, B. (2000) 'George Eliot and Religion', in G. Levine (ed.), *A Cambridge Companion to George Eliot*, Cambridge, Cambridge University Press, pp. 119–138.

Tristram, H. (ed.) (1956) *John Henry Newman: Autobiographical Writings,* London, Sheed and Ward.

Wilson, A. N. (1999) *God's Funeral,* London, Little, Brown and Company.

Chapter Six

Learning the Truth in a Christian University: Advice from Søren Kiekegaard

Murray A. Rae

The contemporary university is a phenomenon of uncertain character. Forces both within and without the academy are conspiring to render the traditional 'idea of the university' more and more redundant in the practical day-to-day existence of our institutions of higher learning. A claim like this requires, of course, some clarification of what is meant by 'the idea of the university'. Much has been written on that topic, notably, of course, by John Henry Newman whose lectures of that title were delivered in the 1850s and published in 1873. Very simply, I mean by 'the idea of the university' a community of scholars engaged in the pursuit of truth. That simple definition, occasioning little demur in times past, is in our own time both controversial and much less recognisable as a description of what universities are in fact doing. Neither the idea of a *community* of scholars nor the intention to pursue the *truth* are taken without question to be constitutive of the university's existence, and they figure hardly at all in the mandatory 'aims and outcomes' of university education. It may indeed be time, as Harold Turner was fond of remarking, for the church to reinvent the university.[1]

Universities were founded, and operated for a long time, under the assumption that we live in a universe, that is, that we are part of an entity that is to be treated as an intelligible and coherent whole. The idea of the university as articulated by Newman presupposed both the interconnectedness of things and the value of learning the truth about the complex interdependence of the universe. It was further believed, by Newman certainly, and by many founders of universities throughout Europe and North America, that the truth of things could only be told within a theological context – within the context, that is, of the creative and redemptive work of God. The reclamation of that belief would be one characteristic, it seems to me, of a university that called itself 'Christian'. My concern in this chapter, in dependence on just such a theological context, is to inquire into what might be involved in learning the truth, and to do so with particular reference to the thought of Søren Kierkegaard.

Can the truth be learned?

In his work, *Philosophical Fragments*, attributed to the pseudonym Johannes Climacus, Kierkegaard takes up the question once posed to Socrates: 'Can the truth be learned?' (Kierkegaard, 1985, pp. 9ff). In *The Meno*, Socrates offers an account of learning that depends crucially on the doctrine of *anamnesis* or recollection. The truth, Socrates contends, is latent within the immortal human soul and is learned through a process of recollection in which reason uncovers that which is already in the learner's possession. Learning, according to the Socratic view, may be conceived as an activity of the individual who discovers the truth through reason alone and without necessary recourse to tradition, to authority, or even to a teacher, though any one of these may serve as a point of departure in a particular instance of learning. 'Viewed Socratically, [however] any point of departure in time is *eo ipso* something accidental, a vanishing point, an occasion. Nor is the teacher anything more, and if he gives of himself and his erudition in any other way, he does not give but takes away' (Kierkegaard, 1985, p. 11). Socrates, accordingly, describes himself not as a teacher but as a midwife. He may assist in the process of giving birth to the truth, but he does not give the truth. The truth lies already within the possession of the learner, so that the teacher's *maieutic* role may be helpful but is not essential. The truth is, in principle, discoverable without the aid of any external authority.

That is one view of the learning process, and a very influential one at that. Kant's dictum, 'dare to think for yourself', captures the spirit of modernity and carries forward the Socratic assumption that our own epistemic capacity provides us with all the resource we need in order to learn the truth. The nature of that capacity is variously conceived, of course. Rationalists, following Socrates, see it as coterminous with human reason; Romantics more closely identify it with imagination; empiricists trust in the rational processing of sense experience, and so on. The common factors across the range of 'modern' epistemologies are an enormous confidence in our own epistemic capacity, the individualism of the learning process, the incidental character of the occasion in which one learns the truth – since truth is generated from within the individual rather than from without – and the dispensability of all authority other than our own. Postmodernity differs only in its downgrading of the notion of truth itself to a relative judgement of the individual. The epistemologies of modernity and postmodernity alike thus bear close resemblance to the Socratic. As Climacus himself puts it, again in *Philosophical Fragments*, 'In the Socratic view, every human being is himself the midpoint, and the whole world focuses only on him because his self-knowledge is God knowledge' (Kierkegaard, 1985, p. 11).[2]

Such are the features of Socratic pedagogy. Johannes Climacus, however, is not convinced that this view of learning is right. By way of a 'thought experiment', therefore, he proceeds to consider an alternative account of how one learns the truth. The alternative account is centred on the decisive significance of the moment in time. On the Socratic view the moment in time – the historical occasion on which the truth is recollected – is of no particular significance because the learner already possessed the truth 'from eternity'. It is embedded in the immortal soul. Nothing new, therefore, is introduced to the learner, and there is no change in the learner's person occasioned by his having been brought into a new relation to the truth. 'The Socratic line of thought', explains Climacus, supposes that 'every human being [already] possesses the truth.' But let us suppose, he continues, that the learner does not possess the truth. The learner exists rather in untruth (Kierkegaard, 1985, p. 13). If this is the case, then the process of learning must be reconceived. The teacher can no longer be thought of in the role of a midwife but is called upon, rather, to give something to the learner. Climacus writes: 'Now, if the learner is to obtain the truth, the teacher must bring it to him, but not only that. Along with it, he must provide him with the condition for understanding it, for if the learner were himself the condition for understanding the truth, then he merely needs to recollect' (Kierkegaard, 1985, p. 14). Two things are to be noted at this stage. First, in speaking of the truth Climacus is concerned particularly with that truth that concerns us ultimately and which is given to be known in the person of Jesus Christ. We might as well designate that, as Climacus himself does, by writing Truth with a capital 'T'.[3] There are, to be sure, some special conditions for learning this Truth, but let us follow Climacus' argument through to see what implications there might be for learning the truth in general. The second point to be noted thus far is that Climacus has not committed himself to the correctness of his alternative view. He is merely setting out what would be the case if the Socratic view is wrong, and, concurrently, he is developing a theoretical account of what an alternative pedagogy would be like. Climacus is not yet in a position to decide between them. As it turns out, Climacus leaves his readers to make that decision for themselves.

It is in such a manner that Climacus presses on with his 'thought experiment' about the means by which the truth is learned. If the learner is not in possession of the truth nor even of the condition for learning the truth, he continues, then what is required in the learning process is that the learner be transformed. Here is a point of particular interest in respect of the attempt to conceive the nature of a Christian university, and, arguably, of any university. Learning is not only about the acquisition of skills or knowledge; it is also about the formation and transformation of persons. Learning the truth, Kierkegaard insists, is not well served by the modern academic ideal of detached objectivity. What is called for, rather, is a passionate commitment to the object of study, and a readiness to have one's thinking and life-view transformed under the impact of the reality with which we are concerned. The adoption of a 'life-view' is a prominent theme of Kierkegaard's authorship. A life-view is a framework of interpretation through which we organise our experience and determine our courses of action. Its adoption amounts to the acceptance of responsibility for one's own life, and, in the academic sphere, for one's own critical judgements. Kierkegaard in his *Journals* writes, 'education should be directed toward letting the individual traverse the stages of life in the outside world, which the world has previously traversed, until his own cue appears' (Kierkegaard, *Journals*, 1/782). Elsewhere, Kierkegaard draws attention to this aspect of learning by placing the emphasis not on *what* is learned but on *how* the learner relates him or herself to the truth (See Kierkegaard, 1992, vol. 1, p. 202). In its best-known formulation, Kierkegaard has Climacus proclaim that 'truth is subjectivity' (Kierkegaard, 1992, vol. 1, chapter 2). Here the truth is conceived not in terms of articles of knowledge but in terms of a relation. The question is not whether the learner 'knows' the truth but whether the learner is *in* the truth, whether the learner is so related to the truth that it becomes a life in him, whether it has transformed him. Kierkegaard offers a comic parable that makes the point:

> A sergeant in the National Guard says to a recruit: 'You there, stand up straight.' Recruit: 'Sure enough.' Sergeant: 'Yes, and don't talk during drill.' Recruit: 'All right, I won't if you'll just tell me.' Sergeant: 'What the devil! You are not supposed to talk during drill.' Recruit: 'Well, don't get so mad. If I know I am not supposed to, I'll quit talking during drill.' (Kierkegaard *Journals*, 1/649)

The teacher here is frustrated in his efforts not because the learner cannot repeat exactly what he has been told, but because the knowledge has not transformed him, it is not manifest in a new form of life. The pedagogical encounter is therefore judged a failure. A Christian university will not conceive of the new form of life in the legalistic terms evident in this example, but it will be concerned with nurturing in its students a form of relation to the truth that manifests itself in a new form of life, a form that finds its prototype in the one who does not merely speak the truth but is himself the Truth, as also the Way and the Life.

A theological understanding of learning

Returning to the musings of Johannes Climacus, we discover that the transformation of which we have spoken cannot be accomplished by the teacher in the role of a midwife, for what is required is a new creation. Between one human being and another, Climacus explains, the midwife is the highest possible relation, but the task of transformation, 'of giving birth', must be done by 'the god' himself (Kierkegaard, 1985, p. 11; pp. 14–15).[4] Here we find a second principle of education within a Christian context. Learning the Truth is a process that is utterly dependent upon God. Christian theology has long recognised this in relation to its own central Truth, the Truth of Jesus Christ, but the principle may fruitfully be extended to all learning of truth. Christian faith confesses that it is through Christ that 'all things in heaven and on earth were created', and that 'in him all things hold together' (Col. 1:16–17). It is in Christ, therefore, that all things have their origin and continuing coherence, and it is by this Logos and not our own that the order and intelligibility of the universe is upheld. It is by virtue of the creative and sustaining Logos of God, therefore, that the truth of things may be apprehended, and the glory of the creation made known.

This means two things for a Christian university, first, that it will recognise this theological context for all its scholarly endeavours, and second, that it will seek in prayer the guidance and the enabling of God for its work of seeking the truth. This does not imply for those universities that recognise no such context and shun the empowering Spirit of God that their endeavours will be without any fruit. Clearly this is not the case. They may be likened, however, to the nine lepers who expressed no thanks to the divine Word by whom they were healed, but who were made clean nevertheless (see Luke 17:11–19).

To speak of the indispensability of divine enabling in the process of learning the truth is to imply that human capacity is limited. Contrary to the Socratic view now widely accepted in our universities, it is to suggest that learning is crucially dependent upon something other than the resources present in the learner. Those resources are inadequate in and of themselves. Climacus has in mind here the resources of human understanding. In its quest to learn the truth, the understanding comes up short. Nowhere is this more apparent than in reason's encounter with the Truth itself, with the God-man, the incarnate Word of God. The Christian doctrine of the incarnation is deemed to be a paradox; it is an offence to reason, an absurdity that the modern mind cannot conceive. But of course it is not just the *modern* mind that stumbles at the rock of the incarnation. Paul already knew in the world of Hellenistic culture that the gospel was foolishness to the Greeks. Kierkegaard reminds us, however, that the apparently paradoxical claim of the doctrine of incarnation does not betoken an impossibility at the heart of Christian proclamation but rather the incapacity of human understanding to apprehend the Truth. Not least among the reasons for this incapacity are the false presuppositions with which reason typically goes to work – that God and the world are mutually exclusive realities that cannot be given together, for instance; that the world can be explained from within itself without reference to God; that what is accessible to human reason exhausts what can be counted as knowledge; that reason is neutral; that it operates without presuppositions, and that it enables us to see the world *sub specie aeterni*.[5] None of these presuppositions are beyond question. In Kierkegaard's view they falsify the account of human knowing and place the rational subject in the place of God.

The incarnation, or more particularly, the incarnate one – called the Anti-Logos by Dietrich Bonhoeffer (Bonhoeffer, 1966, p. 29) – is at once both the Truth and the measure of all truth. Christ is thus the criterion by which the deliverances of human understanding are judged. Climacus writes, 'But if the paradox is *index* and *judex sui et falsi* [the criterion of itself and of the false], then offense can be regarded as an indirect testing of the correctness of the paradox, for offense is the erroneous accounting, is the conclusion of untruth' (Kierkegaard, 1985, p. 51). Kierkegaard means here that the incarnation, judged to be paradoxical according to the prevailing canons of human reason, in fact exposes the limitations of reason and the inadequacy of those paradigms of thought, now dominant in the academy, that suppose the transcendent and the immanent to be mutually exclusive realms and the universe to be entirely explicable, therefore, without reference to God. This 'erroneous accounting' is 'the conclusion of untruth'.

The notion of a Christian university, or of Christian education more generally, is often opposed with the contention that a religious framework constricts academic freedom and places improper dogmatic constraints on the scholarly enterprise. It must be admitted that evidence in support of such fears can easily be found, but on the Kierkegaardian view that we have been exploring precisely the opposite would be the case. That is to say, a theological framework for the pursuit of truth, a framework grounded in the incarnation, reveals the limits of human reason with its naturalistic and reductionist tendencies, and opens up new horizons rather than closing them down. It affords a larger vision of the universe than that offered by the constricting claims of secular rationality, and provides a more secure ground in the incarnate, crucified and risen Lord for the ultimate coherence and intelligibility of the universe as a whole. In this light it is the dogmatic presuppositions of the secular university that appear more threatening to the university's responsibility to seek the truth. In overestimating the competence of human reason, and by narrowing the frame of knowledge to the deliverances of human understanding, the secular university holds the learner in captivity and denies to the learner that larger vision of the universe in which all things are recognised as having both their origin and their *telos* in God. This captivity to a false vision of the universe manifests itself in the increasing fragmentation of knowledge, in a perverse postmodern delight in the incoherence of things, in the alleged absence of meaning, and in the concomitant claim that we are responsible ourselves for the creation of all meaning and truth.

Climacus does not draw back from naming this failure for what it truly is. Just as Socrates equates knowledge of the truth with virtue, Climacus equates existence in untruth with sin (Kierkegaard, 1985, p. 15). There are various ways of describing sin but especially pertinent within this context are the human propensity to do without God and the quest to be as God – all-knowing and all-powerful. Secular rationality has frequently supposed itself to be just that, and the academy has gone along with the dual myth that the solutions to all problems and our progress toward a better world are achievable without God. A university that is Christian in character, however, will content itself with a more humble claim, namely, that by the grace of God its students and teachers are enabled to see through a glass darkly. An appreciation of humanity's incapacity, moreover, ought to engender scholarly humility in the members of a Christian university and the understanding that 'man's highest achievement is to let God be able to help him' (Kierkegaard, *Journals*, 1/54). George Marsden has recently made the same point, in writing that '[t]he best education involves being not only critical, but self-critical. For that, the Christian perspective on the human condition and the deceptiveness of the human heart provides an excellent place to stand' (Marsden, 1997, p. 100).

Acknowledgement of the need of God's help is not to be understood as a prerequisite of God's helping the learner. Climacus insists that the learner's recognition of his existence in untruth, and thus of his need of help, is already contingent upon divine aid. 'It is too much', Climacus says, 'to ask [the learner] to find this out for himself ... only the god could teach it' (Kierkegaard 1985, p. 47). What God teaches in this instance is not an item of knowledge, although it has a propositional counterpart in Christian dogmatics; the 'teaching' rather, is a trans-formation, a movement from being in untruth to being in truth. That transformation, called variously a new birth or conversion in the New Testament, sets the learner in a new relation to the Truth. The learner is no longer departing from the Truth, but now finds, under the impact of revelation, that all her thinking is reoriented to and takes its starting point from the one who is the Truth. In this event of transformation, of reconciliation with and reorientation to the Truth, the learner becomes a new person. 'The shift is not merely perceptual but existential' (Willows, 2001, p. 134).[6] We return here to the point made earlier that a Christianly-conceived education will be concerned not merely with the acquisition of knowledge and skills but with the transformation of persons. It has now become apparent, however, that such transformation is the gift not of any human teacher, but of God. With explicit reference now to the biblical conceptuality that underlies this alternative account of the pedagogical process, Climacus writes,

> What, then, should we call such a teacher who gives [the learner] the condition again and along with it the truth? Let us call him a *savior*, for he does indeed save the learner from unfreedom, saves him from himself. Let us call him a *deliverer*, for he does indeed deliver the person who had imprisoned himself, and no one is so dreadfully imprisoned, and no captivity is so impossible to break out of as that in which the individual holds himself captive! And yet, even this does not say enough, for by his unfreedom he had indeed become guilty of something, and if that teacher gives him the condition and the truth, then he is, of course, a *reconciler* who takes away the wrath that lay over the incurred guilt. (Kierkegaard, 1985, p. 17)

All of this is true of one teacher in particular, of course. Climacus is speaking of Christian conversion, of that 'moment' in which the learner is encountered by Christ and oriented anew to the Truth made manifest in him. In spelling out the transformative logic of Christian conversion Climacus makes clear that for the learning of this Truth, at least, the Socratic recourse to human resources alone is completely in vain. We can no more learn this Truth ourselves than we can give birth to ourselves. This is a pedagogy that makes of the learner a new creation; the question now to be considered is whether this theological account of learning may provide a basis for a renewal of Christian scholarship.

On the teaching of mundane truths

Having considered the theological case, what can be said now of ordinary human teachers who do not possess the power to give new life, and of ordinary truths that one might think may be taught just as well without the theo-logic of Christian conversion? We shall consider these questions in reverse order and ask first, what lessons may be drawn from Kierkegaard's account of learning for the teaching of 'mundane' truths – that litmus paper turns red on immersion in acid, for instance; that the experience of music in a concert chamber depends crucially on the listener's reception of early reflected sound; that the velocity of sound varies with the medium in which it is travelling, and so on. Truths of this nature, it may be supposed, can be discovered and taught without reference to God and without requiring that the learner be somehow transformed. The 'what' of this kind of knowledge can surely be articulated without explicit reference to God. That is undoubtedly so but Kierkegaard's interest in the process of learning focuses not on the 'what', not, that is to say, on the objective content of our knowledge, but on the 'how'. Our attention is directed by Kierkegaard to the manner in which we are personally related to the truth, with how the truth shapes our lives. It is in this respect that orientation to the Truth which is in Christ offers a transformed perspective on the world and a new way of being in the world, the scope of which extends to all the disciplines of the academy (Willows, 2001, p. 153, n. 57). This difference will manifest itself in a Christian university in a variety of ways.

1. *Christian scholarship will concern itself not merely with 'what' is known but also with 'how' it becomes a life in us.*
Despite the appeal of the slogan 'knowledge for its own sake' in the battle against pragmatic and utilitarian constraints on university education, it is a slogan that Kierkegaard would otherwise resist. Education, for Kierkegaard, is not an end in itself but has to do with the transformation of persons and with the fulfilling of what we might call vocation. Entering a vocation, however, is not the same thing as embarking upon a career. The former is a response to God, it has to do with 'hearing one's cue' and becoming an individual *coram deo*, before God (see Kierkegaard, 1980, pp. 83, 123–124). The emphasis upon the individual in Kierkegaard's writings is frequently misconstrued and

might suggest here a recapitulation to the Socratic mode of learning. But becoming an individual is not conceived individualistically by Kierkegaard.[7] The concept of the individual translates, rather, as one who accepts responsibility before God for the life one lives in all its complex interrelationality. The individual, in Kierkegaard's usage, contrasts with those who merely drift with the crowd, on the one hand, or who are selfishly indulgent on the other. Education, or 'upbuilding' as Kierkegaard often calls it, is directed towards the overcoming of both failures, and ought always to remind the learner of her responsibility to the truth.

2. Christian scholarship will be shaped by revelation.

In addition to applying all the resources of human understanding to the task, Christian scholarship will also wait upon that which is disclosed to it of the *uni veritas,* the unity of truth that it is the university's business to investigate. The endeavours of scholars in the Christian university will be shaped by their confession of what has been revealed to them, namely, that in Christ all things hold together (Col. 1:15), and will be brought to fulfilment in him. It is this theological fact that will perhaps make the biggest difference of all to the Christian academy. David Willows puts it well:

> [Christian scholars] must surely not lose sight of the fact that, insofar as Christian education is *a posteriori* to the moment of divine revelation, the matrix of tacit beliefs and assumptions which we bring to bear on a particular concern will always be different; the gift of faith will always transform the 'pattern' that we discern when we look at the facts. (Willows, 2001, pp. 156–157)

Discerning the pattern differently is part of what is involved in the process of conversion (*metanoia*). Kierkegaard describes this seeing as 'the autopsy of faith'. The follower 'does not see with the eyes of others and sees only the same as every believer sees – with the eyes of faith' (Kierkegaard, 1985, p. 102). How could it be otherwise? If the world is the creation of God and if God continues to be creatively and redemptively involved with the world, as is revealed in Christ, then the 'pattern' simply is vastly different than it would be were it not so. If the Christian gospel is true then there can be no sphere of academic inquiry in which it has no relevance. So, while there may be nothing in particular to say theologically about the turning of litmus paper red, or about variations in the speed of sound, the interrelatedness of such knowledge with other things that go on in the universe and its application to our wider human projects will soon give rise to discussions in which the fact that this is God's world and that it is directed towards the fulfilment of his purposes becomes of the utmost importance.

3. *Christian scholarship by its witness to Christ will reject both naturalistic reductionism and the notion that truth is exhausted by the deliverances of human reason.*

Whatever the numerous merits of human intellectual endeavour may be, they do not amount to omniscience. Kierkegaard takes the incarnation, the appearance of the god–man, to be the disclosure not only of God himself, but also of the limits of merely 'human' under-standing. In its encounter with the god–man, human understanding 'collides' with the unknown and human pretentiousness is unmasked. That too is a matter of revelation. 'The understanding cannot come to know this by itself ... if it is going to come to know this, it must come to know this from the god' (Kierkegaard, 1985, p. 46). Christian scholarship, therefore, in contrast with a scholarship determined to confine itself within the limits of reason alone and to shun God's help, will be a scholarship that is more generous in its expectations of what may be counted as truth and more humble in its estimation of how the truth may be learned.

The role of the teacher

We have been largely concerned in this paper with the situation of the learner, but what might we learn from Kierkegaard about the teacher in a Christian university? We have noted above that the power of transforming the learner is not given to merely human teachers: giving birth belongs to the god alone (Kierkegaard, 1985, p. 11). In respect of human teachers, Johannes Climacus approves the contention of Socrates that between one human being and another *maiuesthai* [to deliver] is the highest. The role of the midwife is the appropriate form of relation. Unlike Socrates' conception of the matter, however, Christian teachers will be concerned not with delivering the truth from within the learner but with encouraging students to see the interconnectedness of things, to relish the interwoven complexity and irrepressible richness of the universe and thus to contribute, not to an individualistic divisiveness and competition within the academy, but to a renewed, collaborative discovery and appreciation of the universe in all its divinely bestowed unity and coherence.[8] Christian teaching will 'gesture', furthermore, towards 'a Truth that remains hidden from view apart from the transforming impact of divine encounter' (Willows, 2001, p. 149).

The teacher is thus called upon to become a witness, to become one whose own existence testifies both to the involvement of God in our learning, and to the transformative nature of education. In seeking to aid in the development of another, therefore, the character of the teacher is itself portrayed and revealed.[9] Kierkegaard was mercilessly scornful in this regard of 'assistant professors' whose lives give no evidence of having being transformed by the truth they purportedly profess.[10]

A final warning

What has been said so far may apply generally to education as it is Christianly conceived. We have outlined some principles, for example, that might be adopted by a Christian scholar in a secular university who seeks to be faithful to the broader theological vision of the universe that we have outlined. But this volume is concerned with the idea of a 'Christian university'. That is something else altogether, something about which Kierkegaard's works issue a stern warning. Kierkegaard was relentlessly demanding of institutions claiming the name Christian. In a series of articles in his closing years, subsequently published together as 'Attack upon Christendom', Kierkegaard unleashed a tirade of criticism against the tendency of institutionalised forms to settle into a cosy accommodation with the surrounding culture – in order to win that culture's respect, to secure state funding perhaps, or just because institutions by their very nature require a degree of conformity to the cultural conventions within which they are established. Such conformity, such 'levelling out' as Kierkegaard put it, is likely to obscure or even to abolish Christianity. For 'what Christianity wants is ... the following of Christ.' (This is not the domesticated Christ of Christendom, but the lowly suffering Christ who causes offence in the world and overturns the tables in our sacred institutions.) 'What man does not want is suffering, least of all the kind of suffering which is properly the Christian sort, suffering at the hands of men. So he dispenses with "following," and consequently with suffering' (Kierkegaard, 1968, p. 123). 'And at last one casts the Pattern [Christ] away entirely and lets what it is to be a man, mediocrity, count pretty nearly as the ideal' (Kierkegaard, 1968, p. 117). To put the matter sharply (and extremely, for Kierkegaard readily admits that much of his polemical writing is a corrective that if taken on its own would be a distortion), a truly Christian university, on Kierkegaard's terms, would count amongst its aims that its graduates, by virtue of their non-conformity, should 'suffer at the hands of men', not because suffering is a good to be sought for its own sake, but because suffering of the Christian sort is the mark of those who follow Christ in a non-Christian world. What Kierkegaard says of the duty to love might also be said of Christian scholarship: 'Oh, do this! And then just one more thing! "Remember in good time that if you do this or at least strive to act accordingly, you will fare badly in the world"' (Kierkegaard, 1995, p. 191). That might mean that the graduates of a Christian university are not easily employable, that their qualifications are frowned upon, that they will be rootless in this world and have no place to lay their heads. Christian discipleship begins with dying to the world! Thus must the Christian requirement be set forth at its highest, Kierkegaard insists. It must not be sold off at bargain price. Only then can we situate ourselves properly in relation to it, recognise thereby the degree to which we fall short, and understand our need of grace. As it is for individuals, so also it should be for institutions that claim the name of Christ.

The category of the individual before God is again important here. Individuals may be followers of Christ but crowds are not and institutions are not. The Christian quality of a university, therefore, will not be safeguarded by its institutional form or by such things as its founding charter, but only by the life lived in obedience to God of those who make up its members. In this regard Kierkegaard's own words do provide encouragement: 'Christianity's requirement is this: your life should express works as strenuously as possible; then one more thing is required – that you humble yourself and confess: But my being saved is nevertheless grace' (Kierkegaard, 1990, p. 17).

References

Bonhoeffer, Dietrich (1966) *Christology,* translated by John Bowden, London, Collins.

Hawking, Stephen (1988) *A Brief History of Time,* London, Bantam Books.

Kierkegaard, Søren (1967–78) *Søren Kierkegaard's Journals and Papers,* seven volumes, translated and edited by Howard V. Hong and Edna H. Hong, Bloomington, IN, Indiana University Press.

Kierkegaard, Søren (1985) *Philosophical Fragments,* translated and edited by Howard V. Hong and Edna H. Hong, Princeton, NJ, Princeton University Press.

Kierkegaard, Søren (1980) *Sickness Unto Death,* translated and edited by Howard V. Hong and Edna H. Hong, Princeton, NJ, Princeton University Press.

Kierkegaard, Søren (1990) *For Self-Examination* and *Judge For Yourself!,* translated and edited by Howard V. Hong and Edna H. Hong, Princeton, NJ, Princeton University Press.

Kierkegaard, Søren (1992) *Concluding Unscientific Postscript to Philosophical Fragments,* two volumes, translated and edited by Howard V. Hong and Edna H. Hong, Princeton, NJ, Princeton University Press.

Kierkegaard, Søren (1995) *Works of Love,* translated and edited by Howard V. Hong and Edna H. Hong, Princeton, NJ, Princeton University Press.

Manheimer, Ronald J. (1977) *Kierkegaard as Educator,* Berkeley, University of California Press.

Marsden, George M. (1997) *The Outrageous Idea of Christian Scholarship,* New York, Oxford University Press.

O'Siadhail, Michael (1996) 'Crosslight', in David F. Ford and Dennis L. Stamps (eds), *Essentials of Christian Community,* Edinburgh, T & T Clark, pp. 49–60.

Pattison, George (1997) *Kierkegaard and the Crisis of Faith,* London, SPCK.

Willows, David (2001) *Divine Knowledge: A Kierkegaardian Perspective on Christian Education,* Aldershot, Ashgate.

Chapter Seven

The University Without Question: John Henry Newman and Jacques Derrida on Faith in the University

Gerard Loughlin

I once suggested to a university vice-chancellor that you could not have a university – a real university – without a department of philosophy. He replied that you could have a university without a department of religious studies. Since he was the Vice-Chancellor of what was then my university – the University of Newcastle upon Tyne – and I taught in its department of religious studies, I took his point. The University of Newcastle closed its department of philosophy in the late 1980s, and its department of religious studies in 2004.[1] So the Vice-Chancellor was right.[2] You can have a university without a department of religious studies, as well as without a department of philosophy. But what sort of university do you then have?

Of course you can have religious studies and philosophy, and indeed theology, in a university without such named departments. Indeed, even where such departments exist you might find their disciplines practised elsewhere, and better, in other parts of the university, and of course in other places outside the university. Or one might think that since a university is to be a philosophical undertaking, it should have philosophy everywhere rather than in one particular place.[3] The university should be saturated with the love of wisdom. And the same might be said of a university that was to have theology at its heart. Perhaps a genuinely Christian university would have no department of theology. Like the heavenly city in which there is to be no church, the properly Christian university would have no department of theology, being itself a theological domain, which everywhere pursues truth in the mode of prayer, the ecstasy of joyous praise. (But the same could not be said of 'religious studies', which names an object rather than a condition of study – on which see further below.) But even if a university were to be characterised as in and of itself philosophical or theological, it would still need to have particular sites where these approaches were practised and interrogated, and thereby known as such. For it is through their disciplined profession that they are brought into the light; rendered responsible to themselves and to others.[4]

Though the disappearance of any named department may not indicate the disappearance of its concerns from the university, one cannot and must not assume that such concerns will persist without a department in which they are known and addressed, a traditioned discipline in which they flourish, even as they are put to the question, because put to the question.[5] What matters in the disappearance of a department is the disappearance of its *questioning*, of the particular interrogations by which it helped to constitute a body of debated knowledge. By the questioning of a discipline – which, when healthy, is also a self-questioning – is meant those forms of interrogative debate that lead to conceptual construction and clarification, the constitution of what one might call an epistemological ascesis. Such ways to knowledge are generative of multiple traditions that learn from one other, from their mutual contestations.

The question that must be asked about the university which 'disappears' departments and their disciplines is whether it is seeking to deny traditions, to refuse the kind of questions (whatever they are) which are asked in such disappeared disciplines. In closing departments does the university seek to foreclose on certain questions? Is it the case that the university no longer sees the point of such questions, or is even unaware that such questions could be asked? These concerns must be addressed when closing the sites of any discipline – and philosophy and religious studies are not the only disciplines to have lost residence in recent years. But the questions are particularly pressing when the disciplines in question seek to ask the most fundamental questions of all, the questions that interrogate what we take to be our identity as human beings, our most cherished assumptions about our place in the universe. When the disciplined asking of such questions no longer has a place in the university, what kind of university will we have and is it one that we would want to have?

This essay seeks to explore what the university might be, and the place of theology and religious studies in its possibility, through reading John Henry Newman's now classic discourses on *The Idea of a University*

(1852/1873) and a short essay by Jacques Derrida, on the 'university without condition'.[6] When taken together, these writings propose the university as a culture of universal knowledge in which we are taught – lecturers and students together – to ask the question of our existence, so that, at the last, we might question those who would have us foreclose on the question, and so give up on truth. Newman and Derrida, in their shared stress on discovery through invention, on open and inter-disciplinary investigation, on community over individualism and on faith over rationalism (foundationalism), together present us with a sort of postmodern university, at odds with the utilitarianism of our nineteenth-century inheritance, and open to a future that is to come – impossibly, perhaps, for Derrida; hopefully for Newman.[7]

Teaching culture

John Henry Newman (1801–1890) famously defined a university as a 'place of *teaching* universal *knowledge*'.[8] Many would be unhappy with this definition, which seems to suppose a grasp of universal knowledge that is now, if not already in Newman's day, impossible; and which seems to exclude research, and so – today – resource. The first concern is easily answered, for Newman did not suppose it possible for any one person to gain universal knowledge. Nor did he suppose that it was possible for any one university to teach it, but allowed that universal knowledge might have to be pursued across a range of institutions, and so the lack of a philosophy or religious studies department might not signal a disaster for the university. Indeed Newman allowed for the possibility we have already broached, that a university might be thoroughly theological but without a department of theology.

> Universities would naturally commence with Arts, and might, at least for a time, have no Professor or Teacher of Theology; but the *truths* of Theology would from the first be taken for granted and used, whenever they naturally entered into the subject of the Lectures which were given in Philosophy or (if so be) the Languages.[9]

But Newman does not allow that a university – a real university – would give up on the *idea* of teaching universal knowledge. Thus if a university lacked some departments, it would understand itself to be but a partial realisation of the true university, in which 'all branches of knowledge were presupposed or implied, *and none were omitted on principle*'.[10] Indeed one might think that all actual universities are partial in this sense, since all will lack something, and so at best be harbingers of the university that is to come. But what is to be feared is that the disappearing of departments might be a matter of principle, and so a denial of what the university is to be, and this no matter how inchoate is the principle in the minds of university overseers, and the culture that constitutes and is (in part) constituted by such an institution.

Newman's seeming denial of research in the university is more curious, for surely the university is a place of research, and all successful universities are 'research universities', an appellation which marks out real universities from mere 'teaching universities'? But for Newman, the object of the university is the 'diffusion and extension of knowledge rather than the advancement'. If the object of the university is 'scientific and philosophical discovery', why should it have students?[11] Newman, seemingly, would side with those who see nothing wrong in establishing teaching-only universities, or teaching-only lectureships.

> To discover and to teach are distinct functions; they are also distinct gifts, and are not commonly found united in the same person. He, too, who spends his day in dispensing his existing knowledge to all comers is unlikely to have either leisure or energy to acquire new.[12]

Newman imagines that knowledge is advanced through the work of institutions and academies which may be connected with universities, as subordinate 'congregations', but need not be. Such independent or semi-independent institutions contemplate science, not students.[13] And indeed, Newman's thinking presages what is now happening in many modern universities, where research institutes are created within the larger teaching university, as universities within universities, to which all academic staff may aspire, but to which only a few are called.

Newman's university is surprisingly 'student centred', focused on the good of its chief stakeholders. The object of the university is to turn its students into 'something or other', to mould their characters, form their habits, educate their hearts through educating their minds.[14] The university imparts knowledge, not just for its own sake, but also in order to create a 'culture of the intellect'.[15] Newman did not foresee a time of mass education in Britain, when there would be more university students studying theology and religious studies than were studying across all subjects in Newman's day, and when more than forty per cent of eligible youth would go into higher education, and more than fifty per cent of them would be women.[16] Newman's students were to become 'gentlemen', shorthand for cultivated minds. Newman was concerned with the strengthening, knitting together and toning of boy's minds;[17] turning youth into men of 'good sense, sobriety of thought, reasonableness, candour, self-command, and steadiness of view, ... entering with comparative ease into any subject of thought, and of taking up with aptitude any science or profession'.[18] Equipped with these transferable skills, a gentleman will be able to withstand the 'random theories and imposing sophistries and dashing paradoxes' of modern culture, promulgated, in Newman's day, by the 'periodical literature'.[19] If we allow that such gentlemanly skills are not the preserve of gentlemen alone, then Newman's vision can still speak to our condition. His university is a place where universal knowledge is taught, not as the mere 'transfer' of information but in order to create subjects with the skills of divination and discernment, the ability to reason and judge, in short, to exercise the ancient virtue of prudence (*prudentia*), that is still necessary for combating contemporary sophistries and seeking out truth.[20]

This is the classic view of a liberal education, as a culture in which the heart and mind are cultivated so as to withstand the siren voices of those whose interests are not universal but partial, whose persuasions are not disinterested, but partisan, inciting our desire for their own benefit. Such a view can be traced from Newman, through Matthew Arnold to F. R. Leavis and beyond, and while many commentators want to distance themselves from this idea of the university as intellectual culture, it strangely returns in their own recommendations of the university.

Krishan Kumar, while he distances himself from the elitism of Newman's idea, offers something close to it, and as answering to the predicament of the university in postmodern society. The university can no longer replicate a high culture for an elite, but it can offer a culture of 'exploration and engagement', a social space – to be located in particular places – in which students can together find themselves through 'speaking, writing, performing, playing, imagining, stretching themselves in mind and body'. Kumar argues that the university can no longer be the privileged site for the transmission of knowledge,

universal or otherwise, because such knowledge is already too contested within the university, and anyway is more easily disseminated
through the internet and other media, and, when it requires specialised
skills, through 'professional schools and institutes'.[21] The doctor is to
gain her knowledge through the medical school rather than the university, and if the former is situated in the latter, the latter exists for the
developing of potential doctors, rather than for their training as such.

What the university has to offer cannot be provided in the home, by
mail or the internet, but only by removing students to a different place,
where they live away from their previous, private lives and are
encouraged to engage in communal exploration of human possibilities,
through interacting with their teachers and fellow students.[22] 'Nowhere
else, and at no other time in their lives, irrespective of age, will students
encounter each other with so much time and so many resources to do
so much, unconstrained by the requirements of job or family.'[23]

Kumar was educated at the University of Cambridge and is now
Professor of Sociology at the University of Virginia, Charlottesville,
Thomas Jefferson's 'academical village',[24] in which – as originally
sketched – staff and students were to live close together, creating a
common culture for the new America. These locations may explain
why Kumar's description of the university is already a vision, a nostalgic
or myopic view which answers to a time and culture when students did
not to have to take out loans and do paid work in order to fund their
studies – indenturing themselves to a usurious economy – as is now
common in both British and North American universities. But as a
vision, Kumar's residential establishment answers to Newman's view of
a liberal education, for both envisage the university as a place in which
lives are to be formed, bodies and minds developed, and characters and
enterprises cultivated. No doubt Newman had a much clearer view
than Kumar of the kind of lives thus developed, and, no doubt,
Newman would have been aghast at the idea of simply allowing
students to 'explore themselves' – since he thought students had at first
no foundations on which to build their intellects, 'no discriminating
convictions, and no grasp of consequences'[25] – but he would have
recognised in Kumar a fellow concern with the university as a place for
the cultivation of intellect, if 'finding oneself' can be construed as such
cultivation. For certainly Newman did not rule out exploration and
engagement, finding the university to be a place of 'inquiry and
discovery, of experiment and speculation'.[26]

Paul Filmer is another sociologist who presses hard the changes that have befallen the modern university, while finding for it a role that is not unrelated to Newman's idea. For while universities cannot but engage with larger social trends, they must resist merely replicating that society and becoming factories for the production of suitable, unthinking employees, whose only interest is the larger pay packet that their university certification affords them. Rather, universities are to be those places which 'constitute the environments and provide the expertise and qualities required to reflect critically on contemporary social processes'. Universities are to resist 'instrumental functionality' by becoming places of unconstrained learning.[27] Thus Filmer's ideal university pursues 'disinterested research for its own sake', a 'critical stance in relation to collective, societal politics, purposes and plans' and promotes the 'most effective conditions for the pursuit of epistemo-logical excellence by the most able from among the community which it serves'.[28] If this sounds remarkably like the elite university of Newman's own day, which was, in Newman's vision, to pursue knowledge for its own sake, for the goods that are intrinsic to such a pursuit (above all, detachment from the sophistries of prevailing interests), it should be noted that Filmer supposes such a model for only a few universities, which are to be distinguished from those that are for teaching and training only, and presumably fully open to prevailing market forces. In between is another sector which manages a mixed economy of teaching and moderately scaled research. Indeed Filmer suggests that such a three-fold division is perhaps already with us in Britain. But however that may be, his vision of the university as a place of disinterested enquiry is not unrelated to Newman's idea of a place which pursues independent thought.

That said, if we are to find a resonance between Newman's idea of the university and are own inchoate aspirations, we will have to demur from his sharp distinction between teaching and research, and suggest that teaching needs to be fostered within a research culture, if indeed it is to promote the habits of reflective discernment that Newman advocates. Newman's idea of the researcher is somewhat arcane, since he imagines a secluded individual, free from the distractions of society, living in a cave or tower, or wandering among trees.[29] No doubt some professors aspire to such an idyll and wish for nothing so much as to be left alone with their laptop and books, but it hardly matches to the requirements of most modern research, especially in the social and natural sciences. Nor does it really match with either Newman's imagined university or the actual Catholic University of Dublin, as it functioned under Newman's rectorship. For Newman tells us that in the university the student is to breathe a 'pure and clear atmosphere of thought', which is produced through the 'assemblage of learned men', who, 'zealous for their own sciences, and rivals of each other, are brought, by familiar intercourse and for the sake of intellectual peace, to adjust together the claims and relation of their respective subjects of investigation'.[30] It is unlikely that such men, zealous and rivalrous for their sciences, but also seeking to learn from one another in pursuit of their investigations, are not engaged in what we would recognise as research. And so it proved in the Dublin realisation of Newman's idea, as when the University's journal, *Atlantis*, began to publish scientific research in 1858.[31] Indeed, Newman's idea of the university became so capacious that he likened it to the ordered multitudes of the Roman empire, a vast 'sphere of philosophy *and research*'.

> [The university] is ... the high protecting power of all knowledge and science, of fact and principle, *inquiry and discovery, of experiment and speculation*; it maps out the territory of the intellect, and sees that the boundaries of each province are religiously respected, and that there is neither encroachment nor surrender on any side.[32]

Thus we can endorse Newman's view of the university as a society in which intellectual culture is fostered, where students can gain a 'philosophical habit' of mind from living amongst intellectual zealots.[33] It was such a view of the university that more or less prevailed in British universities up to the 1980s, but which now is almost gone.

Toward the latter part of the twentieth century, British university education ceased to be about the formation of informed and critical sensibilities, and became a means for maximising earning potential. Now the Department for Education and Skills proffers the university as a 'good investment', since those with higher education qualifications are 'likely to earn on average 50% more than those without'.[34] And the universities follow suit, offering their skills and services as means to a better, financial future. Thus, for example, the newly created University of Manchester is quick to assure prospective students that their 'job prospects' will be 'second to none', that Manchester graduates 'are amongst the highest paid in the country'.[35] How very far this is from

Newman's own recommendation of the university. Today there is no mention of anything resembling the 'cultivation of intellect', no mention of the *universal* knowledge by which, for Newman, the intellect is to be cultivated. While Newman did not disparage the gaining of wealth, nor the advancement of social standing though education, he was adamant that the university is for the teaching of knowledge, and knowledge for the contemplation of truth, which alone brings happiness.[36]

Britain may have been nearing the height of its commercial success when Newman began to contemplate his university – in 1851 the Great Exhibition had celebrated the fruits of an empire ruled through trade – but Newman did not have to view the university as itself a market, a place for the selling of futures. His students were not consumers, nor his professors retailers, touting for business. He could foresee a time when this would happen – when the university would be no more than a 'bazaar, or pantechnicon, in which wares of all kinds are heaped together for sale in stalls independent of each other'[37] – but he could still imagine an educational relationship between teachers and taught, in which the latter are inducted into a culture of character formation, rather than groomed for a certified status.[38] His students were to enlarge their minds rather than their earning potential, gaining knowledge 'not only of things, but also of their mutual and true relations; knowledge, not merely considered as acquirement, but as philosophy'.[39]

Theology and universal knowledge

That the university should make some pretence to universal knowledge would seem implicit in its name, Newman suggests, even though its name is more properly derived not from the cosmos but from the corporate body of scholars and students in which the cosmos is thought. But it is a nice conceit, as Newman more or less admitted.[40] The university is to be that place in which the universe is known. Given the aspiration to teach universal knowledge it follows that theology must be one of the subjects that are taught, since theology, for Newman, is a branch of knowledge. There can be no pruning of the university tree. Thus Newman asks if it is 'logically consistent in a seat of learning to call itself a University and to exclude Theology from the number of its studies?'[41] Newman, it may be noted, was arguing not just for the place of theology in the university, but for the idea of a Catholic university, since he was the newly appointed Rector of the Catholic University of Ireland, and he was having to argue with his fellow Catholics in Dublin who would have been quite happy for their sons to have gone to a secular university, as long as it gave them access to the higher reaches of society. Newman wanted to show them that a university needed theology if it was to be a university at all; that a secular university would not do for those who aspired to a university education in the fullest sense.[42]

Newman was of course aware that it was possible for a seat of learning to call itself a university and exclude theology, for there were such universities in his day, as in ours. Thomas Jefferson's academy of American virtue – the University of Virginia at Charlottesville – had been founded in 1819 without a professor of theology. The American Constitution granted equality and freedom to all religious sects, and this precluded preferring any one of them with a professorship. But in Charlottesville there was to be a professor of ethics, who could teach the basic doctrines of deism, 'common to all sects': the existence and rule of a supreme being.[43] Closer to home, and of more concern to Newman, University College London had been founded in 1826 with no denominational tests and no teaching of theology. Newman assumed that theology is a branch of knowledge, a science, but allowed that this assumption might be questioned. Thus at one point he discusses the 'subject of Religion' rather than theology, and today we might feel more comfortable with this broader category, for though religion meant for Newman only Christianity in its various denominations and a range of ancient sects, we may take religion to include all religious traditions, and so its study approach more nearly to the idea of what is now meant by 'religious studies'.

But what is meant by 'religious studies' or, indeed, religion? For it is increasingly recognised that 'religion' – understood as a determinate thing, as a unified tradition of beliefs and practices – is very much a conception of western modernity, used first as a synonym for Protestant Christianity, and then, when pluralised, for such alien forms as Catholicism.[44] It was this already polemical category that was then employed to constitute the forms of cultural piety discovered by Christian missionaries in the non-European world. Thus it was that the West gave birth to such 'worldviews' as Hinduism and Buddhism, which are now so natural as to be used by those whom they characterise and so in part constitute.[45] But while vexed, the problem of 'religion' as a disciplinary construct is no more acute than in other disciplines, which also construct the objects of their study through their study of them. There is no need to abandon the category of religion so long as we recognise its contingency as a term of art.

> What the scholarly vocabulary of religion provides is one of a number of possible ways of cutting across the available data. Provided we remain self-conscious about our use of such a vocabulary, and refrain from postulating entities where we have only abstractions and representations, there is no reason why such vocabulary should not continue to be used.[46]

The related but more pressing problem for religious studies is the nature of the study by which it determines the religious, the constituting gaze by which it makes the object it sees: for this has never really established itself as a distinctive, disciplined, way of looking. Religious studies has borrowed from philosophical, anthropological, sociological and even theological points of view. And where perhaps it has been most distinctive, as in the phenomenological approach associated with Ninian Smart, it made the error of supposing itself to look with an impartial, neutral eye that saw objectively, free from particular interests.[47] But this positivism was always a preference, a particular standpoint that constrained what could be seen. It was no more disinterested than the theological gaze it sought to displace; only less self-critical or transparent.[48]

Yet the very fragility of religious studies has made it the site for modes of contested discourse that have come into their own with the passing of Smartian phenomenology and the emergence of an avowed eclecticism, a 'postmodern religious studies' that now embraces both anthropological approaches to religion and a relatively new formation that is more philosophical, influenced by 'continental philosophy' rather than Anglo-American analytic philosophy of religion. This new sensibility seeks to think religion from a point betwixt and between, as Gavin Hyman has it. It is a peculiarly academic mode of 'religious thought' that is neither theological nor anthropological, but liminal. '*Religion* and *religious studies* have ... become interstitial terms that refer to forms of thought that occur *between* theological thought and thought "about religion."'[49] One may wonder if this interstitial thought – a sort of 'religious' critical theory – is little more than a late, somewhat self-indulgent and degenerate flowering of Matthew Arnold's and Leslie Stephen's pious agnosticism.[50] But its estimate is not the point of the present discussion, which is to remember that the university, as a site for thinking about religion and about the sort of things which religions think and do, has produced an interwoven range of discourses which are either from within or without religion, and sometimes both, and which together constitute a domain which is not itself a tradition, but where traditions encounter their criticism and development. On this reading, 'religious studies' has become – or is becoming – an ideologically empty placeholder for dialogue around the always to be problematised notion of 'religion'. Borrowing from Alasdair MacIntyre, Hyman names this new religious studies 'a community of contested discourses'.[51] While religious studies might be more concerned with knowledge of religions than with that of which they (claim to) know, this distinction may not always be so clearly made, and especially when those who practice theology and religious studies do not seek to foreclose on the question. Can we possibly think the university without such a site for the critical development and mutual interrogation of the multiple discourses that 'religion' produces? And if we can, what sort of university would we then have?

For Newman, the university without theology (read theology and religious studies) is either trading under a false name or assuming that the 'province of Religion is very barren of real knowledge'.[52] Here Newman is assuming that religion gives us knowledge of what he calls the 'Supreme Being'. One may think this at best a speculative claim, but then religion would not be the only area of legitimate thought to proceed by means of speculation or the venture of trust.[53] But even if we think the idea of a 'Supreme Being' is contestable – as would some theologians – we may surely use Newman's argument in defence of both theology and religious studies, if the university is to be that place where religion is known and questioned, and where its questions are also asked and pondered: that place, moreover, where every conceptual assumption deployed in this discussion may be put to the question.

While Newman noted the growth of a practical atheism amongst intellectuals, he nevertheless felt able to insist that theology is a science, with its own body of knowledge. The practical atheism he put down to a growing tendency to view religion as a matter of sentiment rather than reason, a tendency which began with the Protestant Reformation and was in his day promulgated by the Liberal or Latitudinarian. When such a tendency prevails it is as unreasonable 'to demand for Religion a chair in a University, as to demand one for fine feeling, sense of honour, patriotism, gratitude, maternal affection, or good companionship, proposals which would be simply unmeaning'.[54] Even among those who claimed that knowledge of the world led to knowledge of God, many meant by God something that falls far short of what is meant in Catholic faith. For such people God is but 'Nature with a divine glow upon it'.[55] Against such a view, Newman insists that 'religious doctrine is knowledge.'[56]

Newman was well aware that the object of theological knowledge is of a different order from those of other sciences,[57] and that the way to such knowledge differs, in part, from those of other sciences; but he was in no doubt that it is knowledge, and so demands its place in the university which teaches universal knowledge. And the object of universal knowledge is truth, which Newman glosses as 'facts and their relations, which stand towards each other pretty much as subjects and predicates in logic'. These facts include everything, from 'the internal mysteries of the Divine Essence down to our own sensations and consciousness, … from the most glorious seraph to the vilest and most noxious of reptiles'. And all these facts hang together, forming 'one large system or complex fact', and it is the knowledge of this truth which the human mind seeks to contemplate. We cannot take in this single fact as a whole, but must traverse it slowly, short-sightedly, by means of our sciences, which give us 'partial views or abstractions', which sometimes look to the horizon, and sometimes focus on the ground beneath our feet. Moreover, the sciences show us things by showing us their relations, and so they never tell us everything that may be told, nor escape the mediation of their telling.[58]

The labour of knowledge is divided among the sciences, and when 'certain sciences are away' we have a 'defective apprehension' of the truth.[59] All sciences are needed for the seeking of truth, in the university where it is sought. Thus Newman offers us a view of a unified existence, of creation in relation to its creator, which must be studied by us – as particular, limited creatures – through a myriad of inter-related sciences: a truly interdisciplinary labour for the truth. And this common labour includes the co-dependence of theology on other disciplines, through which it learns of its own proper divine subject through their learning of the world which the creator has made and makes to be.[60] On Newman's account, theology does not appear as the 'queen of the sciences', but as the first amongst equals, for the truth which is to be known in theology is the fundamental condition for all knowledge.[61] When Newman does invoke the idea of a ruling science, an architectonic 'science of sciences', he gives it the name of philosophy.[62] However, this science of sciences is not so much a body of knowledge, distinct from the other sciences, as the caste of mind by which those sciences are apprehended and thus united. It is 'an intellectual ... grasp of many things brought together in one'.[63] It is not the unity of a general theory of everything, but of a community. Indeed, it is the university as such, in its universal scope and *idea*. '[I]t is the home, it is the mansion-house, of the goodly family of Sciences, sisters all, and sisterly in their mutual dispositions.'[64]

> Not Science only, not Literature only, not Theology only, neither abstract knowledge simply nor experimental, neither moral nor material, neither metaphysical nor historical, but all knowledge whatever, is taken into account in a University, as being the special seat of that large Philosophy, which embraces and locates truth of every kind, and every method of attaining it.[65]

The university to come

For Jacques Derrida also, the university is to be a place of truth. 'The university *professes* the truth, and that is its profession. It declares and promises an unlimited commitment to the truth.'[66] Derrida is aware that this bold and apparently straightforward declaration is not what might be expected of him, that he is betraying his 'habitual practice.' Moreover, the declaration is made in what he describes as '*like* a profession of faith'.[67] For Derrida, the university − and above all the humanities in the university − is to be that place where the human as such can be unconditionally discussed, without limit. The university is to be a place of 'critical resistance − and more than critical − to all the powers of dogmatic and unjust appropriation'.[68]

Derrida − in typically Derridean fashion − not only complicates his account by reminding us of how we should interrogate the histories and instabilities of all the terms he employs − the endless task of deconstruction – but also pushes his central idea of the 'university without limit' to the limit, where it becomes another figure for the impossible–possible, the recurring (Kantian) idea in Derrida's work of what we must but cannot think. It is in this way that the idea of the 'university without limit' turns out to have a radically 'theological' character.

Derrida's university professes truth through endless deconstruction. It is to be the place of deconstruction, of more than critical resistance to dogma and injustice. That which is more than critical *is* deconstruction, the practice of a ceaseless hypercriticism, having the 'unconditional right to ask critical questions not only about the history of the concept of man, but about the history even of critique, about the form and the authority of the question, about the interrogative form of thought'. So the university is opposed to a great number of powers, political and economic, religious and cultural; to all the powers that 'limit democracy'. And while democracy always receives a certain honour in Derrida's canon, it too is not beyond question, along with the value of the question, 'of thinking as "questioning"'.[69] Thus unconditional resistance includes resistance to itself, to the practice of resistance, to the constant unsettling of the ground from which resistance proceeds. (We may wonder if this is really so, if Derrida has ever really unsettled his liberal values to this extent. Derrida rarely waits around for an answer to his questions.)

The university is (to be) a place of resistance, of endless and unconditional questioning, even of its self-questioning, and it does this in public, which is the mark of the enlightened age. But even as this public commitment to the question is distinguished from a religious commitment to speak the truth and confess all, Derrida's discourse is strangely saturated with religious terms, the university being the place of a certain *confession*, a certain *profession of faith* in the virtue of limitless interrogation.[70] There is a sense in which Derrida's university is akin to (a certain understanding of) the church, just as Newman's idea of the church is 'noticeably similar in some respects to his idea of the university'.[71] Both Derrida and Newman imagine a university/church without condition. For Newman there can be no limit on the subjects which come within the domain of the university. 'Nothing is too vast, nothing too subtle, nothing too distant, nothing too minute, nothing too discursive, nothing too exact, to engage its attention.'[72] While for Derrida there can be no limit on the university's questioning, an interrogative version of Newman's unbounded sciences. The university, for Derrida, is not so much a place for the teaching of universal knowledge – though it is this as the university's craft or know-how – but is more properly, more rigorously, a place of *faith*. The professor is one who promises to keep faith with the university to come, and in promising performs or fabulates the university, in the mode of the 'as if'.[73] The professor, we might think, is the one who announces the eschaton, if the eschaton is the impossible which is to arrive.

There is no question that Derrida imagines an enlightenment rather than a medieval university, one where the humanities are central, and one where the question of the human, of humanity and of human rights – the 'rights of man' – are proclaimed even as they are interrogated. And yet the enlightened university cannot be so far from the medieval, if it is indeed open to the question, as Derrida avows: for while it may be the mark of enlightenment to dislodge the creator in favour of the creature-become-creator, it must nevertheless remember the older story in its questioning, if it is truly (to be) a place of endless self-questioning. If the university is without condition, then it cannot forgo the question of the God who may be,[74] and who makes all to be, even in its questioning. The university must retain theology if it is at all serious about humanity.

The 'university without condition' is to resist all powers that would seek to control its questioning and determine the answers, powers already identified as political and economic, as cultural, commercial and religious. The university is to resist all attempts upon its questioning, all claims to 'unconditional sovereignty', in which Derrida descries the 'heritage of a barely secularized theology'. And yet in maintaining its independence from such sovereign powers – in its practices of resistance and dissidence (insofar as it has them) – the university must itself claim a kind of sovereignty: a sovereignty, one might almost say, that is not of this world. The university without condition – and so without politically determined state funding and commercial sponsorship – is a university without power, without defence. 'Because it is absolutely independent, the university is also an exposed, tendered citadel, to be taken, often destined to capitulate without condition, to surrender unconditionally.'[75] This is perhaps the most remarkable of the 'theological' moments in Derrida's discourse: the sly invocation of a peaceable kingdom that is to come.

It should now be clear that, unlike Newman, who was envisaging a university that was about to come into being, Derrida is imagining a university that exists nowhere, or rather that exists only in the moment of the 'as if', in the moment when the university professes itself to be *as if without condition*. Such a moment is a profession of faith in the university, a promise to keep faith with such a profession; and, at the same time, a confession that such a promise is not kept. Moreover, such a promise, pledge or profession, is in some sense a 'performative' utterance, that produces the event of which it speaks.[76] Indeed, Derrida's essay is a kind of performance, '*like* a profession of faith',[77] as he says at its beginning. It is a pledge to the practice of a university without condition, to a place of questioning without limit, which is to come, perhaps. It is a profession of faith in the university 'that would be what it always should have been or always should have represented, that is, from its inception and in principle: autonomous, unconditionally free in its institution, in its speech, in its writing, in its thinking'.[78]

A performative discourse brings about that of which it speaks – that which it speaks into being – but that of which it speaks can never take us unawares, completely by surprise, because the performative always depends upon a preceding set of conventions, upon practices which allow us to recognise what has come to be. Thus what happens, happens within a horizon. 'No surprise, thus no event in the strong sense.' The event, in the strong sense, in the sense of 'an *irruption* that punctures the horizon, *interrupting* any performative organization', does not arrive through the conventions which permit the performative.

> It is too often said that the performative produces the event of which it speaks. To be sure. One must also realise that, inversely, where there is the performative, an event worthy of the name cannot arrive. If what arrives belongs to the horizon of the possible, or even of a possible performative, it does not arrive, it does not happen, in the full sense of the word. As I have often tried to demonstrate, only the impossible *can* arrive.[79]

Derrida's deconstruction of the performative, which announces both its possibility and impossibility, repeats a move which, as he reminds us, he has performed with many other concepts: gift, hospitality, forgiveness, justice, friendship.[80] And as with those analyses, the deconstruction depends upon taking a word to the limit, taking it in a 'strong' sense, in a way that we might not normally take it, in a direction we would not normally go. We might seek to deflate Derrida's deconstruction by remembering that there are events (unpredictable) and events (predictable), some that are events assuredly, no matter how predictable and conventional; and by refusing the semantic jurisdiction by which Derrida constrains the sense of 'arrival'. Yet we might also find in this and similar deconstructions that Derrida has invoked an almost 'theological' understanding of what may arrive in and through our utterances, an 'eschatological' interruption of the everyday, perhaps.

Moreover, can we be certain that the impossible does not arrive in the possible; so that, as it were, the 'to be' (*esse*) of our existence – which is always with us – might take us unawares, unsettling our complacency, our refusal of the question, of being put to the question. It would be like the rising of the sun, an event entirely within the horizon of our expectations, dependent on the 'convention' of the earth's turning, and yet which each day arises from *beyond* the horizon – expected but entirely new. It is surely such an epiphany that Derrida finds for us in the promise of the performative.

> What takes place does not have to announce itself as possible or necessary; if it did, its irruption as event would in advance be neutralised. The event belongs to a *perhaps* that is in keeping not with the possible but with the impossible. And its force is therefore irreducible to the force or the power of a performative, even if it gives to the performative itself, to what is called the *force* of the performative, its chance and its effectiveness.[81]

Thus the prayed-for arrival – but to whom does Derrida pray? – of the impossible 'university without condition' is the 'perhaps' in every promise to keep faith with the possibility of such a university, and in the promising the making of a place where questioning is not foreclosed. And there is something of this impossible-possibility in every non-utilitarian idea of the university as such: in Paul Filmer's idea of a place of unconstrained, disinterested questioning; in Krishan Kumar's idea of a place where students may find themselves through the exercise of their intellects; and, above all, in Newman's idea of a place where happiness is sought in truth, through universal knowledge. In all we surely find a commitment to the question, to an unconstrained interrogation of human being, to the mystery that we still are for ourselves: the question of our becoming. And if Derrida helps us to see that there is something of the 'theological' in a commitment to such an impossible possibility, in taking responsibility for the finding or founding of such a place as a 'university without condition' – as a matter of keeping faith with that which might arrive at any moment, in our promise to keep faith – then surely Derrida also helps us to see that the university cannot abandon its commitment to know those (religious) traditions which, from the first, have put humanity to the question, and which today still do so. In some sense, the university has to be a way of contemplation or unknowing, of putting to the question, of unlearning our certainties through universal knowledge, which knowledge is always yet to arrive. In church and university we learn, in different but related ways, how to advance into the dark.

At the last, I am reminded of Herbert McCabe's teaching that Thomas Aquinas, in his famous 'five ways' to what everyone names as God, offered us five ways to the question of existence. Invoking God is not to name some thing, but to ask a question: the question of a truly universal knowledge that keeps us questioning, a 'venture into the unknown.'[82] Therefore, if the university is to be a place where universal knowledge is taught, there is no question, no tradition of questioning, which it can resist or refuse. When this is allowed, the impossible *can* arrive, perhaps.[83]

Chapter Eight

Christian Teaching, Learning and Love: Education as Christian Ministry and Spiritual Discipline

Jeff Astley

The question, 'What is Christian about a Christian university?' is susceptible of a variety of answers. Some of these allow the adjective 'Christian' to qualify the practice and processes of higher education (and of education more generally), rather than its content, and do so in such a way as to imply no formal designation or founding of a Christian higher education institution. This is particularly the case when they focus on the dual, and frequently complementary, educational elements of teaching and learning.[1] What form should these activities take and what motivation might undergird them in the case of those teachers, on the one hand, and those scholars and researchers (including the students), on the other, who regard themselves in some sense as disciples of Christ? This will be my concern in the present essay, where I shall argue that Christian teachers may regard their teaching as a pastoral task and an exercise of Christian ministry, and that Christian scholars and researchers may construe their learning as a spiritual discipline. Both groups may then be said to be engaged in some form of 'Christian education',[2] even if they work in secular educational institutions.

I shall begin with, and largely concentrate on, the Christian vocation of the teacher in higher education, partly because the spirituality of learning has so far received more attention, but also because teaching has less often been granted the status it deserves, particularly within the university.[3]

Loving teaching?

It is unfortunately true that teaching, whatever form it takes, is a serious activity that is not taken seriously enough. A recent Anglican report is therefore to be welcomed for encouraging Christians to view teaching as a vocation 'of equal status to the priesthood' and as 'a ministry in, of, and to the body of Christ' (Church Schools Review Group, 2001, p. 50; see also pp. 91–92).[4] These are high claims; can they be defended?

Teaching is a species of pastoral ministry or service, if 'pastoral' is defined, not in the limited sense of a healing concern for those in trouble or distress, but more generally as a 'carefulness ... for the soul', understood in terms of 'devotion to the well-being of ... others' (Mills, 1990, p. 836). William Willimon is representative of those who are willing to treat education as an aspect of pastoral care. He writes that people can be 'healed, supported, and cared for' even through the process of helping them 'clarify their values and concepts', and by 'putting forward a conceptual framework upon which they are able to make meaning of their often disordered world' (Willimon, 1979, p. 125; cf. Durka, 2002, p. 56). Teaching, at any rate proper teaching, can be a task that is as pastoral as any other.

But perhaps this designation is too restricting, for not all care is pastoral care (cf. Day, 2004, ch. 2). Donald Evans has usefully distinguished two types of care or helping 'concern' (which he regards as being itself a dimension of love): the pastoral and the prophetic. The former labels the more usual understanding, the 'good shepherding' that is particularly directed to the needy and powerless; prophetic care, by contrast, is more a matter of telling forth God's will by criticising the powerful of society (Evans, 1979, pp. 141–147). While pastoral concern nurtures and encourages, prophetic concern probes and judges. And, although it may hurt more in the short term, in the end prophetic love can often prove to be more caring than any amount of comforting support. If it is really the truth that we voice, it will not harm – and may even redeem – its recipient. Teaching can also express this prophetic concern, contributing an ingredient that should prevent us from viewing the activity in too sentimental a light.

Jung argued that while we appreciate brilliant teachers, we are *grateful* to 'those who touched our human feelings', those who showed 'warmth'.[5] Yet some educationalists insist that the teacher's relationship with the student does not require affection. Indeed, they argue, affection can get in the way of a proper personal respect for the learner if the affectionate personal relationship is of a selfish nature, 'blinding one to the real interests and welfare of the other, or being pursued irrespective of those interests' (Pring, 1984, p. 29). A stance like this would be in marked opposition to what Bob Graham has described as the learner's 'really having a place in the good enough heart'.

> Sensing that one is truly 'held in the heart' and really free to be 'all there' does not mean one should feel free to misbehave or be indulged in a wash of perpetual, self-denying benevolence. We do not need our teachers to be kind, loving and giving all the time. There is nothing sentimental and nice about this concept of the good enough heart. Teachers with whom I felt able to be all there and truly myself varied greatly in their personalities, temperaments and behaviours ... A good enough heart can be snappish and irritable as well as sunny and equable. ... It is not sweet good-natured people we are looking for. What we must have if we possibly can are people able to provide genuine places in their hearts for all that we are and might become, people who do not have too strong a need to cling on to a limited version of who we are and for whom it is not too difficult or frightening to be on our side ... (Graham, 1998, p. 29)

I imagine that most university teachers would resist attempts to apply affective language to their own teaching. They would reject, perhaps, the description of the significant teacher as one in whose face the student can see 'that my own learning moves her, and that she is committed to me and my learning over the long haul' (Dykstra, 1981, p. 104). But often this sort of language does secure a purchase; it is frequently heard, for example, when people are asked to look back to their college days and talk about the teachers who influenced them. And there is at least one aspect of teaching where the word 'love' is never out of place. The psychologist James Day provides from among the transcripts of his research interviews a telling account of the influence of one teacher in helping a student to fall in love with a subject. 'Sharon' speaks of her maths teacher as one 'who *loved* algebra, and made me feel it meant the world to him that I could love it too' (Day, 1999, p. 267). (In the face of her father's cynicism, we should note, she vigorously denies that this process is the same thing as falling in love with her teacher!) Parker Palmer has written in a similar vein of the teacher's relationship with the subject in terms of the metaphor of a friendship. The friendship 'that binds subject and teacher' is one that the teacher wants to share with his or her students, for the true teacher is not possessive about such friendships. This is not just 'a passion for the subject'; it is also a passion for others to know this subject – 'to meet and learn from the constant companions of [the teacher's] intellect and imagination' (Palmer, 1998, pp. 120, 137).

> The teacher, who knows the subject well, must introduce it to students in the way one would introduce a friend. The students must know why the teacher values the subject, how the subject has transformed the teacher's life. By the same token, the teacher must value the students as potential friends, be vulnerable to the ways students may transform the teacher's relationship with the subject as well as be transformed. If I am invited into a valued friendship between two people, I will not enter in unless I feel that I am valued as well. (Palmer, 1993, p. 104)

Disinterested tuition?

In his heavily autobiographical book, *Spirituality, Ethics, Religion* and *Teaching*, Robert Nash has written on the importance of passionate teaching and passionate learning in higher education (Nash, 2002, pp. 9–10, 198). He characterises this as 'something akin to a lustful enthusiasm' which is fuelled by eros: the 'unapologetic love' of truth, beauty and relationships, 'the primordial human energy that attracts us to each other and binds us together in affection and generosity'. Aware that there are dangers in advocating unguided hot passion in education, however, Nash advocates *cool passion* as the best compromise (p. 16).

This is an attractive phrase, but I doubt that Martin Buber would have been happy even with this qualified language. In his powerful essay on education, Buber argued that eros has only a limited role. 'Erotic man' is a 'monologist', Buber notes in another piece, concerned only with himself (Buber, 1947, pp. 28–30). This is the danger of the earthly love that, in responding to the loveableness of its object, expresses our need for another and for what he, she or it can give us. In education, therefore, eros must be transcended, for there we must turn and open ourselves to the other. 'Only an inclusive Eros is love.' In using this expression, Buber intends to connote a love that is an 'inclusive power', part of a relationship with another person that lives out a shared experience 'from the standpoint of the other' in 'a dialogical relation' (p. 97). He seems here to be moving towards what others have called gift-love: that is, the other-regarding giving of one's self, the unconditional love that seeks no reward. This, of course, is the agapé of the New Testament.

> However mightily an educator is possessed and inspired by Eros, if he obeys him in the course of his educating then he stifles the growth of his blessings. It must be one or the other …
>
> Eros is choice, choice made from an inclination. This is precisely what education is not. The man who is loving in Eros chooses the beloved, the modern educator finds his pupil there before him. From this unerotic situation the *greatness* of the modern educator is to be seen – and most clearly when he is a teacher. He enters the school-room for the first time, he sees them crouching at the desks, indiscriminately flung together, the misshapen and the well-proportioned, animal faces, empty faces, and noble faces in indiscriminate confusion, like the presence of the created universe; the glance of the educator accepts and receives them all. He is assuredly no descendant of the Greek gods, who kidnapped those they loved. But he seems to me to be a representative of the true God. For if God 'forms the light and creates darkness' [Isa. 45:7], man is able to love both – to love light in itself, and darkness towards the light. …
>
> In education, then, there is a lofty asceticism: an asceticism which rejoices in the world, for the sake of the responsibility for a realm of life which is entrusted to us for our influence but not our interference – either by the will to power or by Eros. (pp. 94–95)

Buber thus commends the 'special humility of the educator for whom the life and particular being of all his pupils is the decisive factor'.

Such humility, asceticism and disinterestedness can make real teaching very demanding, which is why most of us at some time fail at it – occasionally spectacularly. 'Lofty asceticism' is a phrase that would not, I suspect, appeal to Nash. But I think that he might accept *passionate disinterestedness*[6] as an appropriate designation for the ideal that teaching is for the learners – that education is not for the teachers' own self-aggrandisement or the satisfaction of their needs. True teaching cannot be a self-serving activity; it must be a self-giving one.

This is what makes it a form of true love. Hence the teacher may sometimes even appear as a Baptist figure, decreasing while the learner increases (cf. John 3:30).[7]

Robert Bolt's play, *A Man for All Seasons*, begins with a discussion between Thomas More and his former pupil Richard Rich, the character who eventually perjures himself to ensure that More is condemned to death. Rich is seeking employment; or rather, it appears, security, money, power and status. More mentions a post where a man 'won't be tempted' by the bribery of high office – a post as a teacher.

MORE: Why not be a teacher? You'd be a fine teacher. Perhaps, a
          great one.
RICH: And if I was who would know it?
MORE: You, your pupils, your friends, God. Not a bad public, that ...

(Bolt, 1960, p. 4)

But it is not a good enough public for Richard Rich.

Stewart Sutherland treats this speech by More as being, in part at least, a claim about the possibilities of human fulfilment. He adds that the difference between the man whose final word is 'vanity of vanities, all is vanity', and Thomas More's 'you will know it ... God will know it', is not just a difference in attitude towards the same world. At the last, Sutherland asserts, there is a difference here about *the way things are*, about the possibilities defined by the structures of their respective worlds, concerning which these different claims are made (Sutherland, 1984, pp. 83–86). So this is not a trivial matter. The difference comes close to the heart of claims about the proper spiritual view of the world and of life. More's comment seeks to shift the other man's perspective, and to raise the question of what it might mean to see things *sub specie aeternitatis*, 'under the appearance of eternity'. That is a matter of seeing things as God sees them, and thus as they truly are.

I would argue that one essential feature of this spiritual view of reality is the recognition of the virtue of disinterestedness. To be disinterested is to be uninfluenced by, and thus unbiased by, one's personal benefit, profit or advantage. As Richard Rich hardly knows the meaning of the word, he refuses to be a teacher. For the same reason, he cannot be trusted by More, or by God. Presumably, Rich would also reject the calling of the scholar, for that also demands a certain disinterestedness and asceticism, as we shall see. But disinterestedness has an even greater role to play in teaching; indeed, disinterestedness may be said to be the engine that drives teaching as a pastoral task and a caring ministry. Perhaps no form of education should properly be called Christian that does not seek to fulfil this calling.

Cautions and qualifications

There is a danger, however, of overdoing this claim – of so emphasising the demand for disinterestedness that we make the ministry of teaching an impossible ideal. Can good teaching not also contain an element of erotic 'need-love'? If eros is a proper part of the creation (as an intended part, not a fallen part), we must be careful to avoid the trap of wholly despising 'interest'.

Theology has sometimes argued that truly to love God or our neighbour requires us to renounce eros entirely, and with it our desire for the beatitude of God's presence and our natural reactions to our neighbour's charms. Anders Nygren famously made such a claim, radically contrasting egocentric eros on the one hand ('a will to have and to possess, resting on a sense of need') and, on the other, unselfish agapé (which 'freely spends itself', bestowing 'itself on those who are not worthy of it'). These are, he wrote, 'direct opposites'; blending them would result in 'an impossible compromise' (Nygren, 1932, pp. 165, 171, 182).

The importance of disinterestedness in spirituality has been strongly underscored recently in the writings of Don Cupitt and Gareth Moore. Cupitt has notoriously argued for a rather austere and energetic disinterestedness in which we should be 'Good for Nothing' – a notion that includes being good without reward or consolation (Cupitt, 1986, p. 164). In more recent writings, however, he has repented of his 'former self-conscious strenuousness' (1995a, p. 116) and adopted a more relaxed, embodied, social and therapeutic form of spirituality, one that 'will lead to the highest happiness there is to be had' (1995b, p. 2). Yet he still regards the spiritual life as a matter of becoming 'fully disinterested and objective' (1995b, p. 45; cf. Astley, 2004b).

In *Believing in God*, Gareth Moore also wrestled with the problem of rewards, while framing a powerful account of Christian spirituality. He argues there that the talk of reward that we so frequently encounter in the New Testament is often not what it seems, but is being used by Jesus only 'in order to encourage people to forget all about rewards'. The depth grammar of Jesus' language is that 'to seek a reward from God is not to seek a reward at all', for the Christian life is presented as an end in itself and not as a means to something further. True spirituality is not a good bet, therefore; it is a matter of the sort of person one should be, *regardless*. Moore himself not only rejects the promises of earthly rewards for pious living, he also appears to dismiss the usual understanding of heavenly rewards.[8] He writes, 'heavenly success is not another form of success I might try to achieve *in addition* to any other goals I might have', since 'treasure in heaven is the treasure you acquire by not being interested in acquiring any treasure' (Moore, 1988, pp. 143, 145, 165, 172).

This takes us to the heart of Christian spirituality. One scarcely needs to add that it does not commit us to a non-realist view of the divine, nor even a non-realist view of the rewards of the Christian life. Disinterestedness is still possible even if it is rewarded. The point is that the reward is not the point; and, in any case, seeking the reward for its own sake is as counter-productive spiritually as seeking happiness for its own sake is psychologically. We must seek first the kingdom of God (Mtt. 5:33).

But agapé need not always resolutely exclude eros. Among the dissentient voices that have been raised against Nygren's thesis, we may note that of Vincent Brümmer. In *The Model of Love*, this author denies that pure agapé ('gift-love') must exclude eros ('need-love'). Brümmer argues the case for a variety of reasons, including that 'giving without receiving is not love but mere beneficence' and that 'it is only through need-love ... that I can bestow value and identity on your person and your love'. In order to engage in gift-love, therefore, we do not have to renounce the blessings we can receive from, and in our turn can give through, need-love. He applies this claim even to God's love for us, arguing that Nygren's position, which asserts that God's love creates value in its object but is indifferent to it, is incoherent. Brümmer writes, 'Only by needing us can God bestow value on us and upon our love for him' (Brümmer, 1993, pp. 240–242). Others have expressed similar views. James Mackey has even argued that a 'defensible and meaningful' use of the term God could be derived from a notion of eros as a pervasive originating impulse of the cosmos (Mackey, 1992, p. 158).

Most would not wish to go that far. But at least we should recognise that to try at the human level to engage in some totally non-erotic, agapeistic love would be a form of madness, an attempt to be God. W. B. Yeats' poem, 'For Anne Gregory', is more realistic:

> 'I heard an old religious man
> But yesternight declare
> That he had found a text to prove
> That only God, my dear,
> Could love you for yourself alone
> And not your yellow hair.'
> (Yeats, 1952, p. 277)

We should not be so silly as to foreswear all need-love. As human beings, to love and to be loved is to need and be needed.

To return to the forum of education: in teaching, too, there can be a proper and natural form of need-love.[9] It is a need-love that must be qualified, added to, transmuted and *transcended*, but never ignored or disparaged. Real teachers need to teach; they want to teach; they are deeply fulfilled by teaching. They love it, as they love their learners' learning. At some moments of real learning, such teachers 'can hardly hold the joy' (Palmer, 1998, p. 1). It is not too much to say that many teachers *need* their learners: they need the joy of watching them learn – of sharing in that disclosure situation in which the student comes to see the truth or masters a skill, or is changed in some other way. This is a desire and a need that may properly be fulfilled, provided that it is recognised, directed and channelled aright.

Perhaps 'disinterested' is too strong a word, then. What is important is that my teaching, like my love, should be *primarily* other-interested; not that it should be without *any* taste, or even any motivation, of satisfaction for myself.

We might note here that the eros/agapé contrast also marks a distinction between an involuntary, passive – and hence uncommandable – loving passion or desire, which is an emotion (eros), and the love that is primarily a function of the will (agapé). This differentiation is particularly important in learning. As learners we sometimes need to grit our teeth and get on with it; we need to exercise our will and ignore our feelings, or lack of them. 'How boring this research is', graduate students say sooner or later (in my experience, usually sooner). So much of real learning is more grind than glory. Sometimes learning is a duty that we will not enjoy. And the same is true of caring, and consequently of teaching.

Yet it is easy to fall into the mistake, which is a common clerical misconception as well as a Kantian error, of claiming that duty is all we need, and that the unusual circumstance of doing our duty solely for duty's sake is the only true morality. This cannot be the case. If St Francis had embraced the leper merely out of duty, he would have been less admirable because his action would have been less expressive of the good (cf. Benn, 1998, p. 168). Further, psychologically we function better, work better and care better when we enjoy it; and, in any case, striving to purge myself of self-satisfying feelings can itself be a form of spiritual pride. To 'forget myself' adequately I need to concentrate on others, not on my self-forgetting.

We will not always enjoy learning and teaching, but – like worship (hence the clerical reference) – if we never enjoy them, it would be far better to give them up. 'The best inward sign of vocation is deep gladness' (Palmer, 1998, p. 30). True caring normally includes deriving pleasure and joy from embracing the other, among which we may rank the other who is the learner and the other that is the truth. I am emphatically not advocating that the joy of learning and teaching should be drained away and replaced by ashen-faced duty; I am only asking that we acknowledge that this rejoicing is not the proper end of education, for my rejoicing is still something about me. So 'disinterested' teaching should never be equated with 'dispassionate' teaching – a word that suggests too cool, even cold, a relationship with others. *Passionate* disinterestedness involves a care for others that is impassioned and fervent, but directed to the other's interests rather than to our own. Both learning and teaching need such passion.

Nevertheless, while we should acknowledge the proper passion of education, we must also protect that passion – and protect our learners – from the seductions that often run along with it. These include the temptation to manipulate others (in teaching) or to manipulate the truth (in learning) to our own ends. University teachers in particular, perhaps, need to be cautious of using others merely in order to satisfy their own needs: as a means to the end of honing the new book, perhaps, or of advancing their own research interests. The important *outcome* of teaching is that the other is taught, and thus is served; his or her learning must be facilitated. That being the case, teachers and scholars need to define themselves and their work in terms of what is other than themselves, just as the church is defined (according to William Temple) as existing for the sake of those who are not its members. We need to structure and direct our actions to their proper end, which is the good of others and the pursuit of truth, rather than our own good and our own pursuits. Teaching, learning and loving are all activities that can greatly fulfil us, but that fulfilment cannot be their object.[10]

What now remains of my main thesis, my celebration of disinterestedness in teaching (and also in learning)? What is left, at the minimum, is a recognition of a creative tension between eros and agapé in all human loving and caring, learning and teaching. What we require is not a third way, a mean between and distinct from two extremes, for it is the contribution of the extremes that is important. Rather, we must look, paradoxically, for a creative catalytic blending of these two types of love. This is only possible, however, in the great majority of our human relationships – including surely all of our teaching – by responding to the demands of agapé. It is the agapé that matters *for the learners* and it is the agapé that transforms the eros; without it our teaching easily becomes wholly self-centred and self-interested.

In the end, assuredly, we are badly in need of grace. In this case it is the grace of the gift of an agapé that can transform need-love, as C. S. Lewis argued, not by substituting divine love for the natural but by taking it up into the highest love. Natural attraction then becomes grace-filled goodness. Although he divides the cake of love rather differently from the way I have sliced it, I want to quote Lewis here. 'All the activities (sins only excepted) of the natural loves can ... become works of the glad and shameless and grateful Need-love or of the selfless, unofficious Gift-love, which are both Charity' (Lewis, 1963, p. 122). This transformation is necessary, Lewis claims. As a Christian, he also believes that it is available.

> There is something in each of us that cannot be naturally loved. It is no one's fault if they do not so love it. Only the lovable can be naturally loved. ... All who have good parents, wives, husbands, or children, may be sure that at some times – and perhaps at all times in respect of some one particular trait or habit – they are receiving Charity, are not loved because they are lovable but because Love Himself is in those who love them. (p. 121)

Love from parents, spouses, children – and teachers also. Charity-within-teaching flows from, and in part constitutes, the character-strength of disinterestedness. This involves not so much a bracketing or a self-conscious disregarding of our self-interest, as its transformation.

At the very least, as teachers and as Christians we need to distinguish our interests in education from those of the learners, and to shift the focus of our concern from ourselves to them. We must, in other words, lovingly teach them for their sakes.

Spiritual learning?

Learning can also be viewed as a religious activity. Learning about the natural world, and much learning about human society, may be understood in traditional terms as thinking God's thoughts after him, in the sense of uncovering the created laws of physical, biological and social interaction. Learning in the humanities is located at only one remove from this: it is thinking the thoughts of God's rational creatures, and/or using my God-given wit to think my own thoughts.

But, beyond this, learning, scholarship and research should them-selves be embraced by the Christian as vocations of high value – of true virtue – and thus as proper expressions of Christianity and another form of love. Again, my main grounds for this claim are that the learner must show the *disinterestedness* that is the mark of true Christian spirituality and ministry. The learner, too, is a servant, here subservient to the truth, and must therefore exhibit a proper submissiveness. 'Humility is the only lens through which great things can be seen' (Palmer, 1998, p. 108); 'Christianity at its best teaches people that they stand not at the center of reality, but on the periphery along with everyone else' (Marsden, 1997, p. 109). The Christian's learning is also a passionate activity, like her love and her teaching; we are deeply 'interested' in the truth.[11] But at its best this interest is not self-serving. The true scholar should be concerned with the truth alone, and hang the glory. *The truth alone*, whatever it is: however ugly and however unrewarding, however little it is concerned with the needs of the scholar. True learning is not done in, or for, our interests. This disinterested love of truth can be very demanding. 'The truth is not always kind. And the rewards for its pursuit may be small.' Therefore research requires not only the intellectual virtues of impartiality, mental discipline and openness to evidence, criticism and cooperation; but also moral virtues such as courage, steadfastness, honesty and a realistic humility about one's own work (Pring, 2000, pp. 151–152).[12]

Undoubtedly, all this is part of the glory of the life of scholarship and its spiritual power. The true researcher is 'devoted' to his subject. Family and friends may complain sometimes that he loves Aristotle or condensed matter physics more than he loves them. That is not a happy situation; but if the scholar reveals a pure love for a subject, a love independent of any recompense, it is a devotion that should be treated with some reverence – and more understanding than it often receives. There is something almost holy about it; those who love their subject for itself alone can give us a glimpse of one form of pure love, a love of a pure learning.

Nevertheless, we must be realistic. Here, too, there are rewards. The rewards of research and scholarship may be tangible – spendable – such as academic promotion and even Nobel prizes; or they may come in a form that is less easily deposited in bank accounts, for instance the respect of our peers. Or they may not come at all, in either form. And it is this last condition that is the true test of the true scholar. Here, too, we are to seek first the kingdom, in this case the rule of the truth. These other things may then be added as well, if we are lucky. But if not? Well, the research, like the teaching, must then be done for nothing. True learning goes beyond the motivation of reward; at its finest it expresses a spiritual stance, resulting from a spiritual discipline. The professional student who is really only studying for the money is no more worthy of respect than the saint who, if he ceased to believe that any rewards were in the offing, would wholly renounce virtue and cease to love.

Although academics, being human, are at least partly motivated by pride, money and status-seeking, not to mention the fear of failure and disgrace, most are unlikely to claim that rewards and punishments of this kind are what the life of learning is all about. For such returns are all about me, and *this* is not. Perhaps that is why some have thought that the ideal of scholarship is anonymity, a theme that is well expressed by the authors of the four Gospels, of whom we hardly know even their names. In the last analysis it is not important to know who first discovered or formulated any particular truth. The library stacks will never be large enough to accommodate all the writings of forgotten academics, but it doesn't really matter. It is the truth that is the important thing. Once again, the song is more significant than its singers.

References

Astley, J. and D.V. Day (eds) (1992) *The Contours of Christian Education*, Great Wakering, McCrimmons.

Astley, J. (1994) *The Philosophy of Christian Religious Education*, Birmingham, ALA, Religious Education Press.

Astley, J. and L. J. Francis (eds) (1994) *Critical Perspectives on Christian Education: A Reader on the Aims, Principles and Philosophy of Christian Education*, Leominster, Gracewing Fowler Wright.

Astley, J. (1998) 'The Christian Vocation of Teaching and Learning', *Tufton Review*, 2, 2, pp. 57–72.

Astley, J. (2004a) 'Christian Ethics in the Classroom, Curriculum and Corridor', *Journal of Christian Ethics*, 17, 1, pp. 54–68.

Astley, J. (2004b) 'Religious Non-realism and Spiritual Truth', in G. Hyman (ed.), *New Directions in Philosophical Theology: Essays in Honour of Don Cupitt*, Aldershot, Ashgate, pp. 26–53.

Benn, P. (1998) *Ethics*, London, Routledge.

Bolt, R. (1960) *A Man for All Seasons: A Play in Two Acts*, London, Heinemann.

Brümmer, V. (1993) *The Model of Love*, Cambridge, Cambridge University Press.

Buber, M. (1947) *Between Man and Man*, ET London, Kegan Paul.

Carr, D. (2003) *Making Sense of Education: An Introduction to the Philosophy and Theory of Education and Teaching*, London, RoutledgeFalmer.

Church Schools Review Group (2001) *The Way Ahead: Church of England Schools in the New Millennium*, London, Church House Publishing.

Cupitt, D. (1986) *Life Lines*, London, SCM.

Cupitt, D. (1995a) *The Last Philosophy*, London, SCM.

Cupitt, D. (1995b) *Solar Ethics*, London, SCM.

Day, C. (2004) *A Passion for Teaching*, London, RoutledgeFalmer.

Day, J. M. (1999) 'The Primacy of Relationship: A Meditation on Education, Faith and the Dialogical Self', in J. C. Conroy (ed.), *Catholic Education: Inside-Out / Outside-In*, Dublin, Veritas, pp. 263–284.

Durka, G. (2002) *The Teacher's Calling: A Spirituality For Those Who Teach*, Mahwah, NJ, Paulist.

Dykstra, C. (1981) *Vision and Character*, New York, Paulist.

Evans, C. S. (2003) 'The Calling of the Christian Scholar-Teacher', in D.V. Henry and B. R. Agee (eds), *Faithful Learning and the Christian Scholarly Vocation*, Grand Rapids, MI, Eerdmans, pp. 26–49.

Evans, D. (1979) *Struggle and Fulfillment*, New York, Collins.

Graham, R. (1998) *Taking Each Other Seriously: Experiences in Learning and Teaching*, Durham, Fieldhouse Press.

Hughes, R.T. (2001) *How Christian Faith can Sustain the Life of the Mind*, Grand Rapids, MI, Eerdmans.

Jones, L. G. and S. Paulsell (eds) (2002) *The Scope of our Art: The Vocation of the Theological Teacher*, Grand Rapids, MI, Eerdmans.

Lewis, C. S. (1963) *The Four Loves*, London, Collins.

Mackey, J. P. (1992) 'Moral Values as Religious Absolutes', in M. McGhee (ed.), *Philosophy, Religion and the Spiritual Life*, Cambridge, Cambridge University Press, pp. 145–160.

McGhee, M. (2000) *Transformations of Mind: Philosophy as Spiritual Practice*, Cambridge, Cambridge University Press.

Marsden, G. M. (1997) *The Outrageous Idea of Christian Scholarship*, New York, Oxford University Press.

Mills, L. O. (1990) 'Pastoral Care (History, Traditions and Definitions)', in R. J. Hunter (ed.), *Dictionary of Pastoral Care and Counseling*, Nashville, TN, Abingdon, pp. 836–844.

Mitchell, B. (1990) *How to Play Theological Ping-Pong: And Other Essays on Faith and Reason*, Grand Rapids, MI, Eerdmans.

Moore, G. (1988) *Believing in God: A Philosophical Essay*, Edinburgh, T & T Clark.

Moran, G. (1997) *Showing How: The Act of Teaching*, Valley Forge, PA, Trinity Press International.

Nash, R. J. (2002) *Spirituality, Ethics, Religion and Teaching: A Professor's Journey*, New York, Peter Lang.

Nygren, A. (1932) *Agapé and Eros*, ET London, SPCK.

Palmer, P. J. (1993) *To Know as We are Known: Education as a Spiritual Journey*, San Francisco, HarperSanFrancisco.

Palmer, P. J. (1998) *The Courage to Teach: Exploring the Inner Landscape of a Teacher's Life*, San Francisco, Jossey-Bass.

Peterson, M. L. (2001) *With All Your Mind: A Christian Philosophy of Education*, Notre Dame, IN, University of Notre Dame Press.

Plantinga, C. (2002) *Engaging God's World: A Christian Vision of Faith, Learning, and Living*, Grand Rapids, MI, Eerdmans.

Pring, R. (1984) *Personal and Social Education in the Curriculum: Concepts and Control*, London, Hodder & Stoughton.

Pring, R. (2000) *Philosophy of Educational Research*, London, Continuum.

Sullivan, J. (2003) 'Scholarship and Spirituality', in D. Carr and J. Haldane (eds), *Spirituality, Philosophy and Education*, London, RoutledgeFalmer, pp. 127–140.

Sutherland, S. R. (1984) *God, Jesus and Belief*, Oxford, Blackwell.

Willimon, W. H. (1979) *Worship as Pastoral Care*, Nashville, TN, Abingdon.

Wolterstorff, N. (2004) *Educating for Shalom: Essays on Christian Higher Education*, Grand Rapids, MI, Eerdmans.

Yeats, W. B. (1952) *Collected Poems*, London, Macmillan.

Chapter Nine

Expectations of the Christian Campus: Ordinary Theology, Empirical Theology and Student Voices

Leslie J. Francis

Introduction

The concept of the Christian university in England and Wales at the beginning of the twenty-first century raises a number of profound theological issues. Among these issues are two primary sets of questions. The first set of questions concerns the nature of the Christian community or the church, and the relationship between the church and the world. The second set of questions concerns the nature of Christian education, and the relationship between Christian education and secular learning. The ways in which these two primary sets of questions can be addressed is shaped by debate concerning the nature of theological discourse itself. Different theological perspectives and different theological methodologies will approach these questions in different ways and bring different insights to bear on illuminating the implications of the questions. Biblical studies, church history, and systematics, for example, may all choose somewhat different starting points. The present chapter begins from the perspectives of ordinary and empirical theology.

Ordinary and empirical theology

In his recent pioneering book, *Ordinary Theology*, Astley (2002) discusses the importance of what he describes as 'listening and looking' in theology. He makes the case that theology, properly conceived, must remain concerned with taking seriously the experience of God in the world as revealed to ordinary men and to ordinary women, to people who have not been schooled and equipped to express their theological insights in the nuanced professional theological vocabulary of the academy, but whose experience of God and of living in God's world may be no less authentic and no less revelatory of theological truth. The job of the student of 'ordinary theology', according to Astley, is to take seriously the theological insights of ordinary people, by listening to their ordinary explanations and by looking at their ordinary practices and experiences. Real theology never remains static. According to Astley, ordinary theology may provide a powerful dynamic for theological development.

A key challenge faced by those wishing to engage in the study of the activity styled by Astley as ordinary theology concerns specifying appropriate methodology for looking at and for listening to the theology of ordinary people. What are the methodological procedures appropriate for this study? Is reflection on ordinary theology an art, or can it draw on forms of scientific rigour? What guarantee have we that the student of ordinary theology can speak with any more authority than the proverbial traveller on the Clapham omnibus, or with any more access to 'truth' than the proverbial chatterers informed by the *Sunday Telegraph*?

As Astley notes, the quest for a methodological rigour to underpin this study of ordinary theology has already been entered upon by the pioneers of 'empirical theology'. Within the Catholic University of Nijmegen the launch of the *Journal of Empirical Theology* in 1987 affirmed the initiatives of Johannes van der Ven to establish empirical theology as a core branch of theological activity. Van der Ven's view is that it is appropriate for theology to take into itself methodological perspectives shaped by the social sciences and to use these methods to provide, inform and test theological insights and debates. There is nothing either strange or outrageous in such a suggestion. Theologians concerned with biblical studies, for example, have for generations borrowed, refined and claimed as their own methodological per-spectives shaped by other disciples. Van der Ven's view is that empirical theology employs the tools of the social sciences in an intra-disciplinary manner, in clear contrast to the social scientific study of religion which may employ the tools of the social sciences to scrutinise the theological universe from without (see van der Ven, 1993, 1998).

In a parallel movement in Wales, Leslie J. Francis has attempted to pioneer a view of empirical theology consistent with van der Ven's intra-disciplinary approach, but which at the same time also emphasises an inter-disciplinary approach which insists that the activity of empirical theology should be subject to the appropriate peer review critique both of theologians and of social scientists (see Francis, 2002).

Against this background, the contention of the present paper is that the concept of the Christian university in England and Wales at the beginning of the twenty-first century needs to be tested against listening to the voices of the 'Christian' students most likely to seek attendance at such a campus, but to do so only in dialogue with the voices of other 'non-Christian' students who may find themselves sharing that same campus. Such an objective faces three methodological problems: how to listen to students on the Christian campus before the university is built; how to operationalise the construct of 'Christian students'; and how to set about the task of listening. Each of these problems will be addressed in turn.

The Christian campus

Prior to the recent formation of the University of Gloucestershire there were no universities as such in England and Wales which made a particular point of emphasising Christian foundations. In England, within the ancient universities of Oxford and Cambridge, the Christian heritage remains well embedded in college names (Jesus, Trinity and Corpus Christi), in college architecture (chapels and monastic cloisters), in traditions (chapel choirs at King's, Trinity and St John's Colleges in Cambridge), and in linking a few remaining posts in theology with ecclesiastic appointments (Regius and Lady Margaret chairs in Oxford), but the universities themselves are secular. In Wales, the nineteenth century foundation at Lampeter, with historic (but suspended) degree awarding powers linking seminary and academy, has been largely de-ecclesiasticised and absorbed within the secular University of Wales (Price, 1977, 1990).

In the absence of a Christian university in England and Wales, the Roman Catholic Church, Anglican Church and Free Churches nonetheless invested heavily in creating teacher training institutions in the nineteenth century and in re-shaping these institutions during the later part of the twentieth century into significant colleges of higher education or university-sector colleges. The history of individual institutions is well related by many commentators, including: McGregor (1981) on Bishop Otter College, Chichester; Rose (1981) on King Alfred's College, Winchester; Naylor and Howat (1982) on Culham College; McGregor (1991) on Ripon and York St John; More (1992) on St Paul's and St Mary's Colleges at Cheltenham; Gedge and Louden (1993) on St Martin's College, Lancaster; Grigg (1998) on Trinity College, Carmarthen; Eaton, Longmore and Naylor (2000) on St Mary's College, Twickenham; Bannon (1999) on Hopton Hall; and Bone (2003) on Westminster College, Oxford. Elford (2003) celebrates and analyses the creation of Liverpool Hope University College in 1996 out of two Roman Catholic and one Anglican college. Thus while there may have been no recent 'Christian university' there have been a number of Christian campuses in England and Wales. On the one hand, the number of these campuses has continued to decline in recent years with an apparently unintentional programme of closure, including La Sainte Union and Southampton (Roman Catholic), Westminster College, Oxford (Methodist), West Hill, Birmingham (Free Church) and Ripon (Anglican). On the other hand, the surviving colleges have tended to grow both in size and in academic breadth.

Given the potential importance of listening to the students who have opted to pursue their tertiary education on these examples of the Christian campus, it remains surprising how little interest the churches have shown in undertaking such research. An initiative was undertaken in this area by John D. Gay in the early 1980s. Gay's wide-ranging enquiry included an examination of student attitudes and expectations throughout a number of church-related colleges (Gay, Kay and Perry, 1985; Gay, Kay, Perry and Lazenby, 1985, 1986; Lazenby, Gay and Kay, 1987). In their summary report, Gay, Kay, Perry and Lazenby (1985) draw a profile of the student body in the following terms.

Students drawn to the colleges tend to be predominantly female (well over twice as many women as men) and middle class (over half of them being from social group 1 and 2) …

The great majority are aged 20 or less when they come to college. The academic level of undergraduate students on entry is fairly modest – three-quarters of them have A grade levels no higher than the equivalent of three Ds or two Cs.

The summary report goes on to suggest that the level of religious commitment of staff and students 'remains high in comparison with similar groups of people in other walks of life'. According to the data three-quarters of the students described themselves as members of one of the main Christian denominations, one-third say that they attend church services most weeks, and around a quarter describe themselves as having 'strong' or 'total' commitment to Christianity.

A decade after the publication of the report by Gay, Kay, Perry and Lazenby (1985), Edward Norman (1996) challenged the view that the Church Colleges remained, in any sense, Christian communities attracting church-related students expecting a distinctive educational environment. Although not making explicit the empirical grounds of his assertions, Norman (1996) argued as follows.

> Students rarely choose colleges for themselves – they are directed by parents and school teachers. Few opt for voluntary colleges because of their religious affiliations; most decisions are made on the basis of courses offered, and the actual location of the campus.

Clearly there is a need to build on Gay's pioneering work conducted in the early 1980s. The Church Colleges of Higher Education may provide valuable insights into the nature of the Christian campus.

Christian students

The task of identifying a subsection of young people on the Christian campus who may be described as 'Christian students' is conceptually complex. The task embraces both theological and sociological issues.

From a sociological perspective the task of defining religiosity within contemporary society is often seen as needing to distinguish between at least thee dimensions (see Francis, 2003). These dimensions are characterised as belief (say belief in God), practice (say attendance at worship services), and belonging (say self-assigned religious affiliation). Theologically each of these three dimensions also carries significance.

Grace Davie's (1994) now classic characterisation of religion in Britain since 1945 as 'believing without belonging' has provided a helpful stimulus to debate. In a recent analysis of Davie's position, Francis and Robbins (2004) have argued for a re-evaluation of this use of language. Instead they have proposed the notions of 'belonging without believing' and 'believing without practising'. This re-formulation is consistent with the kind of trends routinely reported by surveys like the British Social Attitudes Survey among adults (see de Graaf and Need, 2000) and the Values Today Survey among secondary school pupils (see Francis, 2001). More people generally claim religious affiliation than report religious belief. More people generally claim religious belief than report religious practice.

From a sociological perspective, the value of self-assigned religious affiliation as a socially significant indicator of religiosity has been reaffirmed by the introduction of the religious affiliation question within the 2001 Census in England, Wales and Scotland. Moreover, the predictive effectiveness of this indicator in its own right, independent of belief and practice, has been cogently argued by Fane (1999) and empirically demonstrated by Francis (2003). There is every reason, therefore, to accept as conceptually coherent, the definition of 'Christian students' as those who self-identify themselves as Christian in response to a direct question like, 'Do you belong to a religious group?'

Self-assigned religious affiliation is not, however, the only satisfactory way of defining 'Christian students'. In his innovative study, *Churchgoing and Christian Ethics*, Gill (1999) demonstrated the power of church attendance as a predictor of socially significant values. Gill's hypothesis was supported by reanalyses of British Social Attitudes Survey data gathered among adults. Francis and Kay (1995) came to a similar conclusion in their study among 13- to 15-year-olds reported in *Teenage Religion and Values*. There is every reason, therefore, to accept as conceptually coherent, the definition of 'Christian students' as those who attend church on a regular basis.

Listening to students

Accepting the views that Church Colleges of Higher Education may provide a glimpse into the Christian campus, and that it is reasonable to operationalise the notion of 'Christian students' in terms of indicators concerned with self-assigned religious affiliation and self-reported levels of church attendance, the aim of this chapter is to re-analyse data collected from two cohorts of students admitted to one such college in the mid-1990s. A preliminary overview of some of these data were presented by Francis, Robbins and Williams-Potter (1999). For the purposes of the present analyses and discussions, the college will be referred to by the pseudonym of 'St John's'.

Some three weeks after the beginning of term, a detailed questionnaire was distributed to all first-year undergraduates at St John's campus. The students were assured of anonymity and confidentiality. From the total intake of 847 undergraduates over these two years, 517 returned thoroughly completed questionnaires, making a response rate of 61%.

Three-quarters of the respondents (74%) were female and 26% were male. In view of the gender imbalance and of the prudence of analysing the two groups separately, the following analyses will be reported on the 383 female students only, since space does not permit repeating the analyses for males. Of these female students, 74% were aged 18 or 19, 11% were aged 20 or 21, and the remaining 15% were over the age of 21. Half of these female students (50%) were following the BEd programme, 42% were following BA courses, and 8% were following BSc programmes.

In response to the question, 'Do you regard yourself as a religious person?', 35% checked 'no', 61% checked 'Christian', and 4% checked another religious affiliation. The 17 students who self-identified with a non-Christian religious group have been excluded from the following analyses, enabling comparisons to be made on the basis of affiliation between 231 Christians and 135 non-affiliates.

In response to the question, 'Do you go to church?', 22% checked 'never', 28% checked 'weekly' or 'at least once a month', and the remaining 50% checked 'once or twice a year' or 'sometimes'. Comparisons will be made on the basis of practice between 106 students who attend church at least once a month and 83 students who never attend church.

The students' views on the Christian campus were assessed by a series of short, well focused statements, rated on a five-point scale: agree strongly, agree, not certain, disagree, and disagree strongly. The items were constructed to reflect five main areas: coming to the Christian campus; moving away from home; expectations of the Christian campus; experiences of the Christian campus; and chapel and chaplaincy on the Christian campus.

In presenting these data in the following tables the five response categories have been collapsed into two groups: those who affirmed the question (agree and agree strongly), and those who did not affirm the question (disagree, disagree strongly, and not certain). Chi square has been used to assess the statistical significance of differences in response between two groups defined on the basis of self-assigned religious affiliation, and then between two groups defined on the basis of self-reported religious practice. The three conventional probability levels of .05, .01, and .001 have been employed to assess the level of statistical significance of any differences found between the groups.

Coming to the Christian campus

Table 1 presents six items concerned with the students' perceptions and motivations in coming to St John's, analysed by religious affiliation. The students who were not themselves religiously affiliated gave very little priority to St John's being a church college: just 4% said that it was important to them that St John's was a church college, and none of them made a priority of finding out where the chapel was when they arrived. Just 1% chose to come there because it was a church college.

Table 1   Coming to the Christian campus: by Christian affiliation

	No %	Yes %	X^2	P<
I knew that St John's was a church college before I applied	66	76	4.1	.05
I chose to come to St John's because it is a church college	1	9	10.5	.001
St John's was not my first choice of college/university	38	41	0.4	NS
I was not sure that I wanted to come to St John's	16	20	0.7	NS
It is important to me that St John's is a church college	4	29	31.4	.001
One of my first priorities was to find out where the chapel was	0	11	15.7	.001

Nonetheless, two out of every three (66%) were aware that they were coming to a church college, and were not alienated by that knowledge.

The students who self-identified as Christian were significantly more influenced by the Christian nature of the campus. One in ten (9%) specifically chose St John's because it was a church college. Three in ten (29%) say that it is important to them that St John's is a church college, and 11% made it one of their first priorities to find where the chapel was on their arrival at campus.

What is also important from these statistics is that 38% of the non-affiliates and 41% of the Christians had not named St John's as their first choice for undergraduate study. Moreover, 16% of the non-affiliates and 20% of the Christians were not sure that they really wanted to come to St John's in the first place.

Table 2 examines the same six items from the perspective of Christian practice.

Now it is clear that the churchgoers are much more likely to value the distinctiveness of the Christian campus. Nearly half of the churchgoers (46%) say that it is important to them that St John's is a church college, compared with 4% of the non-churchgoers. One in five of the churchgoers (20%) made it one of their first priorities to find out where the chapel was, compared with 0% of the non-churchgoers. Only 22% of the churchgoers had not named St John's as their first choice for undergraduate study, compared with 37% of the non-churchgoers. Nonetheless, only 15% of the churchgoers specifically chose to come to St John's because it was a church college.

Table 2   Coming to the Christian campus: by Christian practice

	No %	Yes %	X^2	P<
I knew that St John's was a church college before I applied	65	77	3.5	NS
I chose to come to St John's because it is a church college	0	15	13.7	.001
St John's was not my first choice of college/university	37	22	5.6	.05
I was not sure that I wanted to come to St John's	22	21	0.0	NS
It is important to me that St John's is a church college	4	46	42.4	.001
One of my first priorities was to find out where the chapel was	0	20	18.5	.001

Moving away from home

The other side of settling into college life concerns the experience of moving away from home, often for the first time. Colleges which welcome young people onto campus need also to be aware of the wider emotional context of the students' lives. Table 3 presents six items concerned with the students' perceptions of moving away from home, analysed by religious affiliation. The students who were not themselves religiously affiliated were significantly more positive about leaving home than the Christian students. Thus, 35% of the unaffiliated students were glad to come away from home, compared with 25% of the Christian students. Similarly, 48% of the Christian students found the prospect of coming to college unnerving, compared with 37% of the unaffiliated students. The Christian campus may need to be sensitive to the higher level of anxiety among Christian students.

On the positive side, 76% of the unaffiliated students and 76% of the Christian students found it easy to make friends during their first week in college. On the less positive side, 42% of the unaffiliated students and 44% of the Christian students felt very disorientated during their first week in college. As many as 14% of the unaffiliated students and 12% of the Christian students felt isolated in their accommodation. Over a third of the unaffiliated students (36%) and 28% of the Christian students wanted to go home during their first week in college. There remains plenty of scope for pastoral care on the Christian campus.

Table 4 examines the same six items from the perspective of Christian practice. The differences between churchgoing and non-churchgoing young people are not great except in respect of two issues.

Table 3   Moving away from home: by Christian affiliation

	No %	Yes %	X^2	P<
The prospect of coming to college was unnerving for me	37	48	3.9	.05
I was glad to come away from home	35	25	4.3	.05
I felt very disorientated during my first week in college	42	44	0.1	NS
I found it easy to make friends during my first week in college	76	76	0.0	NS
I felt isolated in my accommodation	14	12	0.3	NS
I felt that I wanted to go home during my first week in college	36	28	2.6	NS

Table 4 Moving away from home: by Christian practice

	No %	Yes %	X^2	P<
The prospect of coming to college was unnerving for me	36	39	0.1	NS
I was glad to come away from home	37	22	5.6	.05
I felt very disorientated during my first week in college	45	46	0.1	NS
I found it easy to make friends during my first week in college	75	78	0.3	NS
I felt isolated in my accommodation	16	7	4.0	.05
I felt that I wanted to go home during my first week in college	39	33	0.6	NS

The churchgoers have stronger ties with home: only 22% of the churchgoers were glad to come away from home, compared with 37% of the non-churchgoers. Having arrived on campus, however, the churchgoers felt more at home there: only 7% of the churchgoers felt isolated in their college accommodation, compared with 16% of the non-churchgoers.

Expectations of the Christian campus

Table 5 presents six items concerned with the students' expectations of the Christian campus analysed by religious affiliation. For those of no religious affiliation, the key characteristic of the Christian campus is the

Table 5 Expectations of the Christian campus: by Christian affiliation

	No %	Yes %	X^2	P<
I expected a church college to be a specially caring place	36	55	12.5	.001
I expected a church college to be a specially friendly place	54	68	6.6	.01
I expected a church college to have many Christian students	36	46	3.4	NS
I expected a church college to have many Christian lecturers	19	29	4.6	.05
I expected a church college to be conservative in its outlook	13	12	0.2	NS
I expected a church college to discourage sex outside marriage	7	12	2.0	NS

mark of friendliness. Thus, 54% of the non–affiliates expect a church college to be a specially friendly face. A third of the non–affiliates expect a church college to be a specially caring place (36%) and to have many Christian students (36%). A fifth of the non–affiliates expect a church college to have many Christian lectures (19%). A few of the non–affiliated students construe the Christian campus as standing out against the liberalising trends of contemporary society. Thus, 13% expect a church college to be conservative in its outlook, and 7% expect a church college to discourage sex outside marriage.

There are some key ways in which the students who see themselves as Christian hold higher expectations of the Christian campus. While 54% of the non–affiliated students expect a church college to be a specially friendly place, the proportion rises to 68% among the Christian students. While 36% of the non–affiliated students expect a church college to be a specially caring place, the proportion rises to 55% among the Christian students. The Christian students are also more likely to expect the Christian campus to be populated by Christian lecturers. While 19% of the non–affiliated students expect a church college to have many Christian lecturers, the proportion rises to 29% among the Christian students.

Table 6 examines the same six items from the perspective of Christian practice. Churchgoing students are more likely than non–churchgoing students to emphasise the distinctiveness of the Christian campus in terms of being a specially friendly place (65% compared with 49%) and in terms of being a specially caring place (56% compared with 33%). Churchgoing students are also more likely than

Table 6   Expectations of the Christian campus: by Christian practice

	No %	Yes %	X^2	P<
I expected a church college to be a specially caring place	33	56	10.0	.01
I expected a church college to be a specially friendly place	49	65	4.7	.05
I expected a church college to have many Christian students	40	46	0.8	NS
I expected a church college to have many Christian lecturers	22	30	1.7	NS
I expected a church college to be conservative in its outlook	12	12	0.0	NS
I expected a church college to discourage sex outside marriage	8	21	5.4	.05

non-churchgoing students to emphasise the distinctiveness of the Christian campus in terms of being an environment in which sex outside marriage would be discouraged (21% compared with 8%).

Experiences of the Christian campus

Table 7 presents six items concerned with the students' initial experiences of the Christian campus, analysed by religious affiliation. When viewed through the lens of religious affiliation, there are relatively few large differences between the experiences of non-affiliated students and Christian students. Both groups were similarly impressed by the friendliness of the campus: 42% of the non-affiliated students and 49% of the Christian students were impressed by the level of help offered to them during the first week. Few were worried by the attitude toward alcohol displayed by the campus: just 2% of the non-affiliated students and 5% of the Christian students felt that St John's encouraged too much alcohol to be consumed.

By the end of the first week a small number of the Christian students had begun to feel that there were too few Christian lecturers on the campus (6%) or that there were two few people going to chapel (16%).

The Christian students were more likely than the non-affiliated students to have found the help and advice they needed during the first week. Thus, only 10% of the Christian students complained that they could not find anyone to ask for help and advice during the first week, compared with 17% of the non-affiliated students.

Table 7 Experiences of the Christian campus: by Christian affiliation

	No %	Yes %	X^2	P<
I feel that St John's has too few Christian students	4	9	3.3	NS
I feel that St John's has too few Christian lecturers	0	6	7.9	.01
I feel that St John's has too few people going to chapel	8	16	4.2	.05
I feel that St John's encourages too much alcohol to be consumed	2	5	1.9	NS
I was impressed by the level of help offered to me during the first week	42	49	1.3	NS
I could not find anyone to ask for help and advice during the first week	17	10	4.5	.05

Table 8 examines the same six items from the perspective of Christian practice. Here the contrasts between the two groups become more profound. On the one hand, the churchgoing students are beginning to express disappointment that their expectations of the Christian campus are not being fully met. One in four of the churchgoing students feel that St John's has too few people going to chapel (24%), compared with 4% of the non-churchgoing students. Similarly among the churchgoing students, 16% feel that St John's has too few Christian students and 10% feel that St John's has too few Christian lecturers. One in ten of the churchgoing students feel that St John's encourages too much alcohol to be consumed (9%).

Churchgoing students were much more likely than non-churchgoing students to have been impressed by the level of help offered during the first week (53% compared with 31%). Non-churchgoing students were much more likely than churchgoing students to have failed to find anyone to ask for advice during the first week (19% compared with 9%). It seems that the support mechanisms of the Christian campus are more easily accessed by churchgoers than by non-churchgoers.

Table 8   Experiences of the Christian campus: by Christian practice

	No %	Yes %	X^2	P<
I feel that St John's has too few Christian students	1	16	11.9	.001
I feel that St John's has too few Christian lecturers	1	10	6.6	.01
I feel that St John's has too few people going to chapel	4	24	14.7	.001
I feel that St John's encourages too much alcohol to be consumed	1	9	5.8	.05
I was impressed by the level of help offered to me during the first week	31	53	8.8	.01
I could not find anyone to ask for help and advice during the first week	19	9	4.7	.05

Chapel and chaplaincy on the Christian campus

Table 9 presents six items concerned with the students' understanding of the place of the chapel and the chaplaincy within the Christian campus. The statistics demonstrate that the non-affiliated students

Table 9   Chapel and chaplaincy on the Christian campus: by Christian affiliation

	No %	Yes %	X^2	P<
It is important to me that there is a chapel in the college	7	42	49.3	.001
It is important to me that there is a chaplain in the college	8	42	46.9	.001
I think it is important that there are daily services in the chapel	43	64	14.8	.001
I find the chapel a welcoming place	42	62	14.3	.001
The chapel has become an important place for me in the college	1	13	15.8	.001
I feel comfortable within the chapel environment	27	44	10.1	.001

attribute little importance to either chapel or chaplaincy: the chapel is important to just 7%, while the chaplain is important to just 8%. Nonetheless, a quarter of the non-affiliated students say that they feel comfortable within the chapel environment (27%), and even more say that they find the chapel a welcoming place (42%). While neither the chapel nor the chaplain are of importance to the non-affiliated students, 43% of them think that it is important that there are daily services in the chapel.

For the Christian students the chapel and chaplaincy hold a much more important place on the Christian campus. While 43% of the non-affiliated students think it is important that there are daily services in the chapel, the proportion rises to 64% among the Christian students. While 7% of the non-affiliated students say it is important that there is a chapel in the college, the proportion rises to 42% among the Christian students. While 8% of the non-affiliated students say it is important that there is a chaplain in the college, the proportion rises to 42% among the Christian students. Overall, 13% of the Christian students say that the chapel has become an important place for them in the college.

Table 10 examines the same six items from the perspective of Christian practice. Here the contrasts between the two groups become even more pronounced. The chapel and the chaplaincy are of considerable importance to the churchgoing students. The fact that there are daily services in the chapel is important to 67% of the churchgoing students, the fact that there is a chapel in the college is important to 59%, and the fact that there is a chaplain in the college is important to

Table 10   Chapel and chaplaincy on the Christian campus: by Christian practice

	No %	Yes %	X^2	P<
It is important to me that there is a chapel in the college	6	59	56.0	.001
It is important to me that there is a chaplain in the college	10	53	38.8	.001
I think it is important that there are daily services in the chapel	46	67	8.6	.01
I find the chapel a welcoming place	31	69	26.3	.001
The chapel has become an important place for me in the college	0	24	22.6	.001
I feel comfortable within the chapel environment	21	49	16.4	.001

53% of them. For one in four of the churchgoing students, the chapel has become an important place in the college within the first week of being on the campus (24%).

Conclusion

Careful listening to the views of students, given voice through the systematic survey of two cohorts of undergraduates admitted to St John's, draws attention to some of the key characteristics of the Christian campus as it already exists in England and Wales, provides access to the ordinary theological insights of those attracted to such a campus, and focuses issues which require further theological reflection in shaping the Christian university for the future.

The first characteristic of the Christian campus is that it currently embraces at least three easily identified sub-groups of students: those who claim no religious affiliation, those who may be styled as Christians by self-identified affiliation but not by practice, and those who may be styled as practising or churchgoing Christians. There is not one student voice on the campus, but at least three audible voices. The fourth voice, the voice of those self-identified as affiliated with non-Christian religious traditions, was insufficiently represented to be audible through the present survey. In other words, the current reality of the Christian campus is one which embraces and contains diversity. To reflect this reality, the theology of the Christian campus needs to grapple with inclusivity and divergence, and with mission as well as with ministry.

The second characteristic of the Christian campus is that the non-affiliated students show remarkably little interest in the Christian *foundation* of the institution which they attend. Only 1% of the non-affiliated students chose to come to St John's because it is a church college. Nonetheless, large numbers of the non-affiliated students remain positively disposed toward the Christian character of the campus. Thus, 66% came knowing full well that they were coming to a Christian campus. Although none of them (0%) made a point of seeking out the chapel, as many as 43% consider that it is important that there are daily services in the chapel. In other words, the current reality of the Christian campus is one which embraces goodwill toward the Christian presence, even among those who feel that religion is irrelevant to their own way of life. To reflect this reality the theology of the Christian campus needs to grapple with the representative significance of the church, even within a secularised environment and among those who set themselves at a distance from the church.

The third characteristic of the Christian campus is that it provides a context in which those who claim Christian affiliation unsupported by Christian practice are able to express and to assert their sense of belonging to the Christian church. This sense of belonging enhances their expectations of the Christian campus, particularly in terms of the manifestations of religious presence through chapel and chaplaincy. In other words, the current reality of the Christian campus is one which speaks to those standing more at the margins of church life through the traditional signs of the holy: the buildings, the places, and the people set aside to witness to the enduring presence of God. To reflect this reality, the theology of the Christian campus needs to grapple with the roles of chapel, chaplaincy and liturgy within a context in which the boundaries between church and wider community can remain porous.

The fourth characteristic of the Christian campus is that the churchgoing, active, practising Christian students may quickly sense disappointment that the expectations of being part of a vibrant gathered church are not readily met. Thus, significant minorities of the practising Christians felt St John's has too few people going to chapel (24%), too few Christian students (16%), too few Christian lecturers (10%). In other words, the current reality of the Christian campus is one which reflects the minority status of the church within wider society. To reflect this reality the theology of the Christian campus needs to grapple with the problem of nurturing the ideality of a small community of practising believers while avoiding the pitfalls of both exclusivity and disappointment.

The fifth characteristic of the Christian campus is that it displays its religious distinctiveness through creating a specially caring and supportive environment. Here are the hallmarks of practical Christianity which have spoken almost as clearly to the non-affiliated students as to those who self-identify as Christians. Thus, 42% of the non-affiliates and 49% of the Christians reported that they were impressed by the level of help given to them during the first week. In other words, the current reality of the Christian campus is one which tries to put Christian values into practice. To reflect this reality the theology of the Christian campus needs to grapple with the problems of enabling Christian values to penetrate and to inform all levels of institutional life and practice.

Careful listening to the views of the students has begun to open up a large theological agenda for the Christian campus. The caveat must remain, however, that the usefulness of the data generated by the present study is clearly limited by its location in time and space. Research of this nature in ordinary and empirical theology requires proper replication and further extension. Where better could such research be pioneered in order to inform the church of the future than within the Christian university?

References

Astley, J. (2002) *Ordinary Theology: Looking, Listening and Learning in Theology*, Aldershot, Ashgate.

Bannon, E. (1999) *Genial and Authoritative*, Oxford, Lasallia.

Bone, J. (2003) *Our Calling to Fulfil: Westminster College and the Changing Face of Teacher Education*, Bristol, Tockington Press.

Davie, G. (1994) *Religion in Britain since 1945: Believing without Belonging*, Oxford, Blackwell.

De Graaf, N. D. and A. Need (2000) 'Losing Faith: Is Britain Alone?', in R. Jowell, J. Curtice, A. Park, K. Thomson, L. Jarvis, C. Bromley and N. Stratford (eds), *British Social Attitudes: The Seventeenth Report*, London, Sage, pp. 119–136.

Eaton, M., Longmore, J. and A. Naylor (eds) (2000) *Commitment to Diversity: Catholics and Education in a Changing World*, London, Cassell.

Elford, R. J. (2003) *The Foundation of Hope: Turning Dreams into Reality*, Liverpool, Liverpool University Press.

Fane, R. S. (1999) 'Is Self-assigned Religious Affiliation Socially Significant?', in L. J. Francis (ed.), *Sociology, Theology and the Curriculum*, London, Cassell, pp. 113–124.

Francis, L. J. (2001) *The Values Debate: A Voice from the Pupils*, London, Woburn Press.

Francis, L. J. (2002) 'Personality Theory and Empirical Theology', *Journal of Empirical Theology*, 15, pp. 37–53.

Francis, L. J. (2003) 'Religion and Social Capital: The Flaw in the 2001 Census in England and Wales', in P. Avis (ed.), *Public Faith: The State of Religious Belief and Practice in Britain*, London, SPCK, pp. 45–64.

Francis, L. J. and W. K. Kay (1995) *Teenage Religion and Values*, Leominster, Gracewing.

Francis, L. J. and M. Robbins (2004) 'Belonging Without Believing: A Study in the Social Significance of Anglican Identity and Implicit Religion among 13-15 year old Males', *Implicit Religion* (in press).

Francis, L. J., Robbins, M. and M. Williams-Potter (1999) 'Student Expectations of a Church College', in L. J. Francis (ed.), *Sociology, Theology and the Curriculum*, London, Cassell, pp. 145–154.

Gay, J., Kay, B. and G. Perry (1985) *The Future of the Anglican Colleges: The First Year Students*, Abingdon, Culham Educational Foundation.

Gay, J., Kay, B., Perry, G. and D. Lazenby (1985) *The Future of the Anglican Colleges: The Third Year and PGCE Students*, Abingdon, Culham Educational Foundation.

Gay, J., Kay, B., Perry, G. and D. Lazenby (1986) *The Future of the Anglican Colleges: Final Report of the Church Colleges Research Project*, Abingdon, Culham Educational Foundation.

Gedge, P. S. and L. M. R. Louden (1993) *S. Martin's College Lancaster 1964–89*, Lancaster, Centre for North-West Regional Studies, University of Lancaster.

Gill, R. (1999) *Churchgoing and Christian Ethics*, Cambridge, Cambridge University Press.

Grigg, R. (1998) *History of Trinity College Carmarthen: 1848–1998*, Cardiff, University of Wales Press.

Lazenby, D., Gay, J. and B. Kay (1987) *Trinity College Carmarthen: A Profile 1985–86*, Abingdon, Culham Educational Foundation.

McGregor, G. P. (1981) *Bishop Otter College: And Policy for Teacher Education 1839–1980*, London, Pembridge Press.

McGregor, G. P. (1991) *A Church College for the 21st Century? 150 years of Ripon and York St John*, York, University College of Ripon and York St John.

More, C. (1992) *The Training of Teachers 1847–1947: A History of the Church Colleges at Cheltenham*, London, Hambledon Press.

Naylor, L. and G. Howat (1982) *Culham College History*, Abingdon, Culham Educational Foundation.

Norman, E. (1996) 'Coping with a Crisis of Identity', *Church Times*, 14 June, p. 16.

Price, D. T. W. (1977) *A History of Saint David's University College Lampeter: Volume One to 1898*, Cardiff, University of Wales Press.

Price, D. T. W. (1990) *A History of Saint David's University College Lampeter: Volume Two 1898–1971*, Cardiff, University of Wales Press.

Rose, M. (1981) *A History of King Alfred's College, Winchester, 1840–1980*, London, Phillimore.

van der Ven, J. A. (1993) *Practical Theology: An Empirical Approach*, Kampen, Kok Pharos.

van der Ven, J. A. (1998) *Education for Reflective Ministry*, Louvain, Peeters.

Part Two: A Christian Curriculum?

Chapter Ten

The Curriculum of a Christian University

Adrian Thatcher

Curriculum and identity

Once upon a time, there was *'Engaging the Curriculum – A Theological Programme'* [EC]. In 1993 the Council of Church and Associated Colleges [of Higher Education] in England and Wales initiated and sponsored a programme, the aim of which was 'to make available material which aims at fostering Christian insights into most of the Colleges' curricula' (1994). The programme arose out of the, then current, mission statement of the Council (1988), which said the purpose of its member colleges and institutes was 'to provide high quality education in a context in which the practice and study of the Christian Faith are taken seriously'. All the colleges, it solemnly affirmed,

> seek to offer to their members and to their local communities, the chance to encounter Christian insights and experience in the moral, ethical, social, political, religious, philosophical and cultural issues which arise within Higher Education programmes, and to consider these, freely, alongside a variety of other insights.

The programme produced a series of conferences, a regular bulletin, and several books (Gearon, 1999; Francis, 1999; Poole, 1998; Thatcher, 1999). The importance of *EC* for the present volume is the clarity it brought to the problem of the identity of church-related and church-derived higher education institutions [HEIs] in a secular higher education [HE] system. The director of the programme (with an alliterative flourish) explained that identity claims ('Christian distinctiveness') for CCs were advanced in the relevant literature for some or all of the following features of college life:

(i)   its *care for students*;
(ii) its *community ethos* or atmosphere;
(iii) its *chaplaincy* and provision for worship;
(iv) the *Christian context* within which all educational activities take place;
(v)   the *conduct* of its affairs, or style of management; and
(vi) the *curriculum* or course content of its teaching programmes.

He went on to explain that secular HEIs could be expected to be at least as successful as Christian ones with regard to (i), (ii), (iii) and (v). The 'Christian context' was a 'nebulous' and potentially misleading term, since it could 'foster a dualism between education on the one hand, and the context in which it takes place on the other, resulting in the effective relegation of Christian thought and practice to the margins of College life where it is unnoticed and untroublesome' (Thatcher, 1995, p. 111). Only (vi), the curriculum, provided a distinctive content for CCs, that would not also be provided by the majority of HEIs. The distinction between a necessary and a sufficient condition was applied to the identity problem. While CCs shared (i), (ii), (iii) and (v) with their secular counterparts as a sufficient condition for what they all do, only (vi) was a necessary condition for what the CCs do alone.

This analysis of a decade ago remains sound. But *EC* foundered. Advocates of a contemporary Christian university would do well to ponder the reasons why. Many of the staff of the Church Colleges were suspicious of *EC*. Perhaps they had good reason to be, for *EC* set out to challenge the boundaries of what counts as worthy of inclusion in the curriculum of a Christian HEI. While few were hostile, most were indifferent. Theology departments had largely metamorphosed into departments of religious studies. Theologians in the Colleges (with notable exceptions) were unfamiliar with theology of education as a branch of applied or practical theology, so theological analyses of education, of higher education, and of the possible contribution of theology of education to the curriculum of CCs, were rarely undertaken. Principals and Directors were divided by it. Some gave it overt support in their institutions; others ignored it and some were hostile. There was genuine worry (however absurd) that the programme would indoctrinate students. It was whispered that overt identification with curriculum content that derived from, or nourished people in, faith would have a negative impact on recruitment.

EC showed that the CCs were already post-religious, indeed deeply secular, and even fearful of acknowledging their religious roots. The 'Christian context', which still appears in CC mission statements, is little more than a tacit nod, a wink of deference towards a former religious heritage for the benefit of certain members of governing bodies and bishops. The numbers of remaining staff who affirm the Christian ethos of Christian HEIs must by now be very small. In a word, deep secularisation (Bruce, 2002) is pervasive (despite fashionable challenges to secularisation theory) in the CCs, and one of its manifestations is the virtual disappearance of a theological understanding of the purpose of the Church Colleges themselves, even among the Council of Principals. 'Ethos committees' remain in a few CCs, but these can only be 'advisory'. Important though they are, they provide ironic evidence of the power of secularisation in the CCs themselves: i.e., that distinctiveness is a matter of ethos alone. It is not easy to see how the remorseless secularising trend can be countered or reversed. If the term 'Christian university' implies a Christian curriculum, the CCs will not be able to oblige.

Curriculum and critical distance

The long-running Lilly Seminar on Religion and Higher Education (1996–1999) in the United States recently published its findings. The Seminar consisted mainly of participants from universities and colleges that were founded by churches and whose current connections with their founding bodies have become tenuous or non-existent. None of them responds adequately to the challenge thrown down to them by a sceptical participant, David Hollinger, who poses the bruising question 'whether these imperfect academic communities can be improved by diminishing the critical distance from Christian cultural hegemony that they have achieved only after a long struggle' (Hollinger, 2002, p. 40). This question compounds the difficulties described in the previous section.

Many inimical assumptions are carefully crafted into Hollinger's challenge to Christian HEIs in the United States – that they are needlessly coercive; that scholars have found them oppressive places in which to work; that criticism can be safely practised only outside Christian communities; that a state of intellectual warfare has existed between the church and the academy; and that the church has lost the war, producing a gain for everyone else, including thoughtful Christians. Here are three of Hollinger's arguments (in summary form) which he thinks are bound to secure a negative answer to his challenge.

First, Christians, faced with the mounting implausibility of many of the claims they wish to advance as knowledge, now want to change the intellectual rules governing what counts as plausibility in order to re-admit these false or epistemically unwarranted claims to the cur-riculum. They are likely to draw on some version of pluralism in order to obtain their objectives. Second, Christians, faced with the loss of all influence over the curriculum that they once controlled, seek instead to secure more modest objectives, like offering mere 'insights' into aspects of the post-religious curriculum, or claiming that many cultural and moral riches of course derive directly from the weakened matrix that was once Christianity. And, third, post-Christian campuses are said to be far more fruitful places of learning than faith-based ones because they have become places where students of all faiths and none can learn together and from each other.

Many of the charges made against the custodians of the remnants of Christian scholarship can be readily enough conceded. From the per-spective of the twenty-first century, earlier Christian places of learning doubtless seem over-exclusive, intolerant of dissent, and so on. Everyone knows that Christian fundamentalists oppose Darwin, biblical criticism, abortion on demand, and much else; but these zealots themselves make the case for a Christian university where the truth-claims of Christianity can be safely advanced, critically assessed and brought into constructive dialogue with science, with the humanities, and with alternative religious and non-religious traditions. The existence of superficial, anti-intellectual and frankly intolerant versions of Christianity actually demonstrates the need for places of academic excellence where the intellectual heritage of Christian faith can be shared in a milieu of constructive intellectual inquiry.

Again, while Christians are in effect accused of trying to extend the bounds of what counts as sense in order to revalidate their own intellectual nonsense, Christians and other people of faith might justifiably complain that the plausibility structures of the secular academy are themselves too narrowly and uniformly drawn. The secular academy is no de-traditionalised institution affording untainted and impartial views of everything it sees. It belongs to a tradition, that of Enlightenment humanism (which is itself deeply influenced by Christianity). Despite its impressive achievements this tradition is itself not beyond criticism. What determination is there in the secular academy to find achievable ways of ending global poverty? Or to create or strengthen global peace-making institutions so as to make wars less likely? There is, of course, a positive answer to be made to these questions. Departments of economics, politics, peace studies, and so on, grapple with these and other subjects. Doubtless, some of their teachers and researchers are influenced by their Christian faith. But Christians themselves, conditioned as they are by controlling beliefs in, say, the reign of God, the reconciliation of all things to God through Christ, or the non-negotiable imperatives of love of neighbour and of enemy, have additional reasons for inquiring into these matters.

How dependent are secular universities on finance from, for example, tobacco and weapons companies for their supposedly dis-interested research? What critiques of the political institutions and economic systems that support them are, in fact, allowed? Hollinger is more concerned with narrower philosophical questions about what can count as rational, justified belief. These narrow questions have been soundly handled by Christian philosophers of religion for at least half a century, and the discussion about what counts as reason and faith, as understanding and belief, and about the relation between them constitutes a sprawling and growing literature. But there are wider issues about what exists to be known that cannot simply be left to enlightened humanists. Epistemic frameworks (unlike the Ten Commandments) are not fixed, whatever the secular fundamentalists may say. Is there not a growing awareness that positivist, rationalist and now vocationalist frameworks are all importantly reductive?

The charge that Christians now appear uncharacteristically modest in their curricular aims may be true, but if it is true it is too hollow a conclusion to matter. What's wrong about offering insights? Or being intellectually humble? Christians are likely to find much that is congenial in the learning of the secular academy, because they believe that, in the will of God, the world is a creation; that intelligibility is written into it and into our minds as part of it; that inquiry is a proper use of mind; and that wherever there is truth there is God who is Truth (and, long after the demise of poststructuralism, will remain the Truth). This is no matter of colonising or re-colonising for Christ the liberated, secular curriculum. It is to appeal to a worldview rooted in ancient conviction yet capable of revision and re-affirmation in every age. One modest aim of a Christian curriculum might be to point out that much that we take for granted in a post-Christian state derives from, or was influenced by, Christians and churches. But to desire so to teach these things is not to commit any version of the genetic fallacy, as Hollinger charges. There may be other reasons for teaching these things, for example as straight social or moral history, or in order to indicate the peculiar origins of the post-religious world that increasing numbers of students inhabit.

No more plausible is the assumption of the mono-cultural and mono-religious character of the Christian campus. The most multi-cultural campus I have visited in the UK belonged to the Seventh Day Adventist Church. That aside, the argument commits another genetic fallacy, that of supposing that because Christian campuses were once exclusive places, they always will be. Theologians constantly expose these kinds of arguments. Because God was once thought of as an all-powerful absentee landlord, God must always be thought of this way. Because marriage once oppressed women, it must always necessarily oppress them. Because some versions of the doctrine of the atonement are immoral, no version of that doctrine is serviceable. And so on. All such arguments ignore constructive change and discount the promptings of God's Spirit. Why should not a Christian campus positively zing with dialogue, creative dissent, openness to the Other, and to teaching, learning and researching with all people of faith and those of none? Such intellectual engagement is in any case essential to the development of the theological tradition.

Hollinger's arguments, however, are likely to prevail. This is not because they possess persuasive power, but because intellectuals will affirm them anyway. They will affirm them because epistemological frameworks which are indifferent or hostile to religious truth-claims are installed in the academies of a post-religious age. This is of course, unsurprising. The critique of reductive epistemology is likely to be an important task for a Christian university to undertake, but as there is unlikely to be any such institution that task will fall to individual Christian theologians, whoever employs them. Since Christendom is over (Guroian, 1994), Christians cannot expect customary deference when assuming Christian epistemologies. They can expect instead some ridicule, and this will assist their recovery of their prophetic tradition.

The curriculum and pluralism

One of the arguments offered for Christian places of learning draws on the plural character of the societies they serve. I support this argument. Alan Wolfe (in Sterk 2002, p. 34) has offered a 'third way' for Christian universities and colleges in the United States to affirm their distinctiveness. The first way, exemplified by Pope John Paul's *Ex Corde Ecclesiae*, is the way of rejection of modernity (Wolfe, p. 31). The second way, that of 'parallelism', is 'the existence of more than one kind of academic culture within an institution, but structured in such a way that these various subcultures have little in common with each other but instead operate as if they were on parallel tracks' (Wolfe, p. 32). Wolfe calls the third way 'option opportunism'. 'Secular institutions', he says, 'are committed in theory to pluralism but rarely practice it. ... Religious institutions, by contrast, are not pluralistic in themselves but have been forced by circumstances to have a potential for pluralism in practice. By opportunism I mean an effort to try to fill that potential' (Wolfe, p. 34).

This argument for pluralism derives from the United States, but it also has a unique resonance in Britain. In the Thatcher years (1979–1990) HEIs were challenged as never before to rush to 'mission statements'. Many of these were bland. The Department for Education said it welcomed a 'diversity of mission' among HEIs. One of the reasons for this was doubtless ideologically loaded. Students (and their parents) were to be offered 'more choice'. Choice was to be extended. The extension was not simply between academic and vocational, or traditional and modern, or conventional and modular. There would be genuinely diverse institutions in the HE system and students as consumers were to be given sufficient 'product information' (much of it in the form of league tables) to make informed selections. In the early

90s there was some evidence that the CCs would market themselves as 'Christian institutions', adding a genuinely religious dimension for discerning student purchasers in the HE 'market' to consider.

The argument from pluralism may have stronger persuasive force in Britain than in the USA, because Britain is officially a Christian country. Her citizens are the loyal subjects of Her Majesty the Queen who is the Defender of the Faith, and who appoints (through her Prime Minister) the Head of the Church of England and of the Anglican communion worldwide. However fashionable it may be to ridicule these arcane and archaic constitutional arrangements, they do not underwrite the assumption of modernity that the modern state must be (at best) neutral with regard to religion, and must be seen not to favour the religious tradition that has helped to shape it. In any case this modern position is rightly regarded with suspicion by people of faith in other religions, especially Islam. The 2001 Census, the first to ask questions about religion, revealed that more than 42 million people – 71.7 per cent of the population of the UK – considered themselves 'Christian' (*Church Times*, February 21, 2003). For England and Wales, the figure was 37.3 million. Arguments will of course rage about how these figures are to be interpreted. A Christian university would assist not merely in providing diversity of mission in a secular HE sector. It might well prove popular among the majority of 'residual Christians' who, while they do not often show up at churches, still identify as 'Christian'.

The arguments advanced a decade ago within the Church Colleges, regarding the achievement of their distinctiveness in the national HE sector through their curricula, apply equally to a Christian university. But the mere act of proposing such an institution is likely to lead to such controversy, and generate such suspicion, that it will take an act of God to bring it about.

The Christian curriculum as the development of tradition

A Christian university with a Christian curriculum requires funding. Its curriculum will provide what the fundholders require, and they will require Christian purposes to be achieved. What would count as a

Christian purpose? Let us start with beliefs, and then move from these to purposes.

I propose that the identity of Christianity is expressed in part by the creeds, or rather by the beliefs and practices that come to expression in them. The Christian faith assumes God. God is Creator, and the universe and everything in it depends on God for its origination and being. God the creator or father of all is revealed decisively in Jesus Christ, the human face of God. God is revealed elsewhere. The 'Word made flesh' (Jn. 1:14) is also the Word without whom 'no created thing came to be' (Jn. 1:3), and who is already life and light for all humankind (Jn. 1:4). God is Father, Son and Spirit, whose being is a loving communion of persons. By his life, death and resurrection, Jesus Christ has reconciled the world to Godself (2 Cor. 5:18). Estrangement from God (to use Tillich's synonym for sin: Tillich, 1957, p. 51) is manifest everywhere in human selfishness, greed and failure to live in love. But salvation from sin is available partially, now, and is yet to be realised in the final purposes of God. God the Spirit is the inspirer of all that is good in human culture, science, religion and society. The divine love, out of which the universe flows, seeks union with all that has been made.

The last paragraph has drawn some familiar contours onto the standard map of Christian belief. Epistemologically this is 'moderate realism'. But a possible curriculum is easily derivable from these creedal commitments. That the world is understood as a creation *at all* signifies and summons a theology of the environment, which is informed by the environmental sciences, which repents of its former indifference to pollution and plunder, and is able, along with Teilhard de Chardin to praise matter:

> Without you, without your onslaughts, without your uprootings of us, we should remain all our lives inert, stagnant, puerile, ignorant both of ourselves and of God. You who batter us and then dress our wounds, you who resist us and yield to us, you who wreck and build, you who shackle and liberate, the sap of our souls, the hand of God, the flesh of Christ: it is you, matter, that I bless. (de Chardin, 1970, p. 64)

The environmental programme that might be initiated by a Christian university, in partnership with science and people of all faiths, would require a huge academic commitment over several decades. But the environmental agenda that derives from a theology and spirituality of creation is no less daunting than the social, sexual, ethical and political agendas already set by the world that the church exists to serve. Much theological effort is required merely by way of response to the vast, life-changing discoveries of the natural and social sciences and the social practices that follow in their wake. But reflective faith can sometimes manage considerably more than a struggle to catch up with new knowledge. It offers insights, intuitions of wholeness and depth, and over-arching sources of meaning that make ultimate sense of things.

I hope readers will allow me to draw on a personal example of engaged theological work of the type a Christian university might exist to produce. Within the field of Christian ethics I have recently become involved in the study of cohabitation (Thatcher, 2002). Detailed reading of twenty-five years of social and demographic research into the phenomenon of cohabitation was necessary to understand what I wanted to talk about. If presumption was to be avoided, the suspension of judgement and much prior listening was necessary before the easier part, that of drawing and meditating on Bible and tradition, took place. But the drawing on familiar sources was transformed by the prior grounding of theological work in the social facts that, collectively, produce the phenomenon that was once too easily dismissed as 'living in sin'. This sort of theology might be called the theology of correlation (Tillich, 1953, p. 67), or public (Tracy, 1981, p. 3) or practical (Browning, 2003, p. 3) theology. What matters is that the faith 'once and for all delivered to the saints' (Jude 3) conveys fresh life-enhancing wisdom to a culture that has given up on hearing good news from churches. This study, undertaken in the usual way (by a solitary researcher doing small chunks of writing in 'spare' time), might be replicated 1,000 times as Christian scholarship engages with more of the world's social and political problems from the perspective of the divine revelation given in Christ and spread about through the Spirit. In a Christian university such scholarship might be expected, and proper collaborative provision for it secured, as Christians think, listen, learn, pray, converse and finally propose contributions to some of the contemporary debates about, for example, the practice of non-violence, the practice of neighbour-love (love of the different and daunting 'other'), the practice of cloning, or the escalation of individualism into narcissism and greed. Concerted, focused, systematic efforts in these and countless similar areas might provide the core business of a Christian research university.

Whatever a Christian university does it would fail if it did not approach its own identity from the perspective of the plural universe of faiths. There is a wealth of available material about the relation between Christianity and the world religions (D'Costa, 2000); but much of it does not extend beyond theological theory, and specifically to move beyond the paradigms of exclusivism, inclusivism and pluralism which dominated Christian discussion of these matters in the 80s and 90s. Many practical, small-scale, local studies are needed, from all over the world, which document the wisdom of interreligious conversation and cooperation involving Christians and their discovery of God the Spirit in the Other of world faiths. The practice of neighbour-love is a *sine qua non* of Christian faith. How might Christian ethics look if neighbour-love were radically prioritised? How might Christian eschatology look, transposed into a vision of social and economic justice that was theoretically feasible? What futures would be designed as possible models of the divine will? How might they impact upon our real, globalised future, and offered as a sensible counter-alternative, in true prophetic charity and clarity? Or is social criticism to be left to a few philosophers and secular theorists?

Stakeholders in a Christian university may require it to fulfil specific Christian purposes. The education and training of clergy, and of teachers for service in church schools, are two obvious examples. Research into the needs of church schools has scarcely begun. Departments and faculties of education in CCs have yet to be convinced that church schools deserve any kind of special provision or nurture. The report of the Archbishops' Council, *The Way Ahead: Church of England Schools in the New Millennium*, cited 'two major issues' for the Anglican CCs. The first and 'great challenge' to them is 'to sustain and develop their Christian distinctiveness', and the second is 'to continue in being for the long-term as Christian institutions' (2001, p. 68). In other words, they have made no headway on distinctiveness since the demise of *EC* (and *The Way Ahead* offers no further proposals). Indeed, the reasons given above for the abandonment of *EC* apply *a fortiori* to the non-specific exhortation to remain 'distinctive'. And the pressure of increasing vulnerability (two more have disappeared since the mid-nineties) is thought only to require prudent survival strategies to be developed. While several of the CCs have become universities,[1] these, like the colleges themselves, are funded largely by the state, and must therefore provide courses that the government of the day is willing to fund. Meanwhile the Church of England maintains separate institutions for the education of clergy.

Hollinger and many like him see faith-based education as pre-critical, closed to the icy blasts of modern scepticism. But a Christian theology of education has no alternative but to be self-critical, not because it is compelled to import Cartesian methods of inquiry into itself or to assume radical empiricism as the fount of all earthly wisdom, but because its understanding of Christ's death is a 'No' to the adequacy or self-sufficiency of any human endeavour before God. The church and, of course, the traditions of theology which the church has 'authorised' have every reason to be self-critical, for they have also authorised many evils, including racism, sexism and patriarchalism. At one level this is to be expected. The history of science is in part a history of abandoned hypotheses, as more adequate ones have replaced them. A similar judgement might be made about changes in theology. The problem, of course, is that theology is much slower to discard the temporal assumptions and accretions of previous generations, and sometimes invests them with divine status. Christians of all people might be the most self-critical because they possess good reasons for supposing that knowledge, like *praxis*, needs constant correction in the light of the revelation of God.

A contemporary theory of doctrinal development might be expected to posit engagement with secular culture as one of its necessary conditions. As Monti has argued, 'The cosmological and cultural environments of the Church are neither accidental nor only "external", but foundational for what is commonly termed [Christian] "self-identification"' (Monti, 1995, p. 5). There is no space here for an account of the development of doctrine (in any case Monti provides one). The reason why this section of the chapter is entitled 'The Christian curriculum as the development of tradition' is because of the obvious congruence between a distinctive Christian curriculum and the conditions needed for the church to become involved with the intellectual, social, moral and cultural frameworks of the world it serves. The best theology is done by engagement with the 'external world' and the resources of faith, simultaneously. The best Christian university will be one whose Christian identity is forged not merely by its anchorage in traditions of faith and practice, but by its determination that these should grow. Engagement with the intellectual environment within which the church is placed is necessary for Christian scholarship to flourish and for Christian doctrine to develop. This is the business of the Christian university.

What a pity that it is not going to happen (at least in the UK)! How would it be funded? Could 'stakeholders' agree on a 'vision statement'? There are insuperable difficulties preventing the CCs from transforming themselves into institutions of the kind suggested here. The idea of a Christian university is probably daft. But occasionally God uses foolishness to confound the wise. Indeed, that is another way of putting the case for the Christian university: that 'God has made the wisdom of this world look foolish' (1 Cor. 1:20).

References

Archbishops' Council (2001) *The Way Ahead: Church of England Schools in the New Millennium*, London, Church House Publishing.

Browning, D. S. (2003) *Marriage and Modernization: How Globalization Threatens Marriage and What to Do about It*, Grand Rapids, MI and Cambridge, Eerdmans.

Bruce, S. (2002) *God is Dead: Secularization in the West*, Oxford and Malden, MA, Blackwell.

Council of Church and Associated Colleges (1988) *Mission Statement*.

Council of Church and Associated Colleges (1994) *Engaging the Curriculum Bulletin*, 1.

D'Costa, G. (2000) *The Meeting of Religions and the Trinity*, New York and Edinburgh, Orbis Books and T & T Clark.

de Chardin, P. Teilhard (1970) *Hymn of the Universe*, London, Collins.

Francis, L. J. (ed.) (1999) *Sociology, Theology and the Curriculum*, London and New York, Cassell.

Gearon, L. (ed.) (1999) *English Literature, Theology and the Curriculum*, London and New York, Cassell.

Guroian, V. (1994) *Ethics After Christendom: Toward an Ecclesial Christian Ethic*, Grand Rapids, MI, Eerdmans.

Hollinger, D. A. (2002) 'Enough Already: Universities Do Not Need More Christianity', in Sterk, pp. 40–49.

Monti, J. (1995) *Arguing About Sex: The Rhetoric of Christian Sexual Morality*, New York, State University of New York Press.

Poole, M. (1998). *Teaching about Science and Religion: Opportunities within Science in the National Curriculum*, Abingdon, Culham College Institute.

Sterk, A. (ed.), *Religion, Scholarship, and Higher Education: Perspectives, Models, and Future Prospects*, Notre Dame, IN, University of Notre Dame Press.

Thatcher, A. (1995) 'Engaging the Curriculum – A Theological Programme', *Journal of Further and Higher Education*, 19, 3, pp. 109–118.

Thatcher, A. (2002) *Living Together and Christian Ethics,* Cambridge, Cambridge University Press.

Thatcher, A. (ed.) (1999) *Spirituality and the Curriculum,* London and New York, Cassell.

Tillich, P. (1953) *Systematic Theology,* Vol. 1, London, Nisbet.

Tillich, P. (1957) *Systematic Theology,* Vol. 2, London, Nisbet.

Tracy, D. (1981) *The Analogical Imagination: Christian Theology and the Culture of Pluralism,* London, SCM.

Wolfe, A. (2002) 'The Potential for Pluralism: Religious Responses to the Triumph of Theory and Method in American Culture', in Sterk, pp. 22–39.

Chapter Eleven

On Theology's Babylonian Captivity within the Secular University

Gavin D'Costa

Introduction

In this essay I want to advance three related arguments. First, theology as it is generally currently practised in mainstream English universities is not worthy of its name. Most theology is in fact a brand of religious studies, a historical critical approach to texts, with varying uses of sociology, literary theory, and so on. It is, to use John Webster's phrase, not a 'theological theology'.[1] Second, the discipline that has grown in methodological dominance within the university is religious studies. Here I shall argue two things. Religious studies, at least in one of its English historical manifestations, is a pseudo-discipline and requires unmasking (by theology). Then I shall suggest that what we require is a theological form of religious studies, that is a Christian theological reading of the presence of non-Christian religions. These two arguments arise from my own location in an English university as a teacher of theology. But cumulatively they require a rethinking of the very context of the university, not just in terms of the practice of one of its disciplines – theology and religious studies – but rather in terms of all of the academic disciplines. This paper is a call for a Christian university, and a specific type of Christian university if one takes tradition-specific enquiry seriously: a Roman Catholic university. This is not meant in any unecumenical spirit, but I will be arguing that authority and tradition require that we do our thinking on these matters from tradition-specific stances. Only when this has been done to a fairly high level is there any chance of successful ecumenical ventures. Hence, this might be read as an ecumenical proposal for a Christian university, but first coming at the matter from the Christian tradition within which I find myself: Roman Catholicism.

On (not) doing theology in the university

Let me briefly recount two experiences. Story one: a university lecturer begins his lectures in patristics with a prayer. Students complain and he discontinues this practice. Where do your sympathies lie when you hear this story? Tale two takes place in an arts faculty meeting when a change of syllabus is being discussed in the programme of the theology department. After the vote on the matter, thunder and lightning occur. Everyone laughs and the Dean proclaims that the decision has not received appropriate sanction! Those in the named department are not amused. What is your reaction to these academics – both the chucklers and the indignant?

The history of institutional theology in England, as with Western Europe, is tied to the patronage of the church. I will sketch only the bare contours in what follows.[2] For most of Western European history the study of theology remained an ecclesiastical practice. It developed within church schools, in monasteries and convents, which initially meant that both men and women were able to contribute to theology, even though the latter faced all sorts of restrictions.[3] The situation began to change dramatically in the thirteenth century with the ecclesial foundation of the University of Paris and then, subsequently, of a number of major universities throughout Europe. Two of the problematic consequences of the emergence of the university was the exclusion of women from the newly established academy and the continued and inevitable male clerical monopoly over the Christian tradition's intellectual development. Nevertheless, at the beginnings of the European university *both* those who taught and those who learnt in the university believed their task was in service to God, church, and society. They were not bound by academic accreditation by secular authorities. In thirteenth-century Paris, intellectual theology was integrally a socio-political-religious affair. To speak of the sacred and secular in this context would obviously be anachronistic.[4] Despite this clerical monopoly, some argue that the slow secularisation of theology was inaugurated in the thirteenth, rather than in the seventeenth or eighteenth centuries, culminating in the decisive changes that took place within the university curriculum in the nineteenth century when theology was finally dislodged from its pivotal role as the 'queen of the sciences'.

Hans Frei locates this 'great reversal' which shifted theology out of its ecclesial context in the destiny of the University of Berlin at the beginning of the nineteenth century. At this historical juncture the place of theology in the Enlightenment university was deeply problematic. Fichte, like Kant, could only tolerate theology as the practical working out of the truths available via universal reason in a transcendental (Kant), then idealist (Fichte), and later a positivist (Harnack, Strauss) mode. The Enlightenment *Wissenchaft* dictated to theology the preconditions and limits of its enquiry and also regulated its agenda. Both Kant and Fichte reserved pride of place for philosophy, not theology. Frei argues that Schleiermacher's alternative theological proposals won the day over Fichte, although I would question whether this victory signalled any institutional difference in the long run from that envisaged by Fichte. Frei seems to tacitly acknowledge this.[5] The question of the subservience of theology to secular disciplines would not be resolved, although the increasing secularity of the university institutionally favoured one party over the other in the subsequent debate. Witness the struggle between Karl Barth and Adolf von Harnack, and in our own times, Stanley Hauerwas against the liberal university.

The history of the secularisation of the study of theology is of course much disputed. While Frei locates Schleiermacher's Berlin as emblematic of the institutional changes in both the method and content of theology that were already in process starting with the eighteenth-century English deists, others date the 'great reversal' much earlier. Prudence Allen, for instance, traces the crisis right back to Aristotle's influence on Western thinking and his creation of fragmented disciplinary boundaries which were then institutionally embodied in the establishment of the thirteenth-century university. The division between arts, theology, medicine and law, and their self-understandings regarding appropriate methods in relation to their different objects of study, ensured a fragmentation of methodology that resulted in attention to the materiality of human persons primarily within the faculties of medicine and law. Allen argues that the dis-embodied Enlightenment *logos* was already born in these important subject divisions.[6] Francis Martin also suggests that the University of Paris helped to accelerate the process whereby theology became divorced from its proper ecclesial context due to the pervasive influence of nominalism within the university, theology being prised apart from its contemplative monastic context, and the outlawing of any faculty other than theology discussing God, an edict introduced at the end of the thirteenth century.[7]

Relatedly, Nicholas Lash reads Michael Buckley as arguing that the 'great reversal' is located in the thirteenth century, but specifically in the design of Thomas Aquinas' *Summa Theologiae*, which was to become so influential in the development of Western theology. Lash says that Buckley (and others) argue that because Aquinas discusses those things that pertain to the distinction of persons in God *after* discussing what can and cannot be said concerning 'divina essentia', this ordering prioritises philosophy and general categories over revelation and the particularity of the Christ event. Aquinas' ordering presupposes that one can speak of God, persons, creation, providence and final ends, as indeed Aquinas does, prior to and without specific reference to Christ, the Spirit and the Father.[8]

While Buckley is (rightly) unhappy about Lash's interpretation of Buckley and Aquinas, Lash nevertheless does mount a successful and persuasive defence of Aquinas on this count in so much as the argument attributed to Buckley is an argument mounted by others and therefore worth rebutting.[9] Lash himself locates the 'great reversal' not in the eighteenth century (Frei), nor in the thirteenth century (Buckley), nor in pre-Christian Aristotelianism (Allen), but in early seventeenth-century France, in the world of Lessius and Mersenne. Buckley refers to Lessius and Mersenne as seminal figures of transmission, when he writes:

> Diderot's *Pensees* exhibit in miniature the development of natural theology since the days of Lessius and Mersenne. Theology gives way to Cartesianism, which gives way to Newtonian mechanics. The great argument, the only evidence for theism, is design, and experimental physics reveals that design.[10]

The issue between Lash and Buckley is whether Lessius' reading of Aquinas is how Aquinas should be properly read. Lash's conclusion is worth citing for it nicely frames the issue (regardless of the historical question of dating the 'great reversal'). Lash cites Buckley in the opening sentence:

> 'What Lessius presents', in the *De providentia numinis,* 'is not the person and message of Jesus, but those cosmological and historical experiences which are open to any human beings.' Here, in 1613, we are evidently already in the presence of what Hans Frei called the 'great reversal', that shift in interpretative strategy as a result of which theological interpretation became 'a matter of fitting the biblical story into another world' (namely, the world now taken to be constituted by those ranges of experience deemed open to any human being) 'rather than incorporating that world into the biblical story'. In the self-assured world of modernity, people seek to make sense of the Scriptures, instead of hoping, with the aid of Scripture, to make some sense of themselves.[11]

The genealogical picture is extremely complicated, but there are two main points I wish to emphasise. First, the secularisation of theology was a process that reached its culmination in the nineteenth century and we now live in the shadow of the 'great reversal' embodied in the history of the Enlightenment, such that institutional university theology bears many of the marks of this secularised process. Chief amongst these is a resistance to the particularity of revelation and with it a resistance to the particular tradition-specific nature of theological enquiry. Second, the intellectual citadel of theology located within the university inevitably loses sight of the particular trinitarian God of Christian revelation, and instead becomes increasingly concerned with a unitarian deity, forms of deism or agnostic apophaticism – all of which are arrived at from allegedly neutral rational argument. That these two points are interconnected is all important, for some intellectuals who are rightly concerned with the conditions for the flourishing of trinitarian theology have failed to question the very institutions (the university) that nurture new generations of 'theologians'. Hence, in very broad terms our story runs from theology as the 'queen of the sciences' in thirteenth-century Paris to theology as the laughing stock of the arts faculty in David Lodge's fictional city of Rummage.[12] It is not possible here to resolve the genealogical question regarding the origins of atheism.

Ironically John Locke's description of theology at the end of the seventeenth century well expresses the culmination of some of the major currents within the patristic and middle ages' vision of theology. Locke suggests that:

> Theology, which, containing the knowledge of God and his creatures, our duty to him and our fellow-creatures, and a view of our present and future state, is the comprehension of all other knowledge, directed to its true end.[13]

Such a definition presupposes at least three points. First, theology was undertaken by the believing community in the service of the church in response to God – faith seeking understanding, where 'understanding' meant worship, practice and intellectual expression. It involved an intellectual discipline in the context of a particular and practical form of life. It would be correct to say that the epistemological precondition for theology was the community of the church.[14] Second, and connectedly, theology conceived itself as a social (and therefore political) project. Its relation to what is currently called 'praxis' was assumed, and only in fact became detached in the process of the Enlightenment. In this sense liberation theology is not radical or novel. With Marx, it rightly calls into question the disembodiment of reason. Third, the methods appropriate to theology were dictated by the subject matter and not by objects alien to it. For example, inspiration and revelation were basic presuppositions of correct biblical exegesis and not (as in some current practice) the historical critical method. The particularity of revelation was not called into question but, rather, taken for granted and acted upon as the very presupposition of the intellectual enquiry, without it becoming immune from critical reflection.

The contemporary setting of departments of theology in the secular academy has generally institutionally eroded all these assumptions and thereby rendered theology into a graceless, stumbling knave – far from the queen of the sciences. The institutional context is appropriately mirrored in a gradual shift of theological method, so that method (historical positivism), the subject matter of theology (history, not God's action in history) and institutional structure all shore up one another. Hans Frei argues that this 'great reversal' ushered in an interpretative strategy that stood theology on its head. Rather than 'incorporating the world into the biblical story', theology became more and more a 'matter of fitting the biblical story into another world' (which was constructed by secular modernity and 'policed' by its rules and methodology).[15] Or, as Lash put it earlier: 'In the self-assured world of modernity, people seek to make sense of the Scriptures, instead of hoping, with the aid of the Scriptures, to makes sense of themselves.' Within this 'reversal' lies the history of liberal theology, for it was spawned precisely in this reversal, and it is not insignificant that the father of liberal theology, Friedrich Schleiermacher, was also the pioneer of instigating a type of institutional theology at the University of Berlin that heralded the modern period.[16] The end result of this process is that theology is offered as one of the many choices in an Arts or Humanities Faculty curriculum in the secular university. It has become domesticated and secularised. This is in stark contrast to its origins. Also in stark contrast, secular universities clearly assume and explicitly state that access must be equally open to all, in terms of both academic staff and in the background of students. Anything that specified a 'religious' orientation of any kind, for either teacher of student, would be considered anathema (sic).

Hence, on all three counts theology's fundamental nature has been institutionally altered – and therefore rendered into something that is not 'theology' in any historical and theological sense. First, being explicitly Christian in the teaching of theology, or assuming any such starting point by one's students is considered embarrassing. We have the anomalous and anachronistic situation where theology is on offer in our universities to be taught by anyone, learnt by everyone, but apparently only practised in the churches. Recall my first story about the lecturer who began with a prayer. Institutionally, the relationship of the church to academic theology is often ill-considered and *ad hoc,* but rarely openly and explicitly defined in a positive manner. Second, it is assumed that one can study theology (with requisite general academic qualifications) requiring no practical virtues and no appropriate lifestyle in accordance with the subject of study. The subject has been fully 'intellectualised' in terms of a non-Christian tradition (liberal secularism) and its relation to Christian forms of life and praxis have been successfully prised apart. Third, the skills and abilities required for the academic study of theology must increasingly be defined in terms of transferable skills relevant to any other arts or humanities discipline. Thus, the study of theology must be explicitly in service to academic standards dictated by the secular academy and its monetary sponsors.

Intellectually, it could never be stated that university theology operates primarily in service to God, the church, and then, and only then, society. The secularisation of theology's method and subject matter in part explains the important English (Protestant) strength in biblical studies during the heydays of historical criticism. This indebtedness to secular methodologies easily harmonised with the demands and expectations of the secular university. However, this situation is changing as evidenced in a number of recent publications from English New Testament scholars.[17] This process of secularisation also explains, as we shall see below, the emergence of 'religious studies', for both institutionally and methodologically theology has too often given up the fight against being controlled by the secular academy. If it had done otherwise, it might well be arguing for different forms of tradition-specific universities and, within them, varying types of theology departments.

The curious situation, which in part accounts for the laughter from the academics in my second opening story (the lightning tale), is that those who teach in theology departments are often ordained or explicitly practising Christians (but this, one is assured, should not get in the way of their sound teaching), and many who study in such departments are also Christians, but this is usually well concealed except for ordinands feeding in from church colleges and the evangelical Christian who uneasily declares him or herself in class discussion.

Many readers will of course breathe a sigh of relief at these changes, and I do not want to turn the clock back – for that is both impossible and undesirable. Instead, I only want to suggest that what masquerades as theology cannot intellectually and historically meet the description. What now exists is simply a study of texts that are concerned with religious matters. Strictly speaking, one cannot claim that theology departments are there to help teach people to theologise better. What is denied to theology departments is allowed to many others. History departments can claim to produce good historians, and English departments will often actively encourage 'creative writing' within the academic curriculum. However, it is difficult to find a theology prospectus in England that claims to produce 'good theologians'.

On the secular respectability of doing religious studies

It is time to turn to religious studies. In England, as with the United States and Europe, a number of factors are worth noting in tracing the production of religious studies as both bed-fellow and successor to theology. In what follows I will stick with England to avoid generalisations. Clearly, while the contexts are very different, some of the points here will be applicable more widely. The Oedipal configuration is not random, for at one level religious studies explicitly claims to cohabit the academic territory with theology, but if taken seriously, implicitly seeks its destruction for it must rightly and properly claim Christianity as its object of investigation, in the same manner as it claims Buddhism or Islam. Hence, at best, religious studies sub-consciously desires to seize and control the academic territory that concerns the 'divine' from theology. At worse, it explicitly seeks to destroy the albatross that drags it down, as a prominent religious studies supporter notes: the 'theological establishment is [therefore] a problem in that it is a kind of conceptual albatross around the neck of religious studies.'[18] Despite this claim, it would be intriguing to know what would change in the practice and methods of teaching in theology departments, were they to change overnight to religious studies departments. I suspect very little.

The increasing secularity of theology, both institutionally and methodologically, produced a situation where many felt that actually what existed in the practice of theology was the study of religion. Historical accidents meant that the religion so selected was Christianity. Furthermore, in the context of England's multi-religious nature, its colonial conquests, and the growth of Indology and Orientalism, many argued that religions other than Christianity should be taught. If the study of religion were an academic speciality, it seemed right and obvious that to limit the menu to Christianity was parochial to say the least. This trajectory was predictable in the Enlightenment's resistance to the particularity of Christian revelation. By this, I do not mean that the proper study of theology can be done in isolation from engagement with world religions, or that other religions should not mount analogous arguments to the ones here presented. I am simply outlining the manner in which modernity came to homogenise the university. Furthermore, students in the period of the introduction of religious studies to the universities in the late sixties were increasingly from secularised backgrounds. The attraction of Buddhism and Hinduism to these consumers, aligned to the Romantic European idealisation of these traditions, meant that the market was just right for religious studies.[19]

The final factor worth mentioning, and perhaps the most significant in the English context, was the introduction of an allegedly scientific, objective and academic method appropriate to the study of religion: phenomenology. It is no accident that the supporter of such a method in this country, Ninian Smart, was also the founder of the first department of religious studies in England, in Lancaster in 1967, and the author of the albatross statement quoted above. While Lancaster was the first department with this name, the study of 'comparative religion' goes back further to 1904, when Manchester University had the first department of comparative religions, chaired by the Pali scholar T. W. Rhys Davids. Ninian Smart's *The Phenomenon of Religion* (1973) is central for understanding the Oedipal relations between theology and religious studies.[20] It is important to note that the understanding of the 'phenomenological' method and approaches to 'religious studies' is increasingly multifarious, and has a history going back to 1873 when the founding father of comparative religions, Friedrich Max Müller, published his famous study, *Introduction to the Science of Religion*. Eric Sharpe calls this the 'foundation document of comparative religion'.[21] Sharpe's study is one of the best in charting the emergence of religious studies, not only in the UK but also world wide. A constellation of names describes the orientation I'm labelling 'religious studies': comparative religions, history of religions, and of course, religious studies. The first fell from grace due to its evolutionary associations; the second, based on the German *Religionswissenschaft*, is still found in Germany, Sweden and Finland.[22] Hence, the term religious studies in its phenomenological sense has an entirely different European genealogy to that in England.[23]

Returning to England: In explicit contrast to the memory of the dead mother (theology) whose distorted image masqueraded in the universities, the emerging prince of the religious academy proposed a method which definitely and distinctively should not and could not involve faith as its starting point. Faith as a starting point was both unscientific and unscholarly according to the canons then acceptable to the secular academy and the cultured despisers of theology. Hence, the phenomenological method started with epoché or bracketing. Epoché meant the suspension of one's own beliefs, attitudes, and values, in order to avoid contaminating objective description with personal prejudice such as one's own personal religious commitments. It was allegedly only in this fashion that the enquirer could really get at the object of enquiry and understand it correctly, be it Hinduism, Buddhism or Christianity.

However, the very notion of different 'religions', related to each other as species of common genus, was itself a seventeenth-century invention, as Peter Harrison has so persuasively argued.[24] The construction of such a field ('religion') is a project that is partly located in the Enlightenment's refusal to acknowledge the particularity of Christian revelation. Consequently, there followed the creation of a single secular history whereby different religions were organised within the Enlightenment's own overarching narrative, rather than taking seriously the different organisations of time, space and history within the various religions. Such a taxonomy also failed to attend to the epistemological prerequisites required for comprehension specified by some of the religions under examination.

John Milbank makes an interesting connection between the growth of comparative religion in the discipline of religious studies and the assumption that all religions are equal paths to the one divine. He suggests this connection because in the very creation of the field of 'religion' there is an in-built assumption of different species of a common genus, and with this assumption the idea that the common genus is our 'own' religion of which others are various manifestations. Milbank writes:

> The usual construals of religion as a genus, therefore, embody covert Christianizations, and in fact no attempt to define such a genus (or even, perhaps, delineation of an analogical field of 'family resemblances') will succeed, because no proposed common features can be found, whether in terms of belief or practice (gods, the supernatural, worship, a sacred community, sacred/secular division, etc.) that are without exceptions. The most viable, because most general definitions ('What binds a society together', and so forth) turn out to be so all-encompassing as to coincide with the definition of culture as such.[25]

It is no chance coincidence that Smart's phenomenological methodology bears striking resemblance to Descartes' and Locke's stripping
down process to get to the foundations of knowledge; nor is its
similarity to Hume's positivism insignificant. In one sense the new
scientific methodology of religious studies, which was emulated by
theology in its attempt to remain within the academy, was clearly a
child of the Enlightenment.

Admittedly, there has been much debate about Smart's model,
and the point I wish to make is this. While the methodology and
subject matter of religious studies in its institutional setting was
increasingly successful (there are now a number of religious studies
departments, while prior to 1967 there were none[26]), intellectually the
presuppositions of Smart's approach are deeply problematic. Its
problematic nature lies in its Enlightenment marriage to objectivity
and scientific neutrality. Hence, and I must make this clear, my
argument is in no way directed against the study of Buddhism and
Hinduism and other religious traditions in the academic curriculum
(far from it), but rather against the assumptions about how such subjects
are studied and how they are related to theology within the
curriculum.

There are important objections against epoché as a method and
subsequently all that follows from it.[27] As mentioned above, the success
of the phenomenological method was in part due to the social
episteme which looked favourably upon such an enterprise. Such
consensus, though certainly not unanimous, is coming to an end, and
the episteme is shifting in our times, in a period that is often described
as 'postmodern'. The natural and social sciences have tended to move
away from the positivist assumptions they both shared at the turn of the
century – and which were imitated by Smart's religious studies. Both
the former sets of disciplines have tended to eschew objectivity and
neutrality, and increasingly acknowledge that the role of the
investigator and her socio–political location is crucial to the production
of knowledge.

For instance, Thomas Kuhn's notion of scientific paradigms is widely,
though certainly not unanimously or uncritically accepted in the
natural sciences.[28] Kuhn challenged the idea of some kind of neutral
objectivity whereby the scientist can make judgements from a
universally acceptable neutral starting point, as the Enlightenment

episteme assumed. There would be few contemporary scientists who would deny that the language of investigation, the methods and controls of experimentation, and the very questions asked in scientific exploration, are profoundly shaped by the paradigm inhabited by the research scientist. And there is no scientist who is not operating within a paradigm. This insight need not lead to relativism, as some argue, for the very fact of paradigm shifts suggest that the quest for truth is still maintained, even with the recognition that all enquiry proceeds from out of a particular epistemological and ontological tradition. Epoché, in this view, is not only epistemologically impossible (for how could one suspend one's beliefs?), but actually undesirable, for it both masks the operative set of beliefs held by the investigator (thinking they are neutral), and obscures the forceful eviction of contenders for intellectually respectable methods of study (in our case, the dead mother – theology).

Kuhn's point can be seen to have its counterpart in moral philosophy and the social sciences. For example, Alasdair MacIntyre has argued persuasively against the possibility of neutral enquiry or a universal rationality, and has tried to show the tradition-specific nature of all moral and philosophical intellectual enquiry.[29] In his three major books, MacIntyre has confined himself to Western Christian and secular culture and generally ignored the pressures exerted on Western culture from other religions. This is hardly a failing, given his mammoth achievement, but we should keep this in mind in what follows. MacIntyre's argument in his third main book, *Three Rival Versions of Moral Enquiry* (1990), is particularly germane to my own argument, and this book needs to be placed in the context of the other two.

After *After Virtue* (1981), which launched MacIntyre's scathing critique of modernity and the liberalism of the Enlightenment, many suspected MacIntyre of relativism and the worst sort of sectarianism – a withdrawal and isolation from mainstream society. The charge of relativism had also been aimed at Kuhn in his location of scientific enquiry as tradition specific. It is not surprising that this criticism was also made of MacIntyre. His two later books, *Whose Justice? Which Rationality?* (1988) and *Three Rival Versions of Moral Enquiry* (1990), sought to respond vigorously to such criticism. He tried to show how the dynamic interaction of rival traditions might well be resolved, as it was in thirteenth-century Paris in the struggle between Aristotelianism and Augustinianism and the subsequent emergence of Thomism, by critical dialectics between two apparently incommensurable traditions. MacIntyre sought to demonstrate how some forms of rational argument are possible both within traditions and also between them, although the manner and outcome of such engagements cannot be predicted in advance. *Three Rival Versions* illuminates my own discussion, for I have tried to argue that the advance of modernity and secularity within the university and the death of theology as queen of the sciences are intrinsically connected. MacIntyre analyses the secularisation of the university and the imposition of unitary forms of enquiry as a stifling of genuine plurality and pluriform modes of intellectual enquiry. He is charged with sectarianism in resisting the hegemony of the Enlightenment model of the university.

MacIntyre locates his three rival versions of (moral) enquiry within Western society. They are the Encyclopedic, the Genealogical and the Thomist. The first is the Enlightenment project of liberal modernity, so skilfully unmasked in *After Virtue*: the project that is embodied in the ninth edition of the *Encyclopedia Britannica*. It is upon this model of enquiry that the modern university is constructed. Its hegemonic power is criticised by MacIntyre for stifling any real debate between alternative modes of enquiry. The genealogical mode is essentially the Nietzchean tradition and is represented by philosophical post-modernism in the form of philosophers like Rorty, Deluze and Derrida. MacIntyre dismisses this tradition (at times far too quickly) for being nihilistically relativist and ultimately parasitic, for it is only able to deconstruct rather than develop positive constructive proposals. The third form of traditioned enquiry that is suppressed in the Western academy is the Thomistic project. MacIntyre sees Thomism (which is both internally plural and constantly developing) as providing a bridge between the Enlightenment's spurious universal disembodied reason and the untenable relativism of the genealogists.[30] In the last chapter of the book, MacIntyre calls for a postliberal university system in which different universities would be organised around different and distinct forms of enquiry. In this important respect my own argument joins his, 'from below' so to speak, as I have been charting the same malaise within theology that MacIntyre discerns in moral philosophy, and both have the same causes precipitating their respective crises. MacIntyre rightly, though not unproblematically, diagnoses the cure for this atrophy in calling for a radical change in the very institutions of learning that unwittingly claim to facilitate plural forms of intellectual enquiry, while nevertheless being founded on a unitary vision of intellectual enquiry: the Encyclopedic.[31]

There are two particular intersections between MacIntyre's and my own argument that I should like to highlight. First, religious studies as I have been charting it above is part of the Encyclopedic tradition and is properly located within that mode of enquiry. In this sense its murderous Oedipal desire towards theology is now fully exposed. Theology must rightly contest religious studies' autonomous existence and its claim to objective production; although any sensible theologian would also recognise that there are invaluable skills, tools, methods and insights present within the phenomenological approach of Smart's religious studies. The only point I am contesting is Smart's epistemological claims for religious studies. It is not an objective and dispassionate methodology by which to approach 'religions', but a highly biased and historically and philosophically situated enterprise. Second, MacIntyre's material account lacks attention to the intellectual traditions of enquiry within other religions. Rather than MacIntyre's isolation of three traditions of enquiry (liberal modernity, parasitic genealogical criticism and neo-Thomism), each requiring their own institutions of learning as their conceptions of education vary so profoundly (even if genealogy can only exist parasitically on the other two), there are good reasons to consider further traditions for institutional developments within the formal, rather than material, terms of MacIntyre's discussion.

Indeed, this very point has been made by a sympathetic Muslim critic of MacIntyre's, Muhammad Legenhausen. He notes Islam's relationship to the Aristotelian tradition upon which MacIntyre is so dependent, and therefore criticises MacIntyre's inexplicable omission of Islam in the debate. Furthermore, Legenhausen, writing in Iran, also suggests that Islam can account for the aporia within MacIntyre's argument where MacIntyre's espousal of small sectarian communities, after the order of St Benedict, fails entirely to engage with the problem of nation states that MacIntyre identifies as one of the roots of the malaise. Susan Mendus and John Horton make the same point:

> Moreover, given the importance which MacIntyre attaches to the social embeddedness of thought and enquiry, his largely negative view of modernity continually threatens to undermine any attempt to root his

positive proposals in the contemporary world of advanced industrial societies.[32]

According to Legenhausen, Islam, on the other hand, is able to offer a theocratic solution, allegedly avoiding both 'nationalism and liberalism', an alternative that is 'not taken seriously by Western theorists'.[33] Hence, Legenhausen takes up MacIntyre's critique of modernity, but points to the same weakness located by Horton and Mendus within MacIntyre's alternative, and at that point thereby commends Islam. In institutional terms, given MacIntyre's premises, this would amount to an argument for an Islamic university. Certainly the existence of such an entity within Western Europe and the United States might better facilitate systematic theology's rigorous engagement with a living religious intellectual tradition other than Judeo-Christianity. It may also have many other important benefits and consequences. The Jewish community has already established higher level educational institutions within Western Europe, the USA, England and, of course, Israel. Whether and how these arguments and considerations should be related to the various religions and whether such institutions would even be desirable is a question that would have to be pursued by intellectuals within those communities. For example, it seems clear that Tibetan Buddhism presupposed a very precise epistemological and pedagogical set of assumptions in its construction of the four Tibetan universities operating in Tibet prior to the Chinese occupation.[34]

I do not have adequate space to develop my argument, but at this juncture I would suggest the importance of a *theological religious studies*. That is, other religions should be part of a theological curriculum, equal in status to secular culture, the 'dialogue' partner of most modern European theologians. In this respect, theology cannot properly be done without an engagement with other religions. If teaching about world religions within theology were the best strategy, questions would have to be answered as to who did the teaching of other religions, how it would be related to the theological curriculum, how much experience of those living traditions should be facilitated if the tradition was 'alive', and the factors that would dictate the choice of which religions should be studied. For example, it would be clearly important for Catholic universities in Africa and the Middle East to engage with Islam, as it would be for those in India to engage with Hinduism and Islam.

Were the conditions right, one might consider whether students in the theology department within a Roman Catholic university would be better sent to, say, an Islamic institution for a part of their training as theologians. This would facilitate a real richness in interreligious engagement as it would facilitate, in MacIntyre's words, the proper learning of a 'second language'.[35] Such an enterprise of course pre-supposes very fluent first language users prior to their training and acquisition of a second language. Nevertheless, such a requirement, although prohibitive against the pick-and-mix attitude of many modern theology and religious studies departments, would facilitate genuine and costly interreligious encounter, and would call for various contextual theologies of religion, rather than any single over-arching theology of religions.[36]

For the moment, let me recall the second step of my argument. Religious studies was born into English universities partly because of the anachronism of theology being located within the secular academy; partly due to the search for scientific and objective ways of carrying out research in religions to avoid theological sectarianism (but nevertheless creating another form); and partly to gain the approval of the secular academy (which has, in many other disciplines, moved on). Put together with part one of my argument, the cumulative case will require, if it is accepted, at least one of three possible responses, only the third of which I support. One would be to abolish both theology and religious studies departments altogether and integrate them into history, literature, politics and so on. Second, one could rename theology and religious studies as 'the historical critical study of religion' and carry on with what went on previously. Or thirdly, one might allow specific starting points to flourish, label them clearly, and allow them to interact. Within this third option, many different models are possible.[37] My own specific theological option would be to argue for a Roman Catholic university within a pluralist academy on the lines advanced by Alastair MacIntyre.[38] This is not in anyway supposed to privilege, ghettoise or sanctify Roman Catholics, but to recognise that tradition-specific forms of enquiry should be facilitated on good intellectual grounds.

Chapter Twelve

Philosophy and the Idea of a Christian University

David Carr

The unity in diversity of philosophy

Asked to address the question of the place, if any, of philosophy in a Christian university, a philosopher might be expected to 'define' the relevant key terms in much the way that student essayists or trainee researchers are so often exhorted to do. Still, even if it was not way beyond the scope of a short chapter to try to define such complex terms as 'philosophy', 'Christian' and 'university' – upon which so much ink has been spilt by some of the greatest minds of antiquity and modernity – few philosophers would nowadays regard such attempts at definition as conducive to significant conceptual progress. On the other hand, however, since one could hardly even say this in the absence of *some* conception of philosophy and its purposes, it seems reasonable to start – before examining the possible place of philosophy in a Christian university – with some brief account of what the present author takes these purposes to be.

What then is the overall aim of philosophy? At first sight of the bewildering range of philosophical traditions, schools, approaches and methodologies – divided not only by diverse concerns with quite different sorts of questions, but also by apparently irreconcilable approaches to the resolution of common questions – it might be held that no *generally* useful account of the philosophical project is possible. The different traditions and schools of logical positivism, idealism, Marxism, 'ordinary language' philosophy, pragmatism, phenomenology, existentialism, critical theory, structuralism, post-structuralism, post-modernism (to name only the main 'Western' traditions) seem to be so divided over the question of what actually counts as philosophy as to constitute not just one but several different disciplines. Indeed, pheno-menology may seem to be as remote from Marxism as psychology is from sociology (and for not unrelated reasons). What order, then, might be brought into such apparent chaos, in the interests of clarifying the status of philosophy in any educational programme whatsoever?

Of course, one might predictably respond to the apparent scandal of philosophical plurality by observing that to philosophers such dis-agreement and diversity is hardly scandalous. On the contrary, such disagreement is of the very essence of philosophical enquiry, and should the day ever come when philosophers can no longer find anything to disagree about, that day would also mark the end of philosophy. But a second, more contentious, point (no worse, in my view, for that) is that on closer scrutiny, and on a narrower construal of philosophy, there is perhaps less diversity and more unity to the basic philosophical enterprise than readily meets the eye. Thus, I suspect it would be widely agreed that the heart of philosophy lies in a sort of *critical analysis* of human discourse that makes its first clearly recognisable historical appearance in the enquiries of Socrates as recorded in the dialogues of Plato. Indeed, Socrates seems to have been the first to attempt rigorous and systematic analysis of usage of a recognisably modern kind, to the extent that his own analyses of knowledge and virtue are still of paramount modern philosophical interest and logical strategies pioneered by Socrates (such as *reductio ad absurdum*) have since his time been an important part of the stock-in-trade of philosophers of diverse traditions and persuasions.

In short, Socrates, and following him Plato, were centrally concerned with the question of the sense or *meaning* of the terms we employ to describe, express, understand and/or explain the world of human experience. Whether or not Socrates (or Plato) thought that such meaning could actually be captured in strict *definitions*, it is probably fair to credit him with two key insights into the theoretical need for conceptual clarification. First, Socrates sees that there is a pressing need for *coherence* among the terms we use to describe and explain things: the chief sign of conceptual incoherence is contradiction, and – as logicians rightly point out – from a contradiction, absolutely *anything* follows. Secondly, there is an equally compelling need to eliminate *ambiguity* from our talk about the world, since ambiguity seriously spoils or impedes valid reason or *inference*: if we cannot preserve consistent sense from the premises to the conclusions of our arguments, or from one context of discourse to another, then our best dialectical efforts are liable to fallacy and confusion.

The point about ambiguity reminds us that the senses of many familiar terms of ordinary usage – not least of such philosophically contentious terms as knowledge, mind, goodness and beauty – are prone to instability or waywardness in different contexts of employment. Thus, although we may be right to suppose that senses of 'good' in 'This is good weather' and 'Good morning!' are not entirely separate, sensitivity to context shows us that 'good' does not always function as a descriptive term, and that others may not therefore be dissembling if they wish us 'Good day!' in bad weather. In modern times, it took the genius of Wittgenstein to demonstrate that even when terms such as 'good' and 'beautiful' are used referentially or descriptively, they should not be taken to denote some abstract Platonic form conducive to strict context-insensitive definition (Wittgenstein, 1953). Still, one does not need to be a card-carrying Wittgensteinian to recognise that the basic programme of conceptual clarification that he sought to develop is significantly prefigured by the pioneering semantic and logical analyses of Socrates, and that at no subsequent points of major philosophical schism and disagreement is it clear that serious philosophers have reneged on this central Socratic project. In this sense, the founding father of modern phenomenology, Edmund Husserl, seems no less committed to this basic programme of Socratic analysis than does the principal architect of modern analytical philosophy, Gottlob Frege (and indeed, there was important philosophical correspondence between these philosophical pioneers) – just as, likewise, seventeenth- and eighteenth-century post-Cartesian empiricists are no less Socratic (in this analytical sense) than their rationalist rivals.

That said, I believe that this project does need to be distinguished from other enterprises which have sometimes been called philosophical. On the one hand, it needs to be distinguished from the construction of imaginative narratives, stories and sermons of the sort that feature in the work of nineteenth-century romantic essayists, in such post-Hegelian writers as Carlyle, Kierkegaard and Nietzsche, and in their various twentieth-century existentialist and other literary heirs. On the other hand, it also needs to be distinguished from those equally sweeping flights of metaphysical, social scientific, historical, economic and biological conjecture and fancy of thinkers as diverse as Plato,

Hegel, Spencer, Marx and Bergson. To be sure, modern pragmatist heirs of nineteenth-century idealism have strenuously denied any firm boundary between philosophical and natural or social scientific enquiry, but a fairly evident commitment to the searching logical scrutiny of inherited dogmas, prejudices and generalisations, nevertheless places pragmatists mostly in the Socratic tradition of analytical enquiry.

To be sure, the work of such modern natural, social and cultural theorists as Darwin, Freud, Marx and Nietzsche, has engendered some problematic structuralist, post-Marxist, post-structuralist and postmodern erosion of the distinction between Socratic philosophising and grand social or empirical theorising. Ironically, this is nowhere quite so evident as in the radical *anti-theorising* of the postmodern 'philosopher' J.-F. Lyotard: for where Lyotard asks us to accept that there are no 'overarching metanarratives' (Lyotard 1984), Socrates would surely have wanted to distinguish and/or interrogate the potentially different senses of this claim. In this spirit, we might ask: does denying metanarrative mean that no one today can *believe* in any grand theory? (which is clearly false); does it mean that no theory can be regarded as successfully *explaining* what it purports to explain? (which seems doubtful); does it mean that no *single* theory can be taken to *explain* everything? (which is true, but trivial – for surely no one in his or her right senses has surely ever supposed otherwise). At all events, the difference here between the critical philosophising of a Socrates, or modern analytical philosopher, and the social or other theorising of intellectual trends often nowadays referred to as 'philosophy' could hardly be more apparent.

Philosophy, liberal education and the university

It might also go some way towards reassuring those who would regard this view of philosophy as an excessively narrow one, to say that this does not imply any cavalier dismissal of the ideas of Darwin or Marx, or of a Nietzsche or Kierkegaard: on the contrary, such thinkers are key figures of intellectual history who have significantly contributed to our general understanding of ourselves and our world. Even so, it seems hard to deny that a distinction of some importance is at stake here, and that at the very least the *philosophies* of a Marx or Spencer are not *philosophy* in the same sense as the enquiries of a Socrates, Russell or

Wittgenstein. Even if such radical empiricists as Mill, and such key pragmatists as Quine, are right to suppose that the most general laws of logic and philosophical reason are simply high level empirical generalisations – and it remains an open question whether this is so – it may be doubted whether philosophical claims concerning the relationship of mind to body or fact to value are apt for empirical disconfirmation in the manner of Darwin's ideas of natural selection or Marx's economic predictions. In this regard, progress in neuro-physiological research is no better placed to establish that mind is a product or function of the brain, than is psychical research to show that it is not – and philosophical clarification must ultimately rest on analysis and argument that goes beyond any information given. But if such argument and analysis does not depend on received empirical or other theory and evidence, upon what does it depend?

Primarily, I believe that philosophical analysis and argument is concerned with just that rational appraisal of the varieties of empirical or other theory and explanation by which humans have tried down the ages to make sense of their world, and which focuses precisely – and Socratically – on questions of the formal consistency of concepts and the rational validity of arguments: its aim is to map the bounds of coherent sense. There is nowadays, to be sure, much postmodern and other scepticism about the prospects of any such project. One influential line of thought has it that any such enterprise is doomed from the outset, insofar as no such critique could avoid importing the rational categories and logical strategies of some cultural perspective. In that case any 'Socratic' critique of this or that viewpoint must inevitably embody the prejudices of some rival view, and hence be question-begging, if not also culturally colonialist. But such objections seem either trivial or confused. In one sense, of course, any modes of rational appraisal by which we may criticise this or that view will be 'our' modes of appraisal (who else's would they be?), and it is far from clear that Socrates or any other philosopher ever supposed that we might reason apart from some intellectual inheritance. On the other hand, it is hard to see how any human discourse that remained impervious to logical and evidential constraints acknowledging something like (for example) principles of identity and non-contradiction could count as *rational*: from a contradiction anything follows, all reason is thereby forfeit, and any 'philosophy' which defies the authority of such principles cuts off the branch upon which it sits.

Moreover, the virtues of philosophical analysis lately extolled are also largely those that modern analytical philosophers have regarded as integral to intellectual advancement and socio-political flourishing in conditions of liberal democracy, and which also seem to be integral to liberal education conceived as a key condition of effective citizenship in any such society. Although contemporary communitarians have sought to criticise modern liberal social and political conceptions of reason on the grounds that they presuppose a socially detached 'view from nowhere', and whatever the justice of such charges as levelled at more metaphysical (Kantian) versions of twentieth-century liberal theory, it is far from clear that they apply to such nineteenth-century architects of liberalism as J. S. Mill, whose views on mind and reason could hardly enshrine a clearer appreciation of the way in which human enquiry is conditioned by a diversity of often rival cultural traditions and inheritances (Mill, 1859). Indeed, it is significant that the great modern spokesmen of liberal education – from Matthew Arnold in the nineteenth century to Michael Oakeshott, G. H. Bantock and Richard Peters in the twentieth – have invariably been educational *traditionalists*. Unlike progressivists in the tradition of Rousseau, who exhibit a deep distrust of received wisdom and regard it as the key task of education to shield young people from its indoctrinatory effects, the major champions of liberal education have invariably held that there can be no coherent intellectual progress other than by prior immersion – in Arnold's famous words – into 'the best that has been thought and said in the world' (Gribble, 1967, p. 150).

In short, the educated citizen of liberal democracy, or persons educated for liberal democracy, would be those acquainted with the highest intellectual, moral and artistic achievements of their culture, who manifest the values and virtues needed for civil association within this or other cultures, who possess the knowledge and skills required for economic and other practical self-sufficiency, but who further exhibit some capacity for that 'Socratic' appraisal of received views which appears to be the *sine qua non* of any properly ordered human sensibility. It should therefore occasion little surprise that, as well as being themselves philosophers or of a markedly philosophical cast of mind, most champions of liberal education have clearly regarded philosophy – Socratically conceived, as a capacity for critical rational enquiry rather than as mere acquaintance with the views of past philosophers – as a key ingredient of any worthwhile liberal education (see, for example,

Hirst, 1974). On this view, an educated person is someone who is capable of higher-order enquiries concerning the grammar of human knowledge and discourse that are not possible to ask within any particular discipline. For example, where forms of knowledge have been held to conflict, as in the apparent conflict between Darwinian evolution and the biblical account of creation in *Genesis*, an educated person might be capable of framing and/or addressing such questions as: Does this mean that *Genesis* in particular and religion in general is false? Does this mean that evolutionary theory in particular or science in general is false? Does this mean that we need a better account of the grammar of religious or scientific discourse?, and so forth.

Still, despite more recent emphases on critical thinking as a significant goal of general education, not to mention latter-day attempts to develop philosophy as a constituent of the elementary school curriculum, it would appear that modern advocates of liberal education have mostly inclined to regard the university, conceived as a distinctive sector of higher education, as the main bastion of such broader education, and philosophy as a key ingredient in such education in particular. On this view, ably defended by Cardinal Newman and others, although universities might well assume some responsibility for higher vocational or professional training, the key responsibility of the university resides in the pursuit and advancement of knowledge and understanding, not as a means to any social or economic end, but primarily for its own sake (Newman, 1976). Indeed, the university needs to be importantly distinguished, in respect of its concern with the intrinsic pursuit of knowledge and understanding, from any and all other further and higher educational institutions – such as seminaries, teacher training colleges, technical colleges, polytechnics and so on – all of which are fairly evidently concerned with the pursuit of knowledge as a means to other professional, social and economic ends. Hence, with particular regard to philosophy, though one might hope to see this studied by seminarians or student teachers as an aid to the clarification of their several professional projects, one would expect university students of philosophy to study it precisely in the detached Socratic spirit of the pursuit of clarification and understanding for its own inherent worth.

Religion in higher education and the university

That said, it cannot have escaped the notice of even the most ivory tower academic that British and other universities have of late been overtaken by political and economic changes that have greatly served to erode any distinction between the liberal educational concerns of the university and the instrumental goals of other higher education institutions. First, radical changes in higher education funding have put universities under enormous pressure to seek other than public sources of revenue, and to be more financially self-supporting. Such pressure has encouraged them to diversify in more market competitive professional and vocational directions, so that courses of business studies may nowadays appear more economically attractive and viable than courses in ancient history or philosophy. Secondly, recent trends have been generally and inexorably moving in the direction of a fully unified system of tertiary education in which any distinction between the liberal educational role of universities and the instrumental function of other higher education institutions has all but disappeared: former colleges of professional (teacher and other) training have either merged with erstwhile universities or, like the former polytechnics, been upgraded to university status. Thirdly, increasing political pressure towards wider access to higher education (backed by rhetoric of 'lifelong learning') has greatly undermined previous distinctions of ability and/or status between university and other higher education students, and universities have increasingly been forced to adjust to the academic needs of a student clientele for whom they may formerly have less often had to cater. To be sure, such trends are deeply problematic, and have not lacked their critics from the traditional university sectors (see, for example, Graham, 1999; Haldane, 2000; Maskell and Robinson, 2001): but they seem unlikely to be reversed in the short term, and it may well be that the liberal educational character of traditional universities has been altered forever.

In the light of such distinctions and developments, however, we now need to ask what the place of religion and religious studies might be in universities and/or other institutions of tertiary education. First, since religion constitutes a significant dimension – perhaps the most significant dimension – of many people's lives, and since such major religions as Christianity, Islam and Hinduism have exercised profound influence on human cultures, the study of religion would seem to qualify as worthy of pursuit in its own right, and it is difficult to see how someone might count as any sort of educated person in the absence of some knowledge of the cultural impact of religion and religions, and of the effects of this impact on contemporary events. Secondly, given the salvific and pastoral mission of organised religion and the place of public religious observance in many people's lives, there is clearly also a place for religion and the study of religion in advanced professional and vocational training for the ministry and priesthood. If it is proper to conceive church ministry as something more than divinely inspired practice acquired on the basis of 'hands-on' apprenticeship, and the flocks of the faithful are to be tended by shepherds who are thoroughly grounded in the principles of faith, church dogma and proper pastoral procedure, then there would also seem to be a place in the academy for the acquisition of relevant professional knowledge and skills. On the face of it, then, regardless of the 'old' or 'new' status of the university, or of its liberal or vocational credentials, there would appear to be some case for the higher academic study of religion.

The less good news, however, is that few if any of these observations support a case for the idea of a religious (or in particular Christian) university in the sense intended by the present work – especially if philosophy, conceived as radical Socratic critique, is to be located at the heart of universities conceived as agents of liberal education. For clearly, universities are to be regarded as in this sense religious or Christian not merely insofar as they give institutional space to the academic study of religion and/or Christianity, or provide courses of vocational training for professional careers in ministry, but in the much stronger sense of offering a higher undergraduate or postgraduate experience that embodies or exhibits a distinctive religious flavour or *ethos* to which one might expect students of that particular religious orientation to be drawn. The idea of a religious or Christian university in this sense is about the establishment of a learning institution that is also characterised by the values and virtues of a particular way of life to which any and all human enquiry might be seen as ultimately subservient. In this sense, religious or Christian universities would be the tertiary equivalents of 'faith schools' at the primary and secondary levels of education – and this very idea would seem prey to precisely the objections to which such approaches to elementary schooling have been prone.

Indeed, a brief survey of the problems that have recently overtaken religious denominational elementary education in Britain might help to bring some of the key issues about the very idea of a religious or Christian university into sharper focus. In this respect, one may first note not only that British elementary education has been shaped by traditions of close political and cultural association between state and church, but that British schooling has also continued to exhibit a markedly religious denominational character: not only is the religious dimension of British schooling generally apparent in an officially mandated daily act of religious (until recently entirely Christian) worship, but it is more particularly evident in a diversity of religious (mainly Catholic and Protestant Christian, but also other) provision. Indeed, it is probably safe to say that until fairly recently it was widely taken for granted in British society that elementary schools had a perfectly proper role to play in the 'confessional' induction of pupils into the beliefs, values and virtues of an essentially Christian culture.

It is likely that two main developments of the last half century or so have served to undermine this common assumption: first, the rapid transformation of post-war Britain into a multicultural and multi-faith society, in the wake of increasing immigration from former British colonies; second, a post-war reworking of liberal philosophy of education, which – albeit continuous with earlier nineteenth-century liberal educational traditions – has proved highly sensitive to the indoctrinatory potential of faith-based moral and religious education, and to arguments that any liberal education (like the liberal state) should remain neutral between different conceptions of value and flourishing. Needless to say, the increase in numbers of children from other faiths in British schools has seriously problematised the very idea of a daily act of *Christian* worship, and intensified abiding concerns of non-religious educational theorists and policy makers about the public educational propriety of any such religious teaching or preaching. To date, moreover, there have been two principal responses to this issue. The first has been the development, precisely under the pressure of 'neutralist' liberal thinking about the nature of moral and religious values, of a nonconfessional pedagogy which seeks to transform religious education into the religiously unattached study of the devotional practices of different faith communities – with, to be sure, a primary view to the promotion of intercultural understanding and tolerance. On this approach, one may even keep the daily act of 'worship', so long as such acts are even-handedly respectful of all faiths, and emphasise only those elements of different faiths that are concerned to uphold the common procedural moral values of liberal cooperation and tolerance. The other response to the issue of religious education in cultural diversity, however, has been to press for a diversity of educational provision for different faith communities.

A communitarian approach to the place of religion in education

Notwithstanding the widespread endorsement of such nonconfessional approaches to religious education in Britain and elsewhere, and despite their laudable commitment to liberal tolerance, they are clearly open to objections from any substantial faith perspective. One problem is that insofar as religious faiths are not just systems of belief, but ways of life and conduct requiring some practical or experiential initiation, the rather superficial 'academic' acquaintance with different cultural customs that children are liable to derive from such approaches seems to fall well short of genuine religious education. For one thing, just as education in football or woodwork is hardly reducible to telling pupils what these activities are *about*, one might not expect them to gain much sense of what it is like to be Catholic or Hindu in the absence of practical engagement in the worship and rituals of these faiths. For another, it may be that even to understand these faiths as systems of belief, one would need to grasp something of the *reasons* for the beliefs – including the reasons why different people of faith often disagree. But the impetus to liberal tolerance of nonconfessional approaches inevitably places more emphasis on the common moral banalities of different faiths than upon the interesting disagreements that divide them. Indeed, it may be hard for young people to gain any serious sense of why particular religious customs, practices and rituals have exercised such power over the human imagination, if it seems that there is no more to be learned from this or that great religious narrative or parable than the commonplace that we should all be nice to one another.

In this light, recent so-called 'communitarian' responses to liberal social theory and liberal conceptions of education and schooling have been warmly welcomed by many religiously minded educational philosophers and theorists. Indeed, many of the communitarian social and moral philosophers and theorists who have taken greatest exception to liberal conceptions of reason and its identity-constitutive role have been either practising Christians or significantly influenced by Christianity. For present purposes, indeed, it would be hard to find a better example than the contemporary Roman Catholic philosopher Alasdair MacIntyre, who has in several places sought to apply his moral and social theories to educational questions and issues. MacIntyre's perspective on the place of moral, religious and other values in human life is broadly similar to that of other communitarians (see, for example, MacIntyre, 1981). First, he holds that moral perspectives are more a matter of cultural inheritance than of 'objective' disinterested or decontextualised reason, and that they therefore cannot be decoupled from broader religious, theological or metaphysical perspectives on human destiny and flourishing: alternative moral values are therefore rooted in radically divergent forms of life with their own distinctive traditions and practices. Secondly, however, he claims that insofar as the rival moral conclusions of diverse cultures reflect incommensurable intellectual practices and traditions, it is no use trying to evaluate such conclusions from some rational standpoint external to such traditions: there can be no culture-free 'God's eye view' from which we might judge this society's moral values to be better than that one.

But this has led MacIntyre to question the actual coherence of any and all rationalist conceptions of common school moral formation of the sort canvassed in post-war modernity by liberal philosophers of education and cognitive developmental psychologists. In a highly influential educational essay of some years back, MacIntyre (1999) claimed that there is no 'shared public morality of commonplace usage' that might justify a common programme of moral education for the common school, and he proceeded to argue – in a manner highly congenial to many contemporary communitarian educational philosophers – for a diversity of educational provision that might better respect the integrity of different systems of moral belief and practice. In short, MacIntyre's arguments in this essay point towards a further extension of the religious sectarian diversity – most conspicuous in the form of separate Roman Catholic schools – already evident in British and other systems of schooling. Indeed, there is currently much heated controversy over the future prospects of separate British Catholic and other faith schooling between contemporary educational communitarians influenced by broadly MacIntyrean arguments, and liberal educational theorists and policy makers who are equally exercised by the potential for social division that they take to be exemplified in separate educational provision in such strife-ridden regions as Northern Ireland (on these concerns see, for example, Halstead, 1995; Conroy, 2001).

I shall not comment on this issue here, other than to observe that there seems to be some confusion and obfuscation on both sides. On the one hand, the case for separate schools sometimes seems driven by an aspiration to autochthonous religious purity and insularity that has hardly ever been either realistic or desirable; on the other, little in the way of argument nor evidence strongly supports the socially divisive effects of separate faith schools. What is of greater present interest is a more recent argument of MacIntyre (2001) in support of specifically Catholic *universities*. MacIntyre's more upbeat message in this later work is that Catholic Christian and other religious perspectives have precisely a role to play in fostering that broader liberal vision of the meaningful 'connectedness' of things that traditional universities saw it as their purpose to promote, and which has only fairly recently been eroded by a more instrumental focus on narrower vocational and professional concerns. MacIntyre's view seems to be that, although Catholic universities might succumb to contemporary pressures to pursue more instrumental ends, such institutions could nevertheless play a vital role in affirming the relevance of philosophical and theological debate to broader human concerns about the meaning and purpose of human life and endeavour. What seems puzzling about these latest claims, however, is that they are made in the name of a notion of general education that MacIntyre had dismissed in another earlier educational essay (MacIntyre, 1987) as difficult if not impossible to sustain in modern social conditions, and on behalf of a conception of human destiny and flourishing that he has in other places (e.g. MacIntyre, 1981, 1999) held to be significantly quarantined off from external philosophical, moral or other criticisms.

On the face of it, there seems to be some tension between the idea of MacIntyre and other communitarians that the value perspectives of rival cultural or religious traditions have an intellectual or moral integrity that is resistant to external appraisal and requires nurturing in separate educational contexts, and the claim that such traditions nevertheless have a contribution to make to a wider human con- versation about the ends of human life (not just of any particular community) as such. On the one hand, Catholic universities seem committed to justifying and maintaining the integrity of those beliefs and practices that are definitive and constitutive of Catholic faith and doctrine; on the other, they are charged with sustaining a conversation with other faiths and/or modern secularism that MacIntyre has elsewhere judged to be inevitably doomed to cross-purposes. Indeed, whether or not Catholic universities might be capable of some such feat of juggling, it is not hard to imagine cases of faith-based higher education in which the task would surely be quite unnegotiable. How, for example, might a *fundamentalist* Christian university sustain meaningful and constructive dialogue with humanist or other perspectives committed to evolutionary theory, whilst continuing to insist that every statement in the Bible – not least the biblical account of God's direct and episodic creation of fully formed *Homo sapiens* – is literally true? To remain open to rational conversion to the secular scientific view is to risk the loss of fundamentalist identity, but to be closed to the possibility of such dialogue is to refuse any and all entry into that critical philosophical conversation about human nature and destiny which MacIntyre thinks that religious interest in theological and other questions might introduce into a wider university experience.

Conclusion: the possibility of rational religious conversation

The story so far seems to cast doubt on the very idea of a religious university in general and of a Christian university in particular – not least on the largely traditional assumption of MacIntyre and others that universities are seats of liberal learning in which philosophy would have a central role to play in submitting past and present human wisdom to rationally objective critical scrutiny. On the traditional liberal (or liberal-traditional) conception, the university should be open to any and all disinterested enquiry – but to exhibit a particular religious character, it seems bound to exempt some beliefs from the potentially undermining effects of any such enquiry. The communitarian case for separate religious elementary schools is of course largely immune to these points. As sites of more general human formation, such schools would have a wider range of legitimate developmental purposes than universities, and be accountable to the social and moral values of the communities they serve: thus, even in a liberal society there is a case for the promotion by some schools of the religious and moral values of the parents of children attending those schools (so long as such values are not seriously at odds with the liberal injunction to tolerance). But the liberal educational remit of universities clearly finds them differently positioned with respect to religious ethos or influence. From this viewpoint, although there might be Catholic seminaries, Anglican teacher training colleges or Islamic agricultural schools, there could no more be Catholic or Seventh Day Adventist universities (in any sense other than that such institutions were religiously founded, funded or aimed to accommodate students from a particular religious constituency) than there could be Marxist-Leninist or Flat Earthist universities – at least in any sense in which philosophy as unfettered critical analysis might be seriously implicated.

All the same, I shall close with some lingering doubts about some presuppositions of the story so far. To be sure, the argument turns upon accepting that very idea of open liberal reason and argument that MacIntyre and other communitarians have often sought to question as incoherent. Indeed, it seems to be one basic difficulty with MacIntyre's recent essay on the Catholic university that it aims to revive the prospect of Catholic intellectual traditions contributing to the wider liberal conversation about human ends and purposes that he has previously undermined in denying the coherence of any external questioning of rival traditions. However, it might be held that a better way to justify the contribution of religious discourse to the larger educated conversation is not – like communitarians – to deny in the name of hermetically sealed cultural traditions the very possibility of any such wider philosophical conversation, but to reconsider the epistemic status of religious discourse in any such wider conversation. In this light, although one might reasonably question the coherence of a fundamentalist university education which taught that evolutionary theory must be false because it conflicts with the 'truth' of *Genesis*, one might equally question a scientific university education which taught that *Genesis* must be false because it denies the theory of evolution.

There seems to be little doubt that philosophy – not least philosophy of a generally analytical turn – has to date been fairly inhospitable to religious discourse. On the one hand, following in a long positivist tradition in which meaning is largely predicated on correspondence to empirical data, much philosophical theology of the last century tended to support scientific critics of Scripture in regarding much religious discourse as devoid of serious point or meaning (see, for example, Flew, 1966). On the other hand, later Wittgensteinian or 'use-theoretical' traditions of opposition to such positivism, while more sympathetic to the meaningfulness of religious discourse, have inclined to equally reductive affective or noncognitive construals of such meaning: on this view, religious language and practices are meaningful only as expressions of affective, aesthetic or cultural preference (see, for example, Phillips, 1970a, 1970b, 1976, 1993). It may also be that such noncognitive construals of religious discourse owe much to a widely influential (at least on Protestant theology) Kantian separation of faith from reason. At all events, I believe that most influential contemporary trends in the theory of religious education reflect one or more of these generally sceptical positions concerning the rational sense of religious discourse. On the one hand, the retreat from faith initiation of nonconfessional approaches to religious education almost certainly reflects the positivist view that religious stories cannot themselves (since they are unverifiable or unfalsifiable) be taken seriously as ways of interpreting or understanding (either this or) the (next) world – notwithstanding the case for acquainting young people with such stories, and the beliefs and practices in which they are embedded, as historically important forms of cultural expression. On the other hand, however, the communitarian flight from such nonconfessional disengagement into more full-blooded practical religious or other cultural initiation is often embraced in the name of a no less anti-rational separation of faith from reason.

In the space that remains, I can observe only that the common philosophical assumptions underlying nonconfessional and con-fessional approaches to religious knowledge and understanding, and any implied dichotomy between the 'knowing how' of confession and the 'knowing that' of nonconfession, seem to be well overdue serious critical scrutiny. The key philosophical mistake in thinking about these issues may be to suppose that insofar as religious narratives – such as the stories of *Genesis* – are not exclusively (indeed, in the case of many major religions, not at all) descriptive of *empirical* matters of fact, they might not nevertheless be addressed to serious non-empirical (metaphysical or normative) concerns, or expressive of genuine truths about such concerns. One possible source of trouble is that a reasonable recognition that the character of much religious narrative is allegorical or mythopoeic has often led to a reductive aestheticisation of religious meaning that has precisely belied the moral and mortal significance of such narratives. But it seems generally ill-considered to suppose that just because stories are not literally true they can have no other substantial truth – as any serious reader of either Shakespeare's *King Lear* or Milton's *Paradise Lost* might well insist.

In general, it seems neither impious nor implausible to regard religious stories and narratives as part of a wider human literature that has down the ages sought to address issues of serious normative (spiritual, moral and aesthetic) concern in the metaphorical, analogical and allegorical terms of art rather than science – precisely to the extent that, as Kant for one clearly saw, the most profound questions of human freedom, good and evil, love and redemption are fundamentally resistant to reductive scientific explanation. From this viewpoint, to claim that the meaning of Bunyan's *Pilgrim's Progress* or Marlowe's *Faust* is allegorical or mythopoeic rather than empirical or literal need not be to place these beyond the pale of reason and truth, and one may be ultimately less than sympathetic to regarding anyone as a (rationally) educated person who lacks either substantial acquaintance with literature of this kind and/or the intellectual resources to appreciate and comprehend the normative, spiritual and metaphysical issues that it raises. In this regard, it may also be that analytical philosophy has yet to catch up with such other disciplines as anthropology, comparative mythology, textual criticism and psychoanalytic theory with respect to serious engagement with the hermeneutics of religious discourse (though, for some timely work in this direction, see Schilbrack, 2002).

At all events, this is not to claim in the manner of some con-temporary communitarians that Catholic Christian or other faith communities need to be educated in religious 'narratives' in order to be confirmed in their own cultural identity. The point is rather that hardly anyone could count as educated in the absence of some informed appreciation and understanding (in more than a superficial cultural studies way) of the literature of Christianity, Islam, Hinduism and other great faiths. But, in this light, *all* universities worth their salt – not just religious or Christian universities – would have to be places in which Christian and other scriptures are taken seriously as significant contributions to the larger educated conversation of humankind with regard to those profound normative and metaphysical questions of divine providence and human purpose that continue to resist capture in the statistical or other nets of natural or social science.

References

Conroy, J. (2001) 'A Very Scottish Affair: Catholic Education and the State', *Oxford Review of Education*, 27, 4, pp. 543–558.

Flew, A. (1966) *God and Philosophy*, London, Hutchinson.

Graham, G. (1999) *Universities: The Recovery of an Idea*, Aberdeen, Kings College, University of Aberdeen.

Gribble, J. (ed.) (1967) *Matthew Arnold*, London, Collier Macmillan.

Haldane, J. J. (2000) 'The Value of a University', in G. Kirk (ed.), *Scottish Universities in the New Millennium*, Edinburgh, Edinburgh University School of Education, pp. 21–26.

Halstead, M. (1995) 'Voluntary Apartheid? Problems of Schooling for Religious and Other Minorities in Democratic Societies', *Journal of Philosophy of Education*, 29, 2, pp. 257–272.

Hirst, P. H. (1974) 'Liberal Education and the Nature of Knowledge', in P. H. Hirst, *Knowledge and the Curriculum*, London, Routledge and Kegan Paul, pp. 30–53.

Lyotard, J.-F. (1984) *The Post-Modern Condition: A Report on Knowledge*, trans. G. Bennington and B. Massumi, Manchester, Manchester University Press.

MacIntyre, A. C. (1981) *After Virtue*, Notre Dame, IN, University of Notre Dame Press.

MacIntyre, A. C. (1987) 'The Idea of an Educated Public', in G. Haydon (ed.), *Education and Values: The Richard Peters Lectures*, London, Institute of Education, University of London, pp. 15–36.

MacIntyre, A. C. (1999) 'How to Appear Virtuous Without Actually Being So', in J. M. Halstead and T. H. McLaughlin (eds), *Education in Morality*, London, Routledge, pp. 118–131.

MacIntyre, A. C. (2001) 'Catholic Universities: Dangers, Hopes, Choices', in R. E. Sullivan (ed.), *Higher Learning and Catholic Traditions*, Notre Dame, IN, University of Notre Dame Press, pp. 1–21.

Maskell, D. and I. Robinson (2001) *The New Idea of the University*, London, Haven Books.

Mill, J. S. (1859) 'On Liberty', in M. Warnock (ed.) (1970), *Utilitarianism*, London, Collins, pp. 126–250.

Newman, J. H. (1976) *The Idea of a University*, Oxford, Oxford University Press.

Phillips, D. Z. (1970a) *Faith and Philosophical Enquiry*, London, Routledge and Kegan Paul.

Phillips, D. Z. (1970b) *Death and Immortality*, London, Macmillan.

Phillips, D. Z. (1976) *Religion without Explanation*, Oxford, Blackwell.

Phillips, D. Z. (1993) *Wittgenstein and Religion*, London, Macmillan.

Schilbrack, K. (ed.) (2002) *Thinking Through Myths: Philosophical Perspectives*, London and New York, Routledge.

Wittgenstein, L. (1953) *Philosophical Investigations*, Oxford, Blackwell.

Chapter Thirteen

Science in a Christian University

R. J. Berry

The means by which we live have outdistanced the ends for which we live. Our scientific power has out-run our spiritual power. We have guided missiles and misguided men. (Martin Luther King, 1963)

Science is 'knowledge ascertained by observation and experiment, critically tested, systematised and brought under general principles'. For the purpose of this chapter, I define the sciences as all subjects outside the humanities. This should not be taken to imply over-bearing arrogance or an attempted takeover on my part; the distinction does not mean that the sciences necessarily occupy a lesser or a greater part of human intellectual involvement, but it emphasises that science and scientists are concerned with 'the way the world is' (the title of John Polkinghorne's first book, published in 1983, exploring the relationship between science and religion) rather than the way we would like or expect it to be. This imposes a primary rigour and robustness on science, much tighter than on the humanities.

To extreme positivists the discipline of 'the way the world is' excludes the possibility of science encompassing any values or beliefs. There are still scientists who hold this view. A distinguished current proponent is Lewis Wolpert – see his *The Unnatural Nature of Science,* 1992. Wolpert quotes Tolstoy's assertion that science does not tell us how to live; it has nothing to contribute on moral issues. He draws a firm boundary around science, defining it as an experimental methodology: 'It is the politicians, lawyers, philosophers and finally all citizens who have to decide what society we will live in.' But the main repository of such views is among humanists. This had led some scholars to be so impressed with the apparent objectivity and power of the scientific method that they have disparaged the credibility of (particularly) theology to a point where it is hardly worth bothering to affirm or refute its claims. The propaganda of crusaders like Peter Atkins or Richard Dawkins has encouraged this timidity. For example, Atkins has written, 'I think religion kills. And where it doesn't kill, it stifles. Religion scorns the human intellect by saying that the human brain is simply too puny to understand. In contrast, science enables one to liberate oneself; it liberates the aspirations of humanity. ... [Science] gives people answers that are much more reliable, much more plausible than the obscure arguments that religion provides. ... Science can show that there is not a purpose in the universe, and is not going to waste its time worrying about it' (in Stannard, 1996, pp. 167–168).

The inadequacy of the attacks by Atkins, Dawkins and their ilk can be fully dealt with by traditional Christian apologetics (e.g. Ward, 1996), but the debates have been thoroughly muddied from the Christian side by equating normal science with atheism. The most obvious and well-known example of this is the claim that evolution is 'only' a hypothesis and should be taught alongside (and given 'equal time') with other hypotheses; I return to this below. A more insidious charge is that science is pure naturalism and that scientists ignore any evidence that does not fit their preconceptions. It is argued that there are many examples of 'design' (even 'intelligent' design) in nature which undercut the common 'neo-Darwinian' picture of the world and open the way to 'other' explanations, if only the fossilised mind-set of conventional scientists would allow it. Such arguments have been aggressively and forensically developed by University of California lawyer Phillip Johnson (1991, 1995) and mathematician and philosopher William Dembski (1998; Behe, Dembski and Meyer, 2000). They have been answered (at least as forcefully) by Miller (1999) and Pennock (1999), and in dialogue with their proponents in Johnson et al. (1999) and Carlson (2000).

This is not the place to set out the arguments and counter-arguments that are – and have been – employed by scientists and religious people (mainly although not entirely Christians); there are many excellent Christian books examining and probing the interface between science and faith (e.g. Russell, 1985; Brooke, 1991; Houghton, 1995; Barbour, 1998, 2000; Jeeves and Berry, 1998; Alexander, 2001). The point is that there is a complex of issues: scientists attacking superstition (often portrayed as religion); Christians attacking science for misunderstanding and burying their interpretations; the 'secular' world rejecting religion when faced with scientific 'facts'; and a postmodernist espousal of 'spirituality' at the expense of any historical beliefs in revelation of the divine. How should a Christian university approach this morass, both in preparing students for life after university and in witnessing to the Christian faith?

Science and Christianity

There is no evil in the atom; only in men's souls. (Adlai Stevenson, 1952)

The first criterion of any reputable university must surely be a search for and defence of truth at all levels and in all spheres. This does not mean overall comprehensiveness (there is no reason to expect law students to learn physiology or medical students ship–design), but it does imply that any subjects taught should be treated rigorously, including those at the borders of disciplines. Academic biology received a strong fillip in British universities through the requirement for medical students to be taught botany because they needed to identify plants from which many medicines were extracted. It was not necessary to produce professional botanists, but it would clearly have been disastrous for doctors to mis–classify their source of drugs.

An essential component of truth is accurate knowledge. There are such things as universal facts or laws. The Second Law of Thermo-dynamics, the genetic code, the movement of a particular tectonic plate, or the site of the South Pole do not depend on religion, race or philosophy. As Galileo allegedly said when forced by the Inquisition to recant his belief that the earth was not immoveable (as the Psalmist seemed to assert), 'but it does move'. The acceptance of an earth that moves round the sun owes more to the telescope than to theology.

This could mean a never-ending adjustment of theology as science advances, but the situation is much simplified by the recognition that there are only three main contact points between science and religion (Dixon, 1953):

a. the question of *origins,* of the physical and biological worlds;
b. the question of *miracles*; and
c. the nature of *human-ness.*

Unsurprisingly all three have given and continue to give rise to controversy, within both the scientific and religious communities as well as between them. Before examining them in detail, five common errors need to be pointed out:

1. Time-honoured *interpretations* should not determine the likelihood of correctness. Traditional Jewish and Christian datings of the date of creation centred around 6000 years ago, long before Archbishop Ussher calculated 4004 BC: Orthodox Jewry placed it at 3671 BC, Theophilus of Antioch at 5529 BC, and the Venerable Bede at 3952 BC. Radiometric dates suggests a date of around 4.7 billion years ago. There are different implications arising from whether the earth is 'young' (which would give little time for change since its formation) or 'old', but the Bible is agnostic about its age. Expositors too often add to the Bible to support their beliefs: Galileo was persecuted on the grounds that the sun daily crosses the heavens (Ps. 19:6), that 'the earth is established immovably' (Pss. 93:1, 96:10) and 'fixed on its foundation' (Ps. 104:5). But these texts can be regarded as reflecting the reliability of God, not the details of astronomy; 'the Bible teaches us how to go to heaven, not how the heavens go' (Galilei Galileo in a letter to the Grand Duchess Christina, 1615).

Nowhere does the Bible state that true human-ness is determined at conception; the assumption that 'life begins at conception' is derived from a papal bull of 1869 (*Apostolicae Sedis*) because it was an implication of the 'immaculate conception of the Virgin Mary', not because of Bible texts. Prior to this, the 'Christian tradition' as expressed in both canon and common law was that killing a foetus in the first two or three months of gestation was wrong but not punishable as murder (Dunstan, 1984). 'Human-ness' is described in the Bible as being 'in God's image'. Whatever this is, it is certainly not a genetical or anatomical trait. Nowhere are we told if God's image is conferred (or implanted) at conception or at some other time.

2. Biblical language is not so much *un*-scientific as *non*-scientific; it describes phenomena but does not explain them. We do much the same: we happily talk about the sun or moon 'rising' or 'setting' because that is what we see; it would be pedantically odd (and cumbersome) to say that the sun is visible (or not) from our personal vantage point because of the rotation of the earth. The Bible very rarely gives a reason for the phenomena it describes. Exodus 14:21 tells us that 'the Lord

drove the sea away with a strong east wind all night long, and turned the seabed into dry land', thus allowing the Israelites to cross the R(e)ed Sea. The key point here is the timing, not the mechanism: the Israelites crossed safely while the pursuing Egyptians were drowned in the returning waters. John 9:6 tells us that Jesus 'spat on the ground and made a paste with spittle which he spread on the [blind] man's eyes'. Here again we are told of mechanism, in this case an element in the curing of blindness.

3. In general, the Scriptures are concerned with answering 'why' questions while science is about 'how' questions – what causes plants to grow, animals to mate, minerals to form, and so on. The success of science in its own sphere leads on to a false assumption: that if we know one cause of an event, we know everything about that event. This is wrong. For example, we can describe a painting entirely in terms of the distribution of molecules in two-dimensional space. If we knew enough about pigment chemistry, we could give a complete description of the picture in chemical terms. But we can also give a complete description of the same picture in terms of its design and composition, telling why the artist created as he did. Both descriptions refer to the same physical object, yet they do not contradict at all. It is obviously inadequate to describe the picture as nothing but a collection of spatially ordered chemicals; it is equally untrue to assert that it is nothing but an artistic design. The picture has more than one 'cause'; its 'scientific' and 'artistic' explanations can be described as complementary, building on the four 'causes' distinguished by Aristotle in the *Metaphysics* and extended by Niels Bohr from the paradox that electrons can behave – or be described – as either particles or waves to 'situations analysable by alternative conceptual systems'.

4. Science is often accused as being reductionist, i.e., asserting that any process can be wholly explained in terms of its simplest components. This is over-simplistic. It is true that scientific experimentation involves choosing particular variables to study under different conditions, and by implication, ignoring other factors as irrelevant. The correct choice of relevant factors is a mark of a good scientist. But this is operational reductionism and should be distinguished from doctrinaire or ontological reductionism, which is a sort of extreme Occam's razor. Doctrinaire reductionism insists that the most basic cause is the only

one worth considering, and thus ignores threshold phenomena, synergism, emergent properties, etc. Operational reductionism is a necessary part of the practice of science; ontological reductionism is mere assumption. Whilst it is true that many scientists over-focus on their particular experiment or expertise, it is false to claim that science demands or expects that all interactions and effects arising from complexity are unimportant epiphenomena. It could – and perhaps should – be the aim of a sound education to equip scientists and non-scientists alike to appreciate the implications and context of any processes that they study.

5. God (or, at least, supernatural intervention) is the traditional explanation for any unexplained event. G. M. Trevelyan wrote about the pre-modern age:

> The fields around town and hamlet were filled, as soon as the day-labourers had left them, by goblins and will-o'-the-wisps; and the woods, as soon as the forester had closed the door of his hut, became the haunt of fairies; the ghosts could be heard gibbering all night under the yew-tree of the churchyard; the witch, a well-known figure in the village, was in the pay of lovers whose mistresses were hard to win, and of gentleman-farmers whose cattle had sickened. If a criminal was detected and punished, the astonishing event was set down as God's revenge against murder; if a dry summer threatened the harvest, the parson was expected to draw down rain by prayer. The charms that ward off disease, the stars of birth that rule fortune, the comet that foretold the wars in Germany, the mystic laws that govern the fall of the dice, were the common interest of ordinary men and women. In a soil that imagination had so prepared, poetry and Puritanism were likely to flourish loftily among lofty men, basely among the base. The better kind of men were full of ardour, fancy and reverence. The ignoble were superstitious, ignorant and coarse. The world was still a mystery, of which the wonder was not dispelled in foolish minds by a daily stream of facts and cheap explanations.
>
> (Trevelyan, 1938, pp. 53–54)

Science has demolished this: but it has meant that as we have learnt more and more about the causes of disease, of climatic fluctuations, of the determinants of crop productivity, the space for God has been progressively reduced. The longer we persist in using God as an explanation for our diminishing ignorance (a 'God of the gaps' in Charles Coulson's evocative phrase: Coulson, 1955), the smaller our God becomes. Yet a 'God of the gaps' remains one of the commonest apologetics for God: it is used to explain holes in the fossil record and human creativity; for those who argue in this way, such a God is sited in Heisenberg's uncertainty principle, quantum physics or chaos theory. We have to recognise that all these rationalisations about God's relationship to his creation are dangerous and almost certainly mistaken; they make theology subservient to scientific understanding. Newton and Lord Kelvin argued that the earth was only a few thousand years old, basing themselves on inadequate experiments to support their interpretation of the Bible. They were wrong; advances in science have forced a change in understanding of the Bible but have not in any way invalidated the Bible itself. The aim of science is to find out how God's world works; Christians who are scientists need to explore how to understand God's work in his world. For the Christian, there are many signs of God in the world (e.g. Ps. 19:1; Is. 40:25, 26; Mk. 4:41; Acts 14:17; Rom. 1:20), but these are not proofs of his existence as was once believed (most notoriously by Archdeacon Paley).[1]

Contact points

Art is myself; science is ourselves. (Claude Bernard, 1865)

Dixon's three contact points between science and Christianity are not part of science proper. An ability to deal with them should be in the armoury of every mature Christian, but they do not belong to a science course *sensu stricto*. Questions raised by them often occur to science students and need considered answers, but just as scientists have to learn to separate results (or data) from discussion (or interpretation), students have to recognise a clear distinction between the study of the natural world (which is science) and its implications (which is technology or philosophy – or theology).

In a much quoted paper, 'Is the scientific paper a fraud?', Peter Medawar (Edge, 1964) pointed out that the formal presentation of scientific results is almost always very different to the process of thought and experiment that gives rise to the work described in the scientific paper. This does not mean that it is fraudulent, but recognises the need to formulate the work in a way that can contribute to the advancement or challenging of the discipline to which it refers. The disadvantage, as Medawar pointed out, is that this procedure tends to obscure the mistakes and blind alleys that are inseparable from the practice of science and hence present an apparently faultless face. The distinctiveness of science – and this is where it differs and arguably has the advantage over scholarship in the humanities – is that it has an inbuilt monitor and check on its progress. Scientific findings are subject to experimental check and verification (or not). This characteristic has to be born in mind when exploring the implications of science for theology – which I have narrowed down to Dixon's three 'contact points'.

1. *Origins*. There is general agreement that the universe had a beginning, a 'Big Bang'. This is not affected by the argument of Stephen Hawking that there may not have been a simple beginning point in time (a singularity) (Wilkinson, 1993). More contentious is the idea that change has happened since that beginning. Evolution is a concept that divides conservative Christians; indeed denial of evolution is sometimes a requirement for teachers in colleges with an explicitly Christian basis. It is also characteristic of many Islamic institutions. Four points can be made:

a.   The Bible nowhere excludes evolution. Anti-evolutionists support their beliefs by their interpretation of (particularly) Genesis 1, especially that the 'days' of creation represent discrete acts of God rather than markers in a progression. This is by no means the only legitimate understanding: the 'day' framework may mark literal 24-hour days, but it could also describe long periods of time, stages of revelation or a literary device (Blocher, 1984). Indeed – and in contrast to the 24-hour day interpretation – the Bible emphasises change: from chaos to order, garden to city, sin to salvation, etc. It is important to recognise the importance of interpretation in understanding God's revelation in the Bible. The claim that we should (or ought) not *interpret* the 'plain message' of Scripture is unhelpful and mischievous.

b.   Charles Darwin's main achievement was in putting forward a mechanism by which adaptive evolution could take place. Many conservative Christians embraced Darwin's ideas fairly soon after the publication of the *Origin of Species* (in 1859) because they saw natural selection as God's providence in action (Livingstone, 1987). Darwinism was fairly generally accepted within a generation. These earlier debates have no intellectual link to modern-day creationism, which is largely derived from the imaginative expositions of an Adventist, George McCready Price (Numbers, 1992). Indeed, it is worth noting that several of the authors of the *Fundamentals* series in the early twentieth century, which gave rise eponymously to biblical fundamentalism, were happy to accept Darwinian evolution. B. B. Warfield, the father of biblical inerrancy, wrote that evolution could supply a tenable 'theory of the method of divine providence in the creation of mankind' and that Calvin's doctrine of the creation 'including the origination of all forms of life, vegetable and animal alike, including doubtless the bodily form of man [was] ... a very pure evolutionary scheme' (Noll and Livingstone, 2000).

c.   It is often claimed by creationists that more and more scientists are having 'doubts' about evolution. This is false. There are legitimate scientific debates about various aspects of evolutionary mechanism (e.g. punctuationalism, causes of extinction, developmental co-adaptation, etc.) but there is a near unanimous acceptance that evolution has occurred and a wide agreement about the mechanisms by which it has taken place. The dissentients to this consensus include a few philosophers but mostly they are those with religious objections. In fact, the real objections are not to biological evolution as such, but to unjustified extrapolations of it giving apparent licence for racism, communism, capitalism, eugenics, sexual excess, and so on – implications which owe more to the Social Darwinism of Herbert Spencer than to Darwin himself (Ruse, 1999, 2001). In a US Federal Court case brought to challenge an Arkansas Law that evolutionary science and creation science were valid alternatives, Judge William Overton ruled that science involves naturalness, tentativeness, testability and falsifiabilty, and that 'creation science' wholly fails to meet these criteria, since it served only to advance religion (La Follette, 1983).

d.   Modern creationism is deist and unitarian (Moore, 1889), con-centrating on the creating work of God and largely ignoring the redeeming and upholding work of Christ and the Holy Spirit (Col. 1:16, 20; Heb. 1:2, 3; Rev. 4:11). It is therefore sub-Christian; it is also pastorally and evangelistically problematic because it presents evolution as opposed to God's work, rather than as a legitimate complement.

2. *Miracles.* Rather like evolution, miracles were largely unquestioned until the eighteenth century. There were, of course, sceptics, but systematic doubts only began to surface with the modern rise of cosmological and physical science and the notion of the world as a gigantic machine governed by 'laws of nature' as uncovered by scientists like Newton and Descartes. These 'laws' were seen to describe and limit the world, relegating God to no more than a first cause, a creator who left his creation to run along the lines he had laid down at the beginning. Such a creator would be wholly transcendent and unable to affect the workings of the world except by intervening or suspending the laws he had set in place.

In 1748 David Hume (in)famously defined a miracle as 'a violation of the laws of nature', adding 'and as a firm and unalterable experience has established these laws, the proof against a miracle, from the nature of the fact, is as entire as any argument from experience can possibly be imagined.' Although this argument is frequently repeated, it is, in fact, circular. C. S. Lewis (1947, p. 106) is only one of many who has pointed this out: 'Of course we must agree with Hume if there is absolute "uniform experience" against miracles, if in other words they have never happened, why then they never have. Unfortunately we know the experience against them to be uniform only if we know that all the reports of them are false. And we can know the reports to be false only if we know already that miracles have never occurred.'

Science can neither prove nor disprove the occurrence of miracles. It is commonly and often explicitly assumed that science excludes miracles by its demonstration of a deterministic network of cause and effect, leaving 'no room' for God. Attempts to find ways in which God could operate in such a world are all variations of seeking gaps in a causal nexus. It needs emphasising and reiterating that to claim the God is constrained or limited by physical laws is to reduce him to a deist machine-minder. Polkinghorne (1983, p. 55) states the situation clearly:

The problem of miracles is the problem of finding that wider framework in which they can find a coherent place. This is demanded not by science but by theology itself. 'Intervention' is not a word that one can properly use of God in any fitful or *tour de force* sense. His relationship to his creation must be faithful and consistent if it is to be in accord with his eternal nature.

Polkinghorne points out the irony that 'in an earlier age, the miracles would have been one of the strongest weapons in the armoury of apologetic. A man who did such things must at the very least have the power of God in him. ... For us today, by one of the twists that make up intellectual history, miracles are rather an embarrassment. We are so impressed by the regularity of the world that any story which is full of strange happenings acquires an air of fairy-tale and invention.'

New Testament miracles are 'unusual events which are wonders due to God's power, intended as signs' (Berry, 1986). They are a necessary but unpredictable consequence of a God who holds the world in being. Apparent miracles need to be investigated with the same objectivity and rigour as any scientific study. Those who deny the possibility of miracles are exercising their own brand of faith. Miracles are not intrinsically impossible or intellectually unbelievable; acceptance of their existence does not necessarily involve credulity, but it does involve recognising that science has limits.

3. *The nature of human-ness.* As already noted, the biblical distinction between human beings and all other living things is that only the former possess ('being in') God's image (Gen. 1:26–27). The full meaning of this has been long debated. Clearly it refers to characteristics peculiar to God and equally clearly these cannot be tangible, i.e. 'God's image' does not indicate anatomical, physiological or genetic traits.

Secondly, the Bible portrays Adam as a Neolithic farmer, settled in a locality with sons who were agriculturalists and cared for domesticated animals, and at a time when urbanisation and metalworking were beginning (Gen. 4:17, 22). This context can obviously be treated in various ways, but at face value it implies that Adam lived ten to twenty thousand years ago. Taken together with the suggestion in Gen. 2:7 that the creation of humankind was a two-stage process, it is possible that the original humans in the fullest sense (they have been called *Homo divinus* as opposed to *Homo sapiens*) might have been created late in historical time, with the *imago* being conferred by the creator on all members of the species *H. sapiens* alive at the time.

Such an interpretation is speculative but not far-fetched. It is attractive because it makes sense of biblical anthropology. For example, many references to human death must refer to spiritual death (= separation from God) rather than the end of physical life (e.g. Paul writing to living Ephesians, 'You once were dead . . . but God has brought us to life', Eph. 2 cf. Jn. 3:3–6). It also provides a way of looking at the Fall story in Genesis 3 as essentially a break in relationships – with God, self, neighbour and the rest of creation – as a result of disobedience, symbolised by eating a forbidden fruit but derived from failure to observe the first divine command to care and nurture creation (Gen. 1:26; 2:15). Rom. 8:19–22 (the most explicit New Testament reference to the Fall) can be seen as describing the consequences of falling short in our role as creation-carers.

Such an interpretation restores humankind to its role as specially created beings responsible to God whilst not excluding (or contradicting) the genetic and fossil evidence that we are fairly closely related to chimpanzees. It thus avoids the difficulties of accepting that we are nothing but advanced apes on the 'way up' or of denying the relevance of our animal ancestry. It is possible to be both orthodox believers and rigorous scientists.

Conflict of science and Christianity

The aim of science is not to open the door to infinite wisdom, but to set a limit to infinite error. (Bertolt Brecht, 1939)

Religion is always going to be challenged by new discoveries or interpretations. This does not mean that traditional beliefs face constant re-adjustment: questioning may strengthen an existing understanding just as science is based upon the continual testing of existing ideas. There need not be a permanent war between science and faith if science is seen as an endeavour to discover truths about the world as opposed to an objective stick to batter supernatural fantasy.[2] I have dwelt on the 'contact points' between science and Christianity to emphasise that orthodox faith need not fear modern science. However, it is important that fora exist for examining apparent conflicts.

Are Christian universities the proper fora for such examinations? The answer to this question is not straightforward. The concept of a 'Christian' university implies a determination or commitment to protect 'Christianity'. Whilst this is fine in principle, in practice it may lead to a defence of particular interpretations or authority, such as creationism or traditional gender roles or specific sexual behaviours. A university in the modern sense involves buildings, hierarchy, codes of practice, competition for students and finance: an edifice far removed from the debating arenas of ancient Greece, or even the hostels where scholars taught in medieval times and which evolved into Cambridge and Oxford Universities. This does not mean that modern universities cannot (or should not) sponsor debate or enquiry on science-faith contact points, but it recognises that such enquiries are not central or even necessary to such an institution. Although it is far remote from modern academia, Paul's exposition in Athens of God's work and the subsequent debates is the sort of occasion where 'contact points' can be explored.

Current debates on contact points are probably most commonly on ethical issues arising from the underlying contact points – on life issues, nuclear energy, global warming, and so on. They are often sponsored or fostered by pressure groups. Universities or learned societies are usually more profitable arenas for such debates than advocacy by dedicated protagonists, because they can provide a less committed and hence more objective context. It is important that universities take part and encourage interactions of this nature, but it has to be recognised that they are secondary to their main purpose – to gather scholars and encourage research, and to communicate knowledge.

Science, scientists and a Christian university

Science must begin with myths, and with the criticism of myths. (Karl Popper, 1957)

Some years ago, I edited a series of essays by senior scientists who were committed Christians (Berry, 1991). I invited 'senior scientists' because

I wanted the contributors to be people who had reflected on and faced the challenges of the faith-science interface. My only other criterion was to involve people from as many different disciplines as possible. I asked the authors to describe what difference their faith made to their science and their science to their faith. The contributions varied considerably – some were largely apologetic, some autobiographical. But every writer emphasised the universality of science, and most of them wrote how important it had been for them to escape the confining influence of particular Christian interpretations – usually that of a creationism ruled by biblical literalism.

There is always a risk for a scholar in any discipline to become isolated from criticism and intellectual stimulus. It is particularly dangerous for a scientist because his or her work needs to be divorced as far as possible from local, cultural or religious bias. Of course this is a counsel of perfection: it is impossible to isolate oneself completely from history or current developments. But it is important to insist that there is no such thing as Hindu, Islamic, Buddhist or Christian science; nor is there English, American, Argentinean or Indonesian science. Science can – or should be – practised anywhere without difference in its outcome. There is, of course, good science and bad science, but this difference is not dependent on race or religion (Poole, 1995).

However, a factor which affects Christian scholars in all disciplines is the calling to be salt, yeast, lights in the places they are put. Forty per cent of randomly-selected senior US scientists claim to believe in a personal God (remarkably, an incidence unchanged in surveys carried out in 1916 and 1996; the chief difference between the two surveys was that there was a greater proportion of believing biologists and correspondingly less of believing physicists in 1996 than in 1916) (Larson and Witham, 1997). There are no comparable figures for the UK, although it seems likely that the proportion of believers would be less. Yet the influence of Christians in government and academia is generally agreed to be considerably greater in Britain than in North America, despite the many 'Christian universities' in the latter. It is difficult to quantify this effect, but it can be seen as an expected effect of Christians developing their professional expertise in the 'real world' and of the importance of a faith matured by debate over hard and changing questions, rather than defending inalienable interpretations – not faith – handed down from previous apologists. There are technical questions for Christians recognising and presenting issues of science, its data and values in educational settings (Poole, 1995), but these are subsidiary and should remain subordinate to reading and co-relating *both* God's book of words and God's book of works.

On the flyleaf of the *Origin of Species,* Darwin cited from Francis Bacon's *Advancement of Learning* (1605) the advice that no one should think or maintain that it is possible to 'search too far or be too well studied in the book of God's word, or in the book of God's works', but rather 'let all endeavour an endless proficience in both'. Scholars argue whether this was really Darwin's belief or merely a sop to his critics, but it is fair to assume that he did not dissent too radically from Bacon. We find it much easier to read about God in the Bible than in creation, but he is the author of both. Reading one book to the exclusion of the other will almost certainly cause distortion in understanding. We need institutions where each book is studied in detail. We also need mechanisms to relate them together so that science can inform Bible understanding and Christian perception can challenge scientific triumphalism. Whether these mechanisms are best nurtured within or outside a 'Christian university' is a pragmatic not a doctrinal question. But Christians need to nurture them, because no one else will.

References

Alexander, D. (2001) *Rebuilding the Matrix,* Oxford, Lion.

Barbour, I. G. (1998) *Religion and Science: Historical and Contemporary Issues,* London, SCM.

Barbour, I. G. (2000) *When Science Meets Religion,* London, SPCK.

Behe, M. J., Dembski, W. A. and S. C. Meyer (2000) *Science and Evidence for Design in the Universe,* San Francisco, CA, Ignatius Press.

Berry, R. J. (1986) 'What to Believe about Miracles', *Nature,* 322, pp. 321–322.

Berry, R. J. (ed.) (1991) *Real Science, Real Faith,* Eastbourne, Monarch.

Blocher, H. (1984) *In the Beginning,* Leicester, IVP.

Brooke, J. H. (1991), *Science and Religion,* Cambridge, Cambridge University Press.

Carlson, R. F. (ed.) (2000) *Science and Christianity: Four Views,* Downer's Grove, IL, IVP.

Coulson, C. A. (1955) *Science and Christian Belief,* Oxford, Oxford University Press.

Dembski, W. A. (1998) *The Design Inference,* Cambridge, Cambridge University Press.

Dixon, M. (1953) *Science and Irreligion,* London, CPAS.

Dunstan, G. R. (1984) 'The Moral Status of the Human Embryo: A Tradition Recalled', *Journal of Medical Ethics,* 10, pp. 38–44.

Edge, D. O. (ed.) (1964) *Experiment,* London, BBC Publications.

Houghton, J. T. (1995) *The Search for God: Can Science Help?* Oxford, Lion.

Jeeves, M. A. and R. J. Berry (1998) *Science, Life and Christian Belief,* Grand Rapids, MI, Baker Books.

Johnson, P. E. (1991) *Darwin on Trial*, Washington, DC, Regnery Gateway.

Johnson, P. E. (1995) *Defeating Darwinism*, Downer's Grove, IL, IVP.

Johnson, P. E., Lamoureux, D. O. *et al.* (1999) *Darwinism Defeated*, Vancouver, Regent College.

La Follette, M. C. (ed.) (1983) *Creationism, Science and the Law*, Cambridge, MA, MIT Press.

Larson, E. J. and L. Witham (1997) 'Scientists are still Keeping the Faith', *Nature*, 386, pp. 437–438.

Lewis, C. S. (1947) *Miracles*, London, Geoffrey Bles.

Livingstone, D. N. (1987) *Darwin's Forgotten Defenders*, Grand Rapids, MI, Eerdmans.

Miller, K. R. (1999) *Finding Darwin's God*, New York, HarperCollins.

Moore, A. (1889) 'The Christian Doctrine of God', in C. Gore (ed.), *Lux Mundi*, London, John Murray, pp. 57–109.

Noll, M. A. and D. N. Livingstone (eds) (2000) *B. B. Warfield: Evolution, Science and Scripture*, Grand Rapids, MI, Baker Books.

Numbers, R. L. (1992) *The Creationists*, New York, Knopf.

Packer, J. I. (1958) *'Fundamentalism' and the Word of God*, London, Inter-Varsity Fellowship.

Pennock, R. T. (1999) *Tower of Babel*, Cambridge, MA, MIT Press.

Polkinghorne, J. C. (1983) *The Way the World Is*, London, SPCK.

Polkinghorne, J. C. (1988) *Science and Creation*, London, SPCK.

Poole, M. W. (1995) *Beliefs and Values in Science Education*, Buckingham, Open University Press.

Ruse, M. (1999) *Mystery of Mysteries: Is Evolution a Social Construct?* Cambridge, MA, Harvard University Press.

Ruse, M. (2001) *Can a Darwinian be a Christian?* Cambridge, Cambridge University Press.

Russell, C. A. (1985) *Cross-Currents*, Leicester, IVP.

Stannard, R. (1996) *Science and Wonders*, London, Faber & Faber.

Trevelyan, G. M. (1938) *England under the Stuarts*, London, Methuen.

Ward, J. F. K. (1996) *God, Chance and Necessity*, Oxford, Oneworld.

Wilkinson, D. (1993) *God, the Big Bang and Stephen Hawking*, Crowborough, Monarch.

Wolpert, L. (1992) *The Unnatural Nature of Science*, Faber & Faber.

Chapter Fourteen

The Idea of Politics in a Christian University

Nicholas Rengger

In the late 1930s C. S. Lewis read a paper to an Oxford religious society entitled 'Christianity and Literature'.[1] At the opening of the paper, he confessed to having been tempted to refuse the opportunity to present it, since he did not very well understand what it was about. His central point was that, although of course there is 'Christian literature', i.e. literature that represents biblical or hagiological scenes and even literature written by Christians for Christians, in as much as it is *literature*, it would have to conform to the same standards as other literature; as he puts it, 'whatever [Christian literature] chose to do would have to be done by the means common to all literature; it could succeed or fail only by the same excellencies and the same faults as all literature.'[2] Essentially, in this essay, I want to agree with Lewis but apply his reasoning not to literature but to politics considered as an academic activity and to the role that universities play in educating anyone, whatever their provenance – both the student and the university.

This being so, you will realise quickly enough that I am going to argue that, properly understood, the idea of politics in a Christian university is no different to the idea of politics in any other university. The key points, of course, are both what I understand the academic activity of studying politics to involve and what kind of education I assume a university has to offer and I shall get to these points in due course. First, however, I want to look at an alterative position, which would argue that, in contrast, studying politics in a (truly) Christian university is a very different kind of activity from studying it in a secular one.

The 'radical otherness' of the study of politics in a Christian university

These arguments have appeared in a variety of contexts over the last few years and have been expressed by some leading contemporary theologians.[3] John Milbank, for example, has argued both that theology needs to regain the position it has lost within both the university and the wider world and also, at least by implication, that in a Christian university – if one could be found – all subjects would be constituted differently from their secular equivalents.[4] And similar positions have been advocated both by other theologians in 'radical orthodoxy'[5] and others such as Gavin D'Costa.

However, on this occasion I am going to concentrate on the presentation of this view from a rather different theological direction, to wit the version of it one finds in Stanley Hauerwas and in this context a caveat is appropriate first. This is simply to point out that, despite an astonishingly large and wide-ranging corpus, Hauerwas nowhere discusses the *study* of politics (as opposed to its character) in any detail. Indeed, his remarks about the study of politics are mainly located in the interstices of more general discussions chiefly about its character. However, since one of those discussions is the character and flaws of the modern liberal university *in connection with* politics, this is doubly helpful in our current context. A second point is to emphasise, in the light of the above, that my interpretation is inevitably something of a palimpsest. Nonetheless, all this having been said, it seems to me that he expresses with great clarity and commendable honesty a viewpoint that suggests that a genuinely Christian university would do *all* things differently – and that this would of course include the study of politics as an academic activity.

Let me start then with some remarks he makes in the opening essay of his wonderfully (and characteristically) polemical *Despatches from the Front*.[6] In this essay he makes a distinction between two types of politics. The first type, to which he tells us he subscribes himself, 'names those practices necessary over time for a community of friends to exist'. He continues that, as a result of this, 'non-violence is not only the necessary prerequisite for such politics but the creation of non-violent community is the means and end of all politics.' The other type of politics he refers to he describes as that associated with the nation state and adds that this is the sort 'that is studied by most political science departments'. This type, he says, 'I see no good reason to call politics except in the most degraded sense.'[7]

This distinction is then amplified by discussion of the university that, he suggests, naturally mirrors the kinds of 'politics' – and indeed other activities – typical of the wider society of which it is a part. For Hauerwas, the university 'serves the wider liberal polity through the suppression of conflict' essentially through the presentation of 'choice' for students, but the choice is that of a consumer not a real learner; 'students', he suggests, 'are ... inscribed into capitalist practices in which they are taught that choosing between ideas is like choosing between a Sony or a Panasonic.'[8] This is particularly true, he thinks, in those areas where he teaches, i.e. ethics and religion. The biggest problem of all, he thinks, is that universities have lost any sense of who their constituency is or might be, and the result is the increasing 'professionalisation' of the university and the increasing lack of contact between specialised academic disciplines and 'life' or the world outside the academy. For Hauerwas, the root problem is a loss of legitimacy and authority. Academics should want to change people's lives – and yet in the modern secular world no one has given them the authority to do this, and so they abdicate the one thing that would make their teaching truly significant for them and for those they teach. Significantly (for my later argument, that is), Hauerwas predicates this claim on the assumption that the task of the university has something to do with the formation of people who want to know their world more truthfully. More of this in a moment.

As a deliberate contrast to this kind of university, Hauerwas tells us, chapter three of his book is a version of a commencement address he gave at Goschen College, a college sponsored by the Mennonite Church. Here, as he puts it in that chapter, 'political science is not taught at Goschen the way it is taught at Duke [where Hauerwas teaches] since political science at Goschen College is not at the service of nation-state ideologies.' Repeating one of his earlier points, he then goes on,

> I knew, for example, that when I spoke at this assembly there would not be
> an American flag present ... the power of the flag is, by necessity, violent
> ... because there is no flag here Goschen college is potentially a more
> truthful and thus academically more interesting, educational institution

than those that serve such flags ... that is why you know that there is no such thing as a "liberal arts education" in which knowledge is an end in itself. Rather, you know that you have been educated in an institution that constantly reminds you that any truth which is neither based on, nor serves the practice of reconciliation, and thus peace, cannot be anything other than demonic.[9]

What, then, does this tell us about Hauerwas' ideas about the study of politics in a Christian college like Goschen? It suggests, first and foremost, that politics in this context is 'not in the service of nation-state ideologies', because these ideologies (represented, presumably by the 'power of the flag') are necessarily violent and that there is no such thing as a 'liberal arts education where knowledge is an end in itself', and those in a Christian setting (like Goschen) know this. Presumably, then, if knowledge is not an end in itself, it serves something else. And for Hauerwas, and for those who think like him, it would presumably serve Christian truth and, again for Hauerwas, Christian truth is non-violent (which is why politics in a Christian educational setting cannot be dominated by the 'power of the flag').

Thus, we have in Hauerwas a vision of what it would be to teach and study politics in a distinctively Christian setting. It would be different from politics as taught in the secular university, not dominated by the 'power of the flag' and committed to forms of politics that understand the requirements of Christian witness; specifically non-violent action, and committed to, as Hauerwas puts it in a different book, the 'Church as polis'.[10] In the introduction to *that* book, Hauerwas suggests that 'theological politics' is distinguished from (for example) political theology by a refusal to make a political struggle for emancipation the centrepiece of understanding the church's theology and practice and substituting for this the church's story as a counter-story that interprets the world's politics. And he adds, with Arne Rasmusson, that doing this 'not only changes the political horizon but also requires a different understanding of the nature of politics'.[11] It seems fair to suppose, then, that the study of politics in a Christian university, for Hauerwas, would be the telling of the stories about these conceptions of politics and their implications.

This is, of course, what much of Hauerwas' best work consists of, but delving into that here would take me too far away from our topic of concern. We have, however, assembled something of what an influential group of contemporary Christians think about the proper study of politics in a Christian university and why that should be different from what goes by that name in established secular universities. What are we to make of these claims?

The character of education and the idea of a university

I have some sympathy for aspects of Hauerwas' critique of modern universities as well as for aspects of the wider theological positions outlined by him, Milbank and others. It is certainly true, I think, that contemporary universities have come close to incoherence in that it is no longer clear that they understand what their principal purpose is, and it is equally true that expectations at some variance of what I take a university's purpose to be have been added. However, I also think that there are considerable problems with the specific way that Hauerwas develops the position. This is especially so because there is so little discussion of what education in a university itself might consist as such, as opposed to extensive – and often very acute – criticism of what is actually going on in (largely) US universities. To explain this better, therefore, and as a preparatory to addressing what the study of politics should be in a university – and therefore what it might be in a Christian context – let me offer a brief account of what I understand the character of a university education to be.[12]

Of course, to understand what a university is, one must understand that it is, first and foremost, a place in which education takes place. However, the *kind* of education that takes place needs to be specified. After all, education is something we all encounter in some form or other throughout life. Michael Oakeshott has famously suggested that we see education in general as 'an initiation into civilization' and has added that, as such, 'we may regard it as beginning to learn our way about a material, emotional, moral and intellectual inheritance, and as learning to recognize the varieties of human utterance and to participate in the conversation that they compose.'[13] Seen in this way, education early in life is largely composed of learning about oneself, about how to control one's emotions, or use one's limbs, or learn to speak or write, or gradually to understand other parts of the symbolic capital that a civilisation has made available to us (music, for example).

The key to understanding this part of education is that the manner is more important than the matter, but gradually and inevitably this changes. As Oakeshott puts it, 'What is read begins to be significant and to afford an entrance into literature; instrumental music becomes less a thing of the hand and eye than of the ear ... in short the educational capital of a civilization begins to be enjoyed and even used while the dexterities by which it is known and recognized are still imperfectly acquired.'[14]

This process, or something very like it, is what we expect 'school education' to culminate in, I think. And there is one significant point worth briefly mentioning at this point. There are in most societies 'religious' schools, including of course Christian ones. Although there are examples of such schools which directly attempt to limit certain kinds of knowledge, to inhibit the ability of their pupils to 'enjoy or use' various aspects of this civilisational capital – think, for example, of attempts to ban certain kinds of knowledge, like the theory of evolution – in most cases such schools recognise the need to introduce a range of things that are not fully understood. Indeed, in this sense, to quote Oakeshott again, school education is 'learning to speak before one has anything significant to say', and as such is necessarily con-strained but constrained not by the desire to exclude this or that kind of knowledge, but by the requirements that should delimit the learning of *any* kind of knowledge. In this sense, whilst there can be Christian (or Islamic, or whatever) schools, they are all schools *sub specie aeternitatis*, in that they are doing the same thing, whatever particularities they also have.

Education continues after school, of course, but Oakeshott suggests that it continues in at least two different ways. The first way, which he calls vocational education, is understood as learning the skills appro-priate to a current manner of living (a doctor, a plumber, a farmer and so on). And, necessarily, the design of a vocational education is to be concerned with current practice and always with what is believed to be known. Here Oakeshott introduces a distinction that is important for his later argument. This is a distinction between languages and literatures. For Oakeshott, 'texts' are spoken of and read as 'literature', but they are examples of a certain kind of language. Thus, as he puts it, 'what is being studied in a vocational education is a literature or a text. What is being acquired is a knowledge of what has been authoritatively said and not a familiarity with the manner of thinking which has generated what has been said.'[15]

The second way education continues, however, is as university education. Or rather, as Oakeshott puts it, there is a sort of education different from both school and vocational education which differs both in respect of what is taught and how it is taught and which is the sort of education which for centuries has been the concern of what we have called universities. This sort of education is, in Oakeshott's terms, an education in 'languages' as opposed to 'literatures', 'because it is concerned with the use and management of explanatory languages (or modes of thought) and not prescriptive languages'.[16]

This understanding of education also generates a particular account of the university. For Oakeshott, universities are 'associations of persons, locally situated, engaged in caring for and attending to the whole intellectual capital which composes a civilization'.[17] Naturally, such an engagement is not confined only to universities. Oakeshott admits that many other associations may take part in it. However, nowhere else is it pursued continuously and exhaustively, and when universities have been negligent of it there has been nothing equivalent to take their place. The second key point for Oakeshott is that in a university the intellectual capital that it is engaged in caring for and tending is encountered as a variety of 'modes of thinking', each speaking in a voice of language of its own and related to one another conversationally – that is, not as assertion or denial, but as oblique recognition and accommodation. Thirdly, a university is a place where education takes place – the kind of education specified above – and fourthly and finally, a university is an association of persons engaged in formal teaching, and as such, the persons so engaged are concerned with the activity of exploring particular modes of thought in particular connections.[18]

This, then, is the approach I wish to take to the activity called a university education, and the character of the university as such. How does this impact on the study of politics, and what is the significance for the arguments of the theologians and others touched on in the first section above?

The study of politics in the university: secular and Christian

With this as background, let us turn to the specific matter at hand, the idea of the study of *politics* in a university. The first thing to emphasise, of course, is that the education offered in any (coherent) university should not in the least be 'vocational', notwithstanding the equally obvious fact that there is a huge (and continuously burgeoning) literature that is a 'vocational' literature in politics. Of course, the problem in the secular university in general today is that the idea of 'vocational' education has become increasingly significant in general in the university context and so in many fields, especially in the so-called social sciences. Vocational education is often the form of education that is, in fact, on the menu – at least to a very large extent. However, let me put this to one side for the moment – I shall return to it a little later.

Education in politics would, as a university education, be an education in the explanatory languages of politics. So the first question is what these are. Oakeshott is clear that the two basic modes of thought relevant to politics are philosophy and history and that, as a result, these are the modes of thought that the student of politics should acquaint him or herself with, in the context of politics. He adds that 'if it should turn out that politics is an appropriate occasion for acquiring a familiarity with other authentic languages of explanation, then the opportunity may properly be taken.' But he also adds that 'what falls outside these is ... one or other of these manners of thinking disguised in some not so very elegant fancy dress.'[19]

We might agree in general terms with Oakeshott and still suggest that the picture that results could do with elaboration. In most politics departments these days, especially in the USA but to a lesser extent elsewhere, the basic explanatory language is derived from economistic styles of reasoning. Oakeshott, I think, would dismiss these, in as much as they were genuine attempts at explanation, as echoes of either philosophy or history, and in as much as they tried to ape the methodological presuppositions of natural science, as merely inappropriate.[20] But there are, I think, stronger candidates even on Oakeshott's own understanding. What of the language, practice and understanding of law? Surely this is an essential part of politics and surely too there is a long and important body of work that takes legal argument to be in important ways *sui generis* and that it should take its place as a mode of explanation alongside history or philosophy? And then there is also the study of rhetoric. As Oakeshott himself remarks, the earliest recorded European 'chair' of politics in a university, the chair at Uppsala founded in the seventeenth century, was a chair of statesmanship and eloquence – and, he adds, 'doing and talking, the inseparable components of political activity'.[21] So surely we might include in the study of politics the explanatory languages of rhetoric and communication.

Oakeshott might well respond that all of these, to a greater or a lesser extent, could be subsumed under historical or philosophical under-standing. I would not necessarily disagree with this, but would add that perhaps one has to develop a more nuanced account than the one Oakeshott gives us of the character of different explanatory languages and their relation to politics, on the one hand, and to other explanatory languages (perhaps meta-languages?), on the other.

Be that as it may, there is, however, one other possible 'explanatory language' that might be held to be especially significant in the current context. This is, of course, theology itself, or if not theology then Christian witness. After all, does not Hauerwas suggest that this witness is best seen in terms of a story or set of stories that gives an account of the meaning and significance of our lives and circumstances (in this case telling a different story about politics from the one told by 'nation-state ideologies')? And Milbank, in *Theology and Social Theory*, seeks as he puts it, 'to restore, in postmodern terms, the possibility of theology as a metadiscourse'.[22]

Is perhaps the way to reintroduce the idea of a distinct Christian university education to do so in terms of theology as the relevant explanatory language? This, it might seem, is a way of combining the account of a university education offered above, with the concerns of those theologians I discussed in the opening section. In all probability, for theology actually to *be* a metadiscourse for explaining politics, the education would have to be located in a specifically Christian environment.

Yet I think that this way of understanding the possibilities is wrong, and I do so simply because, in the relevant sense, I do not think 'theology' *is* an explanatory language. Rather, 'theology' is one way of understanding, *in the practical world*, the world of conduct and action, and the 'doing' part of life. As students seeking understanding, as opposed to persons seeking guidance, we will naturally look to *differing* modes of thought to explain why theological ideas or movements (or indeed wider religious ideas or movements) were particularly influential or especially powerful. The modes of thought most relevant here will be, I think, philosophical and historical ones. This says nothing about the significance of theological concerns in the world – one might hold, as indeed I would, that a religious sensibility manifests itself in ways of living and that as such it is central to human experience and at its height is simply practical understanding at its fullest[23] – it merely suggests that in the sense we have given here, 'theology' cannot be a metadiscourse that explains all other discourses, because properly understood it is not an explanatory discourse at all.

So if we say that the study of politics in a university should be understood by means of the relevant explanatory languages, and that the chief such modes of thought are history and philosophy, what does this imply for the study of politics in general in universities?

In the first place it implies, I think, that the study of politics is not necessarily implicated in so-called 'nation state ideologies'. It may well be the case, indeed I believe that it *is* the case, that many, perhaps most, departments of political science are dominated by the legacies of the 'nation state' and its travails and dilemmas (though I would add that that, in itself, is rather different from being *in thrall to* ideologies supportive of the nation state), yet my own view is that this is largely because the study of politics in most departments is an uncomfortable mix of 'university' education, as I have defined it here, and 'vocational' education. It is the 'vocational' aspect of it that distorts simply because if one is doing this, then, of course, one tends to focus on those aspects of the 'vocational' education with most obvious practical relevance for our current 'manner of living'. Hence, in conventional political science departments, the focus might well be on the character of the state and contemporary threats to it (sub-state nationalisms, irredentism of various sorts, revolutionary or terroristic violence, however understood, and from the other end of the spectrum, as it were, globalisation, regionalisation and so forth), the politics of particular areas – where inevitably the state, or its lack, still plays a central role – the character, or lack thereof, of the international system of states and its implications, and so on and so forth.[24] None of this is uninteresting and much of it obviously important for any understanding of politics. The question is how is it to be approached.

On the understanding developed here, it should be approached through the explanatory languages of history and philosophy. This would imply, however, that we are seeking to understand 'politics' (in whatever context, local, national, international, religious, secular, etc.) not in any predetermined way but simply in terms of the ways in which historical or philosophical understandings might be relevant. This might be compatible with a focus on the contemporary world or its immediate history, but there is no requirement for it to be so focused. One would simply be exploring the relevant explanatory language in some context that is specifically (and again in some particular way) political. This might indeed include, for example, the claim – made by Hauerwas and discussed earlier – that the appropriate political form is the church and that other forms are in important ways decadent. But one would be exploring such a claim as a 'text' in the context of a language, and not in any other way.

These considerations then clearly imply certain things for the idea of politics in a *Christian* university. The first point to make here is that, if the understanding offered above is plausible, then a Christian university, whether it be Goschen College or the Pontifical Gregorian University, will have to decide first if what it wishes to offer is a *university* education. If so, then it will confront the same questions as would confront any programme for studying politics in any university. However, it might well be the case that, since all such departments are limited (by personnel, expertise and interest), the choice of curriculum would reflect the institution's specifically Christian orientation. It might become, to use a term of Hauerwas, an education in theological politics, though, of course, a *university* education in theological politics; as such it would be fundamentally oriented towards the relevant explanatory languages (history and philosophy) and would offer its education in that light. In other words, while it would be perfectly understandable (and indeed very worthwhile) for a Christian university to offer a curriculum starkly at variance with that on offer in most 'secular' departments of politics – focusing on the presuppositions of the church as polis thesis, perhaps, or narratives of the appropriate institutional setting for a politics of friendship, or the internal logic and coherence of pacifism – the manner in which that curriculum was offered, and the kind of education that resulted, would not differ substantially from that on offer in any other kind of university, if, that is to say, both institutions were, in truth, offering a *university* education.

Conclusion

My conclusion, then, is obvious. The idea of politics in a Christian university might well be different, by some large degree, in terms of *what is taught*, but, if it is to be a university education at all, it cannot be different in terms of *the orientation to teaching it*. A university education in any setting is simply what it is and not another thing. The mistake that Hauerwas and some other contemporary theologians make is to seek to elide the real distinction between manner and matter in this context. All that would do is create institutions called Christian universities that did not really offer a university education at all and simply offered something else which would, I suspect, be merely a version of vocational education in another guise. It may be that some in the Christian world would be happy with this, and certainly many outside Christianity would, especially within the secular frameworks that tend to dominate in contemporary universities. Yet for me, at least, such a division would represent a loss both for the university as such, and for Christianity. Christian ideas have always been part of the wider conversation of our civilisation, at varying times more or less important parts. In as much as universities exist to recover, refine and continue that conversation, Christian thinking needs to remain a part of it. Of course, Christian universities *per se* could do this, if the kinds of study and teaching that goes on within them remains guided by the idea of the university itself. Such a future is surely more fruitful than that which would be achieved by a vocational sectarianism.[25]

Chapter Fifteen

Interdisciplinary Perspectives within a Christian Context

William K. Kay

Introduction

For the purpose of analysis three things which belong together have been separated from each other in this paper. The structure and functioning of *universities* relate to the aims and funding priorities of these institutions. They also relate to the way that teaching is divided up by sub-units (e.g. departments) within the university, and this institutional arrangement is intended to reflect the different fields of *knowledge* or, at the very least, is justified by discourse that claims to be rational. *Christian theology* as the third factor within this composite whole is influenced by the society where the community of faith lives and by the academic and religious traditions espoused by its practitioners.

In an ideal Christian university the institutional structure will be intimately connected with the knowledge-bearing components that comprise it. These knowledge-bearing components will, in some sense, reflect the view of knowledge that allows the university, by definition, to be called Christian. So there is bound to be an interaction between what it means to be Christian and what counts as knowledge. Yet, what it means to be Christian and what counts as knowledge must also be directly influenced by the voice of Christian theology. But first, how should we think of universities?

Universities

In considering a Christian university it is reasonable to strike a balance between the general presumption that 'history teaches us that history teaches us nothing',[1] and the more polemical view advanced by Popper that the account of the unfolding of human affairs according to basic historical or sociological laws is fundamentally flawed: indeed it is vicious and inclines only to a ghastly totalitarianism (Popper, 1961). So there is value in sketching the evolution of the university. They began within the cathedral choir schools, which could date themselves back to the sixth century. By the eleventh century they had become the main providers of learning and scholarship and their expansion and importance followed the economic revival of the century before. Over the next one hundred years the choir schools enlarged further and metamorphosed into the new institution of the university, whose job it was to train the lawyers, clergy and schoolmasters needed by the burgeoning administration of church and state (Bowen, 1975, pp. 105–106).

The organisation of choir schools was taken from the medieval craft guilds; hence the relationship between teacher and student followed that between master and apprentice. The Latin term for guilds was *universitates*. In any major city there had to be enough teachers to make it worthwhile to form themselves into a guild but, once they did so, it took only one outstanding teacher with a well-known reputation to attract students and create the conditions under which a university might come into existence. In Paris after 1180 Abelard was the crucial figure.

Students would usually first learn the pre-Christian liberal arts of grammar, rhetoric and dialectic or logic (the trivium). The term 'faculty', referring to the subdivisions in the guild, appears at about this time and, though the word strictly referred to the studies themselves, it was soon transferred to the groups of scholars attached to each subject. These large groups of people, teachers and students needed a legally-recognised identity within the cities of which they were a part – especially since many of the teachers were clerics and the church wished to incorporate them within its authority structures. In 1231 what was effectively a papal charter was issued to the Paris university. This was a mixed blessing, however, because it enabled the Vatican to stipulate the qualifications of masters and the content and methods of instruction.

By the middle of the thirteenth century the curriculum had settled to the trivium with the addition of Aristotle's logic and the quadrivium of arithmetic, geometry, astronomy and music. The student who completed his studies could pass through the stages of bachelor and licentiate to master. But only after this grounding in the liberal arts might a student progress to one of the three higher faculties of law, theology or medicine (Bowen, 1975, p. 119).

The place of theology in one of the senior faculties within the medieval universities reflected not only the dominant position of the church in medieval society but also the all-encompassing nature of theology as a field of discourse that could include every aspect of life and thought. The curriculum of these universities reflected a non-scientific culture, one that depended heavily on authority and on the written word, whether this word was in the form of legal pronouncements within canon law, or the ethics or logic of Aristotle and the grammarians. The typical student had to learn a dialectical form of argumentation whereby propositions for and against particular inter-pretations or philosophical positions were seriously and formally debated. It was both uninventive and stilted in one sense because the foundational texts were finite in number but, in another sense, the whole process of dispute and argumentation allowed for logical creativity and intellectual rigour (Boyd and King, 1964).

The arrival of science, broadly conceived, began with an examination of 'the book of nature' that is, the natural world, and through experiments and observations gradually shifted the focus of attention from the past to the present and, horror of horrors, was able to show that, in some instances, the renowned authorities of antiquity were completely mistaken in their beliefs.[2] In due course, natural science and the Enlightenment poured an entirely new content into the old university curricular structures. The teaching faculties con-tinued to exist and the degree structure remained but, with the founding of the University of Berlin in the early nineteenth century, the priority that had previously been given to legal and theological discourse was now obviously being given to science and technology (Perkin, 1984, p. 34).

It is surprising how late many of these changes were eventually completed. The University of Oxford underwent considerable transformation in the nineteenth century both in respect of the content of what was taught and also in terms of the internal workings of the university itself. What finally determined the shape of Victorian university life could be traced not to the high-flown forms of knowledge that emanated from philosophical, scientific or religious origins, but to the simple need to provide a career structures for full-time academics (Engel, 1975, p. 344). Once it was agreed that academics ought to be full-time, and not simply clergymen who also gave lectures, and once it became clear that research as well as teaching was of fundamental importance and that there were reliable methods by which research could be done in all fields, then new knowledge was going to be routinely discovered (Schwehn, 2002, p. 55). The university became not so much the transmitter of an ancient culture as a regenerative agency driving what became the processes of modernity.

In the Western world, the university of the twentieth century was characterised by its expansion and its transposition into the mass education systems needed by highly industrialised cultures. While the expansion of the university sector also led to its diversification, there are general patterns and trends that underlie what happened. Fundamentally, education became not only a means by which social change might be affected but also a process that was important to commercial and scientific interests. The creation of a funding stream into universities by patenting the genome is only one example of this. In any event, diversification is less important than the similarity between institutions of higher education. In a scathing critique of the American university of the end of the twentieth century, Bloom (1987) pointed out how the 1960s engendered an extraordinary revolution. Respected university professors became hostage to ideologically-driven students with the result that academic staff might be fired if they thwarted the ambitions of vociferous pressure groups. Academic standards in such an atmosphere came to mean very little – low-grades could be attributed to prejudice or to the manipulations of a student quota system – and academic freedom to teach against the latest intellectual fashions retreated in the face of strident student demands.

When the dust had settled, the 1990s found universities with three major divisions: natural science, social science and the humanities (Bloom, 1987, p. 342). The natural scientists found themselves on 'an island' separate from the turbulence within the humanities. In the humanities the acceptance of incontestable facts had been dissolved into postmodernity, and the cultural achievements of the past had been revalued so as to make room for separate lines of tradition claiming priority over the previously established canons of human excellence. Culture wars raged as competing social groups asserted the moral legitimacy and intellectual credibility of their own positions. Feminist scholars might lock horns with black scholars; right-wing Christians might debate with fundamentalist secularists; Muslim historians might disagree with Jewish intellectuals. In every instance the only harmonising possibility was to consider that each group had its own 'plausibility structures' and that within its own circle what was being claimed was true, or true for it. 'Indeed, the relations between natural science, social science and humanities are purely administrative and have no substantial intellectual content' (Bloom, 1987, p. 350). In Bloom's view, the university sector settled into a kind of superior vocational training in the form of business studies or accountancy at one end of the campus and, at the other, provided the natural sciences that continued in their own insulated high-status laboratories far away from populist pressures. In the middle, and occupying the majority of buildings, the humanities offered a consideration of 'old books' that might, in the end, have some relevance to the entertainment industry but which had no overarching legitimacy.

An equally scathing view of the university scene is given by Roberts (2002) who argued that the imposition by government of the quality assurance mechanisms upon British academic life after the late 1980s produced a set of unnecessary procedures, many of which actually destroyed quality and all of which limited the freedom of academics to pursue their proper callings. The new top-heavy administrative structure of universities damaged their essential nature by destroying the egalitarian community of scholars that had characterised the best of university life since the Middle Ages. No longer could the cloistered quiet of a contemplative life survive and offset the busy materialism of the markets.

This community of scholars, cloistered or not, offered an interdisciplinary space. It allowed those who had made a lifetime study of different disciplines to meet and dine together, to talk informally about their discoveries and their problems, and to piece together a unified account of the world. Once the community of scholars is dispersed, interdisciplinary opportunities vanish. Yet this wistful evocation of a nineteenth-century Oxonian idyll of 'dreaming spires' may have its twenty-first century equivalent. The e-university is emerging and, as a precursor to it, the electronic community of scholars, each at a screen that can communicate with a person half-way across the world as easily as a person in the same building, has arrived. The virtual face-to-face meeting is already facilitated by Internet cams but, even without this visual stimulus, typed words on screen make a new form of conversation possible and, if reports of Internet chat rooms are to be believed, such words may have all the immediacy of the senior common room and considerably greater intimacy.

Interdisciplinary space, having been squashed out by the removal of residential quarters for scholars, has re-emerged electronically. Yet, even without this unexpected bonus, scholars can find themselves in multidisciplinary fields like medicine or education and in area studies like American Literature or French history (Clark, 1984, p. 112). And, as the course of degrees is now almost always modular, students make excursions into one discipline or another in a pre-ordained sequence so as to achieve a degree. Somewhere – usually at an academic board – agreement between different disciplines has to be reached to ensure that the series of modules taken by students is coherent and this practical necessity ensures that faculty members discuss the interrelation of their disciplines.

This survey of the university has shown that an existing institution, the choir school, turned into a larger, more complex establishment to service a burgeoning society's needs for educated personnel. The university, then, has always had a social function and would not have come into existence without it. Being a social unit, the university fell under the sway of the centres of authority within its epoch, whether these were sacred or secular. Papal authority in the thirteenth century is no different in principle from government authority in the twenty-first. The university's structure, on the other hand, reflects the needs of its employees, its masters, more than idealised divisions of knowledge flowing from a timeless realm. The university curriculum, whatever the needs of its teachers, is also answerable to the needs of its students. Thus the curriculum usually follows and matches the slow course of change in patterns of employment. It is rare for knowledge-based revolutions to occur, although a paradigm might be found in the ferment of the Middle Ages when Aristotelian logic was applied to questions thrown up by Christian theology. Such phenomena do occur and bring with them profound consequences.

Knowledge

Of the many starting points that could be used to map out the field of knowledge, the bottom–up approach through child psychology offers a valuable approach. And it is this which will be dealt with first, before looking at the top–down approach that works from the characteristics and conceptions of fully–fledged academic disciplines.

The great advantage of an approach using child psychology is that we begin to see how knowledge might grow, how it might be differentiated from its early and misty beginnings in the mind of the child, through to its more adolescent formulations in what is learnt for public examinations, to the final frontiers at the outposts where new research forges into the unknown.[3] We begin by asking, for example, not what the rules of mathematics are but how it is that the child ever comes to attain a conception of what a number is. Or we wonder why it is that children understand things in one way, whereas when older but without any other apparent change to their circumstances they understand them in quite another way.

This approach to knowledge was formulated and defended by Piaget who spoke it as 'genetic epistemology' (Gruber and Vonèche, 1995, p. xviii). There is a sense in which Piaget 'biologises Kant' (Phillips, 1982, p. 420): that is, shows how the Kantian *a priori* categories of space and causation come to be established as a result of a series of transformations of what is first known through the physical senses. The child begins to explore the universe by touch and by physical orientation in relation to other objects, and the process of acquiring knowledge depends upon remembering what has been felt and seen and in other ways sensorily perceived, and matching this with the internal representation of this perception through manipulable mental structures. The growth of knowledge in the Piagetian account takes place when cognitive structures that have been formed in relation to one aspect of the physical or social world are extended to new objects and situations and when, in their turn, these mental structures are themselves modified in the light of new incoming information. The process is one of assimilation and accommodation. In the former the mental structures encase new information whereas, in the latter, new information causes the structures to be reshaped.

The Piagetian view has been criticised for casting its account into a sequence of four stages on the presumption that the mental functioning of children, but also in principle of adults, takes place within the stage that the person has reached. This means that the child learning maths at one stage will also utilise the same mental operations and structures when learning French or history. Critics of Piaget argue that there is very often evidence that children do *not* operate at the same stage in different domains – that the mind is modular and that different things are learned and understood with different degrees of sophistication depending upon all kinds of personal and other factors.

When this type of critique and its counter-critique are translated into interdisciplinary studies, it is easy to see that we are confronted with a situation where we have to decide whether the individual disciplines are largely as a consequence of the utilisation of the same mental operations with different but essentially compatible content, or whether interdisciplinary studies are domain-specific and require quite different mental abilities and functions. For example, do we presume that learning history or maths or French is a matter of putting historical or mathematical or linguistic facts into the same machine and churning them around? Or do we presume that historical, mathematical and linguistic 'pieces' are so different from one another that they cannot fit into the same machine? Indeed, is the machine a living organism constantly modified by the content being fed into it – in other words, is the machine metaphor completely inappropriate?

The Piagetian account is not the only one on offer, of course; but at this point it is important to note that, in relation to interdisciplinary study, the Piagetian corpus of work does presume the unity of mind, a mind that displays plasticity and versatility in relation to the whole world of knowledge. It also makes the assumption that there *is* an outer world, a world of the physical environment in which biological organisms exist, and an inner world of mental structures and representations by which the organism negotiates its way through the outer world.

In terms of interdisciplinary inquiry the unity of the Piagetian mind is particularly found in the operations which traverse various domains. These operations are largely logical. For instance they presume that something cannot both be and not be at the same time; that the part cannot be greater than the whole; that within a properly-constructed series the relationship between the elements of the series are such as to enable logical deduction to be made about the earlier and later members of the set – for example in a series arranged in the order of size, a, b, c, and d we presume that if a is bigger than b it is also bigger than d. In interdisciplinary terms, the Piagetian account allows for an underlying compatibility within the different domains: knowledge is a whole, truth is a unity and the parts, however diverse they may appear, must cohere. Moreover, if the same logic, the same operations, traverse the different domains then there is a ready-made implication that inter-disciplinary inquiry may without contradiction make use of similar methods to achieve its complex ends. We can then presume, as Piaget did, that where there *are* domain-specific differences in intellectual functioning, these are transient and occur only at transitional points between stages.

A different kind of bottom-up approach might be found in the history of the measurement of intelligence. This contentious area has since its inception produced several accounts of intelligence which, in later formulations, hold in common that there are several multiple modes or aspects of intelligence. Gardner (1983) produced seven distinct intelligences including linguistic, logical-mathematical, spatial, interpersonal, etc., while Sternberg produced the notion of intelligence governed by three separate systems relating to the inner world, the outer world and the role of life experience. The point about this is that it is possible to map certain of the so-called intelligences onto the different academic disciplines. While there is more to the different disciplines than the operation of different kinds of intelligence, the match between mental facility and academic disciplines is suggestive of either a unity of mind or a unity of knowledge or both.

A top-down view of disciplines begins from the different branches of human knowledge and, by philosophical analysis, abstracts their generic features. So we might begin with physics and history and look at the characteristic concepts, methods and rules that operate within each discipline. In physics we would discover concepts like 'mass' or 'force' and their relationship with each other according to empirically-observed regularities (or 'laws') supported by mathematical com-putation. It is the concepts, methods and the rules that make up the discipline, in much the same way as a particular game is made up of particular rules and objects. Chess and draughts both use a board of the same size and they both involve two players but the pieces move differently and for different purposes. So using the Wittgensteinian 'family resemblance' analogy, we can say that disciplines have an underlying commonality even if there are large differences between them.

This top-down analysis also presumes that disciplines are similar enough to be categorised in the same way – which is why they share the name 'disciplines' – and this recognition flows from an almost universal apprehension of their co-belonging. As a consequence, inter-disciplinary inquiry is also by this account possible. Again, to change metaphors, we could argue that, just as money can be converted from one currency to another or words can be translated from one language to another, so concepts within one discipline can be converted into another and 'buy things' there.

But, beyond its characteristic concepts and rules, is there anything that constitutes a discipline? In other words, is it possible to discover how many disciplines there are and whether the number that exists is fixed, or must we presume that there will be an ever-increasing number of disciplines as disparate ones are combined with one another to form new hybrids? One way of answering this is to view disciplines as quests for different types of knowledge.

If knowledge is 'justified true belief' (Scruton, 1994, p. 317, paraphrasing Plato), then anything about which belief is possible may also be an area where knowledge could be found if the corresponding justification were forthcoming. We may therefore see the rules of each discipline as expressing procedures by which area-specific beliefs may be justified. A discipline's rules provide the grounds for admissible evidence. Since the concepts of each discipline must be compatible with its rules, there is a sense in which the rules are derived from the concepts. In any event, once these rules are in place normal academic activity within the discipline can occur simply by gathering in-formation that will contribute to the fulfilment of its rules. For instance, historical research can take place if one of the rules of the discipline is that events may be interpreted best by subtracting the bias of any primary documentation relating to them. To write about historical events one simply needs primary documentation, preferably providing slightly different perspectives, so that the bias can be detected and eliminated.

Looked at in this way, there is no limit to the number of disciplines that might come into existence as fresh concepts are created out of new combinations of existing interdisciplinary perspectives. The real barrier to endless disciplinary invention lies in two directions. In theoretical terms certain concepts can only retain their meaning in the discipline that gave them birth. We could talk about 'gravity' in the discipline of

English literature, but there is no possible synthesis between concepts characteristic of literature and those of gravity: interdisciplinary study between physics and literature fails to function. Second, there are no practitioners to create a new discipline *de novo*. A discipline with one practitioner becomes a language spoken by one person: a dead end. Consequently new disciplines cannot arise casually and at will. They only come into being when sufficient intellectual energy is generated by the attempts to solve new and pressing problems.

And it is this which is indicative of the way disciplines grow. If disciplines are methods by which concepts related to particular sets of beliefs are justified and turned into knowledge, then there is a prior question to ask. How is it that beliefs come into existence? And what happens when incompatible beliefs are entertained about the same object? This disjuncture, this problematisation of existence, is a candidate for the engine of cognitive growth. The discrepancy between contradictory beliefs must prompt an attempt to reconcile them. This is because we can consider a belief as a form of hypothesis related to possible actions. Contradictory beliefs engender or are equal to contradictory hypotheses, and contradictory hypotheses paralyse action. Though this is essentially a Piagetian analysis, it fits well with the earlier description of the growth of knowledge.

It is only a step from here to consider why it is that interdisciplinary research might be undertaken. And the answer must lie in the same direction. Beliefs about a subject that can be deconstructed into different disciplines must engender interdisciplinary hypotheses. So the process that drives the development of an individual discipline is the same as the process that drives the development of many disciplines working together in an interdisciplinary fashion. Indeed, interdisciplinary research may be seen as a sophisticated attempt at reconciling apparently incompatible beliefs.

And this leads into an analysis of the different types of interdisciplinary study that might occur. The most uncontentious form occurs when a single method is applied across a variety of disciplines, as it so often is in the sciences.

Here the basic method of the sciences is used after a theory is advanced to explain physically-observable phenomena.[4] The theory may contain concepts which are not directly observable but which have to be converted into the variables that can be fitted into testable propositions. This is the hypothetico-deductive method: the hypothesis, or several hypotheses, make up the explanatory theory and then from this theory a testable proposition or propositions can be deduced. It is this unbreakable relation between theory and empirical testing which constitutes the essence of the scientific method. And it is this method which, because it can be utilised within various theoretical frameworks, offers a unifying focus within scientific fields, whether these are social or physical.

Where a single method is inappropriate, interdisciplinary work becomes complex. An analysis of the possibilities of interdisciplinary research was advanced by Kay and Francis (1985). They argued that research in each discipline should be judged by appropriate criteria and they proposed four models showing how the sets of criteria relevant to each discipline might be related. These may be set out in the following way. In each case D stands for 'discipline' and C for 'criteria': D1 is judged by the set of criteria, C1, and so on.

(a) D1+D2: C1 or C2
(b) D1+D2: C3
(c) D1+D2: −
(d) D1+D2: C1 and C2

The judgements of interdisciplinary work proposed by these models are as follows. In (a) we see the criteria of one discipline applied to work that is carried out in two. For instance, Freud's *Moses and Monotheism* (1939) is an example of religious phenomena interpreted and judged entirely by psychoanalytic criteria. There is no attempt by Freud to allow the criteria of theology to speak, since he rejects these out of hand. An example of type (d) is to be found in the field of religious education, where Goldman in *Religious Thinking from Childhood to Adolescence* (1964) attempted to satisfy both theological and psychological criteria when looking at religious thinking from childhood to adolescence.

Model (b) presumes the negotiation of an entirely new set of criteria. This is uncharted territory to which we shall return below. Method (c) precludes the use of any preconceived disciplinary basis: it 'allows the data to speak for itself' and lets criteria be set up on a rolling basis. This is most nearly seen in research using 'grounded theory', where theory, data and interpretation are all unique to particular inquiries (Cohen, Manion and Morrison, 2000, pp. 150–151).

And this finally leads to the consideration of a Christian context in which interdisciplinary work might be carried out.

Christian theology

Any comprehensive discussion of Christian theology is precluded by the vastness of the subject. In relation to interdisciplinary inquiry, there appear to be five important things that theology has to offer. First, it offers truth-claims about ultimate reality and, indeed, lesser realities like those found within human history. Such claims are assertions which go beyond preference, meaning or probability: at the very least, they assert the existence of a truth that is beyond contingency and against which other kinds of propositions may be measured. Second, it offers a large framework of meaning for the entirety of the universe and the place of human beings within it. The framework of meaning is large enough to account for all human activities and asserts itself against nihilism, cynicism and absurdity. Third, it is able to offer ethical guidelines or, at the least, to draw attention to issues of value and purpose that have been painstakingly distilled within a lengthy, living multi-faceted tradition. Fourth, it provides a narrative of history that can be projected into the future and, in this sense, places all individual human activities within a huge timescale by which they may be relativised and understood.

Interdisciplinary inquiry may be affected in at least four ways by a theological tradition. First, as is often acknowledged, scholars may find themselves working with religious motivations and being drawn to particular problems. Somebody who adheres to the Christian tradition might attach importance to research problems about abortion or the church or the transcendent simply as a result of a personal reflection on his or her faith. The scholar is nurtured and shaped by the tradition to which he or she belongs and, as a very natural consequence, is incentivised and given an unusual determination to solve problems relevant to the Christian community. Clearly scholars shaped by the same religious tradition, whatever their disciplinary expertise, may find themselves inclined to work together. In this sense the Christian context for enquiry is the Christian tradition.

Second, and similarly, intellectual problems may be thrown up by the Christian tradition and these may require an interdisciplinary response.

For instance, issues relating to free will and determinism might be investigated psychologically, theologically and historically. Again, the context is the tradition.

Third, and more generally, research problems arise from the vision of the universe that religion inspires. The religious view of life is of its interconnectedness – its subsumption under a single divine power – and consequently of an organic unity. For instance, the expectation that scientific laws and explanations apply not only on earth but on other planets, or that the burning of fuels here is analogous to the combustion in the innermost parts of distant stars, can be said to have been formed in a scientific age when God was seen to stand behind everything. A tacit acceptance of interconnectedness may continue to inform inter-disciplinary work in a less religious age.

In the analysis of interdisciplinary work provided above, models (b) and (c) do not use the criteria already implicit within the discipline. In model (b) new criteria are negotiated that are suitable to the disciplines which combine together within an interdisciplinary project. The criteria are open to any discussion by the people carrying out the inquiry and, though they may bring to it their own preconceptions from their own disciplines, the model stipulates that they leave behind their preferences to begin a discussion that has no predetermined endpoint. So, fourth, where a Christian context intrudes on this negotiation, there is room for any aspect of the Christian theological tradition to make a decisive contribution. Perhaps the truth-claims of Christianity will influence the truth-claims of the piece of work that is envisaged. Maybe the framework of meaning that Christianity provides will shape discussion and support certain conclusions. Similarly with the ethical considerations. Perhaps the teleological narrative of Christianity will influence the historical dimension of the project. The point is that the negotiation is entirely ready to accept any inferences that may be made from the criteria that are normally applied to the disciplines involved within the interdisciplinary study *and* also any other agreed factors that relate to the formation of knowledge.

A somewhat similar situation arises with model (c). Here the model presumes that there are, in a sense, no criteria by which the disciplines might be judged and that the criteria for interdisciplinary work are emergent, not decided in advance, but discerned once the normal methods of the different disciplines are applied to the subject matter.

Here again, and fifth, because this model of enquiry either adopts unique criteria or proceeds without stipulating any criteria, no method or series of judgements are excluded and the work that emerges, the grounded theory that is formulated, may come partially from the Christian tradition in all its variety and richness.

In both these last cases, the Christian tradition may or may not be a welcome visitor at the interdisciplinary feast. Yet the decision about what constitutes a properly constituted interdisciplinary programme of research rules out no contribution in advance. We can imagine a situation where atheistic and Christian scholars from different disciplines sit down to find agreement about a programme of research they jointly undertake. They must hammer out a rational procedure for conducting and assessing their work. In these circumstances it is impossible to claim a privilege for specifically Christian epistemology, but it ought to be possible to find conditions for agreement within their common rationality and common humanity. If, on the other hand, interdisciplinary work is undertaken by a specifically Christian team of scholars, although they may find agreement easier it is questionable whether their joint work will be acceptable to other scholars if their faith commitments impinge too much upon the assessment or testing of their work.

In this respect the university of medieval Christendom is surprisingly informative about the possibility of interdisciplinary research within a Christian context today. The medieval university deliberately set up a process of dialectic whereby arguments for and against particular positions were marshalled and determined. Despite the overarching Christian values and principles that informed the vast majority of European scholars at this time, the critical testing of propositions was rigorous and without obvious limit apart from that stemming from the restricted knowledge base from which everyone started. So it is perfectly possible to imagine valuable interdisciplinary research taking place within a twenty-first century Christian context, that is, a context where there are shared fundamental presuppositions. Despite concerns about the privileging of Christian epistemology (Hollinger, 2002), the vital issue does not concern the context – since as we have said this may simply be the source of a variety of ideas and motivations – but the power of the critique to which knowledge-claims are subjected. Moreover, and finally, if the long historical perspective shows anything it is that the university is a mutable institution and one which responds to the needs of the society where it is situated. In this connection the Christian institution may fittingly find a servant role within its parent society.

References

Bloom, A. (1987) *The Closing of the American Mind*, London, Simon and Schuster.

Bowen, J. (1975) *A History of Western Education*, vol. 2, London, Methuen.

Boyd, W. and E. J. King (1964) *The History of Western Education*, seventh edition, Lanham, MN, Barnes and Noble.

Clark, B. R. (1984) 'The Organizational Conception', in Burton R. Clark (ed.), *Perspectives on Higher Education*, Los Angeles, CA, University of California Press, pp. 106–131.

Cohen, L., Manion, L. and K. Morrison (2000) *Research Methods in Education*, fifth edition, London, RoutledgeFalmer.

Engel, A. (1975) 'The Emerging Concept of the Academic Profession at Oxford 1800–1854', in Lawrence Stone (ed.), *The University in Society*, vol. 1, London, Oxford University Press, pp. 305–352.

Feyerabend, P. (1975) *Against Method: Outline of an Anarchistic Theory of Knowledge*, London, New Left Books.

Freud, S. (1939) *Moses and Monotheism*, in *Standard Edition of the Complete Psychological Works of Sigmund Freud*, twenty-four volumes, edited by James Strachey, Alix Strachey and Alan Tyson, London, Hogarth Press, 1953–1974.

Gardner, H. (1983) *Frames of Mind: The Theory of Multiple Intelligences*, New York, Basic Books.

Goldman, R. J. (1964) *Religious Thinking from Childhood to Adolescence*, London, Routledge.

Gribben, J. (2002) *Science: A History 1543–2001*, London, Allen Lane.

Gruber, H. E. and J. J. Vonèche (1995) *The Essential Piaget*, London, Jason Aronson.

Hollinger, D. (2002) 'Enough Already: Universities Do Not Need More Christianity', in Sterk, pp. 40–49.

Kay, W. K. and L. J. Francis (1985) 'The Seamless Robe: Interdisciplinary Enquiry in Religious Education', *British Journal of Religious Education* 7, 2, pp. 64–67.

Medawar, P. (1990) *Advice to a Young Scientist*, New York, Basic Books.

Perkin, H. (1984) 'The Historical Perspective', in Burton R. Clark (ed.), *Perspectives on Higher Education*, Los Angeles, CA, University of California Press, pp. 17–55.

Phillips, D. (1982) 'Perspectives on Piaget as Philosopher: The Tough, Tender-Minded Syndrome', in S. Modgil and C. Modgil (eds), *Jean Piaget: Consensus and Controversy*, New York, Holt, Rinehart and Winston, pp. 13–29.

Popper, K. R. (1961) *The Poverty of Historicism*, London, Routledge.

Roberts, R. H. (2002) *Religion, Theology and the Human Sciences*, Cambridge, Cambridge University Press.

Schwehn, M. R. (2002) 'Where are the Universities of Tomorrow?', in Sterk, pp. 50–59.

Scruton, R. (1994) *Modern Philosophy: An Introduction and Survey*, London, Sinclair-Stevenson.

Sterk, Andrea (ed.), *Religion, Scholarship and Higher Education: Perspectives, Models, and Future Prospects*, Notre Dame, IN, University of Notre Dame Press.

Wolterstorff, N. (2002) 'Epilogue', in Sterk, pp. 247–254.

Chapter Sixteen

Responsibility, Vocation and Critique: Teacher Education in a Christian Context

John Sullivan

Effective teaching, like effective discipleship, is about inventiveness and creativity rather than compliance or reproduction of a pre-specified model. However, the capacity to innovate, to be flexible, to engage in imaginative renewal in teaching and in discipleship rests on a thorough induction into professional, academic and religious traditions. Worthwhile teaching relies upon personal transformation rather than mere transferability – for students and for their teachers. It goes beyond skills and aspires to people-changing, for the teacher is not just an engineer, technician, manager or therapist. A richly developed understanding of teaching entails attention to three central concepts: responsibility, vocation and critique.

In this chapter I shall first consider some current features of life and work in universities that present a challenge for Christians. Second, I shall argue that there is a legitimate role for a faith perspective to play in teacher education, without loss of either academic respectability or professional credibility. Third, I present an analysis of the nature of responsibility, with four aspects of teacher responsibility being exposed for consideration: responsibility *for, with, from* and *to*. Fourth, these four aspects of responsibility are related to the task of promoting theological literacy, which I claim should be a distinctive contribution of Christian colleges and universities in the field of teacher education. Fifth, linked with the development of theological literacy, the fostering of a sense of vocation is highlighted as a central priority for departments of education in Christian institutions. Finally, in order to protect independent thinking, to promote authentic action and to facilitate renewal of professional and religious traditions, the role of critique is briefly addressed.

Education and the university

Originally a university did not only equip its students to be scholars; it also prepared them for careers, perhaps in the church, in the law, medicine or administration. A Master's degree showed not only a level of academic competence; it also functioned as a licence to teach. Although philosophers and other scholars have, for centuries, written about education, its nature and constituent features, its contexts, aims, methods and outcomes, explicit study in universities of the processes of education, study which links academic and professional dimensions of the subject, is nevertheless a relatively recent development. University education departments have existed in this country for scarcely more than a century. In the UK, initial teacher education and training has played a particularly important role in Christian colleges and universities. In fact, historically it has been an integral and essential part of the work of such colleges and the centrality of teacher education to their *raison d'être* remains crucial to their mission and their niche in the market of university level institutions.

It might be expected that the centrality of teacher education to the mission of Christian colleges would ensure that these colleges establish a reputation for being places where there is systematic reflection on the mutual bearing of theology and education, and where there is rigorous examination of the relationship between Christian faith and the practice of teaching. However, this rarely happens. Many factors contribute to this situation. Among these factors might be included the requirements of government policy and legislation, along with the range of priorities that have to be addressed if institutional survival is to be guaranteed for a few more years. Also relevant here is the changing composition of students and staff, the pluralist and secular nature of society and prevailing notions of academic objectivity. These factors are related in complex ways that are too difficult to disentangle here, but their operation is evident.

Thus, external pressures put an emphasis on increasing numbers, reducing the cost of education per student, improving completion rates, widening participation, increasing efficiency, employing new technology and demonstrating accountability on ever more fronts. Institutional leaders have to become more adept at a range of tasks and skills such as strategic planning, internal reorganisation, compliance with bureaucratic requirements imposed by government and other funding agencies, marketing, seeking a competitive edge and managing boundaries. (For perceptive critiques of the current university scene in the USA and UK respectively, see Rhodes, 2001; Graham, 2002.)

Many, if not most, of the staff and students who come to Christian university colleges to work and to learn select that place on grounds other than its espoused connections with the church or its religious ethos. They might be attracted, for example, by its location, its size, the appropriateness of its courses to their needs, its academic reputation, or by the employability record of its graduates. Only a few will come with the expectation that a particular college provides an education and form of professional training that engages seriously with the implications for life and work of Christian – or any other – religious faith. This includes many students and staff who may, in their private lives, consider themselves Christians, but who separate their faith from the academic and work dimensions of life. They do not want to be indoctrinated and they do not want to proselytise. Faith is treated as a private and optional matter, and, in their view, should not intrude into the classroom, even where it flourishes in the chapel, in voluntary study groups, in charitable service and in campus ministry. In recognition of religious pluralism and a highly secularised population, and to avoid false assumptions or cultural 'imperialism', notions of religious truth or significance, especially those that call into question prevailing norms, are 'bracketed out', removed from the focus of study. They are not scrutinised, interrogated and evaluated. Religious traditions are neither explored for their implications, nor deployed as potentially powerful intellectual, social and spiritual resources in aid of understanding, community-building or individual and collective practice. Not being brought into play, they appear unfamiliar, irrelevant and even alien forms of thought. Scholarship and spirituality, reason and faith, religious tradition and academic reflection on education – these are kept apart in ways that render both 'sides' of these pairs seriously deficient (Sullivan, 1997, 1999a, 1999b, 2002a).

With the huge rise in numbers of those attending modern universities, it is no longer clear what, if anything, gives these institutions any lasting unity or coherence. The notion that there might be overarching purposes that govern their diverse activities seems inappropriate and sounds like an act of (unwarranted) cultural domination. Without such an architectonic perspective, however, maintaining connections between their multifarious parts seems a thankless, perhaps impossible, task. The world of higher education is 'multi' rather than 'uni' – in aims, contexts, perspectives, approaches and outcomes. It is neither possible nor is it sensible to seek to turn the clock back to an era when it might be assumed that Christian faith provided the context, foundation, goal and yardsticks for the enterprise of education in general or of teacher education in particular.

A faith perspective in education

Yet surely, for Christians studying and working in the university context, the choice is not simply restricted to seeking a cocoon, on the one hand, or capitulation, on the other. Total isolation from non-believers is not only impossible; it is also undesirable. It would encourage the development of an unquestioning and inadequately-tested and inward-looking faith. None of the mainstream churches seek to establish a sacralised space that supernaturalises the project of teaching and learning, treating education as simply an agent of evangelisation or simply to consolidate the ecclesial community. This would be a narrowing process and unworthy of any institution that aspires to university status. Catechesis – or dialogue between believers for the purpose of maturing faith – does not constitute critical academic investigation.

On the other hand, Christians can legitimately resist secularist assumptions even as they accept secularisation; they do not have to accommodate the methodological atheism, reductionism, relativism or the hermeneutics of suspicion that dominates much contemporary scholarly debate. If they are prepared to expose the foundations of their faith, to bring this into dialogue with alternative (and critical) perspectives, to be ready to be questioned, as well as to challenge (humbly), it should be possible for Christians to engage their faith with their studies in ways that do not compromise either the life of faith or the nature of the academic disciplines. Faith and study (and faith and preparation for a professional career) will not neatly and painlessly coincide; nor, however, should it be assumed that they will automatically contradict one another.

Despite the pressures on teacher educators to comply with secular requirements relating to subject knowledge and to professional competencies, I believe it is desirable, indeed that it is necessary for the health and flourishing of education in general, as well as of Christian education in particular, that Christians seek to reflect deliberately, rigorously and systematically on how their faith, religious tradition and theological insights might have a bearing on the tasks of teaching and learning and influence the way that life, work and leadership in schools might be conducted and construed. I also believe, on the basis of lengthy personal experience of teaching courses in church school leadership, that it is possible to combine a faith perspective with critical academic rigour and the development of professional competence. One can distinguish a Christian philosophy of education in general from the various forms of education in faith, although Christian educators should have an interest (if not a direct involvement) in both (Astley, 1994; McLaughlin, Carr, Haldane and Pring, 1995; Groome, 1998; Peterson, 2001; Sullivan, 2001; Wolterstorff, 2002). For the purposes of this chapter, I intend to restrict my attention to the former.

My own work since 1994 in the field of Christian education at university level includes initial and inservice teacher education and training, directing advanced study (Master's programmes in Christian educational leadership), supervision of research and professional consultancy for schools, colleges, dioceses and seminaries. This experience informs and underpins the normative issues raised here, though of course such experience alone cannot be persuasive for others. But I build on it in the hope that it may reveal the links that may be established between the work of an education department and a Christian perspective and ethos.

All teachers and educational leaders, whether just embarking on their career or moving towards its end, from the most junior to the most senior, need to reflect upon the philosophical, political, practical and personal dimensions of their work. Christians would wish to add to these the theological dimension. Furthermore, they would envisage the theological dimension not as something separate and distinct from these other dimensions, but as integrally implicated in them.

First, one has to be clear about the logical geography, the key concepts that govern the activity of education, its central purposes and essential features. In addition to this, a developed and secure understanding by the teacher of subject matter, appropriate methodology and criteria for evaluation is required.

Second, it is vital for survival that one is sensitive to the political aspects. Whose permission has to be gained for what may be done?

What kind of mandate is granted to teachers? What rules govern, frame, facilitate and constrain educational endeavours? What influences and powers are at work that must be taken into account?

Third, at every level of education teachers have practical questions to address. What will I say in tomorrow's assembly? What material will I put before students in class? What tasks will I set? What resources should be used? How will I assess their learning? How will I keep order? How will I encourage their active engagement? What motivational strategies will I employ? What modes of communication and style of relationship will be deployed?

Fourth, how is what I bring as a person to my teaching influencing, for better or worse, my effectiveness? We each bring to our teaching and educational leadership a particular set of experiences and abilities, of assumptions and convictions, of hopes and fears, of strengths and weaknesses. How are these impacting upon what happens in the classroom and the staffroom? How am I coming across to those with whom I try to teach, or to collaborate or to lead? Is there congruence between my goals and my approaches? Furthermore, what difference is this work making to me? How is it affecting me, positively and negatively, as a person?

All of these questions can easily be explored by people of any faith and by those with no religious convictions. By relating these questions to their theology, Christians seek to connect the tasks of education to their understanding of God and God's relation to the world of nature, creatures and humanity, as conveyed to them via their religious tradition. In doing so they expect to find direction and purpose in the overall endeavour, to detect a sense of significance and meaning even in the mundane, to draw from their faith inspiration to embark on this career, motivation to sustain them throughout its travails, and perseverance when the obstacles to success seem burdensome. By relating their theology to their thinking about education, they should be in a better position to give a reason for the hope that is in them and to render a credible account of their faith to outsiders.

Responsibility

There is already available much valuable literature on teaching as a profession, material which does not depend upon an appeal to religious principles (Carr, 2000; Goodlad, 1990; Hare, 1993; Hoyle and John, 1995; Ungoed-Thomas, 1997; Van Manen, 1993). It is generally accepted that a professional ethic for teaching has built into it a sense of responsibility. One can distinguish here four aspects to this responsibility: *for*, *with*, *from* and *to*. The first two types of responsibility seem to me to be well represented in educational literature, although the second less adequately than the first, while the third and fourth types are usually neglected.

One's responsibility *for* others is about attending to students and it entails a sensitivity to their current capacities and needs; it aims to sponsor, promote and care for their growth, development, learning and change, their confidence and competence. Most of the literature about education relates to this first form of responsibility, including recent emphases on inclusiveness and differentiation.

To emphasise responsibility *with* others is to focus on the many types of collaboration and partnership that are essential for effective education over a period of time, including with colleagues, parents and students. For Christians this includes the notion of partnership with and on behalf of the church. In most educational institutions teaching functions best when it is conceived of and practised as a corporate endeavour. This does not mean by suppressing individuality. It does entail having regard for the company we keep, the quality of the ethos and the kind of community that is being constructed.

By responsibility *from* I am referring to the personhood of the teacher, the one 'within' who is expressed outwardly in the activity of teaching. To make sense of what we do, we need to know who we are (and who we might become). Then, ideally, there is some congruence between our sense of identity, our purposes and our vocation. To concentrate on the subject (rather than the object) who is responsible turns our attention away from the external features of our activity and towards the spirit in which it is carried out. Thus, one might ask about one's activity: Am I its author? Do I own it? Am I being authentic? Without a concern for the aspect of responsibility *from*, there is the danger that teachers become technicians, implementing policies that they have no part in developing, and obeying instructions whose purpose comes from outside themselves, according to external orders.

This links with the fourth type of responsibility, responsibility *to*, which I examine in section five of the chapter. Such responsibility *to*, centrally involves for Christians the ability to respond to God in discipleship and through a particular vocation.

My emphasis here on responsibility *from* is related to a conviction that a major aspect of the nature of teaching has been seriously marginalised in recent years in initial, inservice and higher level study carried out by university education departments. This is the contemplative side of teaching, which has been almost eclipsed by the stress on its active features. Traditionally teaching has been seen as requiring both. The whole battery of competencies and skills required by the Teacher Training Agency for Qualified Teacher Status and for the National Professional Qualification for Headship – including communication, planning, group management, assessment, and the capacity to use information and communication technology – is evidence of the emphasis on the active side of teaching (and leadership).

In the contemplative I include a range of features which receive very little attention. To be contemplative means taking time to let the object of our contemplation touch us, speak to us, impress its presence on us. This requires patience, stillness, silence and humility. It also suggests the leisure and inner space to gaze, to ponder, to admire, to wonder, to listen to, to wait upon, to be open to. Without this the teacher is likely to be merely busy, shallow, a threat to or an intrusion in the lives of learners, lacking openness, inattentive to the needs of others and unappreciative of the presence of God. Contemplation fosters a penetrating and comprehensive 'seeing' and a sense of the true, the good and the beautiful. Beyond this, it is sensitive to the source of these qualities, attends to the whole picture and the goal of life. It allows significance, purpose and meaning to surface rather than to be submerged in a flurry of 'busy-ness'.

To give due attention to responsibility *from* and to the contemplative dimension of teaching, as I have described these two connected features, is linked to the development of vocation and the sense of responsibility *to* that is, in my view, central to the distinctive contribution a Christian college or university should make to teacher education. From the stance of Christian faith, there should be close links between our attitudes to learning and knowledge, to other people, to self, to the objects, tasks and creatures of this world, and to God. A Christian approach to the work of an education department at university will reflect this kind of interconnectedness between all the aspects of life, the importance of communion with others and with

God. It will then differ in important respects from the approach adopted in other such institutions in several ways. The yardsticks or criteria for success that it measures itself by (drawn from the Gospels) will go beyond the usual competencies (though these will still be taken seriously). Attention will be given to the inner resources which help us to carry on even in the face of difficulties and apparent defeat. The perspective in which education is conceived, the purposes which govern it and the priorities that are given attention within it will be more person-centred, holistic, integrated, coherent, open to the spiritual and to the transcendent, and related to a religious worldview than is possible in a secular university. A religious view of human personhood, of our divine origin and eternal destiny, will be taken seriously. Human gifts and talents, as well as weaknesses and shortcomings, will be examined.

Theological literacy

In order to address the kinds of emphasis indicated above, education departments in Christian colleges and universities need to draw upon, to make their own contribution to, and to develop in their students, a theological literacy. (For a richly diverse range of insights into the nature and scope of theological literacy, see Petersen and Rourke, 2002.) I take theology to be a process of systematic reflection that seeks to make sense of the religious experience of a faith community. As one writer put it, 'Theology is a continuous process of interpreting our lives in relationship to ultimate questions – in relation to God. We struggle to discover truths on which we can stake our lives' (Seymour, 1993, p. 29). Although God is the focus of study in theology, we cannot leave aside the rest of our experience, for this would simultaneously diminish our appreciation of God and distort our perception of the world as created. Theology is about seeing all things in relation to God and then responding to this understanding of reality. The purpose of theology is 'not simply to discover "knowledge", but to serve a way of life' (Volf, 2002, p. 247).

Theology displays the four kinds of responsibility that have already been discussed: *for, with, from* and *to.* That is, theology, as a form of responsibility *for* must attend to the needs of the people we encounter and creation in general. An informed intellectual grasp of notions about

God that did not express itself in careful ways to look after God's people and world would be sterile and contradictory.

Second, as a form of responsibility *with,* theology takes place within the context of a believing community. Even when working alone, theologians draw upon the wisdom, insights and experience of a faith community and allow themselves to be formed, nourished, supported, guided and corrected by this community, notwithstanding the fact that sometimes that community needs criticism from theologians for false interpretations and misuses of its tradition.

Third, as a form of responsibility *from,* theology has to engage the multiple dimensions of the life of theologians themselves, not least their spirituality and their moral character. Authentic theology has to be a self-involving activity, one to which we voluntarily give ourselves at a deep level. As a source and compass for our major decisions and actions, it will transcend being merely a compartment of life and will 'spill over' into the way we perceive and respond to all our experience.

Finally, as a form of responsibility *to,* we can claim that a theologian for whom a relationship with God is not real cannot communicate effectively about God's relationship with all things in life. For 'what orders theology as a form of knowledge is its object, God' (Schner, 1993, p. 27). Although theology has to use human language and concepts, and is subject to misleading distortions and severe limitations when it tries to speak of God, ultimately it cannot be reduced to a purely human construction. It will be formed by the quality of relationship that exists between the theologian and God. Eckhart articulated a traditional perspective that has mostly been ignored or forgotten: 'The degree to which the mind is active, and therefore the degree to which it exists, is determined by the actuality of that which it knows' (Davies, 1994, p. xix).

There is not time, given all the other curriculum pressures in education departments, to do justice to the range and depth of studies made possible by theology. But what should be possible is to provide, in conjunction with theology departments, an introduction to the theology of education, one that illustrates the potential contribution that a theological perspective can make to the understanding and practice of teaching and educational leadership. There are many ways this could be done. One could invite students to reach up to the thinking of a particular theologian whose work captures their imagination. They could explore the educational relevance of recent developments in one area of theology of interest to them. Alternatively, one might start from practical issues and questions that arise from the perspective of pupils, parents, teachers, school governors, diocesan officers, and so on and then to seek appropriate theological resources for their resolution. Areas that should receive some attention in education departments are faith and culture; the human person; types of knowledge and truth, including religious knowledge and ways to this; vulnerability, self-acceptance and growth; the role of the worshipping community as a forum for some kinds of learning and development; an introduction to what is meant by perceiving creation in a sacramental perspective; how spiritual development relates to all of these themes.

Xavier Thévenot (1991, p. 281) describes some of the risks in using Scripture in education, which I want to adapt and apply more widely to the use of a theological approach in education. First, it can become ideological, as an aid to our power and position (thereby slipping into domination instead of liberation). Second, we can be selective (and imbalanced) in what we draw from theological traditions and employ only some of the languages of faith and the church. These include *kerygma* (proclamation), *koinonia* (fellowship or communion), *leiturgia* (worship), *diakonia* (service) and *didache* (teaching). Selectivity and omission in using the languages of faith can give a distorted picture. Third, inappropriate or 'blanket' application of theological concepts to the particularity of people and the singularity of situations may prevent an adequate 'reading' of and response to those situations. Fourth, we can fail to acknowledge the cultural embeddedness (and limitations) of some expressions of the tradition. In order to guard against these risks, the skills of critique (see below) need to be applied to theological as well as educational concepts.

Vocation

One feature that should be evident in the work of education departments in Christian colleges is the emphasis they give to the notion of vocation. Vocation can be interpreted as being about my sense of identity, which community I connect myself to, the focus and direction of my behaviour and the sources of significance for me. My vocation provides an answer to the questions: Who am I? Where and with whom do I belong? What should I do and how should I act? To what priorities should I commit myself? Where am I going? In this way vocation provides a thread that links identity, community, behaviour, direction, purpose and destiny. Vocation is a way of living out what we believe and what we value in response to the needs of others. It is nourished and reinforced by our way of worship and those we belong to (see Schner, 1993, pp. 8, 30). It links who we are with what we do. It embodies and expresses our framework of meaning and significance. It functions as a project for us towards wholeness and integration of head, heart and hands.

The primary call for a Christian is the call to become a disciple of Christ, to commit oneself to follow Jesus in one's heart and to express this commitment concretely through one's actions and lifestyle (Pietri, 2002, pp. 26, 121). Although each is called by name, as an individual, the journey of discipleship is one we are called to travel together; it is more true to describe discipleship as a community of life (with Christ and with the body of believers) than it is to consider it as adhesion to a teaching (Pietri, p. 12). To carry out one's vocation as a Christian disciple, one has to take account of two principal modes of communication from God: the word of God as expressed in Holy Scripture and the events and situations in the world. These have to be seen in the light of each other. Karl Rahner puts it thus:

> One can only decipher clearly and fully the message of Jesus–Christ in the book of the world in so far as one has read it in the book of Scripture. But one can and should read it in the book of the world and of human life to have a true and full understanding of what is said in the word of Scripture. (As quoted by Pietri, p. 88)

For Christian teachers, their work can be viewed as a vocation: this is *where* God wants me to be; this is *what* God wants me to do; this is *how* God invites me to share my talents; and, most important of all, this is *who* God calls me to be (Sullivan, 2002b). The personal presence of teachers is a key vehicle for conveying this sense of vocation. Their exemplary role with children, young people and their colleagues relies upon their deepest values, their integrity, their self-knowledge, their sense of purpose in education, their feelings of worth and confidence. In turn, this sense of personal calling connects up with the public dimension: we are called to account because we work not only with, but also for others, and not just for ourselves. My work is merely a small part of a bigger picture than the story of my own life. It serves a greater cause than meeting our own needs or developing our own talents. It is played out on a larger stage than just our own life and its particular concerns and goals. A strong sense of vocation is potentially a very valuable resource for developing in teachers the four aspects of responsibility described earlier.

Critique

If vocation in teaching is an expression of responsibility, a response *to* God that is made *from* within, *with* others and *for* students, neither vocation nor responsibility can be properly exercised without developing the capacity for critique. There are many elements within this capacity. It includes being able to discriminate between the contingent and transient, as compared with what is permanently significant. Teachers need to learn how to adopt a critical stance towards the knowledge, skills and attitudes that are being transmitted, attentive to the reliability of their sources. They must learn how to be sensitive to the voices that they hear, noting which are privileged and which are marginalised in classrooms and throughout the school. They should be conscious of the bases for their judgements and evaluations. They should be encouraged to be alert to the shadow side of life in schools; this includes organisational pathologies and cultural blind spots, the unintended consequences of policies and decisions, gaps between rhetoric and reality, and areas of complacency (Egan, 1994).

If teachers, in both their initial and inservice courses, develop the qualities of critical thinking, this should help them, in the process of committing themselves to a particular school or educational setting, to avoid being too assimilated and thereby losing their own integrity and authenticity. The capacity for critique should equip them to discern which external pressures and opportunities to accept or resist. Sometimes, even at the cost of unpopularity, their vocation will entail teachers playing a prophetic role, with counter-cultural witness being a duty on some issues. Christian teachers, while indwelling their faith tradition, need to be aware of the ongoing and central arguments within that tradition, the multiple interpretations it has been subject to and the current internal and external challenges that require consideration and response. Faced with current educational orthodoxies, priorities and assumptions, for example those relating to pluralism, tolerance and social harmony, or those relating to performance and accountability, or the role of the market in education and the emphasis on the economic dimension in education, they need support in interrogating these in the light of the gospel.

Just as at least some philosophical underpinning is needed for professional practice, so personal spirituality is needed for public ministry. Unfortunately, very little time is given in most teacher education programmes either to philosophy or to spirituality. This means that teachers are ill-equipped to resist the inexorable pressures of the performativity which is so integral a feature of the managerialism in all arenas of education. Outcomes matter more than intentions. People become judged by their apparent success in meeting certain targets. Securing achievement and raising standards can take place while the inner life gets neglected. A focus on the spiritual helps us bridge the gap between the ethical – what we feel we ought to do, and the political, as described above. At the same time, insufficient philosophical reflection leads to an uncritical adoption (or rejection) of current educational 'bandwagons', policies and inducements to compliance. Then teachers leap too quickly to questions about the 'how?', the 'when?' or the 'with what?', before clarifying the 'why?' This might apply in areas such as appraisal, school development planning, citizenship, sex education, study skills or multiculturalism. If this bypassing of clarity about purpose and guiding principles leads to a premature engagement with practical questions, teachers can as a result find themselves busily participating in activities that have the appearance of being collaborative educational and management processes, but which in reality are carried out by people who hold radically different and often incompatible perceptions of what they are doing.

The development of critical thinking, as part of the work of education departments, enables students to enter into conversation with both the theological and educational traditions of enquiry and practice they encounter. The theologian George Schner refers to 'the ability to be in conversation with the tradition of which one is a part, to be enthusiastic for that inheritance. Not a naïve enthusiasm, of course, but a critical one'. He continues:

Teachers who are angry with, uncomfortable with, deeply at odds with the tradition cannot teach it; they can parody it, find fault with it, but not in any real sense teach it. Conversely, the uncritical teaching of the tradition is equally poor teaching. (Schner, 1993, p. 137)

This critical engagement applies as much to their Christian faith as it does to their professional context. As Schner says, 'teachers are not the uncritical purveyors of an established, ahistorical interpretation of the Word of God, nor are students mechanical imitators' (p. 150).

I have argued that there is a legitimate place for a faith perspective to be deployed in education departments in Christian colleges and universities. Furthermore, I have claimed that such institutions have a duty to draw from the Christian tradition ideas and practices that facilitate ways of reflecting on the responsibility of teachers and that transcend current narrowness and limitations. Prevailing models of education, based on a national curriculum for schools and beyond, seem to rely upon a pre-specified picture of what should be learned, how this must be assessed, what kinds of skills are required by teachers to 'deliver' the desired outcomes, and a strictly adhered-to list of competencies displayed by those who manage this work. If education departments developed in their students a critical appreciation of the resources of Christian tradition on issues relating to teaching and if they fostered a strong sense of vocation, far from being a backward step, this would equip new and experienced teachers and educational leaders to make a constructive and effective contribution to students, colleagues, schools and the profession as a whole. If the multiple dimensions of responsibility, vocation and critique, as outlined in this chapter, are taken to heart and a serious effort is made to integrate them, then teachers and leaders who graduate from departments of education in Christian institutions will be well placed to find significance in their work, to regenerate a demoralised profession, to excite students, to model commitment, to convey a sense of purpose, and to operate with clarity, conviction, compassion, courage, freedom and inventiveness.

References

Astley, J. (1994) *The Philosophy of Christian Religious Education*, Birmingham, AL, Religious Education Press.

Carr, D. (2000) *Professionalism and Ethics in Teaching*, London, Routledge.

Davies, O. (1994) *Meister Eckhart: Selected Writings*, London, Penguin.

Egan, K. (1994) *Working the Shadow Side*, San Francisco, CA, Jossey-Bass.

Goodlad, J. *et al.* (eds) (1990) *The Moral Dimensions of Teaching*, San Francisco, CA, Jossey-Bass.

Graham, G. (2002) *Universities: The Recovery of an Idea*, Exeter, Imprint Academic.

Groome, T. (1998) *Educating for Life*, Allen, TX, Thomas More Press.

Hare, W. (1993) *What Makes a Good Teacher?* London, Ontario, Althouse Press.

Hoyle, E. and P. John (1995) *Professional Knowledge and Professional Practice*, London, Cassell.

McLaughlin, T. H., Carr, D., Haldane, J. and R. Pring (1995) 'Return to the Crossroads', *British Journal of Educational Studies*, XXXXIII, 2, pp. 162–178.

Petersen, R. and N. Rourke (eds) (2002) *Theological Literacy for the Twenty-First Century*, Grand Rapids, MI, Eerdmans.

Peterson, M. (2001) *With All Your Mind*, Notre Dame, IN, Notre Dame University Press.

Pietri, G. (2002) *La Vocation*, Paris, Salvator.

Rhodes, F. (2001) *The Creation of the Future*, Ithaca, NY, Cornell University Press.

Schner, G. (1993) *Educating for Ministry*, Lanham, MD, Sheed and Ward.

Seymour, J. *et al.* (1993) *Educating Christians*, Nashville, TN, Abingdon.

Sullivan, J. (1997) 'Blondel and a Living Tradition for Catholic Education', *Catholic Education: A Journal of Inquiry and Practice*, 1, 1, pp. 67–76.

Sullivan, J. (1999a) 'Philosophy as Pilgrimage: Blondel and John Paul II', *The Downside Review*, 117, 406, pp. 1–16.

Sullivan, J. (1999b) 'Von Hügel and Catholic Education', *The Downside Review*, 117, 407, pp. 79–88.

Sullivan, J. (2001) *Catholic Education: Distinctive and Inclusive*, Dordrecht, Kluwer Academic Press.

Sullivan, J. (2002a) 'Scholarship and Spirituality', *The Downside Review*, 120, 420, pp. 189–214.

Sullivan, J. (2002b) 'Leadership and Management', in Michael Hayes and Liam Gearon (eds), *Contemporary Catholic Schools*, Leominster, Gracewing, pp. 91–106.

Thévenot, X. (1991) *Pour une éthique de la pratique éducative*, Paris, Desclée.

Ungoed-Thomas, J. (1997) *Vision of a School*, London, Cassell.

Van Manen, M. (1993) *The Tact of Teaching*, London, Ontario, Althouse Press.

Volf, M. and D. Bass (eds) (2002) *Practicing Theology*, Grand Rapids, MI, Eerdmans.

Wolterstorff, N. (2002) *Educating for Life*, Grand Rapids, MI, Baker Academic Books.

Chapter Seventeen

A Worked Example of the Christian Agenda: The Impact of a Christian Ethos on the Research and Teaching of an Australian Educational Faculty

Patricia Malone

Introduction

Before discussing the impact of a Christian ethos on the Education Faculty of Australian Catholic University (ACU) it is necessary to consider the nature and context of this University. Australian Catholic University came into being in 1991 and the Education Faculty was first set up in 1993, so their development has occurred within a period of great change and complexity both in the field of education and in Australian society. When speaking about current reality in Australia, the social historian Mackay stated:

> We are in the midst of a significant culture shift in which old and new values, old and new attitudes, are finding ways to coexist in a genuinely pluralist society where, possibly for the first time, we are understanding what diversity really means. No wonder it feels to many Australians as if they've been caught in a rip. (Mackay, 1999, p. xviii)

It is in the midst of such diversity and changing values that ACU has had to establish an identity that expresses the Catholic tradition in a way that is appropriate in a multicultural society. Australian Catholic University is one of the new universities which have come into being since 1987, when Colleges of Education were required by the Government to amalgamate with existing universities or to join together to form universities, initially under the sponsorship of an existing university. Latrobe University in Victoria was the sponsoring university for ACU.

Australian Catholic University is Australia's only public Catholic university. It formed in 1991 from an amalgamation of four Catholic tertiary institutions located on eight campuses in Queensland, New South Wales, Victoria and the Australian Capital Territory. It is one of the nationally-funded institutions within the Australian Unified National System of Higher Education. It is set up as a company limited by guarantee under the companies (Victoria) code rather than by an Act of Parliament, which is how the other public universities are established.

Australia has long had a tradition of Catholic schools existing side by side with the state and independent schools. The predecessor colleges to the university had originally focused on training teachers for these schools and were set up by religious congregations for this purpose, although over time they broadened their focus to include nurse education, social work and other fields of education. Notre Dame University in Western Australia is also a Catholic university but it is a private university based on the American model.

Nature of Australian Catholic University

The Memorandum and Articles of the University identify its objects in education, scholarship and research as part of the mission of the Catholic Church. Within that statement and in the name of the university are the seeds of the tension that exist in the current debate to identify and develop what it means to be both university and Catholic within the Australian context. Within its mission statement the University states:

> Australian Catholic University shares with universities worldwide a commitment to quality in teaching, research and service. ... The University's inspiration, located within 2000 years of Catholic intellectual tradition, summons it to attend to all that is of concern to human beings. It brings a distinctive spiritual perspective to the common tasks of higher education.

The University names its contribution to the Catholic mission in language that focuses on the underlying Christian values of the Catholic tradition. It does not use evangelising language and in another section of the mission statement notes: 'it is guided by a fundamental concern for justice and equity, and for the dignity of all human beings.' The University emphasises its inclusive nature and has a slogan 'open to all' in its brochures. The Chancellor, Brother Julian McDonald, in his contribution to the Annual Report, included the following in his description of the University:

> an invitation to staff and students of different or no religious backgrounds to participate in teaching and research that fosters individual growth and humanises the University and the society in which we live. (ACU National, 2002a, pp. 8–9)

To emphasise this inclusivity, and to appeal to an Australian public which still has in its memory fear of the denominational rivalry of an earlier period, the University is now marketing itself as 'ACU National' and includes the following in its list of descriptors (emphasis in original).

- ACU National brings a *unique Catholic Mission* to Australian higher education.
- National university open to all Australians.
- Publicly funded and open to all, *regardless of race, colour, creed or religion*.
- *ACU National is an ethical university*. It empowers its students and staff to consider the moral and ethical dimensions of their study and work. It encourages its staff and students to be socially responsible.
- Engages with and *serves the community*.

(ACU National, 2002a, p. 3)

The first three of the above begin the list and the others are interspersed with statements about areas of study that are available and the quality of the learning process and environment.

In its various statements about itself, ACU National emphasises that 'it contributes significantly and in a unique fashion to the diversity of higher education in Australia' (ACU National, 2002b, p. 11). It states that it 'places values at the core of its teaching and research activities', that it has a national focus and that its profile of teaching and research is oriented towards 'the professions serving the educational, health-care and social needs of the community'. In a response to a Government paper on higher education, the Vice-Chancellor noted that ACU:

offers a special kind of diversity that underpins a system of higher education in a thriving democracy that is searching for meaning. Australia is in need of the specific insights and wisdom that Australian Catholic University provides to Australian people. (Sheehan, 2002b, p. 11)

Catholicity debate

In the general understanding of the contribution of Catholic education to the mission of the church, particularly at the school level, there is often a tendency to overstate the contribution of the educational institution to the life and religious practice of the individual. There is not such an expectation on other Catholic agencies such as health care and social work agencies. Rossiter has commented on this, as follows:

[T]here is a tendency for educators (mainly the Catholic school authorities, school executives, and religion teachers) to use predominantly religious/ecclesiastical language to describe the purposes of Catholic schools; in so doing, they overestimate the extent of the Catholic school's contribution to the mission of the Church. ... In addition, the spiritual development of pupils is framed almost exclusively in terms of a personal relationship with God and in participation in the life of the Catholic Church. (Rossiter, 2002, p. 3)

In its statements the University has avoided this evangelical emphasis and has focused on the underlying values that are consonant with being a Catholic university in a pluralist society. In order to describe the Catholicity of ACU, some people have drawn on aspects of John Paul II's *Apostolic Constitution on Catholic Universities, Ex Corde Ecclesiae* (1990), for language that is more ecclesial. This is a Roman document written for Catholic universities that are generally church-owned and not necessarily part of a public system, yet there are many statements within the document that are appropriate for ACU National and have been incorporated into recent writings. The document states:

Students are challenged to pursue an education that combines excellence in humanistic and cultural development with specialised professional training. Most especially they are challenged to continue the search for truth and for meaning throughout their lives since the human spirit must be cultivated in such a way that there results a growth in its ability to wonder, to understand, to contemplate, to make personal judgments, and to develop a religious, moral and social sense. (John Paul II, 1990, p. 22)

Object 2.1.1 of the University's Constitution states that the University should operate 'in accordance with the beliefs, traditions, practices and canonical legislation of the Roman Catholic Church'. Some consider that this is best carried out by a majority of staff and students who are practising Catholics. These would measure Catholicity in terms of worship and doctrinal orthodoxy and do not accept the reality of the context of the Australian society where, despite an interest in the spiritual, formal religious observance is practised by less than twenty per cent of the population. However, the University does provide opportunity for worship, for the personal spiritual growth of staff and students, and for service and outreach to those in need.

The University, in its official statements, tends to emphasise those dimensions of the spiritual that are part of the Catholic tradition and may be supported by staff and students of various faiths and none. The current Vice-Chancellor of ACU, Professor Peter Sheehan, consistently refers to the University's role as one that promotes the human search for meaning and the expression of a spirituality that is relevant to the contemporary world. He enunciates within his key principles that a Catholic university should be:

'student-centred' and that a 'contemporary Catholic university should be a place where faith and intellect meet in the growth of human potential.' He also argues for an identity that reflects Gospel values and that in 'a contemporary university these values should be integrated through the curriculum and whole University environment.' (Sheehan, 2002a, pp. 131–132)

There are differing perspectives on how these values may be discussed and located within the University curriculum. Some have a narrower view of the educational process and focus on specific disciplines such as philosophy, theology and to a lesser extent religious education, as the locus for such discussions. Sheehan commented:

One of the indirect effects of the current debate about *Ex Corde Ecclesiae* is that the task of forming a Catholic identity is seen to rest too pointedly with those responsible for single disciplines. This has created too much attention on the link between Catholic identity and single disciplines (e.g. Theology). Though Theology is crucial, Catholic identity is integral to the entire scholastic domain and the nature of the total university environment. (Sheehan, 2002a, p. 133)

To appreciate these varying perspectives it is necessary to consider the structure of the University, the varying understandings of the learning process and the specific contributions of subject disciplines within the formal curriculum.

University structure

The University is divided into three faculties: arts and sciences, education and health sciences, and these are located across six campuses in three States and one Territory, and are responsible for developing, implementing and reviewing the various courses. Members of the academic staff are located within these faculties and belong to a specific school of the faculty. The Faculty of Arts and Sciences is the largest faculty and includes the discipline fields of arts, social science, science, business, informatics, philosophy and theology. There are two sub-faculties within this faculty, namely business and informatics, and philosophy and theology. The Faculty of Education is responsible for undergraduate and postgraduate courses in education and has specialisations in teacher education, religious education, adult and community education and educational leadership. The Faculty of Health Sciences is responsible for undergraduate and postgraduate courses in nursing, midwifery and exercise science. ACU National is a small university and there are presently more than eleven thousand students and eight hundred academic staff on the various campuses and studying online.

The University has developed a series of flagships and centres to focus its research output in terms of the specific expertise of the staff and mission of the organisation. These are *early Christian studies; Catholic educational leadership; lifelong learning; mathematics teaching and learning; palliative care; spiritual, moral, religious and pastoral dimensions of education; youth studies; Plunkett Centre for Ethics in Health Care; Social Policy Advocacy Research Centre; and environmental restoration and stewardship.* The focus of the flagships/centres related to the Faculty of Education will be discussed in some detail to illustrate how these respond to the challenge of expressing/reflecting the Catholicity of the University.

As part of a University discussion concerning the articulation of its mission within the degree programmes, each of the faculties reported to the Academic Board in July 2001 on their approaches. McMullen (2001) presented a paper setting out these various approaches which include core and elective units, multidisciplinary units, professional experience placements, service based activities, and the commitment of Faculty and other staff to the values presented in the curriculum. The next section describes and analyses the approach of the Faculty of Education.

Faculty of Education

During the period 1999 to 2001, the Faculty reviewed all its courses and participated in both an internal audit and an external review with respect to the terms of reference identified by the Vice-Chancellor as part of an ongoing strategic planning process of develop–implement–review–improve. The Faculty was proactive in choosing to participate in these processes in a way that would promote collaborative learning of its entire staff.[1] As it stated in the Internal Audit Report:

> [T]he Faculty chose to review itself against its own Goals as well as responding to the Common Terms of Reference provided by the University for Faculty Reviews. It developed a framework in which it considered its six major Areas of Strategic Focus against the elements identified in the Common Terms of Reference and the Faculty's Strategic Goals. (Australian Catholic University, 2001a, p. 4)

It went on to make the following statement. 'The report and the accompanying portfolio reflect a dynamic Faculty with a strong commitment to the mission and values of the University.' The *Areas of Strategic Focus* that related to the major functions of the Faculty were identified as:

- learning and teaching;
- research and scholarship;

- community service and outreach;
- management;
- staffing;
- student needs and student support.

The focus on learning and teaching (and not just teaching) is indicative of the strong emphasis on the learning paradigm at the core of the Faculty. The relationship between research and scholarship and its intrinsic place in the learning paradigm for staff and students reflects a university that reflects the Catholic tradition's search for truth and synthesis of knowledge and life. In a recent response to a Government Paper on *Striving for Quality: Learning, Teaching and Scholarship*, the Vice-Chancellor stated:

> The view of ACU is that there is a necessary and ineliminable connection between good teaching and learning, and the research and scholarship from which it springs, on which it is based, and which continues to give nourishment for further thought. ... It is from the mission of the University, the cognitive endeavours and achievements of the disciplines and fields of study within the University, and the needs of students, that the types of research scholarship and teaching that it commits itself to undertaking are determined. (Sheehan, 2002c, p. 5)

Articulation of the mission in the curriculum

Curriculum includes all the planned activities of the University, and specifically the faculty, to promote learning. There is need for an adequate curriculum theory that appreciates the value of disciplines but recognises that learning is not limited to formal areas of subject and that most learning is transferable across fields. The Faculty set up a committee of the Faculty Board in 2001 to report on the ways the Catholicity of the University was expressed and developed within the courses of the Faculty. Several position papers were presented to the Faculty Board, and after consideration of these and the report of the External Review Committee a Draft Policy Document, *Spiritual, Moral, Religious and Justice Dimensions of the Faculty Curriculum*, was accepted by the Board in August 2002.

The External Review Committee noted that:

The Mission is evident in the commitment and activities of the Faculty directed towards the achievement of quality in teaching, research and service. There is evidence of a recognition of justice and equity issues through the orientation of a number of courses. (Australian Catholic University, 2001b, p. 17)

It did recommend that the Faculty continue to articulate this relationship and ensure that members of staff are given the opportunity to endorse and implement the vision. The Faculty is very conscious of the inclusive nature of its faculty and student body, and in all the discussions within the University had challenged the suggestion that an understanding of the mission was developed principally by 'philosophical and theologically related units' (Rossiter, 2000, p. 1). The Faculty notes in its policy document that it 'is appropriate for any university to address spiritual, moral, religious and justice issues in its curriculum. For a Catholic sponsored university, such a focus is an explicit part of its mission.' This policy document further states that:

> *All* of the Faculty's units are expressions of the mission of the University. Use of the term 'mission focussed' units (in some University documentation) can create problems with the determination of how and why some units may be more mission-focussed than others. (Australian Catholic University, Faculty of Education, 2002, p. 1)

The Faculty offers 'three principal curriculum approaches' as an articulation of the spiritual/ethical dimension. These approaches are:

- **Explicit:** where spiritual, moral, religious and justice content/concerns/issues are the formal content of the units (e.g. religious education units, social analysis units and community service programs).
- **Contextual:** Where these areas are raised in relationship with the substantive content of the units (e.g. ethics in educational and business practice, globalisation issues).
- **General skills and consciousness-raising:** learning and teaching processes in all units which contribute to the 'personal' learning and development of the students and their personal search for meaning and identity.

> (Australian Catholic University, Faculty of Education, 2002, p. 2)

This emphasis on personal development recognises that one of the key roles of the Faculty is to help the students identify their own goals and relate their learnings to their profession and to the whole of their lives. As Bentley noted:

> Active learning projects can help the participants to make connections between ways of knowing things, between situations in which they might need to learn, and between the specific content of their activities and the wider social and personal goals the participants may embrace. (Bentley, 1998, p. 52)

Shephard offers a social-constructivist model about learning that supports the Faculty's approach, maintaining that the search for understanding is also culturally and socially determined. She states:

> From cognitive theory we have also learned that existing knowledge structures and beliefs work to enable or impede new learning, that intelligent thought involves self monitoring and awareness about when and how to use skills, and that 'expertise' develops in a field of study as a principled and coherent way of thinking and representing problems not just as an accumulation of information. (Shephard, 2000, p. 10)

This approach to learning is essential for educators of the future who have not only to use their learning to solve their own problems, but also to assist the next generation of learners to carry out their own search for meaning.

Graduate attributes

A great deal of work has been carried out by the Faculty to articulate the attributes that their graduates should demonstrate. This became the focus for 2002 in response to the Report of the External Review of the Faculty of Education, December 2001, which had as its second recommendation that:

> The Faculty explicitly identify and articulate the skills and attributes required of educators of the 21st century, and that such a list of desired

graduate attributes be spelt out so that they are understood by students (and Faculty members) at the point of commencement and throughout their studies. (Australian Catholic University, 2001b, p. 12)

The Faculty set in train a series of *Revisioning Workshops* so that all staff could explore and discuss the desired outcomes of their programmes so that they could work together to promote the type of learning needed to assist graduates acquire the desired attributes. In the very process of these workshops, the Faculty illustrated the nexus between teaching and research previously noted. Staff who had been involved in two different Government-funded research projects had current scholarship to share with their peers. The Dean and staff representatives, therefore, who had been part of the studies of *Lifelong Learning, Teachers and Teacher Education*, and *Service Learning*, presented theoretical frameworks at each workshop. These workshops contributed to a growing sense of a common vision and the findings were incorporated into the Draft Policy discussed previously.

This focused staff vision and sense of purpose is essential if the ethos of the University is to become part of the student world. Changing curriculum and proposing new forms of pedagogy will not necessarily bring about attitude changes, as various research projects have demonstrated. Values and attitudes, particularly about personal beliefs or concerning issues of race or prejudice, are the most difficult to change simply by formal educational processes. *The Teaching for Resistance Report* (Education for Social Justice Research Project, 1994, pp. 18–19) stated that there are many factors involved in the process of developing prejudice, and that although ignorance is a contributing factor, simply learning about a religion or another culture is not sufficient to change attitudes. This was also reflected by students' comments in research carried out by the author after the introduction of formal religion courses in the senior years of high school. One student said about another religious group, 'I know more about them but I hate them more' (Malone, 1995, p. 6). Most research has shown that to bring about a change in attitudes, knowledge has to be linked to some experience with representatives of the other group and a structure in which the values are actually lived and not just talked about. This is the challenge for the Faculty, and indeed for the University, as all have a responsibility to work towards bringing about a vision of a more open and accepting society in which the spiritual, moral, religious and justice dimensions of the curriculum and of life are afforded their rightful place.

Beare (2001, p. 37) speaks of the need to change our basic approach and suggests that we move from developing clones to developing *clades*. Clades literally mean branches of trees and describe life forms that generate new species in the evolutionary process. At times education seems to have as its focus cloning the existing forms, but these are unable to generate new life forms and the graduates of today's university will need to be able to create a church and a society which, at present, we cannot even imagine.

Unless the students have an active role in their learning and see the value of the learning process no real learning will happen. Staff need to name and work for the dreams of each group of graduates. The Australian College of Education expressed it thus:

> Learning is not simply a matter of pure intellect but must be an engagement by the learner with others and the self in practical action and the expression of personal experience. There ought to be passion in learning, which infuses learners with curiosity long after they leave their institutions. (Australian College of Education, 2001, p. 24)

The energy generated by such a search is essential for the life of the Faculty.

In the External Review Report it was noted that the Faculty has developed a strong culture of participative leadership in which the following were noted:

(i)   Staff endorsement of the mission of a Catholic University with its distinctive spiritual perspective.

(ii) A consciousness of the Faculty's own identity. Although it operates as part of the University and responds to the University's mission, ethos and priorities, it operates independently in its own area of expertise.

(iii) The dignity, respect and loyalty accorded to individual members of the Faculty, their roles and responsibilities.

(AustralianCatholic University, 2001b, p. 9)

This is a significant development within a ten-year period. Initially, the core of the Faculty came from the predecessor colleges and now it is moving into a new phase as many of these come to retirement age.

New members of staff need the opportunity to explore the challenges of the University's ethos and mission and find new expressions for it in the Faculty of the future. The present induction processes need to be constantly reviewed to ensure that they offer the opportunity for new members to grapple with the issues expressed within the tradition, and are not simply given a set of guidelines on how to operate within the vision of the University and its Faculties.

The External Committee also noted that:

> As part of its distinctiveness, the Faculty has a particular concern for developing graduates with a strong sense of social justice. While this value suffuses many aspects of the curriculum, the Committee considered that students should be enabled, perhaps even obliged, to undertake a placement in some community based setting as part of their education. Such settings could include remote, underprivileged or marginalised communities in Australia or abroad. This approach is known as Service Learning, and the Committee believes that ACU could become a leading site for such Service Learning in Australian higher education.
>
> (Australian Catholic University, 2001b, p. 14)

Service learning and community involvement in many forms has been an important dimension of many of the programmes offered by schools within the Faculty of Education. This recommendation provides a new challenge to the Faculty to ensure that there is not just an empty rhetoric about the call to serve the community, and particularly those most in need, and to ensure it is part of an integrated learning process. Processes of critical social analysis are as important as the personal experiences involved, and it is hoped that the critical reflection that accompanies these will become part of the ongoing learning and development of the educators of the future.

Focus of research

As previously noted, the flagships have been developed as a focus for research that is in keeping with the University's mission, and have the capacity to enrich the teaching of the Faculty and contribute knowledge that is essential for the professional development of the graduate. The flagship *Centre for Lifelong Learning* illustrates this very effectively; indeed the first research objective of the Centre is 'to undertake research and development relevant to the university's mission and government priorities'. The very language in which it states its purpose reflects this:

> This Centre was established in an effort to advance the mission of Australian Catholic University, and to contribute to the realisation of lifelong learning for all.
>
> The Centre was established to provide a basis for research and scholarship, teaching and learning, policy advice, and community service and outreach in the area of lifelong learning. It further enhances the University's capacity to promote reflection upon personal and spiritual values in the context of local, national and international communities.
>
> (www.acu.edu.au/fed/LLL_stratfocu.html)

This Centre states that it is able to respond to 'the deliberations of OECD, UNESCO, the European Parliament, the Nordic Council of Ministers, the Japanese Parliament, APEC and the Australian Commonwealth Government [which] reveal a growing commitment to policies of learning across the lifespan' (www.acu.edu.au/fed/LLL/index.htm). This capacity to respond means that the values that are integral to the Faculty are expressed in the approach to the research tasks that the Centre is able to carry out.

Similarly, the flagship *Catholic Educational Leadership* in its very name and focus illustrates the Faculty's contribution to a specific aspect of the church's mission. The flagship's purpose is stated as:

> being shaped by a Catholic philosophy and framework that will assist leaders in Catholic systems and schools to develop an authentic approach to leadership characterised by a commitment to ethics, morality, service, stewardship, spirituality, social justice, equity and compassion.
>
> (www.acu.edu.au/leadership/CEL)

The following, which are stated as being two of the objectives of the flagship, illustrate further the close relationship to the practical world of the profession:

(i) [to] promote and support a research culture with a research agenda developed in partnership with key stakeholders in Catholic educational leadership; ...

(v) [to] create national and international networks of Catholic educational leaders who will engage in critical debate and 'grounded theory building' through discussions on 'best practice' in Catholic leadership.

This flagship, together with the *Cardinal Clancy Centre for Research in the Spiritual, Moral, Religious and Pastoral Dimensions of Education*, provide a focus for many of the doctoral students in the Faculty. Most of these students occupy key positions in the Catholic and other educational systems and help ground the flagships in the real issues of the profession. The inclusive nature of the Faculty is reflected in the fact that one of the two first PhD graduates in the area of religious education was the Principal of a Lutheran Teachers College who researched the educational paradigms in Lutheran schools. The other graduate was responsible for secondary religious education in one of the Catholic country dioceses. Secondary teachers for the Lutheran schools study at ACU National with specialised units in Lutheran theology being offered in place of some specifically Catholic units. There are several doctoral students from other religious traditions studying within the Faculty of Education. Many of the staff are involved in ecumenical and multi-faith associations, both nationally and internationally, which ensures that their perspective is consistently broadened so that they can continue to challenge their students and fellow researchers.

Conclusion

The Education Faculty of Australian Catholic University has its own agenda and structure as it responds to the changing reality and needs of education in the second millennium. This agenda and practice is informed by the traditions of the predecessor Catholic Colleges of Education from which ACU was formed. This agenda is consonant with the vision and mission statements of ACU National. The Faculty uses educational language to express the mission of the Church in ways that are able to inspire and challenge its staff and students who belong to the pluralist, multicultural society of Australia.

References

Australian Catholic University (2001a) *Faculty of Education Quality Review: Internal Quality Audit Committee*, Report August 2001, Melbourne, Australian Catholic University.

Australian Catholic University (2001b) *External Review of the Faculty of Education*, Report of the External Committee established by the Vice-Chancellor of Australian Catholic University to review the University's Faculty of Education.

Australian Catholic University, Faculty of Education (2002) *Spiritual, Moral, Religious and Justice Dimensions of the Faculty Curriculum*. Draft Policy Statement of the Faculty of Education, Australian Catholic University.

Australian College of Education (2001) 'A National Declaration for Education 2001: A Report on the findings *Celebrating the Past, Shaping the Future: Outcomes from the Education Assembly*', *Unicorn*, 27, 2, pp. 5–26.

ACU National (2002a) *Annual Report 2000/2001*, Sydney, Australian Catholic University.

ACU National (2002b) *Performance Portfolio*, Vols 1 and 2. Documents prepared May 2002 for the Australian Universities Quality Agency in preparation for 2002 Quality Audit of Australian Catholic University. Sydney, Australian Catholic University.

Beare, H. (2001) *Creating the Future School: Student Outcomes and the Reform of Education*, London and New York, RoutledgeFalmer.

Bentley, T. (1998) *Learning Beyond the Classroom: Education for a Changing World*, London, Routledge.

Education for Social Justice Research Group (1994) *Teaching for Resistance*, Adelaide, Texts in Humanities.

John Paul II (1990) *Ex Corde Ecclesiae: Apostolic Constitution on Catholic Universities*, Boston, St Paul Books and Media.

Mackay, H. (1999) *Turning Point: Australians Choosing their Future*, Australia, Macmillan.

Malone, P. (1995) 'Does It Make Any Difference? Some Effects of Studying Senior Religion', *Intersections*, 1, 2, pp. 37–58.

McMullen G. (2001) 'How the Mission Statement of Australian Catholic University is Reflected in its Curriculum', *Catholic Higher Education* 22, 1, Fall 2001, ACCU, Washington DC – Document 2: 81–91.

Rossiter, G. M. (2000) *The Catholicity of Australian Catholic University: Implications for the Spiritual, Moral and Justice Dimensions of the University's Curriculum*. Paper prepared for the Faculty of Education as part of University discussions on the Catholicity of the University.

Rossiter, G. M. (2002) *Catholic Education and Values: A Review of the Role of Catholic Schools in Promoting the Spiritual and Moral Development of Pupils*. Paper presented at Colloquium at Australian Catholic University, July 2002.

Sheehan, P. W. (2002a) 'Some Special Challenges Facing a Contemporary Catholic University', *The Australasian Catholic Record*, 79, 2, pp. 131–139.

Sheehan, P. W. (2002b) *Response to Higher Education at the Crossroads*. Submission on Ministerial Discussion Paper to the Minister for Education, Science and Training. Available http://intranet.acu.edu.au/vc/kpaper.html [2002, December].

Sheehan, P. W. (2002c) *Striving for Quality*, ACU National Response to 'Striving for Quality; Learning, Teaching and Scholarship'. Available http://intranet.acu.edu.au/vc/kpaper.html [December 2002].

Shepard, L. A. (2000) 'The Role of Assessment in a Learning Culture', Presidential address at AERA Conference 2000, *ER Online,* 29, 7, pp. 1–14. Available http:// www.aera.net/pubs/er/arts/29-07/shep01.htm [2000, October 20th].

Notes

Chapter 1

1 T. S. Eliot, *The Idea of a Christian Society*, second edition, London, Faber & Faber, 1982, p. 62.
2 D. Munby, *The Idea of a Secular Society*, London, Oxford University Press, 1963, p. 14.
3 Munby, *Idea*, p. 17.
4 This summary is both a summary and a reading that assumes the development of the political liberal tradition that shaped modernity. Locke, in his historical setting, is much more ambiguous. For John Locke's views on toleration, see *Letter Concerning Toleration*, New York, Promethus Books, 1991; for his views on the nature and role of the state, see *Two Treatises of Government*, London, Dent, 1924. For my discussion of Locke's arguments, see *Plurality and Christian Ethics*, Cambridge, Cambridge University Press, 1994.
5 Naturally many theologians would want to dissent from this assertion. In fact one difficulty with the secular view of doctrine is that the social implications of these doctrines are overlooked.
6 Raymond Plant uses this image to good effect in his book, *Politics, Theology and History*, Cambridge, Cambridge University Press, 2001.
7 See Bertrand Russell, *Why I am not a Christian*, London, Unwin, 1967.
8 Grace Davie, *Religion in Modern Europe: A Memory Mutates*, Oxford, Oxford University Press, 2000, p. 1.
9 Davie, *Religion in Modern Europe*, p. 1.
10 See Grace Davie, *Religion in Britain since 1945: Believing without Belonging*, Oxford, Blackwell, 1994.
11 See Michael B. Foster, 'The Christian Doctrine of Creation and the Rise of Modern Natural Science', *Mind*, 43, 1934, pp. 446–468 and 'Christian Theology and Modern Science of Nature', *Mind*, 45, 1936, pp. 1–27.
12 This very condensed paragraph is a summary of an argument that is made in my *Truth and the Reality of God*, Edinburgh, T & T Clark, 1998.
13 See Alasdair MacIntyre, *After Virtue*, second edition, London, Duckworth, 1985.

14 John Henry Newman, *The Idea of a University*, edited by Frank M. Turner, New Haven and London, Yale University Press, 1996, p. 45.

15 *Fides et Ratio: Encyclical Letter of the Supreme Pontiff John Paul II to the Bishops of the Catholic Church on the Relationship between Faith and Reason*, Dublin, Veritas, 1998, 'Conclusion', pp. 101–105.

16 For a good discussion of the Salman Rushdie controversy, see Victoria La'Porte, *An Attempt to Understand the Muslim Reaction to the Satanic Verses*, Lewiston, NY, Edwin Mellen Press, 1999.

17 See Richard John Neuhaus, *The Naked Public Square*, Grand Rapids, MI, Eerdmans, 1984.

Chapter 3

1 Cited in McConnell (1993, p. 309). As another example of this bias against religiously-based schools, the prestigious Phi Betta Kappa Society has denied membership to even the best of the many liberal arts colleges of the Christian College Coalition, as well as to the overwhelming majority of the hundreds of Catholic colleges and universities, on the grounds that any religiously-defined standards for teaching are incompatible with academic freedom (Marsden, 1993, p. 233).

2 See, for example, Newman, 1912; Holmes, 1987; Schwehn, 1999; Van Brummelen, 2001.

3 The controversial Apostolic Constitution, *Ex Corde Ecclesiae*, 'From the Heart of the Church', which Pope John Paul II issued in 1990, begins with this reminder: 'Born from the heart of the Church, the Catholic university is located in that course of tradition which may be traced back to the very origin of the university as an institution.'

4 See especially Marsden (1994, p. 438). For other treatments of the decline of the Christian identity of colleges and universities, see Burtcheall, 1998; Sloan, 1994; Geiger, 1986; Gleason, 1995.

5 See, for example, Thomas Kuhn, 1970; Young, 1971; MacIntyre, 1988; Clouser, 1991; Middleton and Walsh, 1995; and Garry and Pearsall, 1989.

6 McConnell refers, for example, to a statement made by the 1988 subcommittee of AAUP's Committee A on Academic Freedom and Tenure with regard to a possible alternative rationale for the accommodation of religious schools – 'many of these institutions usefully function as "decompression chambers" that ease the passage into the larger world for the religiously provincial.' McConnell continues: 'The condescension – indeed bigotry – of this suggestion seems to have passed unnoticed' (1993, p. 312).

7 Alasdair MacIntyre argues that 'membership in a particular type of moral community, one from which fundamental dissent has to be excluded, is a condition for genuinely rational enquiry' (1990, p. 60).

8 This is the central point of Conrad Russell's insightful treatment of the clash between the British Government and the universities during the debate over the Education Reform Bill of 1988 (1993). For a description of more constraints on free enquiry in academia, see Thiessen, 2001, p. 85 and Father James Burtchaell's response to Roman Catholic opposition to *Ex Corde Ecclesiae* in the *Crisis* magazine, July 1999, reprinted in *First Things*, August/September, 1999, pp. 83–85.

9   See Bloom, 1987; Kimball, 1990; D'Souza, 1991; Rauch, 1993.

10 The qualifier 'normal' is added to follow a paradigm I have adopted in an earlier work (Thiessen, 1993). I have developed this argument further in Thiessen, 2001, chapter 5.

11 David Ciocchi objects to the notion of 'intellectually neutral objectivity' often associated with the free pursuit of truth (1994, p. 57). As Arthur Holmes puts it, 'Objectivity consists rather in acknowledging and scrutinizing one's point of view and testing presuppositions. It is more a matter of honesty than of neutrality. Every scholar has commitments' (1987, p. 71).

12 To gain an awareness of the violations to academic freedom that do in fact exist at secular universities, I would recommend Hamilton's excellent summary of seven waves of ideological zealotry that have swept American universities over the past 125 years and which have threatened, and continue to threaten, the ideal of academic freedom as typically understood (1995, chapters 1 and 2). For a description of widespread violations of academic freedom during the McCarthy era, see Schrecker, 1986. For a description of violations of academic freedom in Canadian universities, see Horn, 1999.

13 On Feuerstein's work, see Sharron, 1987. See also Rutter, 1972, 1980 and Bronfenbrenner, 1979. For a similar argument concerning the development of autonomy, see Thiessen, 1993, pp. 140–143.

14 Quoted in Marsden, 1997, p. 7. Paul Hirst raises this objection in a poignant fashion: 'In particular, there has now emerged in our society a concept of education which makes the whole idea of Christian education a kind of nonsense. From this point of view, the idea that there is a characteristically or distinctively Christian form of education seems just as much a mistake as the idea that there is a distinctively Christian form of mathematics, of engineering, or of farming' (Hirst, 1974, p. 77; reprinted in Astley and Francis, 1994, pp. 305–313).

15 I have attempted a more careful treatment of this problem elsewhere. See Thiessen, 1997; 2001, pp. 167–172.

16 Wolterstorff too suggests that for committed Christians the Bible serves to open our eyes to creation and its normative structure, thus encouraging us to look for norms governing the political, economic, aesthetic and other spheres of life (Wolterstorff, 1980, chapter 2). Marsden uses the notion of a gestalt picture to illustrate the commonality and differences between Christian and non-Christian scholarship (1997, pp. 61–62).

17 George Mavrodes illustrates the problem when he reports that he had occasion to study one of the writers of the Reformed tradition with a group of Christian professors, many of whom had international reputations for their research achievements. He reports that they could not think of 'plausible examples of (say) mathematical conjectures or chemical theories which we might reject because of our Christian commitment, nor of new research experiments in astronomy which that commitment might suggest' (quoted in Heie and Wolfe, 1987, p. 328, n. 6).

18 On the philosophy of mathematics, see Ernest, 1991 and Clouser, 1991, chapter 7; on the history of science, see Matthews, 1989.

19 See also John Rawls who uses the notion of an 'overlapping consensus' in his political liberalism (Rawls, 1987).

20 Although Lord Dormand of Easington was speaking about elementary schools, I believe it would be fair to extend his objection also to universities. 'I believe that by their very nature religious schools are divisive. ... Such schools do not

contribute to social cohesion, tolerance and understanding' (*Hansard*, vol. 526, no. 52, March 4, 1991, col. 1281). In 1989 John Patten stated the following: 'Modern Britain has plenty of room for diversity and variety. But there cannot be room for separation or segregation' (quoted in Halstead, 1994, p. 164).

21 I am well aware of the fact that I am here reflecting a North American perspective which finds it difficult to appreciate the idea of an established church within a society. Indeed, I find this notion antiquated and fundamentally unjust and immoral.

22 McClellan, 1985; Glenn, 1988.

23 Kymlicka, 1989, p. 162. Kymlicka does try to give some value to a plurality of cultures, but only insofar as cultural membership provides a context within which an individual can make choices (p. 166).

24 MacIntyre recounts how, in the great academic battles of the 1860s and 1870s, attempts were made to free the universities of Great Britain from the control of the state church, and they did this by imposing a uniform application of the scientific method to all areas of enquiry (1990, pp. 9–31; also reviewed in Marsden, 1997, p. 21).

25 I review some of this evidence in Thiessen, 2001, chapters 2 and 13.

26 This paper was presented at the annual meeting of the Canadian Theological Society, Congress 2002, in Toronto.

27 Edward Relph says that 'home in its most profound form is an attachment to a particular setting, a particular environment, in comparison with which all other associations with places have only limited significance. It is a point of departure from which we orient ourselves and take possession of the world' (1976, p. 40). On the educational implications of this analysis, see Walsh and Bouma-Prediger, 2003.

Chapter 4

1 Now affiliated to the University of Surrey.

2 Formerly Cheltenham and Gloucester College of Higher Education, it achieved university status in 2001.

3 Marsden, 1997, pp. 101–102 makes a similar point.

4 We retain, like Schutz, the archaic spelling to signal the particular usage of the term.

5 For the Cappadocian Father St Basil, it was the world itself that was 'really the school for rational souls to exercise themselves, the training ground for them to learn to know God' (Pelikan, 1993, p. 320).

6 All biblical quotations are taken from the *Authorized King James Version*.

7 In the opening pages of the *Philosophical Fragments*, Kierkegaard draws attention to Socrates' doctrine of recollection, 'by which all learning and inquiry is interpreted as a kind of remembering' (Kierkegaard, 1967, p. 11). The Socratic teacher, through a dialectic of question-and-answer, acts as a maieutical enabler (or midwife), bringing to life that which lies dormant in the soul (Willows, 2001).

8 These three Fathers in particular are called by present day Greek Orthodox thinkers the 'Three Hierarchs' because of their defining role in establishing Christian *paideia*.

9 By not concerning itself, unlike Kant, with the pursuit of truth, Rousseau's progressive education can be seen as the precursor of postmodern pedagogies designed to encourage children to create their own imaginary worlds on the basis of preference, inclination and desire (Cherryholmes, 1988; Parker, 1997; Usher and Edwards, 1994; cf. Wright, 2004).

10 Though this bifurcation is somewhat ameliorated by the emphasis on research and development.

Chapter 5

1 The standard Newman biography is Ker, 1988.
2 For a detailed, if somewhat colourful and at times biased account of nineteenth-century religious thought, see Wilson, 1999. See also Qualls, 2000.
3 We will consider the question of the 'Christian' university in this essay, although Newman certainly made an important distinction between a 'Christian' and a 'Catholic' university.
4 For a brief historical treatment of this period, see volume II of Hylson-Smith, 1997.
5 Carlyle, 1843, pp. 69–70.
6 Carlyle, 1843, p. 1.
7 See the writings of Herbert of Cherbury (1937 edition). For a concise commentary on English Deism, see Beford, 1979.
8 Newman, 1868, p. 9.
9 Dulles, 2002.
10 The best commentary on this seminal work is Merrigan, 1991.
11 Newman, 1845, p. 35.
12 Ibid.
13 Newman, 1845, p. 56.
14 Newman, 1845, p. 36.
15 Newman, 1852, p. 152.
16 Newman, 1868, p. 216.
17 Newman, 1868, p. 9.
18 Newman, 1868, pp. 9–10.
19 Newman, 1845, p. 48.
20 Newman, 1868, p. 123.
21 Newman, 1868, p. 8.
22 Newman, 1845, p. 37.
23 Newman, 1868, p. 82.
24 Newman, 1868, p. 188.
25 Newman, 1868, p. 89.
26 Newman, 1868, p. 189.
27 Newman, 1845, p. 41.
28 Newman, 1868, p. 79.
29 Newman, 1868, p. 82.
30 Newman, 1845, p. 51.
31 Newman, 1868, p. 131.
32 Newman, 1868, p. 10.
33 Newman, 1868, pp. 135–136.
34 Newman, 1845, p. 37.

35 Ibid.
36 Newman, 1868, p. 97.
37 Newman, 1868, p. 93.
38 Newman, 1868, pp. 220–221.
39 Newman, 1868, p. 199.
40 Newman, 1845, p. 34.
41 Tristram, 1956, p. 259.
42 See Ker, 1988, p. 27.
43 Newman, 1978–1984, vol. II, pp. 117–118.
44 See Newman, 1872.
45 Newman, 1845, pp. 56–57.
46 Newman, 1852, p. 153.
47 Newman, 1852, p. 100.
48 Newman, 1852, pp. 278–279.
49 Newman, 1868, p. 10.
50 Newman, 1845, p. 56.
51 Newman, 1852, p. 100.
52 Newman, 1852, p. 113.
53 Newman, 1852, p. 278.
54 Newman, 1852, pp. 276–277.
55 Newman, 1852, p. 148.
56 Ibid.
57 Newman, 1852, p. 65.
58 Newman, 1852, p. 27.
59 Newman, 1852, p. 66.
60 Newman, 1852, p. 439.

Chapter 6

1   Harold Turner founded the Gospel and Culture Network in New Zealand and it was in pursuit of this work that he made the remark. I am not aware that he ever committed the idea to print.
2   The observation is borne out by Stephen Hawking's celebrated claim that if, as he supposes possible, we arrive at the grand unified theory of everything, 'it would be the ultimate triumph of human reason – for then we would know the mind of God' (Hawking, 1988, p. 185).
3   That convention is not preserved in the 1985 translation of *Philosophical Fragments* that we are using. The earlier translation by Niels Thulstrup (Princeton, Princeton University Press, 1936) is to be preferred in this regard, although it is to be noted, given the customary capitalisation of nouns in nineteenth-century Danish, that Kierkegaard's own intentions are not self-evident.
4   The expression 'the god' clearly follows the identical phrase used frequently in the Socratic dialogues. Climacus retains it both in service of his ironical ploy to think things through in Socratic fashion, and to veil as long as possible the Christian character of his alternative.
5   Kierkegaard was fond of using this phrase to indicate the pretentiousness of human beings in supposing themselves capable of God-like vision. See, e.g., Kierkegaard, 1992, p. 217.

6　David Willows' book referred to here offers an excellent exposition of Kierkegaard's conception of the pedagogical task.

7　For a more extensive account of the 'individual' in Kierkegaard, see Pattison, 1997, chapter 6.

8　My expression of this point owes much to Michael O'Siadhail (1996, p. 51).

9　I owe the point to Manheimer (1977, p. 63).

10　See, for example, the 'Crazy Comedy' in Kierkegaard's *Journals and Papers,* 3:3573.

Chapter 7

1　The University of Newcastle ceased to recruit students to its BA in religious studies in 2004, with the last students on the programme graduating in 2006. The existing full-time academic staff transferred to the renamed Department of Theology and Religion at Durham University. It should also be noted that the departments of philosophy and of religious studies in the nearby University of Sunderland were closed in 2001, but with no assured relocation of staff. Thus one might think that since 2004 there has really only been one university in the North East of England. (The University of Northumbria – at Newcastle – has never had a department of theology, religious studies or philosophy, which is not to say that the shades of these disciplines are unknown in its faculties and departments.)

2　However, the vice-chancellor in question did not oversee the closure of either department, philosophy or religious studies, which were closed before and after his tenure of the vice-chancellorship.

3　Jacques Derrida attributes this view to the philosopher Schelling. See Jacques Derrida, 'The Right to Philosophy from the Cosmopolitical Point of View', *Ethics, Institutions, and the Right to Philosophy*, edited and translated by Peter Pericles Trifonas, Lanham, Rowman and Littlefield, 2002, pp. 1–18 (p. 5). This essay can also be found in Jacques Derrida, *Negotiations: Interventions and Interviews 1971–2001*, edited and translated by Elizabeth Rottenberg , Stanford, Stanford University Press, 2002.

4　For a similar argument, see Derrida, *Ethics, Institutions, and the Right to Philosophy*, pp. 27–28.

5　For 'tradition' as a way of questioning, see Alasdair MacIntyre, *After Virtue: A Study in Moral Theory*, second edition, London, Duckworth, 1985, ch. 15. '[W]hen an institution – a university, say, or a farm, or a hospital – is the bearer of a tradition of practice or practices, its common life will be partly, but in a centrally important way, constituted by a continuous argument as to what a university is and ought to be or what good farming is or what good medicine is. Traditions, when vital, embody continuities of conflict' (p. 222).

6　Newman gave five lectures on the idea of a university to the 'Catholics of Dublin' in May and June 1852. They were published along with four other undelivered lectures as *Discourses on the Scope and Nature of University Education* in 1853 – though the book bore the date of the preceding year. It was a revised version of these discourses, together with a further ten lectures and essays, which Newman published as *The Idea of a University* in 1873. See John Henry Newman, *The Idea of a University Defined and Illustrated: (I) in Nine Discourses Delivered to the Catholics in Dublin (II) in Occasional Lectures and Essays Addressed to the Members of the Catholic University*, edited with an introduction by I.T. Ker, Oxford, Clarendon Press, 1976. Jacques Derrida, 'The University Without Condition', in *Without Alibi*, edited and translated by Peggy Kamuf, Stanford, CA, Stanford University Press, 2002, pp. 202–237.

7 For Newman as a nonfoundationalist, postmodern thinker, see Gerard Loughlin, '"To Live and Die Upon a Dogma": Newman and Post/Modern Faith', in Ian Ker and Terrence Merrigan (eds), *Newman and Faith*, Leuven, Peeters, 2004, pp. 25–52.

8 Newman, *Idea of a University*, Preface, p. 5; Newman's emphases.

9 Newman, *Idea of a University*, 1852 Appendix, p. 440.

10 Newman, *Idea of a University*, 1852 Appendix, p. 440; emphasis added.

11 Newman, *Idea of a University*, Preface, p. 5.

12 Newman, *Idea of a University*, Preface, p. 8.

13 Newman, *Idea of a University*, Preface, p. 7.

14 Newman, *Idea of a University*, Preface, p. 9.

15 Newman, *Idea of a University*, Preface, p. 10. While Newman made much of the distinction between liberal and useful knowledge – insisting that the university is concerned with the former rather than the latter, with knowledge apprehended as beautiful rather than as powerful (Newman, *Idea of a University*, Discourse IX.2, p. 185) – he nevertheless found that liberal knowledge has utility in fitting men for society. The art of the university is 'the art of social life, and its end is fitness for the world'. Newman, *Idea of a University*, Discourse VII.10, p. 154.

16 In 2001–02, there were 2,086,075 students in British higher education (1,171,960 women and 914,115 men), of whom 11,485 were studying theology and religious studies (6,205 women and 5,285 men). Higher Education Statistics Agency (HESA) statistics (which do not quite tally).

17 Newman, *Idea of a University*, Preface, p. 10.

18 Newman, *Idea of a University*, Preface, p. 11.

19 Newman, *Idea of a University*, Preface, p. 13.

20 In this Newman agrees with Thomas Jefferson, for whom education in general, and the university in particular, is necessary for defending democracy; for giving 'every citizen the information he needs for the transaction of his own business', of course, but also for knowing 'his rights; to exercise with order and justice those he retains; to choose with discretion the fiduciary of those he delegates; and to notice their conduct with diligence, with candor, and judgment; and, in general, to observe with intelligence and faithfulness all the social relations under which he shall be placed.' Jefferson, *Writings*, p. 459. So, similarly, Newman taught that the university 'is a place to fit men of the world for the world.' Newman, *Idea of a University*, Discourse IX.8, p. 197.

21 Krishan Kumar, 'The Need for Place', in Anthony Smith and Frank Webster (eds), *The Postmodern University? Contested Visions of Higher Education in Society*, Buckingham, Open University Press, 1997, pp. 27–35 (pp. 31–32).

22 Kumar, 'Need for Place', pp. 33–34. Compare Newman, *Idea of a University*, Discourse VI.9, pp. 129–131.

23 Kumar, 'Need for Place', p. 2.

24 See Jefferson to Littleton Waller Tazewell (5 January 1805) and to Messers Hugh L. White and others (6 May 1810) in Thomas Jefferson, *Writings*, edited by Merrill D. Peterson, New York, The Library of America, 1984, pp. 1149–1153 and 1222–1223 respectively. On the design, building and reception of Jefferson's university village, see *Thomas Jefferson's Academical Village: The Creation of an Architectural Masterpiece*, edited by Richard Guy Wilson, Charlottesville, VI, University Press of Virginia, 1995.

25 Newman, *Idea of a University*, Preface, p. 10. Stanley Hauerwas is a latter day Newman in this regard. 'I tell my students that I do not want them to learn "to make up their own minds," since most of them do not have minds worth making up until I have trained them. Rather, by the time I am finished with them, I want them to think just like me.' Stanley Hauerwas, 'Positioning: In the Church and University But Not of Either', in *Dispatches From the Front: Theological Engagements with the Secular*, Durham, NC, Duke University Press, 1994, 5–28 (p. 5).

26 Newman, *Idea of a University*, Lecture VIII.2, p. 370.

27 Paul Filmer, 'Disinterestedness and the Modern University', in Smith and Webster (eds), *The Postmodern University?*, pp. 48–58 (p. 57).

28 Filmer, 'Disinterestedness and the Modern University', pp. 57–58.

29 Newman, *Idea of a University*, Preface, p. 8.

30 Newman, *Idea of a University*, Discourse V.1, p. 95.

31 Kerr, 'Introduction' to Newman, *Idea of a University*, p. xxvi.

32 Newman, *Idea of a University*, Lecture VIII.2, p. 370; emphasis added.

33 Newman, *Idea of a University*, Discourse V.1, p. 96.

34 Department for Education and Skills website (www.dfes.gov.uk/hegateway/studentinfo/index.cfm), accessed on 27th February 2004.

35 See the University of Manchester website (www.manchester.ac.uk/aboutus/history.htm), accessed 27th February 2004. The new University of Manchester was formed through the merger of the Victoria University of Manchester and the University of Manchester Institute of Science and Technology (UMIST) in October 2004.

36 See Newman, *Idea of a University*, Discourse IV.11, pp. 85–87.

37 The description is actually of the already existing University College London, as defended in the *Edinburgh Review*. See Newman, *Idea of a University*, 1852 Discourse V (p. 421). This discourse was suppressed after 1852 and did not appear in *The Idea of a University* (1873).

38 Similar views were expressed by Newman's contemporary, Mark Pattison (1813–1884), who deplored the introduction of the BA examination at Oxford, believing that education should be pursued for education's sake alone. 'The number of those who seek *education* by means of the University is very small compared with the number of those who seek the degree and the social status it confers.' Pattison, quoted in John Sparrow, *Mark Pattison and the Idea of a University*, Cambridge, Cambridge University Press, 1967, pp. 118–119.

39 Newman, *Idea of a University*, Discourse VI.5, p. 121. Contrast this with modern 'teaching and learning' which is held to consist in what it never is or could be, the *transfer* of knowledge from one mind-machine to another.

40 'As to the meaning of the word ['university'], authors are divided in opinion; some explaining it of a universality of studies, others of students. As, however, it is the variety of its schools which brings students from all parts, and the variety of its members which demands so many subjects of teaching, it does not matter much how we settle the *derivation* of the word.' Newman, *Idea of the University*, '1852 Appendix', p. 442.

41 Newman, *Idea of a University*, Discourse II.1, pp. 33–34.

42 See further, Ian Ker, *John Henry Newman: A Biography*, Oxford, Oxford University Press, 1990, chs 9 and 10.

43 See the 'Report of the Commissioners for the University of Virginia' (4 August 1818) in Jefferson, *Writings*, 457–473, p. 467.

44 See Wilfred Cantwell Smith, *The Meaning and End of Religion*, London, SPCK, 1978 and Peter Harrison, *'Religion' and the Religions of the English Enlightenment*, Cambridge, Cambridge University Press, 1990. '"Religions" existed first in the minds of Western thinkers who thought that the lives of other peoples were governed by the kinds of concerns which were really only characteristic of one episode of Western history. The "world religions" were thus generated largely through the projection of Christian disunity onto the world' (p. 174).

45 See Arvind-Pal S. Mandair, 'What if *Religio* Remained Untranslated?' and Navdeep Singh Mandair, 'Virtual Corpus: Solicitous Mutilation and the Body of Tradition' in Philip Goodchild (ed.), *Difference in Philosophy of Religion*, Aldershot, Ashgate, 2003, chs 6 and 7, pp. 87–113.

46 Will Sweetman, '"Hinduism" and the History of "Religion": Protestant Presuppositions in the Critique of the Concept of Hinduism', *Method and Theory in the Study of Religion*, 15, 2003, pp. 329–353 (p. 350). Sweetman is particularly good at showing how several of those who would dispense with the concept of religion (Frits Staal, Timothy Fitzgerald) merely replace it with concepts – ritual, soteriology – that are as contingent and culturally conditioned as the 'religion' they disavow. See also Will Sweetman, *Mapping Hinduism: 'Hinduism' and the Study of Indian Religions 1600–1776*, Halle, Verlag der Franckeschen Stiftungen zu Halle, 2003.

47 See Ninian Smart, *The Science of Religion and the Sociology of Knowledge: Some Methodological Questions*, Princeton, Princeton University Press, 1973 and *Worldviews: Crosscultural Explorations of Human Beliefs*, New York, Charles Scribner's Sons, 1983.

48 See Gavin D'Costa, *The Meeting of Religions and the Trinity*, Edinburgh, T & T Clark, 2000, p. 19.

49 Gavin Hyman, 'The Study of Religion and the Return of Theology', *Journal of the American Academy of Religion*, 72, 1, 2004, pp. 195–219 (p. 213).

50 See Anthony Kenny, 'Leslie Stephen and the Mountains of Truth', in *The Unknown God*, London, Continuum, 2004, pp. 155–178. 'Stephen's fundamental quarrel is not so much with the content of the creed as with the imperiousness of its demand for belief. His final question is this: "Why, when no honest man will deny in private that every ultimate problem is wrapped in the profoundest mystery, do honest men proclaim in pulpits that unhesitating certainty is the duty of the most foolish and ignorant?"' (p. 178).

51 Alasdair MacIntyre, *Three Rival Versions of Moral Enquiry: Encyclopaedia, Genealogy and Tradition*, London, Duckworth, 1990; cited in Hyman, 'Study of Religion', p. 216.

52 Newman, *Idea of a University*, Discourse II.1, p. 34.

53 '[I]f it turns out that something considerable *is* known about the Supreme Being, whether from Reason or Revelation, then the Institution in question professes every science, and yet leaves out the foremost of them. In a word, ... such an Institution cannot be what it professes, if there be a God.' Newman, *Idea of a University*, Discourse II.2, p. 37.

54 Newman, *Idea of a University*, Discourse II.4, p. 41.

55 Newman, *Idea of a University*, Discourse II.7, p. 48. Newman has Dr Edward Maltby (1770–1859) in view. Maltby was Bishop of Durham from 1836 to 1856.

56 Newman, *Idea of a University*, Discourse II.9, p. 50.

57 'Theology teaches ... a doctrine ... so mysterious as in its fullness to lie beyond any system, and in particular aspects to be simply external to nature, and to seem

in parts even to be irreconcilable with itself, the imagination being unable to embrace what the reason determines.' Newman, *Idea of a University*, Discourse III.7, p. 66.

58 Newman, *Idea of a University*, Discourse III.2, pp. 52–53.
59 Newman, *Idea of a University*, Discourse III.2, p. 54.
60 Newman, *Idea of a University*, Discourse III.4, pp. 57–58.
61 Newman, *Idea of a University*, Discourse III.10, p. 70. 'Theology is one branch of knowledge, and Secular Sciences are other branches. Theology is the highest indeed, and widest, but it does not interfere with the real freedom of any secular science in its own particular department.' Newman, *Idea of a University*, 1852 Discourse V, pp. 427–428.
62 Newman, *Idea of a University*, Discourse III.4, p. 57.
63 Newman, *Idea of a University*, 1852 Discourse V, p. 423.
64 Newman, *Idea of a University*, 1852 Discourse V, p. 421.
65 Newman, *Idea of a University*, 1852 Discourse V, p. 428.
66 Derrida, 'University Without Condition', p. 202; original emphasis. Derrida's most important writings on education, both secondary and higher, are to be found in *Du Droit à la philosophie*, Paris, Editions Galilée, 1990, which has been divided and translated into English by Jan Plug as *Who's Afraid of Philosophy? Right to Philosophy I*, Stanford, Stanford University Press, 2002 and *Eyes of the University: Right to Philosophy II*, Stanford, Stanford University Press, 2004.
67 Derrida, 'University Without Condition', p. 202; original emphasis.
68 Derrida, 'University Without Condition', pp. 203–204.
69 Derrida, 'University Without Condition', pp. 204–205.
70 Derrida, 'University Without Condition', p. 205. Perhaps even more strangely, Peggy Kamuf, in her introduction to *Without Alibi*, hardly notes – let alone comments on – Derrida's appropriation of theological discourse, the very discourse which Newman thought must be found in any university that would be truthful. Instead – ironically – Kamuf focuses on the 'forgetting' of psychoanalysis within the professions of the university, which forgetting Derrida has long combated (p. 26).
71 Kerr, 'Introduction' to Newman, *Idea of a University*, p. lxxiii.
72 Newman, *Idea of the University*, Lecture VIII.2, p. 369.
73 Derrida, 'University Without Condition', pp. 214–215. In the etymology of 'profession', Derrida also finds the sense of 'fable' (p. 214).
74 For this – dare we say Derridean – naming of the 'divine', see Richard Kearney, *The God Who May Be: A Hermeneutics of Religion*, Bloomington and Indianapolis, IN, Indiana University Press, 2001. This is not the God who has traditionally motivated the practice of theology, but it is a God sufficient to motivate the question of divinity – of the God *who is* beyond all creaturely existence – and so the necessity of theology and religious studies in the university.
75 Derrida, 'University Without Condition', pp. 206–207. Here, of course, one will think of all the ways in which universities fail to resist sovereign powers, from the recent failure of British universities to resist the instrumentalisation of higher education that has made of it a merely utilitarian accomplishment, to those graver, more deadly times, when universities capitulate to the most pernicious of state ideologies, as in Nazi Germany.
76 Derrida, 'University Without Condition', pp. 208–209. On the sense of the 'performative' which Derrida invokes, see J. L. Austin, *How to Do Things with Words*, edited by J. O. Urmson, Oxford, Clarendon Press, 1962.

77 Derrida, 'University Without Condition', p. 202.

78 Derrida, 'University Without Condition', pp. 213–214.

79 Derrida, 'University Without Condition', p. 234; original emphasis.

80 See the following works by Jacques Derrida: *Given Time: I Counterfeit Money*, translated by Peggy Kamuf, Chicago, The University of Chicago Press, [1991] 1992; *On Cosmopolitanism and Forgiveness*, translated by Mark Dooley and Michael Hughes, London, Routledge, 2001; 'Force of Law: The "Mystical Foundation of Authority"', in Drucilla Cornell, Michael Rosenfeld and David Gray Carlson (eds), *Deconstruction and the Possibility of Justice*, New York, Routledge, 1992; *Politics of Friendship*, translated by George Collins, London, Verso, [1994] 1997.

81 Derrida, 'University Without Condition', p. 235.

82 Herbert McCabe, *God Matters*, London, Geoffrey Chapman, 1978, p. 2.

83 This essay has benefited from the questioning of an earlier version, which was read to the Religions and Theology Seminar in the University of Manchester (March 2004). Though the questioners may think that more benefit should have been taken from their questions, I would like to thank in particular, Michael Hoelzl, Bernard Jackson, Grace Jantzen and Graham Ward. I would also like to thank Pamela Sue Anderson and Gavin D'Costa for subsequent remarks.

Chapter 8

1 For a range of analyses of these terms and their interrelationships, see Astley, 1994, ch. 2; Moran, 1997; Carr, 2003, parts I and II.

2 On the different ways in which this phrase may be understood, see Astley and Day, 1992, ch. 1; Astley, 1994, ch. 1; Astley and Francis, 1994, part I. While many of the marks of true teaching and learning discussed here are not distinctively (that is, *uniquely*) Christian, they are certainly characteristic or *typical of* Christianity, and therefore ought to be central to any Christian philosophy of general education (cf. Marsden, 1997, pp. 68–70; Hughes, 2001, pp. 136–138, 146–147; Evans, 2003, p. 34; Wolterstorff, 2004, p. 106).

3 Despite Newman (cf. pp. 115–116 above). In this essay I develop my more general discussion of these issues in Astley, 1998 and 2004a.

4 On teaching as a vocation, see also Carr, 2003, pp. 43–47.

5 Quoted in Graham, 1998, p. 26.

6 I owe this term to Philip May.

7 This is one reason why there can seem to be a tension between the teaching vocation of a university lecturer and the same person's commitment to research (that is, to the teacher's own learning), particularly if the latter task is strongly motivated by self-interest. The occasional expression of regret in academic obituaries, that so-and-so's diligence or generosity as a teacher led to his neglecting 'his own work', is rarely shared by his students. (It should be recognised, however, that the *publication* of research also has a teaching role.)

8 A position that he shares with Cupitt, of course.

9 Buber's own position, although expressed in different terms, also acknowledges a bridge from eros to real love (see also Buber, 1947, pp. 96–97).

10 Among other 'erotic' temptations in teaching, Buber calls attention to the temptation of the teacher's concentrating on the attractive mind (nimble, open and interested) at the expense of the dull. This is a considerable temptation for the

university teacher, who quickly discovers that the bright are (superficially?) more rewarding to teach. But the bright are very often the ones who do not need teachers. The real, hard ministry of teaching may well be with the rest of the class. The temptation to concentrate on those who need us least can be a wholly self-interested temptation, a focusing on our own reward.

11   And, of course, to be disinterested is not to be *uninterested*, without curiosity or concern.

12   On the virtues, vocation and spirituality of learning, see also Mitchell, 1990, ch. 7; Marsden, 1997, pp. 96, 107–109; McGhee, 2000, pp. 188–189; Peterson, 2001, pp. 137–139, 152–153; Jones and Paulsell, 2002, pp. 17–47; Plantinga, 2002, pp. 130–133; Nash, 2002, pp. 99, 168, 198–200; Sullivan, 2003, pp. 132–137. For Newman's and Kierkegaard's accounts of learning as a vocation, see pp. 84 and 107–108 in this volume.

Chapter 10

1   The Cheltenham and Gloucester College of Higher Education is now The University of Gloucestershire, and the Roehampton Institute of Higher Education, which comprised four CCs, is now The University of Surrey, Roehampton.

Chapter 11

1   John Webster, *Theological Theology*, Oxford, Clarendon, 1997.

2   See Aidan Nichols, *The Shape of Catholic Theology*, Edinburgh, T & T Clark, 1991 for a good basic overview of the history of the discipline.

3   See Jean Leclercq, *The Love of Learning and the Desire for God: A Study of Monastic Culture*, Fordham, NY, Fordham University Press, 1960 for a masterly overview of the background to the medieval monastic context of the study of theology.

4   See Hastings Radshall, *The Universities in the Middle Ages*, three volumes, new edition, Oxford, Clarendon, 1963, especially vol. 1, chapter 5.

5   See Hans W. Frei, *The Eclipse of Biblical Narrative: A Study in Eighteenth and Nineteenth Century Hermeneutics*, New Haven, CT, Yale University Press, 1974, pp. 51, 325. See also Frei's *Types of Christian Theology*, New Haven, CT, Yale University Press, 1992, where he carefully charts aspects of the debate generated in Schleiermacher's proposals in 'Appendix A: Theology in the University', pp. 95–132. The acknowledgement of the structural reconfiguration despite Schleiermacher comes on p. 132, which might have caused Frei greater consternation.

6   Sister Prudence Allen, RSM, *The Concept of Woman: The Aristotelian Revolution 750 BC–AD 1250*, Quebec, Eden Press, 1985, chapter 5.

7   Francis Martin, *The Feminist Question: Feminist Theology in the Light of Christian Tradition*, Edinburgh, T & T Clark, 1994, chapters 1–2, pp. 49–52, respectively.

8   Nicholas Lash, *The Beginning and the End of 'Religion'*, Cambridge, Cambridge University Press, 1996, pp. 132–149; referring to Michael J. Buckley, *At The Origins of Modern Atheism*, New Haven, CT, Yale University Press, 1987.

9   Buckley's misgivings are noted by Lash, *Beginning*, p. 149, note 40. For someone who does seem to read Aquinas in this fashion, see Colin Gunton, *The One, the*

Three and the Many: God, Creation and the Culture of Modernity, Cambridge, Cambridge University Press, 1993: pp. 138–142 for Aquinas, and pp. 52–56 for Augustine.

10 Buckley, *Origins*, p. 202.

11 Lash, *Beginning*, pp. 147–148. The first and second quotations cited by Lash are taken from Buckley, *Origins*, p. 54, and the third from Frei, *Eclipse*, p. 130.

12 David Lodge, *Paradise News*, London, Secker and Warburg, 1991.

13 Quoted in Alan Richardson (ed.), *A Dictionary of Christian Theology*, London, SCM, 1969, p. 335, under the entry 'Theology'.

14 See Aidan Nichols, OP, 'The Habit of Theology, and How to Acquire It', *The Downside Review*, 105, 1987, pp. 247–259; and the aptly entitled, *Instruction on the Ecclesial Vocation of the Theologian*, London/Dublin, CTS/Veritas, 1990, issued by the Congregation for the Doctrine of Faith.

15 See Frei, *Eclipse*, p. 130, and John Milbank's critical reconstruction of this process in *Theology and Social Theory*, especially part II: 'Theology and Positivism', pp. 51–143, which accounts for my reference to policing.

16 In 1808 Schleiermacher published *Thoughts on German Universities from a German Point of View* and in 1810, *Brief Outline on the Study of Theology* (Richmond, VN, John Knox Press, 1966).

17 On example would be Francis Watson, *Text, Church and World: Biblical Interpretation in Theological Perspective*, Edinburgh, T & T Clark, 1997.

18 Ninian Smart, 'Religious Studies in the United Kingdom', *Religion*, 18, 1988, p. 8. For a more militant US/Canadian version of Smart, see Donald Wiebe, *The Politics of Religious Studies: The Continuing Conflict with Theology in the Academy*, Basingstoke, Macmillan, 1999.

19 For the appropriation of the 'East' by the 'West', see for example, Raymond Schwab, *The Oriental Renaissance*, New York, Columbia University Press, 1984 and Wilhelm Halbfass, *India and Europe: An Essay in Understanding*, Albany, NY, State University of New York Press, 1988.

20 London, Macmillan, 1973. It would be churlish to question Smart's outstanding contribution academically and institutionally. I use him purely as a symbol in what follows.

21 Eric J. Sharpe, *Comparative Religion: A History*, second edition, London, Duckworth, 1986 [1975], p. 35.

22 See Sharpe, *Comparative Religion*, pp. xii–xiv, 294–319.

23 See, for example, the survey in Michael Pye (ed.), *Marburg Revisited: Institutions and Strategies in the Study of Religion*, Marburg, Diagonal Verlag, 1989.

24 Peter Harrison, *'Religion' and the Religions in the English Enlightenment*, Cambridge, Cambridge University Press, 1990.

25 John Milbank, 'The End of Dialogue', in Gavin D'Costa (ed.), *Christian Uniqueness Reconsidered*, New York, Orbis, 1990, pp. 174–191 (pp. 176–177).

26 In the mid 1950s, Adrian Cunningham notes that there were no more than 16 people in theology departments teaching about religions other than Christianity. In 1990 (at the time of his essay) all the relevant departments included at least one option in another religion. In 2003, of the 23 HEFCE departments, all offer at least one option in world religions; only 7 are called only 'theology' or 'divinity'; and the majority have 'religious studies' in the departmental name.

27 António Barbosa da Silva, *The Phenomenology of Religion as a Philosophical Problem*, Lund, Gleerup, 1982.

28 Thomas Kuhn, *The Structure of Scientific Revolutions*, second edition, Chicago, IL, Chicago University Press, 1970.

29 See Alasdair MacIntyre, *After Virtue*, London, Duckworth, 1985, second edition; *Whose Justice? Which Rationality?*, London, Duckworth, 1988; and *Three Rival Versions of Moral Enquiry*, London, Duckworth, 1990.

30 He addresses the plurality within Thomism in *Three Rival Versions*, chapter 3, as well as in 'How Intellectual Excellence in Philosophy is to be Understood by a Catholic Philosopher', *Current Issues in Catholic Higher Education*, 12, 1, 1991, pp. 47–50.

31 Some of the many problems with MacIntyre are discussed in John Horton and Susan Mendus (eds), *After MacIntyre: Critical Perspectives on the Work of Alasdair MacIntyre*, Oxford, Polity Press, 1994.

32 Horton and Mendus, *After MacIntyre*, pp. 13–14.

33 Muhammad Legenhausen, extended book review of *Whose Justice? Which Rationality?*, in *Al-Tawhid*, 14, 2, 1997, pp. 158–176 (p. 169).

34 Anne Klein, *Knowledge and Liberation: Tibetan Buddhist Epistemology in Support of Transformative Religious Experience*, New York, Snow Lion, 1986, p. 49.

35 See MacIntyre, *Whose Justice*, chapter 19.

36 See, further, my *The Meeting of Religions and the Trinity*, Edinburgh, T & T Clark, 2000.

37 See, for instance, Alan Wolfe, 'The Potential for Pluralism: Religious Responses to the Triumph of Theory and Method in American Academic Culture', in Andreas Sterk (ed.), *Religion, Scholarship and Higher Education*, Notre Dame, IN, University of Notre Dame Press, 2000, pp. 22–39.

38 Such 'plurality' already exists in the USA, but the extent to which it represents real 'plurality' is called into question by such detailed studies as James Tunstead Burtchaell, *The Dying of the Light: The Disengagement of Colleges and Universities from their Christian Churches*, Grand Rapids, MI, Eerdmans, 1998 and Philip Gleason, *Contending with Modernity: Catholic Higher Education in the Twentieth Century*, Oxford and New York, Oxford University Press, 1995.

Chapter 13

1 John Polkinghorne has argued that natural theology is undergoing a revival, 'not so much at the hands of the theologians (whose nerve, with some honourable exceptions, has not returned) but at the hands of the scientists'. But it is also a *revised* natural theology concerned with law and circumstance 'rather than particular occurrences (such as the coming-to-be of life or of the eye). These latter questions are legitimate subjects for scientific investigation but the attempt to capture them for theology is just the error of the God of the Gaps' (Polkinghorne, 1988, p. 16).

2 Jim Packer wrote in *Fundamentalism and the Word of God*: 'We need to be constantly searching Scripture to find what lines of approach it indicates to the problem raised by secular studies – history, natural science, philosophy, psychology and the rest. ... Our attitude must be determined by the principle that, since the same God is the Author both of nature and of Scripture, true science and a right interpretation of Scripture cannot conflict. ... We shall, therefore, continue loyal to the evidence of both Scripture and of empirical enquiry, resolved to do justice to all the facts from both sources while we wait for

further light as to the best method of relating them together. Meanwhile, we shall look to see whether the appearance of contradiction is not due to mistakes and arbitrary assumptions, both scientific and theological, which a closer scrutiny of the evidence will enable us to correct. ... Not only does the book of Scripture throw light on the meaning of the book of nature; the book of nature reflects some of that light back on to Scripture, so that we may read its message more clearly. *It is through the ferment of thought created by such interaction that theological insight is deepened and the relevance of the gospel more fully grasped*' (Packer, 1958, pp. 134–135, my italics).

Chapter 14

1 Now included in Lesley Walmsley (ed.), *Essay Collection and Other Short Pieces*, London, HarperCollins, 2000, pp. 411–420.
2 Ibid., p. 412.
3 This section of the paper draws on an earlier paper on Hauerwas' political thought given to the research seminar of St Mary's College, the St Andrews School of Divinity. I am grateful to all present for their comments and for Alan Torrance's invitation to address the seminar. I was also grateful for the opportunity to listen to Hauerwas' Gifford lectures at St Andrews, now published as *With the Grain of the Universe: The Church's Witness and Natural Theology*, London, SCM, 2002, as well as the discussions which followed the lectures, which helped me to understand his (always interesting) positions much better.
4 Milbank's magnum opus to date is, of course, *Theology and Social Theory*, Oxford, Blackwell, 1990, but for additional refinement of his position see his *The Word Made Strange*, Oxford, Blackwell, 1996.
5 This term is usually applied to a number of theologians, most usually Milbank, Catherine Pickstock and Graham Ward. See, in addition to the books cited above, John Milbank, Catherine Pickstock and Graham Ward (eds), *Radical Orthodoxy*, London, Routledge, 1999.
6 Stanley Hauerwas, *Despatches from the Front: Theological Engagements with the Secular*, Durham, NC, Duke University Press, 1994.
7 Ibid., p. 10.
8 Ibid., p. 13.
9 Ibid., p. 87.
10 Hauerwas, *In Good Company: The Church as Polis*, Notre Dame, IN, University of Notre Dame Press, 1995. This was, in itself, taken from a book by Arne Rasmussen, *The Church as Polis: From Political Theology to Theological Politics as Exemplified by Jürgen Moltmann and Stanley Hauerwas*, Lund, Lund University Press, 1994.
11 Hauerwas, *In Good Company*, p. 6.
12 As will be seen, I am here essentially agreeing with and paraphrasing, with some small emendations of my own, the understanding of a university and its character offered by Michael Oakeshott in his many writings on education. See especially, Tim Fuller (ed.), *The Voice of Liberal Learning: Michael Oakeshott on Education*, New Haven, CT, Yale University Press, 1990.
13 Oakeshott, *Rationalism in Politics*, Indianapolis, IN, Liberty Fund, 1991, new and expanded edition (original edition, 1962), p. 188.
14 Ibid., p. 189.

15 Oakeshott, *Rationalism in Politics*, p. 309.
16 Ibid., p. 310.
17 Ibid., p. 310.
18 Ibid., see pp. 311–312.
19 Ibid., pp. 328–329.
20 The impossibility of this sort of thing is commented on extensively in Oakeshott's work.
21 Ibid., p. 329, n. 2.
22 Milbank, *Theology and Social Theory*, p. 1.
23 This is also Oakeshott's view. See *Experience and Its Modes*, Cambridge, Cambridge University Press, 1933, p. 293 and also *On Human Conduct*, Oxford, Clarendon Press, 1975, p. 85.
24 Obviously this is merely scratching the surface. There are many other ways in which the curricula cake could be cut.
25 I am grateful to Gordon Graham, Ian Hall, Trevor Hart, Renee Jeffery and Ian Markham for discussion of the themes of this essay and, in a couple of cases, very helpful written comments.

Chapter 15

1 The claim comes essentially from Hegel, who wrote in the introduction to his *Lectures on the Philosophy of History*, 'What experience and history teach is this – that people and governments have never learnt anything from history, or acted on principles deduced from it.'
2 One of many examples comes from Gribben (2002, p. 63) who relates how the supernova observed by Tycho Brahe violated Aristotle's assumption that stars were fixed and eternal.
3 The concentration on Piaget here is made for reasons of space. Vygotsky does not contradict much of the Piagetian account and the interaction in the former's account between culture and maturation does not deny the mental unity that is important in principle for interdisciplinary studies.
4 Wolterstorff (2002) argues that the epistemology of the sciences is shown to be distinct from the actual functioning of science. In other words, the notion of a scientific method is misconceived because science just does not work as neatly as the methodological rigorists would like. But, although he has support from those like Feyerabend and his famous *Against Method* (1975), there is heavy evidence the other way. Not only is Gribben (2002) in his historical survey of four centuries of science able to point to an identifiably constant method, but also those like the Nobel-prize winning Peter Medawar (1990) are happy to assent to the liberating truth they found in the conception of science as a dialogue between daring imagination and tough testing.

Chapter 17

1 The author was chair of both the Postgraduate Review Committee and the Internal Quality Audit Committee and is therefore aware of the large amount of consultation that took place within the Faculty with all relevant sectors of the University, with students, the wider community and key people in the field of education.

Contributors

Jeff Astley is Director of the North of England Institute for Christian Education, and Honorary Professorial Fellow in Practical Theology and Christian Education at the University of Durham, UK. He is the author or editor of twenty-five books on topics in Christian education and theology, including *Critical Perspectives on Christian Education* (1994), *The Philosophy of Christian Religious Education* (1994) and *Ordinary Theology: Looking, Listening and Learning in Theology* (2002).

R. J. Berry was Professor of Genetics at University College London from 1978 to 2000; he is now Professor Emeritus. He is a former President of Christians in Science and of the British Ecological Society. His books include *God and Evolution* (1988, 2000), *God and the Biologist* (1996), *Science, Life and Christian Belief* (with Malcolm Jeeves) (1998) and *God's Book of Works* (2003).

David Carr is Professor of Philosophy of Education in the University of Edinburgh School of Education. He is the author of *Educating the Virtues* (1991), *Professionalism and Ethics in Teaching* (2000) and *Making Sense of Education* (2003), as well as co-editor (with Jan Steutel) of *Virtue Ethics and Moral Education* (1999) and co-editor (with John Haldane) of *Spirituality, Philosophy and Education* (2003). He has also published numerous philosophical and educational articles, many exploring the moral, religious and spiritual aspects of education.

Gavin D'Costa is Reader in Christian Theology and Head of the Department of Theology and Religious Studies at the University of

Bristol. His books include *The Meeting of the Religions and the Trinity* (2000), *Sexing the Trinity* (2000) and *Theology and the Secular University: The Case for an Alternative* (2005). He has also edited *Christian Uniqueness Reconsidered* (1990) and *Resurrection Reconsidered* (1996). Gavin D'Costa is a consultant to the Church of England, the Catholic Bishops' Conference and the Vatican (Pontifical Council for Interreligious Dialogue) on issues regarding other religions.

Leslie J. Francis is Director of the Welsh National Centre for Religious Education and Professor of Practical Theology, University of Wales, Bangor, UK. He is author or editor of over forty books on topics in practical and empirical theology, including *Drift from the Churches: Attitudes Toward Christianity during Childhood and Adolescence* (1996), *Church Watch: Christianity in the Countryside* (1996), *Gone but not Forgotten: Church Leaving and Returning* (1998), *The Values Debate: A Voice from the Pupils* (2001) and *The Naked Parish Priest: What Priests Really Think They're Doing* (2003).

William K. Kay is Senior Lecturer in Religious and Theology Education, King's College, London and Director of the Centre for Pentecostal and Charismatic Studies, University of Wales, Bangor. His books include: *Inside Story* (1990), *Prophecy!* (1994), *Pentecostals in Britain* (2000), and the edited collections *Pentecostal and Charismatic Studies: A Reader* (2004) and *Religion in Education*, volumes 1 to 4 (1997, 1998, 2000, 2003). He has also written numerous articles and chapters on issues relating to his two broad fields of interest: Pentecostalism and religious education.

Gerard Loughlin is Senior Lecturer in Religious Studies at the University of Durham, UK. He is the author of *Telling God's Story: Bible, Church and Narrative Theology* (1996) and *Alien Sex: The Body and Desire in Cinema and Theology* (2004).

Patricia Malone, RSJ, is Adjunct Professor, Australian Catholic University, having retired in 2002 after twenty-two years in the School of Religious Education in ACU and its predecessor colleges to take up a leadership role in her religious congregation, the Sisters of St Joseph. She is co-author of *Sound the Trumpet: Planning and Teaching Religion in the Catholic Primary School* (1994) and *Exploring the Religion Classroom: A*

Guidebook for Catholic Schools (1996), as well as many articles, papers and teacher resources on curriculum development and the use of the web in religious education.

Ian S. Markham is the Dean of Hartford Seminary, Connecticut and Professor of Theology and Ethics there. Prior to this, he was the first holder of the Liverpool Chair of Theology and Public Life at Liverpool Hope University College. He is the author of many books, including *Theology of Engagement* (2003), *Truth and the Reality of God* (1998) and *Plurality and Christian Ethics* (1994). He is the editor of the Blackwell's journal, *Conversations in Religion and Theology*. In December 2004, he will deliver the Teape Lectures in India.

Murray A. Rae taught until recently in the Department of Theology and Religious Studies at King's College, London, and is now Senior Lecturer in Theology and Ethics at the University of Otago in New Zealand. He is author and co-editor of a number of books including *Kierkegaard's Vision of the Incarnation* (1997) and *The Practice of Theology* (with Colin Gunton and Stephen Holmes, 2001). He is currently co-chair of 'The Theology and Built Environment Colloquium' under the joint auspices of Theology Through the Arts (University of St Andrews) and the Institute of Christian Worship (Calvin College, Grand Rapids).

Nicholas Rengger is Professor of Political Theory and International Relations at St Andrews University. He has published on many different aspects of political philosophy, intellectual history, international ethics and international relations. He is currently completing a study of three competing philosophical approaches to world order, entitled *Visions of Order*.

Denis Robinson is a researcher at the Catholic University of Louvain in Belgium. He has a special interest in nineteenth-century theology, particularly the work of John Henry Newman. He is also involved with the research project 'Orthodoxy: Product and Practice'. Recent publications include *Theology and Religious Pluralism* (co-edited with Terrence Merrigan) and *The Mother of Wisdom: The Parabolic Imperative in the Early Work of John Henry Newman* (2003).

John Sullivan is Professor of Christian Education at Liverpool Hope University College. He is author of *Catholic Schools in Contention* (2000) and *Catholic Education: Distinctive and Inclusive* (2001), and of more than sixty articles and chapters on religion and education. Previously Reader in Catholic Education at St Mary's College, Twickenham, he teaches in the areas of formation for ministry and in the connections between theology and education.

Adrian Thatcher was formerly Professor of Applied Theology at the College of St Mark and St John, Plymouth. He is now Professorial Research Fellow in Christian Ethics at the University of Exeter. His recent publications include *Living Together and Christian Ethics* (2002), *Celebrating Christian Marriage* (2002) and *Marriage After Modernity* (1999).

Elmer Thiessen has recently taken early retirement after having taught philosophy and religious studies at Medicine Hat College, Alberta, Canada for over thirty years. His research speciality has been the philosophy of education, in which area he has published two books, *Teaching for Commitment* and *In Defence of Religious Schools and Colleges* (McGill–Queen's University Press, 1993 and 2001). He has just completed a manuscript on 'The Ethics of Proselytizing'.

Andrew Walker is Canon Professor of Theology, Religion and Culture in the Department of Education, King's College, London and until recently visiting Professor of Evangelisation at Perkins School of Theology, Southern Methodist University, Dallas, Texas. He is presently working on patterns of catechesis in the Anglican Communion on behalf of the London Diocese of the Church of England. He is the author and editor of several books, the most recent being (with Martyn Percy) *Restoring the Image: A Festschrift for David Martin* (2001) and (with Kristin Aune) *On Revival: A Critical Examination* (2003).

Andrew Wright is Senior Lecturer in Religious and Theological Education at King's College, London and chair of the Association of University Lecturers in Religion and Education. He is presently working on a book on truth in religious education. His recent publications include *Spirituality and Education* (2000) and *Religion, Education and Post-modernity* (2004).

Printed in the United Kingdom
by Lightning Source UK Ltd.
103950UKS00003B/46-408